RELIGION AND REPUBLIC

RELIGION AND REPUBLIC

The American Circumstance

Martin E. Marty

BEACON PRESS : BOSTON

Beacon Press
25 Beacon Street
Boston, Massachusetts 02108

Beacon Press books
are published under the auspices of
the Unitarian Universalist Association of Congregations.

92 91 90 89   2 3 4 5 6 7 8

Library of Congress Cataloging-in-Publication Data
Marty, Martin E., 1928–
Religion and republic.
Bibliography: p.
Includes index.
1.   United States — Religion. 2.   United States —
Religion — 1960–   .I.   Title.
BR515.M329 1987   277.3   86-47755
ISBN 0-8070-1206-8

Text design by David Ford

To Norman Lear
To honor his regard for religion, the republic,
the circumstance, and his friends

Contents

Contents

Introduction

On July 4, 1776, the Continental Congress named a committee of three to prepare a device for a Seal of the United States of America. The committee members, John Adams, Benjamin Franklin, and Thomas Jefferson, chose as the motto a Latin line that derived from Virgil and was used by St. Augustine: *E pluribus unum*. The motto referred to the federal republic. These founders were very much concerned with the problem of how thirteen colonies, virtual mininations, could come together to form one nation, a republic.

E pluribus unum soon came to be applied by analogy to other aspects of national life. It has turned out to relate more to process than to product. That is, exactly how the "one" Republic and the "many" states relate has never been permanently settled and probably could not and should not be settled. Similarly, how other components of the nation relate to it and each other is an issue that cannot be settled. This is particularly true of groupings of people, whether one is referring to their ethnic, cultural, regional, or religious contexts.

Religion, long dismissed as one of the quieter and safer dimensions of national existence, has suddenly reappeared as a factor in American political and social dynamism. It seems to be near the center of many decisive conflicts: the struggle for civil rights, debate over nuclear armament, and "social agenda" items such as abortion and school prayer are typical. Such issues connect the United States with world trends, for *tribalism* (the experience of

1

"the many") has interrupted national life (the existence of "the one") in places as diverse as India, Lebanon, Northern Ireland, Sri Lanka, and many African states.

Conflict among the "many" in some of these nations has been of a military sort, as it has not been in the United States. One feature that has helped assure relatively civil address to the issues in the United States has been the polity fashioned by the men who designed the seal and chose the motto, along with their colleagues. They were learned and dedicated people, informed by reading in philosophy and religion—persons who reflected on the meaning of a republic.

This book reflects on that dimension of republican life to which religious communities address themselves. On the one hand, as will become obvious, American religious groups have been generally supportive of national consensus, cheerleaders at the patriotic parades, and ready saluters of the flag of this nation "under God." At the same time, most of them have not yielded to the "one" what they believe properly belongs to the "many." This includes the freedom to cling to ultimates independent of any governmental direction, along with the freedom to hold to and propagate their beliefs in open competition with other religious groups. They promote ethical and moral systems, stimulate the nurture of new generations, and undertake measures of care. In the public sector they want the right to speak up for justice on their own terms and to protect themselves from government intrusion. Sometimes they have pressed their own rights so insistently that they have shown little regard for the Republic. At other times, this very pressing has proved to be a creative test of the nature of the Republic. In both cases, they have provoked debate on the nature of pluralism, which becomes a code word for Republican life in America.

The subtitle of this volume sets this historic account and contemporary debate into an environment. Readers will soon see that I am preoccupied with questions of land and landscape, city and cityscape, people and peoplescape. That is, the environment itself, as I shall on occasion declare, has been seen to be somehow revelatory and redemptive in often overtly and consistently quiet ways. This dimension of the work reflects a career-long interest in the perspectival philosophy, the circumstantial outlook, of the Spanish philosopher José Ortega y Gasset.

Introduction

Ortega's frequently stated theme, his virtual life motto, was "I am I and my circumstances . . ." I have always taken this to mean, among other things, something dialectical. Were we to say "I am I," it would charter pure egotism and issue in solipsism. Were we to say "I am my circumstances," this would be an affirmation of or acquiescence to determinism. For Ortega, "life is essentially a dialogue with its circumstances" and "to think is to converse [*dialogar*] with one's circumstances." In the chapters that follow, the "I" reflects on the American circumstance, colored as it is by pluralism. Circumstances constantly change; the choice of pluralism as a topic at this period of national history may require some explanation.

Pluralism, especially religious pluralism, suffers everywhere today, but it deserves celebration. The totalitarian powers throughout the century have tried to abolish pluralism by abolishing religion. Tribal forces use their bonds of religion-culture-ethnicity-race to resist polities of pluralism. They set out to kill each other. In the free world, subtler forces take advantage of popular weariness with pluralism. In order to establish values to propagate, they argue, they must promote legal privileges for majority religious cultures. Few would set out to eject or legally reject diverse religious minorities. Yet they exploit public confusion over morals and values. They propose that if their society were dominated by a single set of people or a single construct—in the case of the United States this is usually "Christian America" coded as "Judeo-Christian America"—all would be well, or at least better.

To that end public officials, philosophers, and publicists often invent or idealize homogeneous pasts. They force the national founders into a single mold. They appeal to nostalgia for a Golden Age when a Little Red School House and a Little White Church controlled the values of "sameness" in communities. That a species or two of the Protestant version of a Christian American, inside a Judeo-Christian civilization, did exercise awesome power in the nineteenth century is demonstrable. I chronicled its rise and extent in *Righteous Empire: The Protestant Experience in America*. That these species have been jostled by new forces of new pluralisms since World War II is equally demonstrable. I have devoted three decades to writing on the "before" and "after" shapes of these pluralisms. This book, a collection of essays, presents numbers of (chiefly historical) chapters on the subject.

3

Introduction

The chapters appear as "celebrations," which does not by any means imply lack of critical distance. Yet overall the argument is an affirmation of beleaguered and beset pluralism. The American experiment with a polity that protects diversity and trusts plural sources of cultural energy came late in history. It has always been fragile, precariously poised between temptations to dominators and lapses into chaos. This polity is a rare prospect in the late-twentieth-century world. Pluralism, like politics, does not save souls, make sad hearts glad, or solve all human problems. It permits humans to face their problems in a spirit of freedom and open engagement for argument and toward possible consensus.

What do we mean by pluralism? It can signal several kinds of phenomena. First, the term can refer to the mere variety of religious-cultural groupings coexisting in a time and a place. "There's an awful lot of religion out there, and there are plenty of groups to promote it." Without such diversity there would be no reason to reach for the term *pluralist* to describe a society. Yet here pluralism is taken to include the polity that assures freedom for such diverse groups to coexist creatively. (These essays rarely refer to philosophical pluralism, which implies a metaphysical commitment. It is a doctrine that suggests that reality is made up of many ultimate substances. Support for cultural and religious pluralism can come from philosophical monists and pluralists alike.)

Why has pluralism become an issue now? At mid-century much of the cosmopolitan world lived by an ecumenical ethos. The United Nations, World Council of Churches, United World Federalists—these were a few institutional expressions of a uniting dream. "Global village," "the human family," and "spaceship earth" served as metaphors for a vision of convergence. Today around the world, counterforces have disrupted the dream and challenged the vision. Now peoples employ religious symbols to reinforce their claims and to bond their groups over against other groups—and to kill in the name of tribalism. The convergent ethos allowed for one style of pluralism, for it did not deny but only limited the values of particularity. The tribal ethos allows for another style of pluralism, but not within a single polity. The clerisy or clerocracy of Shi'ite Muslim Iran shows what happens when one tribe comes to dominate. The civil chaos of Lebanon illustrates what occurs when no

4

polity protects civil peace and pluralism comes to mean the war of each people against all peoples.

America knows neither the totalist nor tribal extremes. Religious pluralism has survived and proven hardy. Yet the weariness we mentioned persists. New powers have come on the scene, eager to rewrite history and control the present and the future. They are not the first to aspire to such scripting or dominating. If today many of these moves come from people called conservative, once they were initiated by liberals. As late as 1951 the liberal Protestant journal with which I am associated, *The Christian Century,* could banner on its cover an editorial titled "Pluralism—A National Menace." Several years later the editors had come to affirm a new pluralism as the best possibility for society.

Pluralism is unattractive to those whom injustices exclude from civil power. There are limits to the promise of pluralism. It is unappealing to those who are losing their status as dominators of a culture. Pluralism appears as a code word for a conspiracy that would prevent new aspirants to power from gaining it. Thus to many of the putative conservatives today it covers for a more menacing phenomenon that they call "secular humanism."

One can see ironies in a situation such as America's today. Diversity in religion and peoplehood continues to grow. There may be two to five million Muslims; there are hundreds of thousands of Hindus and Buddhists; hundreds of intensive religious groups—called cults by their enemies and New Religions by their friends—stand outside the Judeo-Christian tradition. While a secular humanist conspiracy does not exist, there are millions of secular-minded and nonreligious humanists who do not form institutional groupings but who claim a place under the Republic's sun. Millions of Hispanics present new problems and promise to acculturated fellow Catholics and other Americans. Many seek the norms of "privatization," as they determine styles of living, thinking, and believing entirely on their own. Their ideal of pluralism is a republic of 230 million independent world views and outlooks, one for each citizen.

The situation may not be ironical, however. It may result from discernible causes. The very mention of so many options points to a condition that can promote weariness of spirit, a sense of powerlessness, an edge of chaos. The chapters that follow take seriously the fragile character and the modest promises of the pluralist polity in the face of strong criticisms and stronger distaste for it. Yet for reasons that these pages will demonstrate, pluralism demands and deserves celebration. Here are "fifteen big ones," cheers for it.

The book opens with a survey of contemporary religion, accenting the discovery of its abundance in a society legally constituted as and long called secular. A parallel chapter points to pluralism in its context, selecting five main traditions of American religion.

The second part elaborates on the concepts of public religion, civil religion, and public theology. These three concepts are matched by three others: spirituality, in a secular setting; scripturality, the devotion to the Bible; and experiment, the vision of a pluralist republic through the eyes of foreign visitors.

Part 3 begins with two generic chapters. The first deals with the pressures created for pluralism as the landscape turned to cityscape. The second points to the thickness of pluralism by connecting ethnicity with religion in the concept of "peoplehood." A transition chapter begins by discussing one group, Roman Catholics, in its ghetto existence, and then shows how many other ghettos there have been and are. This section then concludes with three particularist samplings. The chapters discuss groupings that were once seen to be outside the mainstream: southern evangelicals, fundamentalists, and Mormons. Modernity has been a challenge to the first two, historical consciousness to the third.

The final part and chapter summarizes the transpositions of powers late in this century. An epilogue points to signals that might inspire confidence in a time of travail for pluralism.

Eleven of these chapters appeared first in journal form and four as chapters in other persons' books. Three have reappeared in books after their journal publication. It is hard to picture any devotees of the author devoted enough to have tracked all of them as essays in disaparate journals and books, so the coherences and elaborations of the argument have hitherto been apparent only in my mind. I hope the readers will find them in what I conceive of as a coherent and elaborate book. Anyone who writes historical articles for journals or as book chapters knows that they can often be as demanding as whole books: I was pleased, therefore, to respond to the suggestion of Caroline Birdsall of Beacon to prepare this book.

Introduction

I thank publishers for permissions to reprint these revised essays. Parts of only two of them (Chaps. 10 and 11) have drawn on sources and developed arguments similar to those drawn upon and developed in a chapter or two of my books (in the first case, a chapter in *A Nation of Behavers;* in the second, some paragraphs in *The Irony of It All*). Almost all readers will find almost all of the volume to be a fresh encounter. While these essays appeared over a seventeen-year period—a very short time in the eye of a historian!—they are not period pieces. I have chosen only chapters that speak to current circumstance and have updated where necessary.

Chapters 1 and 6 originally appeared in *Daedalus*, Journal of the American Academy of Arts and Sciences, as respectively, "Religion in America Since Mid-Century" (Winter 1982), and "The Spirit's Holy Errand: The Search for a Spiritual Style in Secular America" (Winter 1967). Chapter 2 appeared first as "The American Tradition and the American Tomorrow," in Samuel Sandmel, *Tomorrow's American* (Oxford University Press, 1977). Chapters 3, 5, and 8 were first published in the *Journal of Religion*. Chapter 3 appeared as "A Sort of Republican Banquet," 59 (October 1979); chapter 5 as "Reinhold Niebuhr: Public Theology and the American Experience," 54 (October 1974); and chapter 8 as "Experiment in Environment: Foreign Perceptions of Religious America," 56 (July 1976). Chapter 4 was originally "Two Kinds of Two Kinds of Civil Religion," in Russell E. Richey and Donald G. Jones, eds., *American Civil Religion* (Harper and Row, 1974). Chapter 7 first appeared as "America's Iconic Book," in Gene M. Tucker and Douglas A. Knight, eds., *Humanizing America's Iconic Book* (Scholars Press, 1982), and is reprinted by permission of the Society of Biblical Literature. Chapter 9 was originally published as "The Land and the City in American Religious Conflict," in *Review of Religious Research* 18 (Spring 1977). Chapter 10 appeared in *Church History* 41 (1972), as "Ethnicity: The Skeleton of Religion in America." Chapter 11 was first published in *The Catholic Historical Review* 68 (April 1982). Chapter 12 was published as "The Revival of Evangelicalism and Southern Religion," in David Edwin Harrell, Jr., ed., *Varieties of Southern Evangelicalism* (Mercer University Press, 1981). Chapter 13 first appeared as "Fundamentalism as a Social Phenomenon," in *Review and Expositor* 79 (Winter 1982) and then in George Marsden, ed., *Evangelicalism and Modern America*

(Eerdmans, 1984). Chapter 14 was originally an address presented at the annual meeting of the Mormon History Association funded by a grant from O. C. and Grace Turner, and was published as "Two Integrities: An Address to the Crisis in Mormon Historiography," in *Journal of Mormon History* 10 (1983). Chapter 15 was first published as "Transpositions: American Religion in the 1980s," in *Annals* 489 (July 1985).

In addition to Caroline Birdsall, I would like to point to others who deserve acknowledgment. My dean, Franklin I. Gamwell, and my colleagues at the University of Chicago have given encouragement and insight, while the graduate students there have made substantial contributions through their participation in seminars and during dissertation writing. Judy Lawrence helped greatly with manuscript preparation. Graduate assistant Stephen Graham performed yeomanly, as often before, with tasks of selection and editing. Harriet Marty, also as before, lent her good eye in editing and proofreading. My brother, historian Myron A. Marty, offered wise editorial counsel. Final thanks go to that marvelous cast of characters who give life to what could be an abstraction, American religious pluralism. I hope these chapters capture something of the color and texture of their lives.

THE PRESENT AND THE PAST

1   Rediscovery: Discerning Religious America

For a great many years until mid-twentieth century, religion in the United States gave every indication of becoming increasingly secular, institutionalized, and less influential in American life. Yet the years since then have brought unanticipated changes in the relationship between religion and culture, and as a result, academic theorists have sought—and developed—fresh theories to account for these surprising cultural shifts.

First, contrary to expectations, religion is very much in evidence, which means that the secular paradigm and prophecy that had dominated Western academic thought have come to be questioned.[1] Second, rather than being contained within formal institutions, religion has unmistakably and increasingly diffused throughout the culture, and has assumed highly particular forms in the private lives of citizens. Third, traditional religion has not fallen away, as expected, but has survived and staged an impressive comeback, establishing itself firmly and enduringly in large subcultures.

Before exploring these shifts, three important points must be made. The first is that continuity—especially with regard to religiosity and secularity, the social locations of religion, and the durability of traditional faiths in the face of change—has long been a fundamental feature of American religious culture. Though academic theorists have often overlooked it, it has not gone entirely unnoticed. The "consensus historians" of the 1950s, for example, took note of it, and by minimizing the stresses and strains of American life, accented the "givenness," the stable threads of American religion.[2] Halfway through the period, historically informed sociologists, while impressed with the changes taking place, were able to keep their balance in the face of such change. In 1963 Seymour Martin Lipset, for example, in *The First New Nation* used the observations of both foreign visitors and American chroniclers to show that all-pervasive religion had characterized American culture through the years. While trying to do justice to the persistent secularity born of American pluralism—a secularity that manifests itself in the practical American temper—and the moral, as opposed to the transcendental, motif in much American faith, Lipset saw that voluntaryism was the source of religious strength. American citizens *chose* to be religious because they were free not to be; religious organizations survived because they had to compete for loyalty.[3]

Second, academics trained in the sociology of knowledge—theorists in theology, religious studies, and humanistic or social scientific disciplines—were tuned in to certain of the more subtle shifts in American culture. They saw that most of those living *in* the culture have fewer options for their lives than is generally realized, fewer tools for analysis, and many motives for resisting change. John Murray Cuddihy recognized that some core-culture analysts were theorists writing "from within the eye of the hurricane of modernization, where all [was] calm and intelligible." He knew that "for the underclass below, as for the ethnic outside, modernization [was] a trauma."[4] In their humble dwellings, they had neither the peace nor the time to reflect on possible alternative courses: the wind was coming their way, and they had to put up the sandbags, move on, or be destroyed.

Another way to put this is to caricature American society in terms borrowed from the comics and playpen; such an exercise leads to interesting results:

> Society can be diagrammed in a shape more or less like Al Capp's cartoon creation the Shmoo. The Shmoo's motion is largely in its head. A broad middle and a leaden bottom keep it earthbound. The child's roly-poly toy, all beaming and motion-filled in the face, is ungraspably broad in the middle, and burdened by

weights so that it lands right side up when buffeted, and quickly comes to rest.[5]

The academic specialist naturally notices exaggerated tilts of the head among elites; mass communicators consistently report on all signs of novelty and sensation. Thus, when late in the sixties, for example, the offspring of certain professors, mass media communicators, and middle-class suburbanites took up astrology and began to express a belief in omens, the media at once exploited this "occult explosion," while theologians and social thinkers felt called upon to come up with fresh theories about neo-religiosity or transcendence. In fact, the number of the new devotees did not significantly alter the proportion of the population that had always believed in such phenomena. The body of the societal shmoo—or the weighted portion of the cultural roly-poly—had barely moved. Both head and body merit observation; theories drawn from observing only one are inevitably vulnerable.

Proof of religious continuity in American life can be found in many ways, not least in the polling data. Thus, for example, in a poll taken in 1952 as compared with one in 1965, the data seemed to show a widespread, if shallow, *revival* of religion, followed immediately by a sort of *revolution* in religion. There were "startling indications of change and . . . more puzzling indications of non-change."

> Some . . . recalling the drama of the last dozen years, may look for more in these polls than they will deliver. Often . . . readers may have "felt in their bones" that epochal change in the world of science and the mass media or education will have induced epochal change in one or another of the sectors of the churches' lives. They will consult the statistics of those sectors and find a relatively undramatic change in percentages from 1952 to 1965.[6]

Polls today show that continuity persisting. This is not to say that there have not also been certain quite sudden documentable and dramatic changes. Attendance at mass and other religious observances, for example, fell off significantly after Vatican II, when true voluntaryism hit Roman Catholicism. Mainline Protestant and Jewish organizations have shown a continuing decline in their relative place among denominations, though it must be noted that this follows a trend as old as the one that began with the Methodist and

Baptist revivals around 1800, when Episcopalians, Congregationalists, and Presbyterians began to lose primacy. The fundamentalist, Pentecostal, and evangelical churches have clearly gained in visibility, morale, and strength; their code words have become a part of American culture. Recent Gallup polls, for example, have found Americans more ready than ever to identify themselves as "born again."[7] Yet such shifts tend to occur within the borders of an "all-pervasive religiousness" and a concurrent and "persistent secularity."

It is essential to think of these issues in a context that takes account also of generations—our third point. Two or more must always coexist. If there are two generations of Americans with different religious experiences, there are as well two generations of academic theorists with quite different outlooks. A generational shift appears to separate the period from roughly the end of World War II (or the beginning of the Eisenhower era) through the mid-sixties, from the late sixties into the 1980s. Still, the concept "generation" cannot be taken too literally in the biological sense, or too narrowly in the cultural sense. Robert Wohl in *The Generation of 1914* shows how the generational approach to self-understanding may confine and mislead if it is the only norm used for measuring cultural possibility.[8] In trying to grasp something as elusive as culture, however, the generational handle can be quite valuable. José Ortega y Gasset saw this; he defined culture as

> only the interpretation which man gives to his life, the series of more or less satisfying solutions he finds in order to meet the problems and necessities of life, as well those which belong to the material order as the so-called spiritual ones. . . . [Culture is] the conception of the world or the universe which serves as the plan, riskily elaborated by man, for orienting himself among things, for coping with his life, and finding a direction amid the chaos of his situation.[9]

These interpretations, these "more or less satisfying solutions," tend to appear along generational lines. Ortega was almost certainly too mechanical in his idea that cultural generations occurred fifteen years apart; he was more subtle when he recognized that several generations of coevals are alive at the same time. Those who have undergone a similar set of experiences at decisive stages in their life-careers tend to develop common outlooks. This is as true of those within the culture who endow with meaning both their fortune and their suffering—the religious—as it is of those who recognize and label the cultural change they perceive. The latter belong also to the *Zeitgeist,* perhaps more than many of them realize. If their particular task is to analyze and understand their culture, they sometimes extrapolate on the basis of what they see emerging, inevitably prophesying futures that do not always unfold as they predicted. This is most obvious in the paradigm shifts that they experience or initiate. I use the term *paradigm* here to mean both the "disciplinary matrix . . . the entire constellation of beliefs, values, techniques, and so on shared by the members of a given community" *and* the "exemplars," those "concrete puzzle-solutions that, employed as models or examples, can replace explicit rules as a basis for the solution of the remaining puzzles of normal science."[10]

THE SECULAR PARADIGM QUESTIONED

In the years following mid-century, as theorists not only found more evidence of religion than they had foreseen, but had to account for it as well, they began to waver in their support for the secular paradigm. They were committed by their academic "upbringing" to the view that, over the long haul, industrial societies like America could not do otherwise than become increasingly secular, yet plausible explanations were needed to account for the postwar revival of religion. Why, going against all trends, was so much favor shown to religious institutions in the 1950s? Theorists like Lipset believed that the revival was no more than a continuation of the all-pervasive religiousness of American life. Charles Y. Glock believed that there was more *talk* about revival than revival itself.[11] And as Michael Argyle looked at America from England, he tried to make sense of the signs of revived religiousness in America, noting their absence in Europe.[12] He cited Thomas Luckmann, who argued that, while "traditional church religion in Europe kept its religious functions and was pushed to the periphery of modern life, . . . in the USA, church religion has undergone a process of internal secularization, which has kept it 'modern' and visible." Religiosity was merely a veneer covering a deeper secularity. Argyle found a psychosocial explanation for religiosity in work done by Marcus Lee Hansen and

15

Will Herberg in 1952 and 1955: they saw American religiousness as a secular search for identity, a "third generation return." Americans, they said, feel "alienated and unidentified unless they belong to one of the major religious divisions." Argyle also cited earlier conventional explanations that tied religiosity to immigration, ethnicity, and urbanization, and found it plausible to assume that "religion in America . . . is mostly secularized."

Scholars who looked at the problem in these terms tended to see religious people as being, in Cuddihy's terms, "underclass" or "ethnic" and marginal. Yet in the core-culture, the majority were entering the mainstream of Western industrial, technological, and hence, secular culture. Avant-garde theologians, reared in the same "disciplinary matrix" as humanists and social scientists, began to use the paradigm—and even exaggerated it—in what came to be called "secular theology," a school that emerged precisely at the end of the first of the two generations. By now it is no longer rude, it is merely boring, to keep showing how wide of the mark their theories and extrapolations were. But it *is* important to ask why these theories seemed so plausible at the time, and to see whether we can learn, from the experience of that generation, something about cultural direction.

As Western, if not world, citizens, scholars in the eye of the hurricane could discern all the European and Canadian trends that were noted by S. S. Acquaviva in *The Decline of the Sacred in Industrial Society.*[13] Their vision of America was by no means invented out of whole cloth, however selective it was. There was much that made the religious revival superficial. The 1950s were a time when Western faith in general, or religion in particular, produced few profound ethical responses. Yet, although a religious veneer often covered some very secular uses of religious institutions, the secular theologians overlooked the symbiosis of religious all-pervasiveness and persistent secularity that was continuous in America.

Acquaviva ended his book on a somber note, for he believed that religion in the Western world was in a state of almost universal decline:

> From the religious point of view, humanity has entered a long night that will become darker and darker with the passing of the generations, and of which no end can yet be seen. It is a night in

which there seems to be no place for a conception of God, or for a sense of the sacred, and ancient ways of giving a significance to our own existence, of confronting life and death, are becoming increasingly untenable.[14]

The views of Argyle and Acquaviva were shared by many secular American social thinkers. In 1967, for example, Herman Kahn and Anthony J. Wiener, in a "surprise-free . . . basic long-term multi-fold trend analysis" offered as "a framework for speculation on the next thirty-three years" a scenario that managed to be challenged during the following three. They looked forward to "increasingly Sensate (empirical, this-worldly, secular, humanistic, pragmatic, utilitarian, contractual, epicurean or hedonistic, and the like) cultures." Kahn and Wiener were right about only the secular side of the religio-secular polarity and interplay.[15]

American theologians, however, in wanting a theology to match the increasingly agnostic and godless trend, had a more complex agenda than did social scientists. How could they square what looked like a religious boom with what, at the same time, they theorized about long-term religionlessness in the West, and then the world? American piety was undoubtedly "bad faith." The development of "religionless Christianity" or even "Christian atheism" would act, they believed, as a liberating force. To their critics, these relevance-hungry theologians, in attempting to "square the circle," to make faith and reason congruent, had sold out the faith.[16]

Despite the criticism, the secular perception and paradigm prevailed through the mid-sixties. In 1967 Larry Shiner, sorting out the uses of the term *secular,* found five basic meanings. It could mean the simple decline of religion; mere conformity with the world; demystification, or desacralization of the world; disengagement from society (an ancient definition that had survived); or, as in its derivative, *secularization,* the transposition of belief and patterns of behavior from the religious to the secular sphere.[17] The theologians of secularization did not see these meanings as adding up to anything like Acquaviva's dark night. Instead, they were part of the daylight of human freedom, a movement beyond spiritual adolescence to adulthood. Drawing on Friedrich Gogarten's concept that desacralization was what the Bible had in mind all along, or Dietrich Bonhoeffer's that "religionless Christianity" squared with much of the biblical design, they developed native American

17

visions.[18] Gibson Winter called his *The New Creation as Metropolis*, just before the cities burned—not to be replaced by phoenixes and utopias.[19] Harvey Cox had the bad luck to write a best seller, *The Secular City*, that in the public mind made him captive to the secular paradigm, even though he broke away shortly after.[20]

Sociologists, however, became increasingly wary of the secular paradigm's monopoly. In England in 1965, David Martin, in an essay called "Toward Eliminating the Concept of 'Secularization' from Sociology," cautioned that most uses of the term grew out of rationalist, Marxist, existentialist, or other ideological motivations.[21] In *Unsecular Man* (1972), a far more polemical work, Andrew Greeley set out to replace the secular paradigm with the mythosymbolic view of humanity, by drawing on earlier theorists to support the durability of nonsecular models.[22] Peter Berger, at the threshold between sociology and theology, in 1969 published *Rumors of Angels: Signals of Transcendence in the Modern World*—a signal that, among some sociologists, words like *transcendent* and *sacred* pointed to experiences that were available in the culture.[23] And among the theologians, Harvey Cox went back to the drawing board and came up with *The Feast of Fools*, also published in 1969, wherein he celebrated the very magic, myth, mystery, and mysticism of religiousness that only a few years earlier had seemed to be waning.[24] Clearly, a shift was occurring in communities of religious elites. The new generation that the Bergers and Coxes spoke to and about simply spurned the realities that the secularization paradigm pointed to.

At the very least, to make uncritical use of the secular perception and paradigm after the late 1960s was to deprive oneself of a range of instruments and theories needed to do justice to a variety of religious phenomena. What Clifton F. Brown saw in the black movement of 1968 and called "religiocification" was happening in many subcultures.[25] Religion was not disappearing, it was relocating.

THE DIFFUSION OF RELIGION

Humanists, social scientists, and theologians, it appears, are as susceptible to fads as other mortals. In the second of these generations, they saw religiousness everywhere, for by 1970, religion was "in." Scholars who at one time could account for its signs merely by saying that religiousness was an underclass phenomenon, or that it belonged on the ethnic margins of society, could no longer do so. Too many of their own children were caught up in cults and the occult. The Beautiful People were "into" an alphabet of phenomena, from astrology to Zen. Middle-class Catholics and Episcopalians were "speaking in tongues" in pentecostal enclaves.[26] Certainly, the fervent evangelical culture could not be classified as "marginal" when successive presidents—Ford, Carter, and Reagan—openly claimed membership in it. All this occurred, paradoxically, while a moderate, but still marked, decline in support of mainline religious institutions was so clearly taking place.

The cultural turn that was evident among elites, and the durable, but newly visible, "pervasive religiousness" in the broad culture, found theorists with explanations in hand. Some employed a neo-Marxist view that saw religion as the "opiate" for the failed "revolution" of the late sixties. Freudian observations about the need for new illusions, Sartrean suggestions of bad faith as evasions of reality, or Weberian notions about how authentic and deeply held religious views could alter the social and cultural environment were used by others. None need concern us here. Instead, our focus will be the fundamental shift in paradigms; here "modernity," which could include diffused religions, replaced—or at least challenged— "secularity," which had to explain religion away. This occurred, first, when scholars redefined religion and saw it diffused in culture; and second, when they amplified the model of what it is to be human in culture. For the redefinition of religion, the notion of modernity as differentiation was rescued from Talcott Parsons's macrotheory. Cuddihy summarized well the "differentiated modernity" motif:

> Differentiation is the cutting edge of the modernization process, sundering cruelly what tradition had joined. It . . . separates church from state (the Catholic trauma), ethnicity from religion (the Jewish trauma). . . . Differentiation slices through ancient primordial ties and identities, leaving crisis and "wholeness-hunger" in its wake.[27]

To this, Robert N. Bellah added the idea of diffusion, a motif he retrieved from oft-discredited evolutionary models. Bellah defined evolution as a process of increasing differentiation and complexity of organization that endows the organism, social system, or whatever the unit in question may be with greater capacity to adapt to its environment, so that it is in some sense more autonomous relative to its environment than were its less complex ancestors.[28]

Bellah tracked this definition through five stages, toward "postmodern religion," where it was "precisely the characteristic of the new situation that the great problem of religion, . . . the symbolization of man's relation to the ultimate conditions of his existence, is no longer the monopoly of any groups explicitly labeled religious." Religion, it appears, is diffused throughout the culture, difficult to grasp or observe. It has become a private affair, its fate no longer tied to organizations and institutions. Thus it had only been *apparently* paradoxical to observe that in the earlier generation religious institutions prospered while they shrouded a deeper secularization, yet in the second generation they languished while religion itself thrived.

We can summarize the change in religious definition in the phrase "from Thwackum to Geertz." Sidney E. Mead, historian and polemicist, looked back on the cultural laggards who had confined religion to institutions, and called them sectarians, temple-ists, or Thwackumites, after Henry Fielding's Parson Thwackum:

> When I mention religion I mean the Christian religion; and not only the Christian religion, but the Protestant religion; and not only the Protestant religion, but the Church of England. And when I mean honor, I mean that mode of Divine grace which is not only consistent with, but dependent upon, this religion; and is consistent with and dependent upon no other.[29]

Although Mead, like Bellah, believed that religion extended beyond churches and synagogues into civil or republican faiths, Luckmann, and others, saw it as diffused to the point where it had become "invisible" in private life. "Religious institutions," he wrote, "are not universal," but the very "social processes that lead to the formation of Self [are] fundamentally religious." Thus a new note was introduced into cultural anthropology in the West: the means that people use to transcend their mere biological nature, and all the symbolization and socialization that are part of these means, are inherently religious. In that sense, religion is universal and inescapable; it is, furthermore, incapable of disappearing.[30]

20

1. Discerning Religious America

Expansive new definitions of religion began to appear. The most widely accepted one, that of Clifford Geertz, defined religion as (1) a system of symbols that act to (2) establish powerful, pervasive, and long-lasting moods and motivations in men, by (3) formulating conceptions of a general order of existence, and (4) clothing these conceptions with such an aura of factuality, that (5) the moods and motivations seem uniquely realistic.[31]

Suddenly, the problem of definition became, "Where does religion *stop?*" If everything is religious, is then nothing religious? Obviously, superhuman beings or forces, as well as belief, dogma, and institutions, have no place in Geertz's definition. It points clearly, however, to the diffusion of "pervasive religiousness" in culture, even at those times when sacred institutions are enduring a crisis of legitimacy. This protean religion is ubiquitously available; it can be found in self-help books on airport newsstands, on television, in therapy groups, in university classes that deal with religion, or in the private search of lonely metaphysical windowshoppers and spiritual shoplifters as they put together individual world views.

In Geertzian terms, scholars whom the Vatican Secretariat for Non-Believers gathered periodically to study "the culture of unbelief" found only "cultures of *other*-belief." But true unbelief or pure-form secularization was found only rarely, least of all in America.[32]

Yet broad definitions of religion often met with protest, as, for example, when the U.S. Supreme Court called secular humanism a matter of "ultimate concern," and thus, in Paul Tillich's version, a religion. Theologian Julian N. Hartt, fully aware of Buddhism and Taoism, sounded provincially Western when he tried to provide limits: "We ought to say that a man is not really religious unless he feels that some power is bearing down on him, unless, that is, he believes he must do something about divine powers who have done something about him." James Gustafson wanted to reserve the word *religious* for that "dimension of experience (in which not all persons consciously share) that senses a relationship to an ultimate power that sustains and stands over against humans in the world."[33] Anthropologist Melford Spiro agreed; the symbol system required the inclusion of "superhuman" forces or powers. Yet even these confinements, moving religion, as they did, far beyond Thwackumism, allowed for its extremely wide diffusion in American culture.[34]

American religion thus seeped into the cultural cracks and barnacled itself to nonreligious phenomena.

The shift from the secular paradigm to religion as all-pervasive forced theorists, perhaps *enabled* them, to look for dimensions they had at another time ignored. Certain social scientists were able to confirm trends in their earlier work. Daniel Bell began to speak up for the values of the sacred and the transcendent.[35] Philip Rieff awaited the recovery of the sacred after the triumph of the therapeutic.[36] Scholarly definitions of *the sacred* were perhaps not what ministers, priests, and rabbis had in mind when they spoke of God. Humanistic thinkers, however, have often been in advance of theological thinkers; in this case, certainly, for avant-garde theologians who had accepted the secular paradigm now had to account for the survival of the sacred. The counterculture, the Age of Aquarius, the Jesus People, all had come and gone, leaving as their marks new evidence that humans seemed to be durably religious.

The new danger now is that the persistent secularity of American culture will be forgotten. The nation is as pluralist as ever, and in the operative aspects of its national life—in the university, the marketplace, or the legislature—America remains secular, with no single transcendent symbol to live by. Unless theorists and theologians reckon with *both* all-pervasive religiousness *and* persistent secularity, they will again be left stranded with each cultural shift, in search of theories to match their perceptions. The double paradigm will no doubt diminish the audaciousness of certain prophecies and projections: bold predictions of the purely secular city or a thoroughly sacral culture are obviously highly dramatic. But these predictions are as likely to be wrong as right, as the human record in general, and the recent American generational shift in particular, show.

At the end of the first of our generations, I argued that "*a preferable alternative seems to be the religio-secular model of indeterminacy, open to infinite transformations and toward the development of new kinds of consciousness.*" Admittedly, then as now, "the coinage 'religio-secular' to characterize the past, the present, and the tendency of American society, is not very fortunate, but we have not heard more elegant alternatives." But it is a historically accurate model, one that is evident in very many cultures—from

Greco-Roman through Enlightenment to recent American—and both more true to what Wilfred Sellers has called "the manifest image of man," and richer for projecting the probable path of culture.[37]

RESURGENT ANTIMODERN RELIGION

Through the two generations when secularism reigned, one large subculture resisted its sway. It included Hassidic and other mystical or orthodox movements in Judaism; numbers of American-born "sects" like the Latter-Day Saints, Jehovah's Witnesses, and Adventists; Pentecostal and charismatic movements in conventional Christianity; traditionalist Catholicism, to a lesser extent; and to a greater one, evangelical and fundamentalist Protestantism. That subculture is now resurgent. In 1980 it could claim the loyalty of all three major presidential candidates, along with entertainers and entrepreneurs, athletes and beauty queens. Obviously, such a subculture can hardly be described as marginal.

Its recent gains come in substantial measure from the selective use of secular techniques and modern technology; it is characterized by certain signs of secular "worldliness" and modern "diffusion." Yet these appear to be inadequate to account for the survival and strength of this steadfastly antimodern force. If religion elsewhere in the culture is so diffuse, why is it here so organized? If most religious institutions have become "refined" and civil, why are these so belligerent and aggressive? If a good deal of religiosity dissolves into the culture, why does this variety remain lumpish, unwilling to be filtered?

Cuddihy's concept of "dedifferentiating" and "demodernizing" cultural elements points to an embracing theory. Modernity meant differentiation and diffusion; if carried too far, they could leave a "wholeness-hunger" in their wake that only antimodernity could address. But Cuddihy was no determinist: modernity was not an inevitable culminating stage of evolution. One could choose to go behind it or beyond it.

Demodernization, from Marx to Mao, is dedifferentiation. . . . Inward assent to the disciplines of differentiation, the practice of its rites, may be viewed as the *paideia* of the West. "Ideology" is the name we give to the various resistance movements mounted to stem the onslaught of the differentiation process. Essentially these movements are demodernizing, dedifferentiating, rebarbative.[38]

This "old-time" religion never really disappeared; packaged in modern forms and transmitted through sophisticated media, it came back with a vengeance during the second of the two generations. In its Catholic form, it survived in various traditionalist movements or in its selective support for certain of the more conservative policies of Pope John Paul II. Among Jews, it became a charismatic movement, attracting those who had a predilection for Hassidic or mystical forms of Judaism, as well as those whose faith encompassed biblical claims to the land of Israel. Among the elites in mainline Protestant denominations, it took form in movements of "lay concern" against liberal theology, and in opposition to liturgical revision.

The most interesting and apparently most durable of these phenomena by far was the Protestant fundamentalist resurgence. Threatened with extinction around 1925 after the Scopes trial, fundamentalists went underground. There they endured, learned modern techniques, and worked their way back to cultural visibility. Calling themselves evangelicals, the moderates among them gathered power through the benign ministry of Billy Graham in the 1950s and after. Fundamentalism was eclipsed by the secular theology, liberal civil rights and antiwar movements, the civil religion of the New Frontier, and Vatican II, but only momentarily, for it came back to new vogue—and with new force—during the late sixties.

By the early seventies the evidence was in: conservative churches clearly were growing, and overly modernized mainline ones just as obviously declining. In an apparently secular and certainly diffusive religious America, the "strong" churches were paradoxically prospering, perhaps precisely because they were antimodern—absolutist, fanatic, conformist, highly committed to the group, rigidly disciplined, and zealous to proselytize. They were, in short, uncivil.[39]

But it was not long before much of the new conservatism had become civil and moved into the cultural mainstream. In 1974 then-conservative congressman John B. Anderson pointed out signs of the times at a meeting of the National Association of Evangelicals in Boston, signs so obvious that one needed no opinion poll to confirm them:

> It was [the liberals] who denied the supernatural acts of God, conforming the gospel to the canons of modern science. . . . It was *they* who found financial support for architectural monuments to their cause. It was *they* who were the friends of those in positions of political power. *They* were the "beautiful people," and *we*—you will recall—were the "kooks." We were regarded as rural, reactionary, illiterate fundamentalists who just didn't know better.
> Well, things have changed. Now *they* are the "kooks"—and we are the "beautiful people." *Our* prayer breakfasts are so popular that only those with engraved invitations are allowed to attend. *Our* evangelists have the ready ear of those in positions of highest authority. *Our* churches are growing, and theirs are withering. . . . *They* are tired, worn-out nineteenth century liberals trying to repair the pieces of an optimism shattered by world wars, race riots, population explosion, and the spectre of worldwide famine. *We* always knew that things would get worse before the Lord came again.[40]

The media, in their extensive coverage of the Protestant New Christian Right and the pressure it can bring to bear so effectively on vulnerable "public" institutions—schools, legislatures, broadcasters, and others—have been accused of focusing disproportionately on a not fully representative front. Yet by doing so, they draw attention to the groups' more militant counterparts around the world, the tribalisms that Harold Isaacs spoke of:

> We are experiencing on a massively universal scale a convulsive ingathering of people in their numberless groupings of kinds—tribal, racial, linguistic, religious, national. It is a great clustering into separatenesses that will, it is thought, improve, assure, or extend each group's power or place, or keep it safe or safer from the power, threat, or hostility of others.[41]

Wary as Americans must be of analogies to social movements elsewhere, they are yet mindful of the acute versions of tribal fundamentalisms in Hindu-Muslim subcontinental conflicts in Asia, in Tribal Africa, in Jewish-Muslim rationales behind struggles in the Middle East, or Protestant-Catholic versions in Northern Ireland.

These elements in world politics, vivid and startling as they obviously are, might reasonably be expected to lead social theorists and theologians to conclude that these fundamental tribalisms are the only portent in America's cultural future. But if the polity holds, Americans are not likely to jettison their traditions of pluralism and civility, and in doing so, yield entirely to one or another of the contenders. These forces by now have perhaps brought into the fold all those in the culture for whom the fundamentalist message rings clear and true—though without, of course, having exhausted all of the uses to which well-organized minorities can be put. Furthermore, they will undoubtedly stimulate backlashing and counterorganizing coalitions. Finally, by making too much of them, we may overlook the creative apathy of much of the public, which, by ignoring them, usually outlasts them.

There are, however, good reasons for taking the extreme Right seriously. Much of its power comes from Lipset's voluntaryism. Just as voluntaryism once helped assure the life of strong denominations, this American response to the separation of church and state has now proved to be an effective instrument for rallying the demodernizers. Mainline religions—Catholic, Jewish, and Protestant—have become so bureaucratized, so remote from the aspirations of their adherents, that they are ineffective. But because the Right depends upon constant voluntary financial support and response to direct mail, it keeps in constant touch with its constituents, has its finger, so to speak, on their pulse.

In many ways the new traditionalisms—or newly visible old traditionalisms with new glosses—illustrate the antimodern or demodernizing impulse. First, they are frankly nostalgic, longing for that simpler, ordered, homogeneous world that once satisfied the "wholeness-hunger" of individuals, subcultures, and the larger culture, that prepluralist world in which Catholics dominated Christendom, Jews were at home in shtetl or ghetto, and Protestants ran the American empire. Second, they attract those discontented with the chaos of pluralism, the hallmark of modernity. Just as Marx and Mao accomplished dedifferentiation by ideologies that coerced the masses, these new voluntaryists look to both legal instruments and persuasion to overcome the Babel of voices that cancel one another

26

out. Third, they are intolerant of the pluralist society's moral anomie, its apparent inability to generate positive values for common action.

These themes are grounded in others. One is a hunger for authority. A century ago, in a similarly erosive situation, absolutes could be found in Roman Catholic claims of papal infallibility and Protestant appeals to biblical truth. Now, in a similar and more intense crisis, infallibility and inerrancy have again become symbols of potent absolutisms.

The newly assertive forces are not, however, merely content to exact intellectual fidelity to absolute propositions. The craving for experience is part of a larger "wholeness-hunger." In its compromise with secular, dissected religion, modern religiosity ministered to this hunger only passively. Yet modernity creates great pressure for the individual in culture who is seeking meaning for all of life, including the experiential dimensions. That is why so many of the new movements include glossolalia, or tongue-speaking, fervent devotional movements, and the like.

Finally, in what may appear to be a paradox—since it cancels out the aims of these parties to shape more than their own subculture, to have their way, that is, in much of the society around them—the Protestant Right tends to be explicitly premillennial. In their reading of history, the world will worsen in anticipation of the end of history and the Second Coming of Christ, who will restore all order and beauty. Why, then, bother to reform America if it is soon to pass away?

Here one must point to an adaptation of the older millennialisms. Present-day propagators of the vision take care not to set the date for the Second Coming. There is time for enjoyment of the world God gave, even if he will soon cause it to burn. Authors of bestsellers on impending Armageddon regularly and unabashedly flaunt Rolls-Royces, or plow their royalties into long-term real estate investments. On evangelistic television we see a frankly hedonistic side to the new Christian Right. And America, though not here to stay, has, of course, been elected by God to train evangelists to rescue individuals before the end. Humanism and pluralism will only deflect it from its mission. In this regard, the new premillennialism matches Marxist and other eschatologies, since it gives its adherents a sense that they alone know exactly where history is going.

In all these respects, the movements show that neither simple diffusion nor any single style of rationality or experience is acceptable to everyone in a pluralist culture. These forces attract people wary of what Robert Lifton calls the "protean" personality style, favoring, rather, the "constrictive" style. The protean satisfies "wholeness-hunger" with nibbles from many cuisines; the constrictive type favors spiritual home-cooking, in great gulps.[42]

Here are Cuddihy's people in the path of the hurricane of modernization. They do not all reside in humble dwellings; many of them are moving into higher social classes. The outsider has the perspective to make relative judgments on the many versions of religious traditionalisms, but those inside either lack such a perspective, or if they do not, perhaps set aside the problem because of other satisfactions in sharing a particular vision.

It may be that the traditionalisms may soon be bought off by the danegeld that is abundant in American life. They may, in the process of enlarging their subculture and winning some points, find themselves joining the mainline, and in doing so, bartering away their own particularity. To William McLoughlin, a historian of the revivalism from which the movements draw strength, they represent a partly permanent feature of American life, but also—and here, drawing on Anthony F. C. Wallace's "revitalization" theory— a passing stage. After a "period of individual stress" when an old cultural synthesis breaks up, there is a second "period of cultural distortion" before a new orientation takes shape. These prospering groups are part of this second stage. In that phase, a "nativist or traditionalist movement" arises, wherein older generational leaders, decrying the ecclesiastical and civil systems, call for a return to the ways of the fathers, the old-time religion.

In a risky scenario for the early 1990s, McLoughlin expected a new consensus to emerge. It would thrust into leadership a U.S. president committed to the kind of fundamental restructuring that followed previous American awakenings—in 1776, 1830, and 1932. The new vision, he thought, would "not come from Marxism or the Orient but from our own cultural past." Revitalization and reorientation are by definition syncretic; this combination would fuse some "softer" elements with more formal inherited Judeo-Christian and civil covenants.[43] Some political analysts contended that in the 1980s such restructuring was beginning, though it appeared to be doing so without the "softness" McLoughlin envisioned.

McLoughlin's scenario, like so many others, presumes that there will be some sort of national consensus. Robert Heilbroner, in a script that foresees the collapse of the present American polity and ethos, agrees, but thinks it would be an imposed one. Although this looks very much like demodernization—presaging as it does the rise of a coercive state religion, a deification of the state itself, and the minimizing of pluralism—Heilbroner remains sanguine, believing that some sort of congenial socialist pattern will emerge.[44] The record of the American past, however, suggests that if this kind of mild Maoism were to appear, something called "Christian republicanism" would more likely be the nominal ideology to cover the adjustment to a new approved social contract.

We are left now with a many-layered culture. Legally, at base, and in many parts of the ethos, America is a secular, nonreligious culture; in practice, a pluralistic one. But that culture houses an impressive number of religious institutions that attract the loyalties of three out of five citizens, and the weekly participation of two out of five—and are likely to continue to do so indefinitely. Over these is a layer of particled religion, whose institutions count for less and which may take the form of private support. Some would put the whole complex in a container called "civil" or "public" religion, the consensus that presumably holds America together. Meanwhile, as we await a *new* consensus, traditionalist religion thrives. Through it all, a paradigm that seems ambivalent and equivocal, combining as it does both religious and secular elements, does justice to the viscous aspects of American cultural life.

The rediscovery of American religion implies a long tradition, one whose several elements we shall explore in the next chapter. For the present, at the very least, informed Americans are learning that their university, communication, literary, governmental, and intellectual elites overlook the dynamism of religion at their peril. In the emerging generation, during what appears to be a major cultural restructuring that goes from the nation's capital to its most remote precincts, to misperceive the role of religion, in what Ortega called the effort "to meet the problems and necessities of life, as well as those which belong to the material order as the so-called spiritual ones," will be more foolish than ever before.

2 The American Tradition: Five Continuities in National Life

Contemporary American religious pluralism develops within a continuity that we may fairly describe as "The American Tradition." That description is bold but could on the appearance of things look foolish. It demands examination. Whenever historians define the terms in their titles, we expect them to say something like this: "Every word in my title gets me into trouble except, of course, the definite article." In the present case, however, the definite article may be the occasion for the greatest trouble. How can one speak of *the* American tradition? Before we make any attempt at finding coherences which will make sense, it is necessary that we be reminded of the incoherences of American society and its many subcultures.

An illustration of those incoherences might come from the index section of any book that tries to deal in broad terms with America. Doing so almost gives one license to agree with Emmett Grogan that "anything anybody can say about America is true."[1] No outlines of an American plot or tradition seem at first glance to emerge. Take a book with an appropriate title for our circumstances, *Coming Apart*,[2] which is "an informal history of America in the 1960s," years that ever since have symbolized chaos to many. It was written by William L. O'Neill, whose terms merit revisiting in the subsequent period of reaction to that decade. Where might one find coherences in it?

Within the index of that book one may choose any section. I'll select one that, for reasons of ego and alphabet, comes naturally to me. I am told that William F. Buckley once sent a copy of one of his new books to novelist Norman Mailer, an old foe of his. Buckley wrote his little greeting next to Mailer's name in the index section, knowing that there Mailer would immediately get the message. Buckley assumed that authors have giant egos and great curiosity, and that Mailer would look for his own name before he would read the book. On similar terms, my section of choice would naturally be words beginning with *Ma* (which includes *Mc*). This section will serve typically, and well. We can explore it as a sample to search for what was then part of *the* American tradition.

What sense shall we make of the following conglomeration? There in the index are Eugene McCarthy and Robert McNamara, on opposite sides of the sundering Vietnam War. Joseph McCarthy is remembered near Mao Tse-tung, a non-American who helped divide America. Malcolm X is there, but so is Lester Maddox, at the other end of the racial pole. Marshall McLuhan, who told us, in effect, that in the media world whatever was, was right, is listed near Herbert Marcuse, who said the opposite. *Machismo* shares space with the Mattachine Society, a homosexual organization. Norman Mailer, of course, is there, but so is the Maharishi Mahesh Yogi. Marist College and Charles Manson, Jayne Mansfield and Abraham Maslow, "Mass-cult" and maxiskirts, the *Making of a Counter Culture* and MAAG (American Military Mission), John L. McClellan and Floyd McKissick, George McGovern and Mad Dogs, Manufacturing and Marijuana—all helped make up the 1960s. Those names represent only half of the entries under a one letter-combination of one-seventieth of one index of one book from one year from one corner of one library. Is there a *the* American tradition?

A second problem in the title is the word *American,* which seems to be at the same time too small and too large an entity for attention. Too small—in our global village or on our spaceship earth it seems provincial, even chauvinist, to isolate something so small as one nation for a discussion of values. George M. Cohan, the Broadway showman who knew how to use patriotism, reminded us that "many a bum show has been saved by the flag." Should we not speak of the human family, the race itself, the human tradition? But "American" is also too large a category. Most of the citizens of this nation draw their main inspiration from their subcommunities, sub-cultures, religions, tribes, racial and ethnic groups, movements and causes. Tribal deities often have more potency than does the God of the nation. Why use the national experience, a middle-range term, for those purposes?

Nor can we easily slide past the term *tradition* in a society usually seen as producing what Crèvecoeur called "this new man, the American." We are told that ours is a culture that constantly consumes or forgets its past, steel-balls its historic buildings, neglects its archives, produces "Now" people, and blurs the very concept of tradition. For how many people is a living tradition a source of values at all?

Hidden behind the three words of the title is another assumption. At this point we have to ask why anyone should connect the word *religion* with *tradition*. Dare we equate the two, or should we see religion as integral to tradition? Let me begin by defending the assumption that the two have much to do with each other, an assumption based on a theme of Paul Tillich which argues that religion is the soul of culture and culture the form of religion. One would not think of interpreting cultures that derive from Buddhist, Islamic, Hindu, or similar influences without some awareness of their religious grounding. Every visitor to American shores who wishes to make sense of life in this nation also finds it important to reexplore the religious roots of this culture, as many natives do not. While we cannot write "religion equals tradition," we can see that the deepest sanctions for the tradition are religious.

By traditional, I refer in part to what Ortega y Gasset called the *creencias* and *vigencias* of a people. *Creencias* are the ideas that we are, and not merely those we hold. They are the small pool of constitutive beliefs that are so deep they seem to be part of us. *Vigencias*, on the other hand, are the binding customs of the culture, the habits and manners, the ethos and style that become characteristic of wide elements in it. Countercultures know very well what they have to counter when they face those beliefs and ways. Beliefs and customs come to us from history, from the past. Hannah Arendt, with William Faulkner, believed that

"The past is never dead, it is not even past," and this for the simple reason that the world we live in at any moment *is* the world of the past; it consists of the monuments and the relics of what has been done by men for better or worse; its facts are always what has become (as the Latin origin of the word: *fieri-factum est* suggests). In other words, it is quite true that the past haunts us; it is the past's function to haunt us who are present and wish to live in the world as it really is, that is, has *become* what it is now.[3]

That past is mediated through that partly artificial entity called the nation, which provides at least one kind of grasp on universal reality. Our task now will be to try to discern not some outlines of "religion in America," but "American religion." Whoever addresses such an issue inevitably selects and produces a construction of reality. No two people will come out with exactly the same outline, for they deal with elusive realities. One feels almost like the daring and reckless child in a story of encounter with her mother:

   Mother: "What are you doing, daughter?"
   Daughter: "I am drawing a picture of God."
   Mother: "Don't be silly, darling. No one knows what God looks like."
   Daughter: "They soon will."

No one knows what the American (religious) tradition looks like. But, in a sense, they soon will.

One cautionary word: there is no claim here that the five elements to which I shall point are unique to America. They are distinctive. They are sufficiently widely shared in America and not sufficiently widely shared by other nations or peoples who are apart from or who preceded the American precedent to warrant some measure of identification.

PLURALISM

Pluralism is the obvious fact about America, and it is certainly distinctive. With the spread of technology, mobility, and mass media, an increasing pluralism is known all over the world today, in many nations. America is not the first country to include more than one religious grouping, to be sure. But nowhere before or elsewhere has there been variety on the scale experienced here, or such a widespread acceptance of the grounding of that diversity, or such celebration of its positive values. No foreign visitor fails to observe it. In a sense, to say that our tradition is pluralistic seems to say that America has no tradition: how can the "many" be a "one"? Yet Americans have dealt with their "many" in a way that has caused a kind of "one" to emerge.

On the fact of the variety one need not long dwell. *The Yearbook of American and Canadian Churches* annually lists between 220 and 230 widely recognized church bodies. Some Roman Catholic authors who want to perpetuate an old tradition that finds Protestantism to be false because it is both diverse and divided provide longer lists. Israeli scholars, who have to keep tabs on every millennial or apocalyptic sect in America because so many of them have their eye on Israel's role in the plot of history's end time, can list hundreds more. And those listings refer only to more or less formal groups. They do not even begin to reach out to the attitudes of private citizens, or to the ephemeral clusters, cells, movements, and impulses that can be discerned in the index to *Coming Apart*.

What is further distinctive about American pluralism in the religious tradition, beyond its sheer quantity and scope, is the fact that it has generated an assumption: "Any number can play." Most pluralisms have been based on the idea that there should be a host culture and then there can be guest cultures. First there is an official, legal establishment, and then dissenters are allowed to exist in the society on some terms or other. Assent is present so that there can also be dissent; conformity is present so that there can be nonconformity. Parity is another question entirely. The United States, of course, learned its new plot very slowly. It took a couple of centuries before a true legal basis was provided, and down even into the middle of the twentieth century it was still hard for privileged religious groups to learn that in mores and ethos they had to yield privilege and share equal space and time with groups they had once considered to be marginal.

In Holland there existed a pattern called *Verzuiling*, a columnization based on completely separate Protestant-Catholic-Jewish institutions and idea-structures. In many nations there were spatially divided territories in which one religion would be present with a monopoly, while at some distance another had to be reckoned with in its territory. But America became a crazy quilt of overlapping religious groups. The believers invented denominations in order to house their separate impulses. They have kept their sense of peoplehood and tribalism. At times they take them seriously, and at other times they neglect them. But all in all, there is a recognition that, as Father John Courtney Murray has said, religious pluralism is the human condition. It is written into the script of history. Nowhere has it been so manifest or taken so seriously as in the United States, the pioneer and the parable for the modern world in that respect.

EXPERIMENTALISM

While pluralism in religion has been at the heart of the tradition, experimentalism or the experimental spirit has been what has made it interesting. If less obvious, it is no less important. I consider it the basic element in the American experience of spirituality. When we use the word experiment, we refer to the fact that in religion, as in so many other respects, Americans are always ready with "Plan B." But Plan B is not argued on purely pragmatic grounds; it is seen to derive out of a consistent set of principles. There is always room for testing, for trying again, for changing.[4]

Are not all nations religiously experimental? Some of them may be turning toward this temper. Change is the law of life, and people can be dragged into it almost anywhere. But that change is usually slow and subtle, and yielded to grudgingly. It is important to look at characteristic ways of regarding religion elsewhere and in the past. In primitive religion the task was to adhere to the cosmos and the universe of meanings that were already given. The witch doctor, the shaman, and the priest all existed to monitor the ceremonies and ritual acts that grew out of a myth that explained the world. There was no thought of change, only of conformity. While biblical messianism should have meant change in the European world, that world which provided American ancestry, the establishment of Christianity in the fourth century and the forcing of Judaism into the ghetto (while Islam was kept at bay geographically), led people again to see religion as fixed, never to be tampered with. The European tradition of sociology of religion, because it converged, with Émile Durkheim, on "the elementary forms of religious life" or because it drew on Europe's traditionalist religious construct, tended to regard religion only as an apprehension of a given world.

Even Alexis de Tocqueville, that sophisticated observer of American variety and change, brought such assumptions with him. He believed that in the moral and religious world "everything is classified, systematized, foreseen and decided beforehand"; it was only in the political world that "everything is agitated, disrupted, and uncertain." Religion evoked "a passive though a voluntary obedience," while it was politics that inspired "an independence scornful of experience, and jealous of all authority." He did not believe that in the religious world things could be "agitated, disrupted, and uncertain . . . malleable, capable of being shaped and combined at will."[5]

Yet the American religious tradition *was* malleable. Change may be disguised under what sociologist J. Milton Yinger called "symbols of nonchange." "Changes are . . . obscured by the continuity of symbols."[6] That means that American religionists characteristically have had to refer to a script, to a code or canon. They have had to reassure themselves that their changes were in line with a past that had come to them by revelation. But in the context of that revelation were endless possibilities for adaptation and innovation. They might even despise the term *innovation*—as New Englanders in colonial times most certainly did. Then they innovated.

Jacques Maritain saw a carryover of experimentalism in all of American life. Americans embodied Hegel's "infinite elasticity" of the spirit, resilience and versatility. "At the origin of this *fluidity* there is the activity of the mind at work in the people, in the humble ways of daily life."

> Americans seem to be in their own land as pilgrims, prodded by a dream. They are always on the move—available for new tasks, prepared for the possible loss of what they have. They are not settled, *installed*. . . . In this sense of becoming and impermanence one may discern a feeling of evangelical origin which has been projected into temporal activity.[7]

While in its Protestant versions experimentalism took on an optimistic and progressivist cast, the Catholics who came here, even if they still carried along some sense of fate and fixity, also were observed to be experimenters. George Santayana wrote that Catholicism "is ancient, metaphysical, poetic, elaborate, aescetic, autocratic, and intolerant. . . . Everything in American life is at the antipodes to such a system. Yet the American Catholic is entirely at peace. His tone in everything, even in religion, is cheerfully American."[8] Eric von Kuehnelt-Leddihn, the conservative Catholic, in 1950 was again and again "cheered by the American [Catholic] readiness and freshness in tackling organizational problems; the old pioneering spirit is far from dead."[9]

The word *experiment* courses through American religious history, from John Clarke's colonial support of its "lively experiment" in religious freedom, to Thomas Jefferson's "fair experiment" of separating religious and civil spheres, to Philip Schaff's observation that "voluntaryism" was the great "experiment" in church history, to Hilaire Belloc's concern lest Americans devise a kind of civil religion which would be their "experiment" with a new religion.[10] Jews saw America as their Zion; so did blacks.

Those experiments could not have gone on had not Americans come to regard their environment itself as being somehow revelatory and redemptive. The sense that God was working new things here, that, as Reverend John Robinson said in 1620, "the Lord hath more truth and light yet to break forth out of his holy Word," was possible because they took security from knowing that there *was* a Word. American experimentalism has not been mere pragmatism. In a snide passage the maverick European Marxist Ernst Bloch has written that "to understand Marxist practice and propaganda as well, we must hold fast to the view that something is true not because it is useful, but always because, insofar as, and to the degree that something is true, it is useful." He contrasted that to American bourgeois pragmatism, "which holds that the truth value of any knowledge is to be measured by its success—which brings profit and common utility—and that any truth apart from this bourgeois type oriented to profitability is impossible and senseless. This may be true in a country where everybody is a salesman, a seller of himself, but surely *this* kind of 'theory-practice' is useless for us."[11] There may be elements of such styles of bourgeois pragmatism in American religion, but over all it must be said that every evidence shows that the people felt free to experiment because they felt that they were operating on the basis of a truth that would become utile because it was true. It was located in God's holy Word and in a benign environment.

Over against "Plan A" and against fate or fixity, Americans posed "Plan B," freedom, fluidity—experiment. Our history has been marked by positive and negative experiments, by innovations and revisions and reversals—all of them perceived by us to be in a continuity, making up a tradition. Our basic experience has been our own revolution in religion—the lively and fair experiment of religious freedom, the separation of Church and State, and "voluntaryism." Most of our subsequent experiments have been corollaries of the basic move and shift. Alexis de Tocqueville pondered it thus:

> Two things are astonishing about America, the great changeableness of most human behavior and the singular fixity of certain principles. . . . Men living in democratic societies . . . are forever varying, altering, and restoring secondary matters, but they are very careful not to touch fundamentals. They love change, but they dread revolutions.[12]

Here Tocqueville was either blighted by his European concept of fixity or he did not notice that in religion America had had its revolution, or felt that it had. It had devised a new fundamental element on the basis of which a wide range of experiments was possible.

To some, this experimental attitude is deadening to the spirit. T. S. Eliot saw it as a disease, a passion:

> The endless cycle of idea and action,
> Endless invention, endless experiment,
> Brings knowledge of motion, but not of stillness;
> Knowledge of speech, but not of silence;
> Knowledge of words, and ignorance of the Word.[13]

Yet Americans believed that they were not ignoring the Word in their alterations. On its basis they came to convert the Indians—and then they removed or killed them, finding scriptural justification for the move. They both supported and abolished slavery in part on grounds of "the Word." They came to establish monolithic and monopolistic theocracies and developed diverse and pluralistic democracies in religion. They brought along with them and adapted and transformed all the faiths known to Europe, and some from Africa and Asia, but felt free to invent an astonishing new range of sects and cults. The Protestants developed ideology for empire and then yielded it to pluralist impulses. The courts argued that they themselves should be "wholesomely neutral" and then, after saying that our civil institutions presuppose a Supreme Being, limited the attention to that Being in public schools and allowed for conscientious objection as being sacred even if there is no reference to that Being in the mind of the objector. The Americans invented the denominational system and the voluntary pattern, lacking precedent for both. They changed their polities on the basis of both practical necessity and ecumenical encounter, and then went on to explain how the changed version was what God had had in mind all along. Fortunately for all of them in all these moves, their scriptures were sufficiently deep, obscure, and manifold to permit many interpretations and impulses!

SCRIPTURALISM

This whole discussion of experimentalism so far relied on a sense that American religious life was somehow pre-scripted. It was from a holy Word that God's further truth and light was to break. Jerald C. Brauer linked "a constant free experimentation and search for a fuller manifestation of God's truth and will" with "a sustained effort to avoid going beyond the truth and light already known in the Bible and codified in certain basic beliefs and confessions."[14] Such resort to the scripted and the codified went far beyond Protestantism.

It has often been pointed out that even in the radically non-Christian counterculture of the 1960s, young Americans who wanted to leave the Bible far behind were also scriptural people. The Hare Krishna youth hawked their scriptures in airports and exegeted them endlessly. The followers of Sun Myung Moon in his Unification church had their own scriptures. So did the radical Americans who possessed the writings of Chairman Mao. People who lived in communes read the *Whole Earth Catalog* not as literary critics read a text, nor as aesthetes do for enjoyment, but as a kind of canon. So to move beyond the Bible does *not* mean to move beyond a scripture.

Scripturalism did first come to America, however, on biblical terms. Despite all the subsequent changes in our national life, nothing has displaced the Hebrew Scriptures and the New Testament from their positions of privilege. The antecedency helps; the people who give names to a culture hold power for an indefinite period. Americans may be increasingly biblically illiterate, but biblical lore is so bonded to their heritage that whenever they become thoughtful, whenever they reach deeply into their political lore (as with Abraham Lincoln) or into their literature (as with Nathaniel Hawthorne, or Herman Melville, or even William Faulkner), they are going to come across biblical nuances and promises.

The elites among the colonists were very explicit in stating that their lives were lived out as a new reading of the plot of books of Exodus and Exile. Christian though they were, they did not use the New Testament to set up their theocracies or their Bible commonwealths (as William Penn called his), because the New Testament's sense of an imminent end of the world limited its usefulness as code or canon for laws in the earthly city. For that reason, Jews have seldom had basic difficulty with the American legal or literary traditions. While America may be a *communitas communitatum,* a community whose subcommunities may disagree on the choice of scriptures or the content of the agreed-upon scriptures, the *communitas* itself has been marked by the scriptural and even biblical sense.

From the scripturalism have come many *creencias* of American life. Among them are the notions that this is a nation "under God"; that this nation has been pushed into history, and is being pulled from the future, by the biblical God or by a Supreme or Kind Providence, or whatever; that America has a mission, a destiny. Dangerous ideas of chosenness those may all be, but they also endow the people with a sense of worth and value. America is "genetically programmed" to take the Bible relatively seriously. But even though biblical meanings are thinned out, attenuated, progressively forgotten, or transformed beyond recognizability, the scriptural sense is likely to live on. There is no mythical past, no given cosmology that gives life to the people. In the midst of pluralism, arguments and representations have to be made on the basis of texts that are endowed with sacred or normative status in the many subcultures.

ENLIGHTENMENT

The Bible did not hold a unique position at the time of the birth of the nation, that moment from which so much later American life derives. For it happens that in the quarter-century surrounding the birth of the nation a new set of ideas had come to prominence. We refer to them as an "American Enlightenment." Europe, of course, had an Enlightenment at the same time, a more extensive, consistent, full-blown event. But the European Enlightenment ordinarily worked *against* religious claims and opposed the standard religious tradition. In America the Enlightenment was absorbed into the religious claims and either supported or had to coexist with the religion of the churches and subgroups.

In 1749 Benjamin Franklin, despairing of the churches' ability to get themselves together enough to give basis to the nation or to provide it with morals and virtue, spoke of "the necessity of a *Publick Religion*."[15] That public religion was grounded not simply in the Scriptures—though Franklin, Washington, Jefferson, and their kith and kind showed respect for them apart from their supernaturalism. Now religion was also to be grounded in social process, in a reason and nature that were both accessible to all people of thought and good will or good intentions. Here was a modified deism, a post-Christian style of religious philosophy. While it was soon countered by Protestant revivalists and Catholic or Jewish immigrants and fled from by secular folk who did not want to be identified with the excesses of the French Revolution, the Enlightenment did leave its stamp on American institutions. Taught as the truth about life by no known philosophy department in America, and seen as the creed in no church today, it still provided the basis for the nearest thing there is to a national creed—the Declaration of Independence—and was an element in the forming of the constitutional, legal, political, and educational systems in America. It provided the public with just enough hint of ideology to make it possible for them to adhere both to their particular faiths and the general ethos or code.

Earlier visitors were and modern commentators still are puzzled at American toleration, the ability of this people to combine almost fanatic faith in the creeds or ways propounded by separate groups with the relaxed faith in the ways of Enlightenment toleration, and public or generalized religion. In the next chapter we observe Gustave de Beaumont, Tocqueville's traveling companion, observing American religion.[16] He found what he thought was indifference, tolerance based on lack of zeal, combined with a paradoxical zeal for one's own religion. He believed the tolerance had to be born of superficiality. He was not wholly wrong. But he also overlooked the range of ways in which thoughtful and scholarly people have been able to combine their separate scriptures with Enlightenment universalism—or to see that the Enlightenment itself was not universal, but was sometimes its own sect!

That Enlightenment ethos, whose detail never had much following, but whose outline remains strong in our institutions, is therefore seen in America to be a religious positive, even though in Europe it was regarded negatively, as a displacement of historic faith. In America the two kinds of faith are seen not as contradictory (which they sometimes are), but as complementary, overlapping, mutually supportive, and—in the minds of the most reflective—both grounded in a still deeper order of Being that may always elude mortals who in their finitude cannot reach its extent or depth. But from fundamentalism to Unitarianism, in highly varied ways, Americans celebrate and live out many of the intentions of Enlightened religion.

VOLUNTARYISM

Were one able to separate the historical forms that the term *evangelical* connotes in America from its theological content, the word would be useful for describing an important element in the stamping of American religion. However, because evangelism refers to the Gospel of Jesus Christ, it would be inappropriate for application to Judaism and other non-Christian faiths in America. And though Roman Catholicism is devoted to that Gospel, Catholics would find the word too colored by Protestant history. Even within Protestantism the seizure and preemption of the term *evangelical* by a single sect renders it at least momentarily suspect even as a formal category.

For that reason I have chosen to characterize the American style of experience and affiliation as *voluntaryism*. Note the *y*. It is not *voluntarism*—"one or other theory or doctrine which regards will as the fundamental principle or dominant factor in the individual or in the universe" (*Oxford English Dictionary*). Voluntaryism, instead, is "the principle or tenet that the Church and educational institutions should be supported by voluntary contributions instead of by the State; any system which rests upon voluntary action or principles." The accent is on volunteering, not on the will. And while the dictionary definition accents the fiscal and legal implications, voluntaryism in America carries with it a heavy burden of assumptions about the personal agent and his religious experience along with reference to the character of the associations that are formed by the experiencers.

Included in the concept of voluntaryism is a competitive spirit. Daniel J. Boorstin has shown how encompassing such a spirit is, for it also includes Judaism, which has seen itself as being in no way missionary or evangelistic, nor given to advertising. Yet what Boorstin calls "Instrumentalism" has taken over. "Even Judaism—or at least its reformed branch—has become pretty well assimilated to this instrumental emphasis. One Jewish congregation has for the motto of its Sunday School, 'Sinai never does anything halfway.'"[17] When the revivalist calls the potential convert out of the world, he is not really asking the evangelized one to turn his back on it. He is offering a ticket to the "OK world," and is participating in a cultural initiation rite wherever evangelism has been pervasive.

The voluntary style is not necessary where there is no pluralism. There all citizens would be, virtually by the fact of birth, members of the single church. It is not plausible where there is no experimentalism, for it represents the opposite of the sense of fixity and fate that has characterized so much of what was called primitive and what was ancestral and is even now European religion. It draws on scripturalism, but scriptures are commended more "for the services they perform than for the truths they affirm," to use Boorstin's summary of the theme. (That is not to say the truths are not affirmed; they simply are not pushed forward as the main advantage for followers of a code or an invitation.) And voluntaryism draws heavily on the Enlightenment gift of toleration, for it assumes that, religiously, "any number can play," and that support for such playing exists in our law and ethos. Further, voluntaryists tend to rely on a second American Enlightened presupposition: that the separate churches can go about their business without disrupting the commonweal, that the various groups share enough ideas or beliefs to make possible a society, and not a jungle.

The Great Awakening of the eighteenth century may best be seen as the moment when the revolution toward voluntaryism occurred. From then until now the religion of experience has been somehow seen as more religious than is the religion of interpretation or action. Someone is *really* religious if he or she can cite and discourse upon a profound conversion experience, can engage in intense meditation or prayer, is especially devotional and attuned to the transcendent. Those features may not all be admired in the culture, but critics as well as apologists use them as marks for measuring and designating the truly religious. The Awakeners of the 1730s and 1740s and their successors ever since—including those in Catholicism—have stressed experiential religion. Some even called this experimental religion. They stressed the location of religion in the passions and the affections, the will and the emotions. Here was religion of heart and not just of mind and hand. Yet most previous religion was somehow heart religion. One could there and then go deeper in one's apprehension of an existing faith. But in America one first went deep in the art of choosing a faith. "Are you born again?"

While a communal context for experiential decision has always been applied, there is also something personal and even isolating about the voluntaryist appeal. "Do you accept Jesus Christ as your personal savior?" is a question somewhat different from the biblical ones, in which a person is saved with a people. But in America the covenantal community was always in the process of eroding, evaporating, being blurred, being reshaped. The evangelizer who called for voluntary decision called for a personal appropriation.

Voluntaryism's communal concept is also not so much a "given," as an a priori, a part of fate and fixity, a church that exists in the mind of God and the plan of the universe. No matter what the theology of the church may be, in America, where as H. L. Mencken observed, one "gets religion" and is enjoined to "go to the church of your choice," the religious organization is seen as in part a product of the sum total of conversions and choices. Theological exceptions abound, but the psychology and sociology of American religion strongly reinforce the voluntaryistic outlook.

The American Tomorrow

It remains to revisit the five themes and look briefly at their prospects. The American resolution as I have described its tradition is fragile, delicate, veneer-thin, gossamer, and possibly ephemeral. Experiments in social forms tend to have those characteristics. Two main choices lie ahead. On the one hand, our citizens may continue to pursue loneliness and drift from vestigial senses of community into religious isolation. Religion becomes only what one does with his solitariness. It is "doing one's own thing," "doing it my way," inventing "do-it-yourself" syntheses. Thomas Luckmann, in *The Invisible Religion*, has depicted such a tendency as normative in industrialized societies, where mobility and media prevent people from finding support for their belief and behavior in their primary and secondary associations. That invisible religion is the religion of the high-rise apartment, the faith of the television dial-twister who selects the evangelist of his choice, subscribes to a mail-order faith, visits the friendly neighborhood astrologer, and the like.

The other extreme, which strikes me as a kind of mild Maoism in religion, would rise out of despair over the alienation and anomie engendered by religious individualism. It would come as an ideology that would explain and reinforce postrepublican and postcapitalist turns in the larger society. Robert Heilbroner typically foresees such a religion being generated as the business civilization drifts toward the planned economy.

I suspect that a major force for the transformation of business civilization will be a new religious orientation, directed against the canons and precepts of our time, and oriented toward a wholly different conception of the meaning of life and a mode of social organization congenial to the encouragement of that life.

. . . A high degree of political authority will be inescapable in the period of extreme exigency we can expect a hundred years hence. This augurs for the cultivation of nationalist, authoritarian attitudes, perhaps today foreshadowed by the kind of religious politicism we find in China. The deification of the state, whatever we may think of it from the standpoint of our still-cherished individualist philosophies, seems therefore the most likely replacement for the deification of materialism that is the unacknowledged religion of our business culture.[18]

That religion of the state would be an extension of Franklin's *"Publick Religion"* or Bellah's "civil religion" at the expense of the separate faiths. The "invisible" choice would issue in an almost desperate experimentalism (for which the 1970s give considerable precedent), an atomization of pluralism, a continuing accent on scripturalism, an exploitation of Enlightenment presuppositions, and fulfilled voluntaryism. The collectivist alternative would mean the move toward a final experiment, the end of effective pluralism, the development of a new scripture or selection of a single old one, a despair of Enlightenment toleration, and the closing off of voluntaryist styles. I am not predicting that either will prevail. In the short term, the individualizing types are stronger, while it is in the longer range that many foresee the collectivizing system becoming attractive to greater numbers of leaders and people.

Pluralism. In the immediate American tomorrow there seems to be no threat of a diminution of pluralism. *Ex uno plures* has been the religious model of recent years, as a new denominationalism and a new ethnicism in religion have inspired tribal thoughts and practices. The calls for a civil religion or a resuscitated "religion of the republic" represented attempts to bring some order to the chaos in the early 1960s, but they were followed by new chaos and effervescence later in the decade. What seems necessary is the development of publicly accessible theories and theologies by which pluralists can ground their particular faiths in some sort of universal, ways by which they can relate their peculiarities to something general. Otherwise there will be only tribal soliloquies and solipsism and the death of the *communitas communitatum*.

Experimentalism. For the moment, Americans remain poised between the two resolutions of their two centuries (and more) old approach to religion. As Dwight Eisenhower might have put it, "Things are more like they are now than they ever were before." The people are free to set up shop and hang out a shingle for any religion, faith, superstition, or magical system ever known to humans—or to try to cancel out them all. They are able to do that because of the security they continue to draw from their environment, which, even in our secular era, is still perceived as having at least vestiges of promise, possibilities of revelatory power. Trying and testing go on.

Adaptation is as strong among the new groups as it is among the old. Not long after they began to appear on the scene, proponents of Krishna consciousness found it advisable to wear wigs in airports in order to accommodate themselves to prospects who might be put off by too much exoticism. Only months after their founder's death, the major Black Muslim faction's leadership began to invite the white Beautiful People to their events, even though a year earlier whites had represented devils to them. Transcendental Meditation, only a few years after it was first propagated in the United States, began to turn partly commercial and secular, leaving behind its Hindu roots but still offering quasi-religious benefits. The short-lived "Jesus freaks" took on new life as they turned straight and square. Pentecostalists and charismatics first called for spontaneity and then shortly wrote guide books for precision at prayer meetings and often tried to install authoritarian disciplinary systems. So the environment works its magnetic and erosive effects at once, while new groups and new emphases constantly keep appearing to offer still different ways for American spirituality. That experimentalism, however, verges on the atomism of "invisible religion" and has diminishing social effect. It would hardly be useful to the magistrates who might seek a religion for cementing new social bonds. So its future is not wholly assured.

Scripturalism. The standard question that ensues when biblical backgrounds to American culture are discussed is this: what will happen to the substance of the vision as the years pass? The schools are increasingly secularized, the Sunday schools fail in promulgating biblical traditions, the home has broken down as a teaching agency. How will a new generation be shaped around even the mere reminiscences of biblical patterns and thoughts? Will not America seek a "new myth," a new set of symbols? Why has not the boom in Bible translations and sales resulted in an increase of either biblical literacy or the restoration of biblical impulses in the public sectors of life?

If the Bible becomes ever more a sediment and a residue in American ideologies, it remains to be stirred up and activated. But though the biblical impetus has been diminishing, scripturalism seems to have a future, and would be assured whether America took a turn toward more individualism or more collectivism, toward more pluralism or more homogeneity. There seems to have to be a textual reference point for believers in the midst of the storms of modernity.

Enlightenment. As a formal philosophy, Enlightenment is in difficulty. The professional philosophers tend to disdain it: its language does not "check out." Many theological revivals among biblical faiths since mid-century have called its naturalism into question. The irrationalisms of an existentialist age counter its reasonableness. Lacking fresh articulation, it survives chiefly because of the way it made public institutions legitimate. As Sidney E. Mead once remarked, in an indelicate but apt phrase, Americans, especially the evangelicals, have had to swallow the Enlightenment's ideas in order to buy into its system, but they have been able neither to digest nor to regurgitate them.

But if the substantive philosophy of the Enlightenment is eclipsed, the formal cast remains as a set of intentions voiced in Walter Lippmann's "public philosophy," Father John Courtney Murray's attempt to transcend mere pluralism, Reinhold Niebuhr's ironic vision of American history, and the like. That public philosophy lacks widely recognized proponents today, and its liberal version is hardly visible. A moderately conservative call for tradition and continuity recalling some of its principles is present in the writings of Daniel Bell, Robert Nisbet, and others who are concerned about the loss of intention and authority in culture.

If the public philosophy is not regularly voiced with clarity and power in public, it is in even worse shape in the religious organizations. There the experiential prevails, and little premium has been placed on reason. Many an apocalyptic pitch in popular religion is a thinly disguised call for a new Dark Age.

Voluntaryism. In the short range, it is hard to see a disappearance of the experiential note that is basic to voluntaryism. There are signs that the frantic and even faddish lust for experience is diminishing. But if people wish to be religious tomorrow, it is likely that they will use their religion as a sphere in which they can have experiences that metropolitan and technological life ordinarily deny them. There is a new personalism and intimacy in the therapies and "small group movements" that have characterized religion for some years. And voluntary associational instincts are likely to remain strong. But those trends are qualified both by the attractions of the "pursuit of loneliness" and the "invisible religion" on one hand and the homogenizing corporate style of civil religions on the other.

The script for the future, then, breathes very much the sense of what I have here characterized as the American tradition. It is seen as a process and not a product, a stewardship based not on a belief in progress, but on a recognition that the alternatives are less promising. "The authority of the eternal yesterday," as Max Weber called it, has never been consuming in America. But after over two hundred years it is being heard among other authorities. Not all who invoke it do so in order to settle arguments, to lay upon society the dead hand of the past. Many see in it the basis for better disagreements than those we have known, livelier debates, and some measure, at least, of freedom.

The terms for these debates have long histories, and the rules and etiquette for participation developed slowly, sometimes reflexively and sometimes with philosophical bases. What was needed was both a polity and an ethos. Metaphorically, philosopher William James advanced the cause with his picture of a "republican banquet." It is time to set that table.

ii

DIMENSIONS OF PLURALIST
EXPERIENCE

3 *Public Religion: The Republican Banquet*

In late spring of 1831 two young French noblemen spent nine days observing Sing Sing prison in New York. After Sunday worship one of them, Gustave de Beaumont, wrote a letter to his mother. Each week, he reported, a minister belonging to a different communion preached to the captives. "All the prisoners attend the service together, without perhaps knowing the difference between the sects to which their preachers belong. If they don't, so much the better," he mused. But if they do know the difference, "they must find themselves much embarrassed to choose between the various cults the best and only true one."

From views of the hard benches at Sing Sing, Beaumont leaped in imagination to conclude that nothing was more common in America than "indifference toward the nature of religions." Yet, he continued, this indifference did not "eliminate the religious fervour of each for the cult he has chosen." The writer was puzzled over what he called "this extreme tolerance on the one hand toward religions in general—on the other this considerable zeal of each individual for his own religion." How could "a lively and sincere faith . . . get on with such a perfect toleration?" How could a person have "equal respect for religions whose dogmas differ?" What real influence on the moral conduct of the Americans, he wondered, "can be exercised by their religious spirit, whose outward manifestations, at least, are undeniable. Would it not be from their outward show of religion that there is more breadth than depth in it?"[1]

Upon landing in America that May, Beaumont's better-known colleague, Alexis de Tocqueville, asked an instant question: "How can the variety of sects not breed indifference, if not externally, then at least within? That is what remains to be known."[2] He, too, found at Sing Sing a "pretended toleration that had to be nothing else than good round indifference."[3]

The two visitors carried their questions and their prejudices with them on the road. Congressman John Canfield Spencer, at his summer home in upstate New York, gave them the popular defensive explanation for the tolerance they found as he cited "the extreme division of sects (which is almost without limits). If there were but two religions, we should cut each other's throats. But no sect having the majority, all have need of tolerance.[4] Voltaire had earlier voiced just such a notion about England, and James Madison later restated it for America, where, he said, security for civil and religious rights consisted "in the multiplicity of interests . . . and . . . the multiplicity of sects."[5]

Spencer then pushed on to a second "generally accepted opinion" which held that "some sort of religion is necessary to man in society, the more so the freer he is."[6] In his classic *Democracy in America*, Tocqueville showed how he here agreed with the attorney. Instinctive Ciceronians that they were, he and Spencer thought that a republic needed a *consensus juris*, a profound agreement about values undergirding law and society. Cicero had gone even further: "Each commonwealth has its own religion, and we have ours" ("Sua cuique civitati religio est, nostra nobis" [*Pro flacco* 2:8]).[7] The sects, in their understanding, had to be tolerant of each other for the sake of consensus.

On July 22, soon after the pair of Frenchmen arrived at the "fine American village" of Detroit, Father Gabriel Richard provided a third rationale for American tolerance. This former congressman, a Catholic elected by Protestants, argued that citizens knew how to bracket their sectarianism in order to show tolerance: "Nobody asks you *of what religion you are, but if you can do the job*."[8] Yet Americans demanded some sort of religion from everybody. In Maryland that autumn Richard Spring Stewart argued that the belief of Americans was sincere, but their competitive churches did exert social pressure on people to choose one or another among them. Unbelief itself was not then socially permissible. "Public opinion," Stewart added, "accomplishes with us what the Inquisition was never able to do."[9] The sober French visitors shared this public concern for religion because they thought it necessary for "the moral conduct of the Americans," or for what I prefer to call social or public morale.[10]

The tolerance coupled with indifference that they both wanted to find and then seemed frightened to encounter blinded Beaumont and Tocqueville to the raw intolerance that still blighted the United States. They missed much by tending to stay close to lookalike people of old Protestant stock who had not yet headed out in full array on a nativist crusade against Catholics. Tocqueville did find the handful of American Catholics taking advantage of the tolerance that their former adversaries showed them while they themselves remained, as he put it, "still at bottom as intolerant as they have ever been, as intolerant in a word as people who believe."[11] True belief, in his mind, allowed for no tolerance.

Visitors who found as little conflict between sects as did Beaumont and Tocqueville were clearly out of physical range of noisy frontier Methodist and Baptist revivalists who, with larynxes and fists alike, competed for souls. They could not know, for example, that also in New York at that time a new group called the Mormons was gathering; they would soon be victims of persecution. They overlooked the ways plantation owners then dishonored black slave religion and kept the slaves from freely congregating. Yet even they reported on their glimpses of sectarian spite. While swatting mosquitoes at Saginaw in Michigan, in a "corner of the earth unknown to the world," Tocqueville counted six conflicting religions. He noted formidably immobile and absolutely dogmatic Catholics, religiously anarchic Protestants, and ancient pagans there battling for that earth. In the midst of the wretchedness of solitude and the troubles of the present, he heard the Lutheran condemn the Calvinist to eternal fire and the Calvinist the Unitarian, while the Catholic embraced them all in a common condemnation. The more tolerant Indian, in his rude faith, merely exiled his European brother from the happy hunting ground he had reserved for himself.[12] The next winter, in a southern town, a diplomat friend named Joel Roberts Poinsett agreed with Tocqueville that all of these groups would burn each other "if the civil power was given to any of those persuasions. There is always deep hatred between them."[13]

Not for their glimpses of intolerance, but for their perplexities over the character of tolerance, do later generations remember Beaumont and Tocqueville on American religion. They were right to stress how, as moderns, Americans "must choose" a sect because their religion no longer came with the territory, nor was it passed along with the genes. Second, people were truly fervent and zealous in loyalty to their own sects in those days. This they still are, and they prove it by fighting not between church bodies but within and over them. Parties in each denomination fight for control with a passion and finesse that proves the point of John Dewey: people "do not shoot because targets exist, but they set up targets in order that throwing and shooting may be more effective and significant."[14] Thus they would rather fight than switch; and many never did shift loyalties, despite a tradition of constant prophecies by observers who thought that mobile and intermarrying Americans would casually break denominational ties.

It is their third theme, that tolerance in the United States had to be born only of ignorance, indifference, and superficiality, that has misled succeeding observers, including myself when young, more than any other statement they made on the subject. I propose to challenge their notion and to supplant it with other explanations for American attitudes. Beaumont and Tocqueville came by their prejudices on this subject naturally. In Europe, official Catholicism always had opposed tolerance and inspired a horror of indifference even among those who, like Tocqueville, were lapsed members. For classical Protestants, the Reverend Nathaniel Ward in Massachusetts expressed the imported and enduring attitude. Ward derided the English people when he first sniffed among them the dangerous signals of friendliness across sectarian lines. "He that is willing to tolerate any Religion, or discrepant way of Religion, besides his own, unless it be in matters meerly indifferent, either doubts of his own, or is not sincere in it."[15] To this day, taunters like to suggest that the really religious are those who believe enough to be fanatic and intolerant.

Americans, on these historic terms, were damned if they did

show intolerance, because it led to the bloodshed of holy wars, and damned if they did not, because then they looked indifferent and superficial. Now, while it is true that religion did intensify some of the most savage conflicts in national history, including the war over slavery, sectarian strife itself left few corpses. As for the charge of superficiality, it would be difficult if not impossible to prove that the Americans were less profound in religion than the European common people against whom visitors compared them.[16] Between these two sets of damns, however, citizens improvised a third way, which the author of *Democracy in America* helped cause later observers to overlook. In this context, Perry Miller thought that Tocqueville's pages on religion were "probably the least perceptive he ever wrote," because his "Gallic logic failed to encompass the spectacle of American irrationality."[17] But was Miller here his usual perceptive self? I shall contribute to ongoing debates by challenging the charges of both simple indifferentism and irrationality.

All those who study American religion and not merely religion in America have to join United States citizens in wrestling with the classic and here central problem of "the one and the many." The great philosophical jouster with this problem, William James, once provided an image for it that grew out of an analogy to a political idea. Since analogy works both ways, I shall carry his back to its source to offer an image that is designed to replace those of the sullenly tolerant inmates at Sing Sing and the swatting sectarians around Saginaw. In a passage written to counter absolutism in philosophy, William James once asked a question that applies as well against exclusivism in religion: "Why may not the world be a sort of republican banquet . . . where all the qualities of being respect one another's personal sacredness, yet sit at the common table of space and time?"[18]

William James, of course, was at the time busying himself with apparently contradictory qualities of being, while we are depicting apparently contradictory sectarian positions or, better, groups that were forced to sit at a metaphoric common table. They were able to do so most creatively when they began to show "respect for one another's personal sacredness." The republican image is appropriate for the American scene. Rich and diverse as it was, it still filled up with so many conflicting kinds of peoples and sects that they were compelled to devise a compact of mutual tolerance, unless they wanted to repeat unproductive ways determined by the old laws of the religious jungle. Forced thus to come to terms with each other, they developed what Abraham Lincoln called "bonds of affection" and "mystic chords of memory" because of common experiences of a sort that were denied their ancestors.[19]

The beginnings of tolerance, then, grew out of empathy born of firmness, not superficiality. Gabriel Marcel has remarked that tolerance cannot be manifest before intolerance: "tolerance is not primitive." It is "ultimately the negation of a negation, a counter-intolerance. . . . The more it is tied to a state of weakness, the less it is itself, the less it is tolerance." To the extent that I am aware of sticking to my opinion, I can conceive the opinion of another "to be worthy just because of the intense conviction with which he holds it; it may be that my awareness of my own conviction is somehow my guarantee of the worth of his." Mutual understanding, in that case, grounds itself not in doubt or skepticism, says Marcel, but in transcendence, where respect for "one another's personal sacredness" takes shape.[20]

Even to James, any sort of republican banquet demanded argument; it was not a gathering of crapulent or smug diners. "The obstinate insisting that tweedledum is *not* tweedledee is the bone and marrow of life," he elsewhere asserted. "Look at the Jews and the Scots, with their miserable factions and sectarian disputes, their loyalties and patriotisms and exclusions,—their annals now become a classic heritage, because men of genius took part and sang in them. A thing is important if anyone *think* it important."[21] So James allowed that, were he called to address "the Salvation Army or a miscellaneous popular crowd," he would try to break up and ventilate faiths and help "blow their sickliness and barbarism away."[22] No indifferentist himself, he wanted "the freest competition of the various faiths with one another, and their openest application to life by their several champions." They "ought to live in publicity, vying with each other."[23]

Not only self-described pluralists like James debated "the one and the many." Father John Courtney Murray, S.J., a recent contender, typified those from other camps who pondered its implications. Murray was sure that his Catholicism was "the best and only true" church, yet he respectfully entered what he called the conversation with others. "Religious pluralism," as we have heard him say, "is against the will of God, but it is the human condition; it is written into the script of history. It will not somehow marvelously cease to trouble the City." American pluralism seemed to him to be especially lamentable. "Many of the beliefs entertained within society ought not to be believed, because they are false; nonetheless men believe them." Unlike the Jamesians, Murray did not believe that the truth would "always be assured of conquest if only it were subjected to the unbridled competition of the market place of ideas." Yet the priest readily agreed with the United States Supreme Court that it was not the function of government to resolve disputes between conflicting truths, "all of which claim the final validity of transcendence." Murray feared not the barbarian who came to the republican symposium in bearskins with a club in hand, but the person who wore a Brooks Brothers suit or academic robe and threatened others with scholarly footnotes that came from his ballpoint pen. The priest saw no choice but to keep the republican debate going, hoping that it might move some citizens past mutual confusion not to simple agreement but to better disagreement and from thence to a more civil argument.[24]

Just as pluralists and monists shared the table of the Republic, so did those who, like Murray, believed that a *consensus juris* must help glue society together and those, like James, who were less sure of this. In his *In Defense of Politics*, Bernard Crick asked skeptically for representations of this tradition: "Where is the *consensus* in Canada, for instance? Or anywhere, between Catholic, Protestant (High or Low), Muslim, Hindu, Jew, Sceptic, Agnostic, Freethinker, Atheist, and Erastian, who commonly share some common political allegiance—if they take their fundamentals seriously and take them to be directly applicable to politics?" Crick doubted whether any consensus at all could go much further in outline than the merely existential *cri de coeur* of Groucho Marx: "Take care of me. I am the only one I've got."[25]

The majority of Americans, of course, have believed in a consensus, whether somehow achieved or in process, though periodically they call its existence or substance into question. Huge minorities of them, then, set up for themselves the problem of intolerance before they could achieve counterintolerance. What James called their "passional nature" led them to make sectarian choices when options that were living, forced, and momentous faced them. James could sound like an evangelist at altar call: "To say under such circumstance, 'Do not decide, but leave the question open,' is itself a passional decision . . . attended with the risk of losing the truth."[26] So, in a third pairing, citizens also felt called to choose between the conventional sects and those that claimed to represent the very religion of the Republic itself. The latter group today provides the most lively case study for our hypothesis about the nature of counterintolerance at the sort of republican banquet.

FOUR STAGES OF PUBLIC RELIGION

Americans have never begun to agree on what to call the clusters of republican sects. Tocqueville leaned toward "enlightened," and sometimes toward "natural religion" (which the Unitarian former president John Quincy Adams took pains in his presence to distinguish from Unitarianisms), and sometimes to "pure Deism." At Baltimore, Richard Spring Stewart, a physician, fumbled around among words as he told Tocqueville that the vast majority of the enlightened people in America were "truly *believing*" and that they tolerated no anti-Christianity or unbelief. Then he curiously linked *irreligion,* or the absence of firm belief, with deism. Stewart agreed with President Adams that such enlightened deism had been losing ground for forty years and that by 1831 its progress in the United States was very slow. But historically he could anchor it in the faith of respectable national founders. Jefferson, Franklin, and John Adams were "decidedly deists," though Stewart seemed to think that their colleague George Washington was less decidedly one of their company.[27]

We have already recognized that it was Benjamin Franklin who began the advocacy of republican piety when in 1749 he pointed to "the Necessity of a *Publick Religion*." He argued that it would be useful to the public, advantageous in promoting a religious character among private persons, and helpful—was he here twitting the regular sects?—in countering "the mischiefs of superstition."[28] Later, in his *Autobiography,* Franklin defined the substance of pub-

lic religion when he spelled out "the essentials of every religion."
He took pains to exclude all elements of what the Christian majority
called saving faith and kept for his canon only "the existence of the
Deity, that he made the world, and govern'd it by his Providence;
that the most acceptable service of God was the doing good to men;
that our souls are immortal; and that all crime will be punished,
and virtue rewarded, either here or hereafter." Then, as is well
known, he announced his "different degrees of respect" for the
sects, depending on the degree to which these essentials were
"more or less mix'd with other articles" that did not promote public
morale and that did divide citizens.[29]

Just as familiar was the second half of the fundamental canon that
Thomas Jefferson professed in the Declaration of Independence.
Fifty years later he was still sure that the "self-evident truths" there
stated were "the expression of the American mind."[30] They
grounded human equality and the power to govern by consent in a
moral order under a divine endowment of unalienable rights and a
higher law.[31] Jefferson, who had less use than Franklin for the
churches, did allow that "difference of opinion is advantageous to
religion. The several sects perform the office of a *censor morum*"[32]
and thus contribute to social morale. When, however, Jefferson divorced religion from morals—otherwise, he asked, "whence arises
the morality of the Atheist?"[33]—or urged that "it does me no injury
for my neighbor to say there are twenty gods, or no God,"[34] he
suggested what its proponents often overlook, that republican religion had to be voluntary, no more a part of fundamental law than
was churchly religion. Yet even Jefferson worried over how the liberties of a nation would be secure if removed from "their only firm
basis, a conviction in the minds of people that these liberties are
the gift of God."[35]

Presidents of the United States soon became the priests of public
religion. George Washington bade citizens farewell with the view
that "religion and morality are indispensable supports"[36]—he significantly differentiated the two and called them twin pillars—for
political prosperity. John Adams followed in 1798 with the formal
claim that the nation need ask "the protection and the blessing of
Almighty God" for the "promotion of that morality and piety without which social happiness cannot exist nor the blessings of a free

61

government be enjoyed."[37] Abraham Lincoln was later to weaken somewhat the Jeffersonian self-evident truths to propositions, yet he still proceeded to call the declaration his creed and to offer his life for it.[38]

The second stage, which concerns us least here because it has less regularly found official support, took diverse shapes in the writings of nineteenth-century literary figures after enlightened deism faded or lost out to aggressive sectarians. Ralph Waldo Emerson, Henry David Thoreau, Walt Whitman, Herman Melville, and Horace Mann all largely bypassed the historic and divided churches in their proposals. In the interest of social morale they tried to embody a new but often self-contradictory set of public faiths in the form of communal experiments, public schools, or the nation itself. In the end, however, this style of public religion found voice only in the writings of solitary geniuses who attracted reading clienteles, not congregations.

Then, in the middle third of the twentieth century, advocates of a public religion, still united against the churchly sects but disunited about their own alternatives, made new claims. Thus, in 1934, philosopher John Dewey promoted *A Common Faith*, which took democracy as both its setting and its object, over against inherited church religion. Leaving behind the founding fathers, he now wanted a godless religion to turn "explicit and militant." With verbal sleight of hand, he joined the great cloud of witnesses to public religion in the act of conceptually reducing the great number of sects down to only two. "Never before in history," Dewey began his book, "has mankind been so much of two minds, so divided into two camps, as it is today." The educator did not want religious belief any longer to be organized "in a *special* institution within a secular community," evidently not regarding the public school, which would have been the established church of this common faith, to be such an institution. Dewey would allow churches to survive if they dropped their supernaturalism and then celebrated or reinforced naturally in "different ways and with differing symbols" the one "fund of values that are prized and that need to be cherished."[39]

Fear of chaos after World War II led the followers of Dewey to promote social morale through such a naturalist and democratic faith. J. Paul Williams typically argued that denominational faith was a useless distraction because it was not "shared with the members of a whole society." After blasting the churches for being imperial and exclusivist, he called on government to become so by asking it to teach "the democratic ideal *as religion*." More alert to ritual than many of his colleagues, he hoped democratic society would support such a religion with metaphysical sanctions and ceremonial reinforcements that would be more effective than those of its Nazi, Fascist, or Communist counterparts. "Democracy must become an object of religious dedication. Americans must come to look on the democratic ideal (not necessarily American practice of it) as the Will of God or, if they prefer, the Law of Nature."[40] Horace M. Kallen summarized this case by the Dewey school: "For the communicants of the democratic faith it is the religion *of* and *for* religions. . . . [It is] the religion of religions, all may freely come together in it."[41]

A generation of us who came to maturity in the 1950s gathered under the banners of Reinhold Niebuhr, John Courtney Murray, and sociologist-theologian Will Herberg to react against this version of public religion as a "secular humanism" that was threatening to establish itself. To Herberg, who used biblical prophetic motifs to judge civic faith most severely of all, this was a "particularly insidious kind of idolatry." The "common faith" of American society he thought ought to remain implicit and never be pushed to what he considered a logical conclusion that few others found latent in it. To the mass of Americans he wrote that civic faith was "not a superfaith but a common faith," one that made "no pretensions to override or supplant the recognized religions, to which it assigns a place of great eminence and honor in the American scheme of things." But, he added ominously, "all the implications are there."[42]

In the next decade Will Herberg himself displayed a more benign view of the now more benign versions of public religion, including the by now familiar call by Robert N. Bellah in 1967 for Americans to celebrate a civil religion which was "elaborate and well institutionalized," as Bellah thought, "alongside of and rather clearly differentiated from the churches."[43] Bellah, whose program came at the end of an episode that lasted through the third of a century, was friendlier than others to denominational religion. He also emphatically backed off from a religion whose object would be democracy, toward a transcendental theism that evoked texts of Franklin and Lincoln. Then, soon after Bellah had spoken up for this common piety, some renewed religious sects and, more frequently, racial or ethnic groups challenged the very need for consensus and often pressed private interests, neglecting those that promoted social morale. The drastic character of this climatic change in the decade after 1967 occasions a fresh appraisal of the subject.

The "time of troubles"[44] that befell the civic faith is not likely to end calls for public religion. Historians deal with pasts, but it is valid to report on scripts for the future. Many futurists foresee a fourth stage for public religion after the collapse of the present American polity. Typically, as we have seen in chapter 2, economic historian Robert Heilbroner pictured that in the next century, concerns over survival would call American society to generate nationalistic-religious values to replace pluralism. He expected that a new religious orientation, a new social organization, and a kind of deification of the state would ensue. Heilbroner, convinced that the passing of the old order would not likely be mourned, looked for little freedom of expression in the forthcoming form of public religion. The republican banquet would certainly end.[45]

Through the years, then, advocates of public religion, while divided over whether it requires a God or not, or whether it should be voluntary or coerced, and though themselves chopped apart by many competing philosophies, have often successfully conveyed the idea that public faith is one big agreed-upon thing over against schismatic church religion. In their eyes the zealous sectarians, who are able to be tolerant only when indifferent, put their energies into religions that are somehow irrelevant to or that distract from or are at least irresponsible about the causes of social morale. Despite the changes, most members of denominations continued to feel at ease at the republican banquet. They regularly moved far beyond the mere respect for "one another's personal sacredness" that circumstances and empathy inspired to some substantive positions that merit analysis.

THREE SUBSTANTIVE POSITIONS

First, the American laity, often without benefit of clergy, as it were, came to differentiate sharply between what we may call ordering faith and saving faith. They did not, of course, all use those terms or invent the hoary distinctions on which they are based. From their sacred books they inherited a wild variety of models, none of them directly applicable to pluralist America. What Beaumont and Tocqueville saw going on at Sing Sing or around Saginaw was an effort of a people who were being forced to rewrite the old charter for Christendom or replace the one that came from the days of Augustine in the fifth century, Thomas Aquinas in the thirteenth, and Calvin and the Puritans in the sixteenth and seventeenth. The Americans, not able or willing to legislate a formally Christian polity, faced a new condition and needed new outlooks.

Though they did not need to cite him, most believed with Augustine that civil society must be rightly ordered (*bene ordinata, bene constituta*). They took a far more positive view than did he of the sacred dimension of government in the Earthly City. For him, there could arise at best an amoral "republic of a certain kind" in Rome, but even the ruler who was Christian there must despise "those things wherein he is and trust in that wherein he is not yet." On such terms, because *vera justitia*, true justice, belonged only to the City of God, which Rome and America were manifestly not, there could not be a real *res publica*. Only the crabbiest few American prophets have seriously asked, in agreement with Augustine, "Justice removed, what are kingdoms but great robber bands? And what are robber bands but small kingdoms?"[46] Americans might never experience full and true justice, but theirs was a republic that, as Abraham Lincoln and, one day, their pledge of allegiance to the flag would have it, they saw to be located "under God." In this respect they were closer to the view of Thomas Aquinas, who smuggled into his Augustinian outlook the idea of Aristotle that public values are themselves to be valued, though Americans did not need a Christian state for expression of those values.[47]

Tocqueville came close to developing the new public distinction when he remembered that society itself, having "no future life to hope for or to fear," was not in the business of providing salvation. For that reason, individual citizens banded into groups where "each sect adores the Deity in its own peculiar manner, but all sects preach the same moral law in the name of God."[48] The essentials of all religions served well enough to order government, but they did not save souls, make sad hearts glad, give people wholeness, or provide them with the kind of identity and sense of belonging they craved. For salvation, then, millions of Americans kept on making their choice of the "best and only true sect" for themselves, while, for purposes of order, the canon of Franklin and Jefferson—though not the variation of Dewey and company—agreed with their own, though, they thought, it could never bring salvation at all.

Second, when critics have spotted this form of differentiation, many of them have charged that, because the needs of order for society and salvation for individuals or groups differed, denominational members must always experience contradiction between the public religion in its various manifestations and the particular sects. In a study of anomie, Sebastian de Grazia thus feared a confusion of directives or chaos when people tried to serve two masters.[49] Taking content of belief and the cognitive parts of these faiths for the whole, historian Sidney E. Mead, to further this case, pressed for a resolution of conflict when he reduced Voltaire's many "peaceful and happy religions" to two.[50] Then, fearing, with him, lest "they would destroy each other," Mead hoped that the religion of the Republic alone would prevail, evidently not fearing, as Voltaire had, that the despotism of a single religion "would be terrible."[51]

As recently as 1975 and 1977, Mead wrote of "unresolved tensions" and a "mutual antagonism" between the two "mutually exclusive faiths" of the denominations and the Republic. The two, he thought, had to be "intellectually at war," producing "anxious misery," "wasting sickness," and the "danger of collapse" of the Republic. Along with other evolutionists, Mead believed that when two allied species shared a limited environment "the less successful form" must be forced to migrate or become extinct. Like the French visitors of 1831, he thought and thrice wrote that "religious commitment is an all-or-nothing business" and then pronounced the religion of the particular sects "heretical and schismatic—even un-American!" Mead, finding the counter attitude expressed by "several absolutist Christians toward the 'civil religion,'" cited American folklore in this situation: "This here town just ain't big enough for both of us."

In the eyes of Mead, sectarians still pathetically tried to hold their beliefs in "separate mental compartments" and to live with "split" or "bifurcated" or "schizoid minds." Told that an animal that cannot regurgitate will be killed if it accepts as food what it cannot digest, the historian diagnosed in denominationalists "a psychosomatic indigestion resulting from an inability either to digest the theology on which the practice of religious freedom rests or to regurgitate the practice." The delicate need fear no mess on the tablecloth at the republican banquet; the end of the sectarians, he thought, might come before that. "The prognosis," Mead concluded, "cannot be a happy one."[52]

While possible intellectual contradictions are familiar in religious faiths that allow for paradox, they must be faced. Even William James, despite his zest for "booming, buzzing confusion," thought people could not long tolerate ambiguity. In *Principles of Psychology*, he noted that "we cannot continue to think in two contradictory ways at once."[53] In practical politics, of course, matters are different, as the lively British socialist Jimmy Maxton once observed when he noted that "a man who can't ride two bloody horses at once has no right to a job in the bloody circus."[54] Over the long haul, however, religion called for more than practical adaptation among its professors. The testimony of novelist F. Scott Fitzgerald tantalizes: "The test of a first rate intelligence is the ability to hold two opposed ideas in the mind at the same time, and still retain the ability to function." But those lines occur, we are reminded, in a novel called *The Crack-up*, and a group is not likely to function well or long if posed as Fitzgerald suggests.[55]

Must we, however, even agree that there was such simple contradiction between the functions and content or practice of these two ways of seeing religion as ordering or saving? Most thoughtful sectarians in America showed few signs of recognizing one. They claimed "the essentials of all religion" to be their own for ordering government, but these could not save people. The more modest and less aggressive, and they were legion, also were ready to turn around and say that their particular saving faith could not order the Republic. Reams of documentation show that, after differentiating clearly, most stood with Father Gustave Weigel, S.J., when he observed that "the moral code held by each separate religious community can be reductively unified, but the consistent particular believer wants no reduction."[56] Believers simply translated the generalized deity of a nation "under God" to their own perceived God. Protestant John C. Bennett also urged that "when the word 'God' is used it should mean to the citizens not some common-denominator idea of deity but what they learn about God from their religious traditions."[57] Even the American Council on Education warned them to resist the specter of a saving common core that suggested "a watering down of the several faiths to the point where common essentials appear," since this might "easily lead to a new sect—a public school sect—which would take its place alongside the existing faiths and compete with them."[58]

Denominationalists ordinarily felt little contradiction because they regarded their spiritual antecedents to have been "present at the creation" of public religion. Their religious group, they thought, provided "the essentials of all religions" on which Franklin drew. He himself flattered them by listing among the benefits of a public religion its ability to show "the Excellency of the CHRISTIAN RELIGION above all others, ancient or modern."[59] Since the canon came from and agreed with the Hebrew Scriptures, Jews did not feel left out, either.[60] But Christians were in the majority. So proud of ownership did they feel that Hannah Arendt finally felt called to remind enthusiastic Christians that they at least ought to send a card of thanks to secularity or modernity for making possible the liberation of revolutionary germs that they claimed but which had been all too hidden during the centuries of Christian dominance.[61]

From fundamentalists to Unitarians, from the political right to the left, sectarians found their own visions confirmed in men like George Washington or the least-churched president, Abraham Lincoln. Because of Jeffersonian antisectarianism and the clarity of his deism, however, it took decades before grudging church people could feel at home with that "infidel," though some kinds of Baptists were his allies from the first.[62] While it was true that he left the words of saving Christian faith cut out in snippets on the White House study floor, President Jefferson had pasted together what was left over in a four-language scrapbook called *The Life and Morals of Jesus of Nazareth*.[63] For purposes of order and social morale, how could the Christians repudiate this offspring adopted by someone else—or see a contradiction between it and their churchly ordering faith?

3. The Republican Banquet

The churches also claimed that they were supporters of republicanism before either the Enlightenment polity or faith emerged. Some of their efforts to produce tickets to the banquet look humorous in retrospect. Thus, before Catholics were secure, Bishop John England and Archbishop John Hughes both pointed to tiny, papally protected, Catholic San Marino as "the most splendid specimen of the purest democracy" for 1,400 years.[64] In 1887 convert Father Isaac Hecker even jostled the Protestants at the banquet-hall door when he claimed that no republican government ever rose under Protestant ascendancy. "All republics since the Christian era have sprung into existence under the influence of the Catholic Church"; also, there existed a necessary bond and relation between the truths contained in the Declaration of Independence and the revealed truths of Christianity.[65]

Religious lay people, again often without benefit of clergy, voiced many ways in which the God of their saving sect was active in general in ordering the world. Biblically, first of all: when Jewish Theological Seminary honored Baptist president Harry S. Truman for his part in helping Jews found Israel, he remembered how the Second Isaiah called the Persian King Cyrus the shepherd or anointed of Yahweh, even though he was not one of Yahweh's people. Truman showed no ignorance or indifference and certainly no contradiction in his response of joyful bravado. We are told that he said, "A man who contributed much? I am Cyrus. I am Cyrus!"[66] The even more sectarian Jimmy Carter also evidenced no felt contradiction between his saving faith and a cosmic republicanism when, over oatmeal at the 1978 Presidential Prayer Breakfast, he told the assembled pious to give thanks for the faiths of Muslim president Anwar el-Sadat and Jewish prime minister Menachem Begin.

Such improvising laity have come up with a whole catalog of devices familiar to professional theologians, all designed to match up the two ways of seeing religion. In an Augustinian mood, some have found the same God to be active in different ways through *justitia civilis* or civil righteousness, on one hand, and through his saving righteousness in the City of God, on the other. Calvinist and Puritan ideas of their God being active beyond the sects through "common grace" or his "covenant of works" have found countless translations.[67] Christians at Boy Scout banquets, American Civil Liberties Union meetings, Rotary Club lunches, and Masonic ceremonies often anticipated Catholic theologian Karl Rahner with his concept of "the anonymous Christian," without ever yielding their desire to find "onymous" ones in the search for salvation. The idea stated by Paul Tillich that a living religion can break through its particularity at a certain stage[68] took life in the harmless minister-priest-rabbi jokes that pointed to a universalism among people who would never dream of transferring particular care of their souls, or the interpretations of that care, from one of these clerics to another sort. It seems unfair to congratulate professional theologians for finding ways to make things come out right while deriding as indifferent the common people who showed tolerance on principle but remained tenaciously supportive of their particular creeds.

Third, and most ironically, at the republican banquet today the burden of supporting public religion has fallen largely to the very inept and distracted sectarians whom the enlightened expected to see excluding themselves, suffering indigestion, or dying at the banquet door. Through the years the polls showed that the non-theistic versions of John Dewey's common faith had almost no followings.[69] But now we must ask where outside denominational religion are theistic or deistic dimensions of public religion regularly attended to at all. Academic philosophy and political science departments, we must presume, do not teach the canon of public religion as the truth about life. Formal philosophers would dismiss as unverifiably metaphysical the creeds of the enlightened founders and deplore as mystical most later versions of democratic faith.

Fortunately, late in the century the public philosophy began to be revived among thinkers as diverse as pioneer Hannah Arendt, socialists like Michael Harrington, moderates like Robert N. Bellah, conservatives on the order of Daniel Bell, Robert Nisbet, Seymour Lipset, Irving Kristol, and George Will, while Peter Berger in that camp joined Bellah in introducing rumors of transcendence and commenting explicitly on the social and institutional shapes of religion in the republic.

Public religion is not only intellectual; it must be ritualized. What Elihu Katz and Michael Gurevitch call "the secularization of leisure"[70] has undercut the ritual abode of this religion in public places. W. Lloyd Warner was still able to see Memorial Day rites as the American cult of the dead.[71] Since 1959 when he wrote, however, the Congress has turned Memorial Day and most other civil holidays into movable feasts in order to prolong weekends. In doing so it cut these off from their historical roots, local communities, or most communal observances of any sort. Televised football has taken away the public religious dimensions of Thanksgiving Day, and the pathetic if overblown attempts to restore them at halftime ceremonies are poor substitutes. Public school rites had largely disappeared before the Supreme Court acted against devotions in 1962 and 1963. Administrators, when polled, reported that in exactly 99.44 percent of their districts moral values were taught, but only 6.4 percent of the Midwest schools and 2.4 percent of the West Coast ones knew anything like homeroom devotional practices.[72] The people ritually "took God out of the schools" before the Court did.

The law itself remained the last repository of formal public religion. In 1892 and 1931 Mr. Justice Brewer and Mr. Justice Sutherland continued to call this a religious nation and Americans a Christian people who acknowledged "with reverence the duty of obedience to the will of God." These were purely historical notions, as was the first half of the dictum of Mr. Justice Douglas in 1952 that "we are a religious people." Douglas had no legal ground for adding that our "institutions presuppose a Supreme Being," and he slunk away after the immediate dissent by Mr. Justice Black, who protested "invidious distinctions between those who believe in no religion and those who do believe."[73]

Thereafter the "wholesomely neutral" Court progressively removed these distinctions while broadening the definition of what it is to be religious. In 1931 Chief Justice Hughes still defined "the essence of religion" as "belief in a relation to God involving duties superior to those arising from any human relation." By 1965, borrowing a concept from Paul Tillich, the Court backed away from such a slot in theism to declare that "a sincere and meaningful belief which occupies in the life of its possessor a place parallel to that filled by . . . God" among other people would serve civil and legal purposes.[74]

By 1970, in *Welsh* v. *United States*, the Court went still further, judging that a conscientious objector to military service did not even have to claim to be godlessly religious, so long as the Court judged that his or her "moral, ethical, or religious belief about what is right and wrong" was "held with the strength of traditional religious convictions." The last trace of religious substance was now gone. Mr. Justice Harlan complained that in 1965 the Court had engaged in surgery but in 1970 "performed a lobotomy." He then went on anyhow to write that Congress "cannot draw the line between theistic or nontheistic beliefs on the one hand and the secular beliefs on the other" in issues.[75] At last the issue was bare and bald for all to see: from the beginning in the United States public religion was itself a congeries of voluntary sects, some of them privileged, but none of them ever established by law.

THE REPUBLICAN BANQUET TODAY

In 1950 the United States Supreme Court invaded the American sanctum with its dictum that the law knows no heresy and is committed to the support of no dogma. This judgment made visible an aspect of American common life that metaphorically parallels what Pompey was said to have found in 63 B.C. when he finally crashed into the Temple Holy of Holies in Jerusalem: it was empty.[76] The American sectarians of republican and denominational religion alike have, of course, persistently sneaked their own sacral appointments and scrolls into the shrine for their particular rituals and reflection. Enough of them have agreed on essentials of republican order that they can plausibly speak of consensus. Some have done so with such enthusiasm that the critics within their camps faulted churches themselves for promoting civil idolatry. Robert Bellah wryly remarked that "perhaps the real animus of the religious critics has been not so much against the civil religion in itself but against its pervasive and dominating influence within the sphere of church religion."[77] During the national bicentennial, denominations arranged religious civil ceremonies while their own prophets criticized them. The surrounding society more regularly neglected such rites and instead invited the public to watch the tall ships in the Hudson or the fireworks above the Potomac.

Why had the churches taken over so many seats at the republican banquet? It takes no originality to point out that selfish interests motivated the beginnings of their involvement. In the Massachusetts Election Sermon of 1780, the Reverend Samuel Cooper was already calling for a "happy union of all denominations" in support of national government because it provided equal protection to all. "Warm parties upon civil or religious matters,"[78] however, were injurious to the state. In 1958, Father Gustave Weigel, S.J., feared what some have called "repressive tolerance" because he saw the secular society "trying to make a deal with the churches," saying "give us your unswerving support in the pursuit of the objectives we have before us; in return we will cover you with honor."[79] Then, in 1961, William Lee Miller went on to point out that because tax-exempt religious groups could not advertise their worth as peddlers of dogma or mysticism they had to tout their value as agents of social morale—whether they were revivalist or modernist or representative of the sects of "the deistic and rationalist strand."[80] And so, indeed, they have presented themselves.

After this self-interested beginning, the partakers at the banquet did not simply proceed to write out invitation lists for competitors. Most of them at first found each other to be at best what James once called "half-delightful company."[81] In 1954 Perry Miller was crass enough to remind readers that "we got a variety of sects as we got a college catalog: the denominations and the sciences multiplied until there was nothing anybody could do about them." So citizens gave out tickets to the common table, called the result freedom, and found "to our vast delight, that by thus negatively surrendering we could congratulate ourselves on a positive and heroic victory. So we stuck the feather in our cap and called it Yankee Doodle."[82] High principle, if it came, had to arrive later, after respect for persons had developed.

Through the years the guest list of participants kept growing. Even today, however, when groups overtly fuse their saving faith with ordering faith, they exclude themselves or are rebuffed by others. Jehovah's Witnesses are the classic case; they see human governments to be ordered by Satan, and they salute no flags of earthly states.[83] The Nation of Islam or Black Muslim movement began as an outsider with similar views of the white majority but now is knocking on the door.[84] In order to resist being swallowed up or abused, some religious American Indians are turning down tardy and grudging invitations by other religions to partake.[85] Beginning in Kanawha Country, West Virginia, and then spreading from Texas to state after state, fundamentalists began to sniff unwelcome natural or secular religion in textbooks on evolution or atheistic communism in public schoolrooms. They then either staged their own banquets or, like silent film star Gloria Swanson, they came to the public one but insisted on bringing all their own food.

Other groups begin by first ignoring the gathering, but they join it later on terms they learned from the Enlightenment. The Baptists and Quakers are among these. Originally they were what George Santayana called "pensive or rabid apostles of liberty" who sought "liberty for themselves to be just so, and to remain just so for ever," vehemently defying anybody who might for the sake of harmony ask them to be a little different. In the course of time they learned that for liberty they needed what Santayana called "a certain vagueness of soul, together with a great gregariousness and tendency to be moulded by example and by prevalent opinion." Santayana also knew what many have always overlooked: that it took passion to defend the very idea of the banquet. Enthusiasts for democratic liberty, he said, were "not everybody's friends" because they were enemies of "what is deepest and most primitive in everybody" and since they inspired "undying hatred in every untamable people and every absolute soul."[86]

The career of the Mormons best illustrates the process of change. British visitor D. W. Brogan rightly found them to be the only genuine example of religious persecution in modern America because they followed two sacred books.[87] Their Book of Mormon both looked and was different from the Bible in its ordering of society. Though founders Joseph Smith and Brigham Young were super-American people who regarded the founding documents of the nation as being inspired from on high, they insisted these were only temporary charters until God's Kingdom, in Mormon hands, would achieve "domination over all the earth to the ends thereof."[88] When the Latter-day Saints later dropped the offending practice of polygamy and muted their claims of the kingdom, they finally were welcome to the banquet as patriots—by fellow citizens who still remain as hostile as ever if they see Mormons in the act of being aggressive about their way of salvation.

Most debate at the banquet occurs when someone spots another sect apparently mingling elements of its particular saving outlook with the general essentials of ordering faith power. Here the Catholic case is most instructive. The example of San Marino did not make Catholics secure in the eyes of others. Many scores of years of participation beyond suspicion in republican life in America did not help. Not until 1960, when one of their own became president, were they themselves seen to be thoroughly at home. After 1965, when the Second Vatican Council, acting on American impetus, acknowledged a development of Catholic doctrine and declared religious freedom to be a right, there was no longer any basis for complaints of antirepublicanism against official Catholicism.[89] Even so, as in the case when Catholics or anyone else today become accused of trying to legislate what looks to others like a particularistic element of their faith—such as prohibitions against the abortion of fetuses—there develops the kind of confusion Murray feared, sometimes the clarified disagreement he hoped for, and on rarest occasions a higher level of civil argument.

The republican banquet, be it remembered, is not the only show in town. Many citizens still choose the enlightened sects of public religion, and many millions of them select one sect or another of denominational religion, thereafter often to put few energies into the common weal. But millions more who share some beliefs are not available as part of any kind of social force, because they have made religion a wholly private, individual, and even invisible affair and thus no contributor to the causes of social morale. Around them are self-described secular people who ignore the whole debate on all its terms. The courts have been clear: one need not believe in a *consensus juris,* and certainly not in a religious base for one, in order to be a full citizen, in the legally responsible senses. Those who are partakers at the republican banquet have shown myriad ways in which they wish to be responsible both to their focused visions and to the common good, without being superficial or indifferent about their life and thought. It is not now possible, nor will it ever be, to chart the infinite number of ways they have done so. Like Beaumont after Sing Sing, thoughtful people shall find puzzles remaining. We, too, stand humbly at the side of the French visitor to declare that we "would gladly know" more about the marvelous and troubling ways of a contentious republican people.

One of these ways, Benjamin Franklin's "publick religion," found a Rousseauan counterpart two-thirds of the way through the twentieth century, when sociologist Robert N. Bellah observed a "civil religion." This looked to some less like a banquet and more like a prescription. It promised or threatened "sameness" and seemed to run against some of the notions associated with pluralism. Yet such civil religion, it soon came to be clear, was also episodic and sectarian. The fact that it has its own varieties has made it one more element in a pluralist society. It is time to see just how this has come about and keeps coming about.

4   *Civil Religion: Two Kinds of Two Kinds*

Civil religion does not exist in the same sense as, say, the Roman Catholic church exists. It was possible for the late comic Lenny Bruce to say that the Catholic church "is the only *the* Church." Its dogma, liturgy, authority, and tradition were specific and represented a kind of "given." Civil religion is not the only "*the* religion." It represents no defined or agreed-upon faith at all, nor does it suggest the only way of being "civil." No doubt it is a species of a genus which might be called "Way-of-Life Religion." Somewhere between the attention given the specific religion of the sects and the general religious apprehension of reality is a zone where symbols are bartered, in Thomas Luckmann's picture of a "sacred cosmos."[1] Somewhere in that zone civil religion purportedly lies.

I should like to stress that not everything having to do with how one puts a life together—even in the patriotic or nationalistic realm of life—must be viewed religiously. Some anthropologists and sociologists define religion so broadly that nothing can escape it.[2] If everything is religious nothing is religious. In this sphere as in others it is important to allow for a cool, agnostic, disinterested approach.

Having noticed the nonreligious possibility, it is also important to suggest that the civic realm makes room for what has been called "religiocification" more readily than do most other modes or locales of human activity. In historical definitions, the religious would include preoccupation with ultimacy, especially when this is accompanied by the language of myth and symbol, is ceremonially and ritually reinforced, appealed to with metaphysical or quasi-metaphysical sanctions, compelling some sort of socialization, and exacting some sort of behavioral consequences. It is sometimes suggested that such a definition of religion lacks the universal ingredient, deity. Such a definition, however, is Western, influenced by biblical religion; numerous world religions including many schools of Buddhism and—unless one wishes to call it only a philosophy—Confucianism, lack reference to a deity.

The nation, state, or society is one of the most potent repositories of symbols in the modern world, and can often replace religious institutions in the minds of people. The nation has its shrines and ceremonies, demands ultimate sacrifice, and specifies behavioral patterns (e.g., the care and handling of the flag, saying the pledge of allegiance),[3] and in other ways takes the place which formal religions once did. Thus when in 1964 Ernest Gellner restored the concept of civil religion he saw it as a rival to and replacement of the specific traditional faiths. He related this to a kind of ideology with which a society comes to its new approved social contract, with which it moves "over the hump of transition" to that new status. Ordinarily the civil religion will have admixtures of old faiths; in Russia, Marxism served, and in the West Jewish-Christian resources were fused. The result is a division of labor between, on the one hand, symbolic, unifying ideas, communal banners, which once were fullbloodedly cognitive but whose "cognitive import is now shrouded in semi-deliberate ambiguity; and on the other hand, the cognitively effective but normatively not very pregnant or insistent beliefs about the world." Thus it is contemporary Christianity and Judaism itself that

> have now become *civic* religions, inculcating primarily devotion to the values of the community in which they exist (rather than a selfish and anti-social concern with personal and extramundane salvation); and they are held in a manner which allows complete toleration of rival objects of worship.[4]

Needless to say, not all civil religion has that much Judaic or Christian reminiscence.

Civil religion as a species has been referred to with sufficient frequency that it somehow now "exists"; it has subspecies, much as the Christian faith has its denominations. The presence of internal varieties is not a special problem for such a religion. Roman Catholicism has room for votaries all the way from the garlic-and-babushka style of the vestigial Catholic ghetto to the social sophistication of liberation-minded priests and nuns; Protestantism allows for everything from tent revivals to incense-shrouded ritual. Similarly, civil religion is perceived differently down at the friendly Veterans of Foreign Wars or American Legion and up at the halls of ivy where the designation was reborn and revivified.

What makes civil religion different is that at this stage it functions chiefly as what Peter Berger and Thomas Luckmann call "a social construction of reality." After decades it remained chiefly the preserve of the scholars' worlds; the person on the street would be surprised to learn of its existence or to know that he or she is one of its professors. Gradually it came to be worked into the public vocabulary in isolated situations. Thus six years after Bellah's essay, at a presidential prayer breakfast, the well-read Senator Mark Hatfield urged a probably noncomprehending clientele that America should not worship the captive tribal god of civil religion but should be open to the God of biblical faith.

If sociologists would call it a social construction of reality, historians might say it is the result of the endeavor which creates "symbolic history"—much as the Renaissance, industrial revolution, Reformation, and Middle Ages did not "occur"; they are, Page Smith says, "symbolic names that depend for their power, not on specific, clearly defined episodes, but on their ability to evoke broad generalized movements, long-range trends and developments." They are "the creation of the historian. . . . Events in this category are not given names by those involved in them; they are named, and thus called to life, by historians." Civil religion is a kind of cluster of episodes which come and go, recede back to invisibility after making their appearance; only gradually are they institutionalized and articulated in organizational form.

If civil religion as a designation of scholars points to an otherwise overlooked reality, it is valid to ask what void it fills. It serves the function of giving a name to incidents or phenomena which the namer ordinarily likes or does not like; it refers to some skein of objective realities. How does it arise? We have noted that while people in society may be merely or utterly secular, godless, or religionless, yet in practice in a complex culture their lives cohere around certain symbols and myths. If they did not, there could be spiritual anarchy and anomie. The churches and synagogues, it is said, do not fulfill the old function of providing enough coherence for enough people. The sectarian, particular, private faiths tend to divide people.

They therefore naturally cohere around national symbols. William Butler Yeats once said that "one can only reach out to the universe with a gloved hand—that glove is one's nation; the only thing one knows even a little of." The nation provides many with a source of identity and power. The nation thus becomes more than the locus of political decision; it provides some context for meaning and belonging.

A construct as loose as civil religion is can be used to fill different needs at different times. It can be seen, for example, that liberal intellectuals in the academy favor it when the nation's chief executive represents broadly their school or style of politics. Thus the modern round of talk about civil religion reflected the late stage of Kennedy-Johnson Camelotism. In such a period these intellectuals will tend to deride those critics in various particular or prophetic traditions who have taken civil religion apart from some normative (e.g., Hebrew prophetic or biblical religionist) point of view. Thus Sidney E. Mead[5] in the middle of the 1960s attacked Will Herberg, who had criticized civil religion of the Eisenhower era, for having possessed those very features which Ernest Gellner has said commend civil religion to a society.

When later presidents like Richard M. Nixon and Ronald Reagan filled the chief sacerdotal role and set the style for the nation's civil religion in their administrations, the same intellectual designators and appreciators, Bellah visibly among them, tended to flee for cover. They struck out in frustration or rage against Nixonian and Reaganesque interpretation or heresy and pointed to the existence of a more nearly *true* civil religion somewhere else. Having criticized the Herbergs of the world for measuring the best in their historic faith against the worst in civil religion, some of them turned docetic and moved away from incarnationalism to contend, for example, that civil religion hardly ever touched ground. While adherents of church and synagogue religion slosh around in inauthentic faith, civil religion at least existed once in a speech or two of Abraham Lincoln.

Why in the positive or affirmative moments did the liberal advocates of civil religion criticize the critics? For one thing, they had overlooked the positive values of a civic religion. They underestimated the need for some measure of social bonding. They tended to use double standards for measurement. They may have feared competition for the sects. Defenders of civil religion in the academy during the moments when they could cheer one or another of the current manifestations of this faith are often social realists.

If civil religion is episodic, a creation of historians' symbol-making functions or sociologists' ability to perceive how people socially construct reality, it might be observed or concluded that there are an infinite number of apprehensions of civil religion. In these terms, there would be as many civil religions as there are citizens. Because they are present to a world, they are condemned to meaning (Merleau-Ponty), and in this condemnation they reach for the state. On these terms not much passion is associated with civil religion. Citizens are enraged when the national anthem cannot be played at an athletic event, but do not sing it when it is. They favor by a four to one majority a constitutional amendment which would allow for prayer in schools, but did not pray there when the option was licit.

In practice there are not 230 million civil religions, one each for every citizen in America. Citizens tend to concentrate at any time on only several subspecies or sects of such religion. But before we notice these, it is important to regard for a moment the particularist survivals that work against the idea or practice of civil religion. These often have been and could be the denominations of the major faiths. In the 1950s Will Herberg saw some consent to as well as some dissent from civic faith in three large symbolic clusters: Protestant, Catholic, and Jew.[6] Then in the 1970s various ethnic, age, gender, and interest groups offered resistance. Some blacks thought it a WASP invention, and some women called it male dominated and patriarchal. Jews might sometimes step back from Christianized versions of civil faith. For a time, non-WASPS liked to point out[7] that most civil religion, at least recent academic versions, was not so neutral as claimed, but reflected a WASP universe of moral discourse.

Denominational, tri-faith, and ethnic particularist alternatives are partly accidental. But different conceptions are also available, and I shall concentrate on four of them. With them in mind, it is possible to judge civil religion in the context of what it sets out to do and not what scholars think it should do. On those terms Will Herberg need not have seen all forms of civil religion as potentially idolatrous, nor need Sidney E. Mead have had to declare it superior to church religion. Many articulators of civic faith appear in a different light when we understand their roles, self-concepts, and intentions.

In this reading, there are two kinds of two kinds of civil religion. I shall eschew neologisms—let me disappoint those who are seeking novel designations. The stress is here on common sense and traditionally approved terms.

One kind of civil religion sees the nation "under God." Somehow a transcendent deity is seen as the pusher or puller of the social process. He or it may be conceived variously personally or impersonally, as intensely involved or aloof, as providence or progress or process. But somehow there is a transcendent objective reference of a kind which has traditionally been associated with deity. The other main kind stresses "national self-transcendence." It does not see people, left to themselves, automatically given to self-worship. But either references to deity disappear entirely or "God" is drained of earlier cognitive imports and may appear terminologically only out of habitual reference.

Within each of these two kinds there are two kinds of approaches or analyses. With due apology to those Old Testament scholars who do not like to see the line drawn too severely, but with due appreciation to those sociologists who keep drawing the line anyhow, with common-sense application of the terms, let us speak of these as "priestly" and "prophetic." The priestly will normally be celebrative, affirmative, culture-building. The prophetic will tend to be dialectical about civil religion, but with a predisposition toward the judgmental. The two are translations of Joseph Pulitzer's definition of the compleat journalist or, in my application, of the fulfilled religionist: one comforts the afflicted; the other afflicts the comfortable. Needless to say, no adherent need always express only one side or kind; in traditional faiths the priestly and prophetic interact and overlap, though probably most spokesmen or leaders are associated more with one approach than with the other. Thus a priest may judge and a prophet may and often does integrate people into a system of meaning and belonging. But the priest is always alert to the occasions when such integration can occur and the prophet is always sensitive to the fact that he may have to be critical of existing modes of such integration.

THE NATION UNDER GOD: THE PRIESTLY MODE

The phrase "under God" appears in Abraham Lincoln's addresses and after the middle of the twentieth century was smuggled into the pledge of allegiance to the flag (by a secular Congress, after the minister-author of the original pledge had neglected to include it). No doubt a content analysis of historic civil religious assertions in the American past would show that the overwhelming majority of references would stress the reality "under God." Civil religion would normally exist, similarly, for priestly reasons. The prophet Joel speaks for Yahweh when he says, "Sanctify a fast, call a solemn assembly" (Joel 1:14). So would a president of the local chapter of a veterans' group or of the United States.

The God under whom the nation lives will probably be pictured and symbolized in terms similar to those used by the particular religions within a nation. This deity gives identity, meaning, and purpose to the nation and its citizens. God, on these terms, exists prior to and independent of the state and may be expected to transcend and outlast the civil society. This God may be the Trinity, or the God of Jesus Christ, or the Supreme Architect or Benign Providence of the American founders. In any case, the deity represents a promissor to the nation; in this terminological reference one speaks of "the promise *to* American life" more readily than of the "promise *of*" America.

While this may be the conventional pattern of the majority of civil religionists, it is likely to be that of the critical liberal intellectuals who are wont to use the term. The God of a nation "under God," it has been implied in the quotation from Ernest Gellner, may and probably will undergo constant transformations. But, then, so does the God of historic faiths, as any student of the history of Christian (or Buddhist, or Hindu, or Muslim) thought and "doctrine" will know.

For example, at one time the nation was said to be "under God" of a kind of deist reality, the center of power and meaning for most of the national founding fathers. They were usually members of historic Christian churches, but their effectual symbolic references had become deist. This is the case with Benjamin Franklin, George Washington, and Thomas Jefferson, to name just a few obvious examples.

More Americans probably draw their reference to life "under God" from Puritan, evangelical, Catholic, or Jewish forebears than from the deist few who were successful at introducing some of the ethos of the Enlightenment into the political sphere. In these latter readings, an addressable God created, guided, and led a nation toward its destiny. This God mandated a mission, demanded loyalty that went beyond loyalty extended to the state—though a conflict of loyalties was rarely pictured. Thus the churches could give enthusiastic support to this version of civil religion.

Civil religion "under God," in its priestly form, normally appears as a fusion, then, of historic faith (as in Jewish or Christian traditions) with autochthonous national sentiments. Usually it will have as its main priest the president, since he alone stands at the head of all the people—and civil religion would be inclusive—and he has greatest potential for invoking symbols of power. Dwight D. Eisenhower was a particularly gifted priest, who appeared in a decade of cold war when the nation needed its anxieties ministered to and when it needed divine sanction for its adventures. For many critics of civil religion, Eisenhower's carrying out of his priestly roles acquired almost normative status.[8] The strength of this approach lay in the fact that it did bring a nation together in a sort of "era of good feeling"; its liability: it may have contributed to moral pretension in support of American participation in the cold war as a *jihad*, a holy war.

Critics who were shocked at the Eisenhower role would, if they engaged in structural and functional analysis, find reason for their surprise and shock to disappear. The president is normally expected to play a priestly role. Even Abraham Lincoln, everyone's favorite civil religionist-as-prophet, normally was the priest. Edmund Wilson said he regarded the union with an awe usually associated with religious mysticism. But at one or two crucial turns he remarkably moved to a prophetic vocation, and for this he is remembered.[9] But presidents could not be presidents if their main function was to call God down in judgment on his nation's policies.

In the priestly spirit, Eisenhower could say that "America is the mightiest power which God has yet seen fit to put upon his footstool. America is great because she is good."

Not until the 1980s did America again have a president who performed the priestly roles with such power. Ronald Reagan, an expert communicator through mass media, used his office to draw a Manichaean portrait of good and evil in the world, with America representing God's good instrument against, for example, the "evil empire" of the Soviet Union. Reagan exploited specific "Judeo-Christian" symbols in barely veiled critiques of pluralism.

THE NATION UNDER GOD: THE PROPHETIC MODE

Mention has just been made of the way that in rare occasions the nation's chief priest may step into the prophetic role. Historically such a passage is rare, but extremely potent. Just as Christians measure their faith by the cross of Christ in self-giving love, or by the quality of witness of the Hebrew prophets in their canon, so civil religionists measure their faith by central and epochal statements of national faith in the prophetic style.

If Joel, speaking for Yahweh, could "call a solemn assembly," Amos could speak in the same name and say, "I despise the noise of your solemn assemblies." We have seen something of the dialectical-judgmental potential at several important turns in American history. The men whom many regard as the two greatest native-born theologians, Jonathan Edwards in colonial times and Reinhold Niebuhr in the recent past, gave voice to the two kinds of witness that are in tension with each other. Jonathan Edwards can be remembered both as the angry prophet of God against all the works of humans and as a postmillennialist who thought that in his community, colony, or in what was to become the American nation, the "latter-day glory" would appear. The "nation" was clearly under God; but God expected more of chosen people than of others.[10]

Lincoln regarded the nation with a sense of religious mysticism. But he then could remind the people that the Almighty has his own purposes. In the classic texts of prophetic civil religion "under God," he reminded both sides in the Civil War that both sides prayed to the same God, read the same Bible, and the like—but both could not win. Both liked to claim God on their side; Lincoln said they should instead try to conform their wills to God's own mysterious will, so far as it could be known.[11]

In the middle of the twentieth century, Reinhold Niebuhr affirmed the civil society and participated in it, as consultant to national figures like George Kennan, Dean Acheson, Arthur Schlesinger, Jr., and Hans Morgenthau and as participant in partisan politics. But when he found a prideful nation acting in the name of God, he would speak in the words of the psalmist: "He that sitteth in the heavens shall laugh." His favorite category in civil religion was "The Irony of American History."[12]

Perhaps these three figures should be thought of as critical public theologians as opposed to votaries of civil religion. It may be unrealistic to picture most adherents using their religion over against their own identity, integration, or power—just as one would not be likely to picture most Christians remaining in range of a pulpit simply to be put in their place. In all three cases, however, these public theologians are prophets from within the tradition. The outsider never has the same kind of credentials.

The employment of, say, biblical prophetic motifs over against national pretensions, is potent. When Protestant evangelicals, for example, relied upon their conservative faith in the Bible and invoked prophetic language against American injustices or ignorance, they often possessed a power, at least to one large constituency, that was not available to those who had less reliance on a transcendent scriptural word.

The prophetic mode has to be dialectical. If it comes unilaterally from outside or is totally rejective from within, it does not belong to the civil religion, which is an expression of a somehow-covenanted group of insiders. The dialectician says "both/and": God both shapes a nation and judges it, because he is transcendent in both circumstances. The main critics of civil religion from both the left and the right are those who come in the name of a transcendent deity. Thus Senator Mark Hatfield in the comment that has already been mentioned:

> If we as leaders appeal to the god of civil religion, our faith is in a small and exclusive deity, a loyal spiritual adviser to power and prestige, a defender of only the American nation, the object of a national folk religion devoid of moral content. But if we pray to the biblical God of justice and righteousness, we fall under God's judgment for calling upon his name but failing to obey his commands.[13]

The classic picture of the prophets of God versus the prophets of Baal comes to mind in this interpretation of civil religion "under God"!

In order to introduce the other kinds of civil religion it is necessary to set a stage. We picture some secularization: that is, that spheres of life which were once interpreted in the light of a transcendent reference now are construed simply "as they are," so much as possible. This secularization is accompanied by a new openness to religious transformation, particularly to the intrusion of religions of the East. They are full-bodied religions, but they lack objective reference to a transcendent deity. To a lesser extent, the Afro-American movement has shown how alternative ways of interpreting reality have been present in African religion.

When Bishop Ian Ramsey said that we have a "spirituality devoid of God," he was doing some Christian complaining about styles of being spiritual but not "under God." Yet many today would say that "spirituality devoid of God" is a legitimate and positive expression in our day. In the Christian world some radical theologians spoke of this as "this-worldly transcendence." Some of the theological language associated with "process" uses divine references in these contexts. God symbols are not necessarily purged, but they play a lesser role. Terminological neatness is not possible. When the Gallup people poll Americans, between 95 percent and 98 percent of them say that they believe in God. But to interviewers they display a broader range of options. And it is possible to believe in a transcendent deity and be among the 95 percent majority, and at the same time see the possibilities of a self-transcendent nation as being not necessarily the object of worship but the locale of power and meaning or spirit.

In a sociological essay that stands in the Meadian historical tradition of affirmation of civil religion, Robert N. Bellah in 1967 noted this transformation, first in negative terms (just as in a later essay he saw the positive side of this-worldly transcendence).

> The civil religion . . . is . . . caught in another kind of crisis, theoretical and theological, of which it is at the moment largely unaware. "God" has clearly been a central symbol in the civil religion from the beginning and remains so today. . . . But today . . . the meaning of the word *God* is by no means . . . clear or . . . obvious. There is no formal creed in the civil religion. We have had a Catholic president; it is conceivable that we could have a Jewish one. But could we have an agnostic president? Could a man with conscientious scruples about using the word *God* the way Kennedy and Johnson have used it be elected chief magistrate of our country? If the whole God symbolism requires reformulation, there will be obvious consequences for civil religion, consequences perhaps of liberal alienation and of fundamentalist ossification that have not so far been prominent in this realm. The civil religion has been a point of articulation between the profoundest commitments of the Western religious and philosophical tradition and the common beliefs of ordinary Americans. It is not too soon to consider how the deepening theological crisis may affect the future of this articulation.[14]

In the intervening years there has been considerable talk about transcendence which may or may not go on "under God." New models were being sought. Some revolutionaries of Marxist stripes, some philosophers, many people who spoke for Eastern and African cultures and religions, spoke of transcendence without deity. Or at least they could speak of transcendence without seeing deity integral to the language. This was transcendence "from below," as it were, what philosopher Ernst Bloch called "transcending without transcendence." After a generation, this was something held open for a possible but continually undecided future in this vacant place—or, as French poets of the symbolist school called it, "empty transcendence." Something of Martin Heidegger's "the understanding of being" is implied here. Most seekers along this path, it may be noted, may not need civil religion as the focus, but some do.

4. Two Kinds of Two Kinds

THE NATION AS SELF-TRANSCENDENT:
THE PRIESTLY STYLE

When the language of civil religion shifts from talk about the promise *to* America (from a transcendent deity) to the promise *of* America, and national self-transcendence, the signal of priestly civil religion, is raised. Usually this has occurred at the margins of American life. Thus Robert Welch, the author of the *Blue Book* of the John Birch Society, fused an evolutionary cosmic vision with national purpose to produce a priestly "this-worldly transcendent" civil religion. Modern fascisms have this element, and should a version of these become strong in the American future, it would probably be an expression of priestly civil religion.

While marginal priestly civil religion is rare and relatively impotent, there are moderate versions of the same expressed occasionally on higher levels and in more responsible circles. In John F. Kennedy there were occasional references to the nation which saw it in the place where God had once been. Kennedy either by instinct or with the aid of sophisticated speech-writing *periti* reminded a nation that here on earth God's work must truly be our own. There was here an almost Teilhardian sense of co-creatorship; but the reference to deity seemed to be more than nominal.

Not long after his classic essay, Robert Bellah found a case study, almost a classic one, of civil religion gone wrong. In Richard M. Nixon's vocabulary, the nominal reference remained, but subtle shifts had occurred. Advocates of prophetic biblical religion were nervous about such a shift, but it was not universally railed against—and was, indeed, to reappear to popular acclaim in Ronald Reagan's rhetoric. But in the Nixon case already, Gerald Strober and Lowell Streiker, writing an apologia for the emerging conservative religion of middle America, used terms abhorrent to prophetic religionists:

> Henderson, Fiske, and Gary Wills have all criticized the President for his "lack of a sense of transcendence." But the America of American civil religion is scarcely less "transcendent" than is the God of the Judaeo-Christian tradition.[15]

The Henderson referred to in that positive reference is Charles B. Henderson, Jr., who wrote a full-length dissection of Nixon's view of the nation as self-transcendent or even as the object of transcendent reference. He concluded:

> Nixon systematically appropriates the vocabulary of the church—faith, trust, hope, belief, spirit—and applies these words not to a transcendent God but to his own nation, and worse, to his personal vision of what that nation should be. . . . Lacking a transcendent God, he seems to make patriotism his religion, the American dream his deity.[16]

Given the president's willingness to make reference to deity and Billy Graham's assurance that the president does believe in a transcendent God, it may be a bit unfair to say, "lacking a transcendent God." But it was not unfair to say back then, as Henderson did, that Nixon took the vocabulary of transcendence and applied it chiefly to his personal vision of the nation. His was talk about the "promise *of* American life" as a religious ultimate. This did not mean that Nixon never used the language of prophecy. At a presidential prayer breakfast in 1972, his speech even quoted Abraham Lincoln's dialectical references.

Mention might here be made in passing, at least, to a "left-wing" alternative to the views of the Welches at the right and the Nixons at the center. In my own writing on civil religion in 1959 I stressed both the Eisenhowerian version "under God" and the religion-in-general or religion of the American Way of Life as expressed in the tradition of A. Powell Davies, John Dewey, Horace Kallen, Agnes Meyer, and J. Paul Williams. In the liberal intellectual tradition of John Dewey's *A Common Faith* or Walter Lippmann's *A Public Philosophy* there has been room for a quasi-transcendent set of values which emerge from the social process itself. This is a democratic humanism with overtones of religious ultimacy. Rarely, however, has explicitly religious language been associated comprehensively with this point of view.

An exception was J. Paul Williams in *What Americans Believe and How They Worship*. If Williams did not exist, we should probably have had to devise him for this category, because he was an "ideal type" who showed that the priestly approach to national self-transcendence in civil religion does not always belong to the political right and center. Williams said that "democracy must become an object of religious dedication." "Systematic and universal indoctrination is essential." There must be what Williams himself called metaphysical sanctions, "open indoctrination of the faith that the democratic ideal accords with ultimate reality . . . that democracy is the very law of life." And there will be ceremonial reinforcement, a "devotion to democratic ideals like the devotion given by ardent believers in every age to the traditional religions." "Ignoring the lack of spiritual integration invites disaster. Relying on the haphazard methods of the past will not meet the need. . . . Governmental agencies must teach the democratic ideal *as religion*."[17]

In the years since that was written, the Democratic left has suffered many setbacks and by the 1980s, the Ronald Reagan era, had all but disappeared from view. When here and there critics of priestly civil religion made tentative appearances, there were always governmental or conservative and New Right churchly leaders who relabeled them "secular humanists" and drove them off the scene. The democratic left, in short, lacked the potency to give voice to such appeals. Should its forms of humanism ever return to power, we should expect reappearances of such expressions.

THE NATION AS SELF-TRANSCENDENT: THE PROPHETIC STYLE

The second kind of the second kind of civil religion has to be matched with the Lincolnian dialectical version. It is ecumenical, unwilling to see civil religion exhausted by one nation's purposes. Usually it is advocated by people with strong monistic and integrative impulses. The spokesmen are tolerant and allow for many particularities and demonstrate awareness of the rights of peculiar sects to propagate. But they are impatient with them and uneasy about too much pluralism. At the same time, they are cautious lest civil religion be seen as idolatry, as worship of the nation. Thus, for Sidney Mead,

> to be committed to an ideal world beyond the present world and to the incarnating of that ideal world in actuality [is an element in what he calls the "religion of the Republic"]. Seen thus the religion of the Republic is essentially prophetic, which is to say that its ideals and aspirations stand in constant judgment over the passing shenanigans of the people, reminding them of the stan-

dards by which their current practices and those of their nation are ever being judged and found wanting.[18]

The religion of the Republic did *not* mean worship of state or nation, said Mead. He blamed people under European theological influence for hinting that it does or might. In the older language, "one most constant strand in its theology has been the assertion of the primacy of God over all human institutions." But this God-reference had been attenuated symbolically, intellectualized and spiritualized beyond recognition, toward a "cosmopolitan, universal theology."

"Our final concern . . . is to assure ourselves that our attitude toward the nation does not become idolatrous; that the state does not become God; that the Republic does not become heteronomous vis-a-vis other nations." In this succession, Robert N. Bellah was to argue that "the civil religion at its best is a genuine apprehension of universal and transcendent religious reality as seen in or, one could almost say, as revealed through the experience of the American people."

He concluded with a "since" that assumes that something has been established:

> Since the American civil religion is not the worship of the American nation but an understanding of the American experience in the light of ultimate and universal reality, the reorganization entailed by . . . a new situation need not disrupt the American civil religion's continuity.

With more sensitivity to the ecumenical and nonidolatrous idea of national self-transcendence than to the problem of the faiths of other people in other nations who do not share much of the American way of looking at reality, he continues:

> A world civil religion could be accepted as a fulfillment and not a denial of American civil religion. Indeed such an outcome has been the eschatological hope of American civil religion from the beginning. To deny such an outcome would be to deny the meaning of America itself.[19]

By the time reference to a "world civil religion" is made, God-talk has been thinned out; the question of "the meaning of America itself" is a heavy-laden theological term (since one cannot know the meaning of America until the end of its history); problems abound in these two paragraphs. But they do illustrate that the intention of dialectical-prophetic civil religionists is not only to affirm what is, but to avoid idolatry and move toward an *oikoumene*. "Our nation stands under higher judgment." In a later essay, Bellah went on: "Every society is forced to appeal to some higher jurisdiction and to justify itself not entirely on its actual performance but through its commitment to unrealized goals or values."[20]

Such language is possible to those for whom the idea of the "nation under God" is no longer satisfactory. Thus Roger Garaudy, French Marxist who participated in dialogues with Christians before he broke with Marxism, wrote:

> As far as faith is concerned, whether faith in God or faith in our task and whatever our differences regarding its source—for some, assent to a call from God; for others, purely human creation—faith imposes on us the duty of seeing to it that every man becomes a man, a flaming hearth of initiative, a poet in the deepest sense of the word: one who has experienced, day by day, the creative surpassing of himself—what Christians call his transcendence and we call his authentic humanity.[21]

In the future it is possible that this kind of language will be refined and propagated with more comprehension in the American environment.

So far as the future is concerned, it may be that culture will be ever more sensate and secular or it may turn newly religious. Perhaps a new style of consciousness will emerge. In the latter instances, public theologians in the civil religious traditions will probably look for what Tillich denominated "Catholic substance and Protestant principle," not in any denominational sense but as priestly and prophetic realities in tension with each other. If the two elements can be built into civil religion, it will not be so ominous to its critics, nor so simply enjoyable and utilizable by its priests. In the meantime, some creative apathy against its claims— some foot-dragging, finger-crossing, thumbing-gestures, and puckish good humor—are in order. The tradition of Mark Twain, Mr. Dooley, Will Rogers, and others should be invoked to prevent people from taking the claims and counterclaims of civil religion so seriously. Maybe some division of labor is in order. We are told that when Harold Macmillan was criticized for not giving his people a sense of purpose, he replied that if the people wanted a sense of purpose they should go to their archbishops. The particular communities—be they religious, ethnic, or oriented around interest groups—can creatively refract generalized civil religion through specific prisms. They can contribute to peoples' identity and power, their search for meaning and belonging. We shall probably continue to hear advocacies both of a "world civil religion" and for the reformation of the existing centers of value which are now embodied and contended for apart from the civil realm. The future belongs, no doubt, to neither but only to both.

Publick religion or civil religion, however denominated and defined, obviously presents a pluralistic republic with puzzles and challenges. Citizens, especially religious believers among them, have needed and on occasion welcomed profound interpreters who could help them discern between priestly and prophetic utterances and trends, and impel them toward discriminations and choices. Rather than meander through sourcebooks and deal lightly with more superficial interpreters, we choose to take a classic case, twentieth-century America's most profound public theologian, Reinhold Niebuhr, and use him for close-up examination, taking special care to show his rootedness in particular religious communities. This means a visit to a small Protestant parish in Detroit and a large interdenominational seminary in New York, whence Niebuhr gained his vantages for interpreting America.

5   Interpretation: The Classic Public Theologian

The character of both nations and individuals may be defined as a pattern of consistent behavior, created on the one hand by an original ethnic, geographic and cultural endowment, and on the other hand by the vicissitudes of history, which shape and reshape, purify, corrupt and transmute this endowment.

We are always part of the drama of life which we behold; and the emotions of the drama therefore color our beholding.

REINHOLD NIEBUHR[1]

ECCLESIASTICAL AND NATIONAL TRADITIONS

The main strand of American religious thought has drawn together the work of various figures who have interpreted the nation's religious experience, practice, and behavior in the light of some sort of transcendent reference. Roman Catholic theology in its most formal sense was not really free to do this until the middle of the twentieth century. But earlier Catholicism also included various popular figures and publicists—one thinks of Father Isaac Hecker or Orestes Brownson—who in informal ways made their contribution. Jewish thought has been consistently circumstantial, incorporating frequent references to the meaning of Judaism in America. In the course of the decades, theologians in the black community informed their contemporaries about the long lineage of reflection on the value of their peoples' experience in the New World.

The strand has been most consistently visible at the point of juncture between certain styles of Protestant thought and the representation of a "religion of the Republic" which drew on Enlightenment resources. While the nation has produced a number of philosophers of religion who have written without much reference to situation, the more characteristic thinkers have taken on themselves the burden of interpreting experience and behavior as these have been embodied in religious groups and in the nation itself.

From the ecclesiastical side the great colonial focus was Jonathan Edwards, whose philosophy was shaped in constant reference to his painstaking observation of people in the midst of their conversion and awakening. Book titles such as *A Faithful Narrative of the Surprising Work of God etc.* or *Religious Affections* are typical of his empirical concerns. His charter for a fresh mode of theology was to have been "a great work, which I call a *History of the Work of Redemption,* a body of divinity in an entirely new method, being thrown into the form of a history."[2] In sermonic outline it concluded with reference to the awakenings in America and in Edwards's own ministry.

More than a century later Horace Bushnell, working out of a pastorate at Hartford, Connecticut, not many miles downriver from Edwards's Northampton, Massachusetts, used the raw material of his own contemporaries' religious behavior and experience to fashion his seminal *Christian Nurture* (1861) and other works which were theological reflections on alternatives to revivalism. Similarly, half a century later, Walter Rauschenbusch represented another significant turn in what came to be called the Social Gospel. His situation began with a ministry in Hell's Kitchen in New York and became one of observation of and participation in various seminary-based attempts to alter social circumstances. His *Christianity and the Social Crisis* (1907) and *Christianizing the Social Order* (1912) were in part theological extrapolations on these perceptions.

If Edwards, Bushnell, and Rauschenbusch represent what might be called public theology from the churches' side, their contemporaries Benjamin Franklin (or, later, Thomas Jefferson), Abraham Lincoln, and Woodrow Wilson used specifically deistic or theological materials in order to make sense of the American experience.[3] They were in every case uncommonly informed about the practices of religious people in the churches. They also looked for what appeared to them to be a broader and eventually deeper repository of religious motifs: the nation itself. Just as there have been more abstract and acontextual philosophers of religion than those cited here, so, too, there have been political philosophers who reasoned without much reference to their American circumstances. Their impact has been highly secondary to that of these statesmen-philosophers who served as public theologians.

THE TWENTIETH CENTURY: REINHOLD NIEBUHR AS MODEL

In the middle third of the twentieth century these two traditions came together in one person as never before through the career of Reinhold Niebuhr. His first book appeared in 1927, but at the turn to the second third of the century, with *Moral Man and Immoral Society* in 1932, his impact first began to be widely felt. A third of a century later in 1965—though editors were still to bring forth a couple of compilations from his earlier work—his literary career began to come to terminus in *Man's Nature and His Communities*. Its introduction detailed his debt to the practitioners of religion in the American environment. After several years of relative confinement because of ill health, he died in 1971. He and his brother, H. Richard Niebuhr (whose *The Social Sources of Denominationalism* and *The Kingdom of God in America* [1935] have been as determinative as many of Reinhold's essays on national themes),[4] towered over all other native-born theologians in their time. Together they offer the best personal paradigms of the emerging American public theology style.

Given Reinhold Niebuhr's book titles and main subjects, it may seem gratuitous to name him the century's foremost interpreter of American religious social behavior. Yet this has been a neglected theme, one to which the numerous major interpretations of Niebuhr make scant and sometimes even apologetic reference. The reasons for this slighting are manifold. First, Niebuhr himself was surprisingly diffident and reticent, despite the range of his public commitments, to make the kind of autobiographical comment out of which interpretations based on his situation would grow. Almost every analyst is moved to comment on Niebuhr's reluctance to place himself visibly near the center of his work.

He could not completely and permanently avoid such references. His first book was dedicated to his pastor father and to his mother "who for twelve years has shared with me the work of a Christian pastorate," one which was memorialized in his most nearly autobiographical work, a sketchbook called *Leaves from the Notebook of a Tamed Cynic*. He dedicated that book to his "friends and former co-workers in Bethel Evangelical Church, Detroit, Michigan,"[5] where he had spent thirteen years of formative ministerial life. After his move in 1928 to New York's Union Theological Seminary, the locus of his subsequent career, the number of specific parochial comments progressively declined.

Only occasional later references reminded Niebuhr's readers of this factor in his life. In a rare twenty-page "Intellectual Autobiography" he acknowledged that the Detroit "facts determined my development more than any books which I may have read."[6] When autobiography was almost forced out of him in a *Christian Century* series in 1939 he alerted his readers: "Such theological convictions which I hold today began to dawn upon me during the end of a pastorate in a great industrial city." There he had seen how irrelevant simple moral homilies were in the realm of "human actions or attitudes in any problem of collective behavior." Even at Union "the gradual unfolding of my theological ideas [had] come not so much through study as through the pressure of world events."[7]

After his interpreters pay lip service to his own self-interpretative clues, they usually move on to formal analysis of his theological and philosophical ideas on an almost entirely literary base of reference. Some of this skewing may be the result of their own predilections for discerning as more enduring the styles characteristically associated with historic European theology. Or they may be dismissing his circumstantial thought as being the ephemeral context out of which the permanent more abstract philosophical work emerged.

Niebuhr himself often threw people off the trail not only because of the paucity of autobiographical references, but because some of his major works took on an apparently more abstract character. His most solid and most studied book is *The Nature and Destiny of Man*,[8] the Gifford Lectures delivered in Scotland where an American accounting would have been largely beside the point. Yet hundreds of editorials and journalistic occasional pieces rich in American comment went into the background of that formal work. The American references in his other works preoccupy us here.

PHILOSOPHER OF AMERICAN PRAXIS

For all the range of his topics, Reinhold Niebuhr's thought was grounded in his perception that he was a servant of and, in a sense, a prophet to America-in-*praxis*. He conceived America as a nation of behavers and experiencers and not very often as theorists about their belief. But his reportorial perceptions were never reproduced as ends in themselves. Instead, he turned them into much of the stuff of his theology.

This "Professor of Applied Christianity" dealt constantly with the language of a believing and practicing ecclesiastical and national community. His primal vision as "a kind of circuit rider" in a secular age was that of one who had "never been very competent in the nice points of pure theology." He confessed that he had "not been sufficiently interested . . . to acquire the competence." He shared Tocqueville's observation of "the strong pragmatic interest of American Christianity in comparison with European Christianity," a distinction he thought to be valid a century later. When the "stricter sects of theologians in Europe" goaded Niebuhr to prove that his "interests were theological rather than practical or 'apologetic'" he made no defense, "partly because I thought the point was well taken and partly because the distinction did not interest me."[9] So much for page one of his intellectual autobiography. A billboard could hardly have made the point more boldly.

Niebuhr's historic allusions displayed his consistency. When he contrasted his generation with Rauschenbusch's, he noted that the "difference was created not by the triumph of one philosophy over another or by the triumph of Comte over Spencer, but by the beneficent play of cultural and social forces in a free society. In this development, creeds and dogmas were transmuted into a wisdom better than that possessed by any dogmas."[10] His recall of the industrializing generation in America was not of theorists but of "American go-getters."[11]

Niebuhr could mourn the failure of good ideas in America. He was constantly critical of the way Puritans in practice corrupted their idea of taking "prosperity and adversity in its stride [into] a religion which became preoccupied with the prosperity of the new community." In doing so they came to see Jefferson's "'useful knowledge' as the only valuable knowledge," it was "knowledge 'applied to common purposes of life.'"[12]

The Irony of American History developed this theme most extensively. Chapter 5, titled "The Triumph of Experience over Dogma," condensed the Niebuhrian approach. Thus in the presumably ideological clash with Marxist nations, the fact that Americans developed reasonable degrees of justice was "due primarily to our highly favored circumstances"—the wealth of natural resources, and the like. The author then moved on to legitimate discussion of some ideological dimensions, but even there he remarked on how American practice compromised ideology, dogma, and theory. When housing, medicine, and social security became matters of public and political policy, "all this [was] accomplished on a purely pragmatic basis, without the ideological baggage which European labor carried."[13]

As in national affairs, so in religion the affective and observable side mattered most to his compatriots. Niebuhr liked to quote the *London Times Literary Supplement* on the doctrinal point he had done more than any contemporary to revive: "The doctrine of original sin is the only empirically verifiable doctrine of Christian faith." One Niebuhrian interpreter took a line from James Thurber to talk about that chief visible doctrine in the peoples' behavioral pattern: "We all have our flaws, . . . and mine is being wicked." The Union Seminary theologian became the chief chronicler of American structural wickedness and of the relative justice that was achieved in spite of it.[14]

The abstract sphere represented cowardice and escape. In the earliest stages of his career Niebuhr had observed his own behavior to note how hard it was to amass courage so that one could deal with the concrete in religious communities: "One of the most fruitful sources of self-deception in the ministry is the proclamation of great ideals and principles without any clue to their relation to the controversial issues of the day. . . . I have myself too frequently avoided the specific application of general principles to controversial situations to be able to deny what really goes on in the mind of the preacher when he is doing this."[15] His later career made him ever less vulnerable to such a point of self-accusation.

THE RELOCATION OF THEOLOGY

Where did this love of the concrete and historical pattern leave religious thought? For Niebuhr, theology was simply relocated. He possessed a rare gift for relating idea to circumstance. The circumstances might change, but the ideas born of reflection on them could survive and be transformed. Thus when in 1960 he reintroduced his book from 1932 for fresh publication, he had to say that "naturally many of its references are dated," but "despite these dated references I consented to the republication of the book because I still believe that the central thesis of the book is important and I am still committed to it." Though he had changed his mind about many things in almost three decades, he thought that "our contemporary experience validates rather than refutes the basic thesis."[16]

While he admitted that he had experienced "boredom with epistemology" as a Yale student, he later found it necessary to interpret his practical experience in theological terms.[17] Niebuhr knew how little the churches regarded such terms. "Here [in Detroit] I have been all these years in a conservative communion and have never had a squabble about theology."[18] Liberalism in the social realm was what always got his colleagues into trouble. Yet he himself had a positive appreciation of dogma and its history. It has "achieved a hated connotation in the lexicon of modernity, for it connotes the arbitrary assertion of what can not be proved scientifically. As a matter of fact, it was intended to avoid the arbitrariness of private interpretation and *to assure the 'public' character of the truth*. . . . Dogma, at its best, represents the consensus of a covenant community which lives upon the basis of common convictions and commitments" (emphasis mine).[19]

Niebuhr's own movement had been from practice through ethics toward theology. His awakening first came at Detroit through his temporary abandonment of the idea of "worrying so much about the intellectual problems of religion" when he began "to explore some of its ethical problems."[20] His first book depicted this movement through his judgment that "morality is as much the root as the fruit of religion; for religious sentiment develops out of moral experience, and religious convictions are the logic by which moral life justifies itself. . . . If religion is senescent in modern civilization, its social importance is as responsible for its decline as is its metaphysical maladjustment." Metaphysical thought could be a luxury, since it was a characteristic of "those classes which are not sensitive enough to feel and not unfortunate enough to suffer from the moral limitations of modern society. . . . The fact is that more men in our modern era are irreligious because religion has failed to make civilization ethical than because it has failed to maintain its intellectual respectability. For every person who disavows religion because some ancient and unrevised dogma outrages his intelligence, several become irreligious because the social importance of religion outrages their conscience." Yet "the metaphysical problem of religion cannot be depreciated," for religion must be able to impress the minds of moderns with the essential plausibility of its fundamental affirmations.[21]

Throughout his later career, then, Niebuhr appropriated behavioral and ethical perceptions while his thought took on an increasingly metaphysical guise. In his later formal works the constant references are to Aquinas and Aristotle and Augustine or to Calvin and Hegel and Marx more than to the industrialists of Detroit or the seminarians of Morningside Heights. The *use* he made of these major thinkers is what was most significant. He readily admitted that he rarely studied them painstakingly for their own sakes. Rather he plundered their thought for that in them which could be reflected back into the American moral community.

THE DOCTRINE OR PRACTICE OF THE CHURCH

Niebuhr's thought was shaped by his vision of the American religious circumstance. Grasping the substance of that vision is important for any assessment of his role or for further development of the charter and vocation of any public theologian. Since Niebuhr was not a reporter but a transformer, it is not surprising to note that he dealt with virtual stereotypes of his contemporaries' behavioral patterns in their religious communities. He was quite uninterested in idiosyncratic or exceptional experience. He came to treat religious social behavior on nomothetic lines. He lacked the historians' taste for surprise and serendipity. People were expected to act in certain ways depending upon their situations and classes. They had to be able to be counted on almost as if they existed for the interpretations Niebuhr would provide. What he lacked in historical finesse he gained in social power.

He never developed an extensive ecclesiology. To quote John Bennett: "Niebuhr is basically a theologian who sees the implications of his theology for Christian ethics, but he has never addressed himself primarily to the Church as Church." "I doubt if we can make a very clear distinction between the substance of what he says explicitly as a theologian and churchman, and what he says when he speaks to the public." "Most of the critics of Niebuhr, whenever they write criticism, generally say he doesn't have a doctrine of the Church."[22]

Wilhelm Pauck "wondered about Niebuhr's ecclesiology, churchmanship, *not in the practical sense . . . but more in the theological sense*" (emphasis mine). Pauck thought that Niebuhr had a "strangely spiritual concept of the Church."[23] (Niebuhr had strangely spiritual concepts of hardly anything. He merely had an undeveloped sense of or curiosity about the borders of the church.) Harold R. Landon defended Niebuhr for having held in practice a concept similar to that of Paul Tillich's "latent church" and for having served the church faithfully without having developed a corresponding doctrine. But Landon could also cite a succinct and significant statement on the church from *Beyond Tragedy*. Niebuhr there had said that "the Church is that place in human society where men are disturbed by the word of the eternal God . . . it is also the place where the word of mercy, reconciliation and consolation is heard. . . . The Church is the place in human society where the kingdom of God impinges upon all human enterprises through the divine word, and where the grace of God is made available to those who have accepted his judgment."[24]

Another editor added to the defense by eventually culling a great number of Niebuhrian essays that had reference to the church and publishing them as *Essays in Applied Christianity*. In that collection D. B. Robertson succeeded in showing how frequent were Niebuhr's ecclesiastical preoccupations but failed to show him much devoted to definition of the subject.[25]

If Niebuhr produced and employed stereotypes, this was not because he felt that once one reduced behavior to patterned outline, it could be used for simple prediction: "No scientific investigations of past behavior can become the basis of predictions of future behavior." He cautioned against trying to reduce the drama of history's confusion to some kind of simple meaning. Biography serves to disrupt "the analysis of uniformities and recurrences of behavior under like conditions." He considered the biographical and personal factor a good counter to determinism in social sciences: "The impulse to falsify the facts in order to bring them into a comprehensible pattern assails the scientists who try to manage detailed facts and small patterns. Another analogous temptation assails the philosophers and ontologists who try to make sense out of the larger patterns of history and to comprehend the whole drama of history as meaningful."[26] In many respects Niebuhr can himself be accused of falling into both temptations because of his broad level of generalization and his reluctance to deal with exceptions to patterns. The picture of religious community that came to him in the beginning of his career stayed with him to the end, however mellowed he was by the time of his last book.

Though there are notable exceptions, that vision was often informed more by Marxian than Weberian analytic tools. That is, Niebuhr less readily saw the consequences of religious belief in, say, the Puritan community. More frequently he isolated the status, class, and context of a community and then elaborated on the almost inevitable character its religious ideology would take. This debt to Marx he acknowledged, however scornful of imposed Marxist ideology he was to become. "In a sense the word of Marx is true: 'The beginning of all criticism is the criticism of religion. For it is on this ultimate level that the pretensions of men reach their most absurd form. The final sin is always committed in the name of religion.'" Thereupon he diagnosed these sins on Marxian lines, seeing religion as the sanction of capitalist order or noting that many in the church declared politics to be irrelevant to the religious life or seeing part of the church to be content with "insufferable sentimentality," or, finally, with being legalistic.[27]

He could then turn around and comment on the Marxian shortsightedness for having seen religion as a "pie in the sky" refuge from the world, whereas in America it was actually used to enhance and legitimate worldliness and material prosperity.[28]

THE OBSERVATION OF COLLECTIVE BEHAVIOR

To see Reinhold Niebuhr, Professor of Applied Christianity, as a theologian who wrote theology out of his observation of America's collective religious behavior might lead one to treat him as a "theologian with the theology left out." His empirical sense; his choice of theological themes based upon what he considered to be a relevant address to the human situation; his journalistic avocation; his involvement with contemporary policymakers—all these prevent one from seeing him as an ivory-tower dweller with abstractions. When he dealt with churchly or national religious behavior, he did so without explicit reference to a literary tradition. Almost everything was based on observation. Proper nouns in these paragraphs and chapters were rare. He cited no major figures and seemed to be influenced by few. Niebuhr used his own eyes and assumed that readers saw the religious world roughly as he did. All he need do was convince them that what he did with the observation was appropriate.

His rather gloomy *Reflections on the End of an Era* (1934) included passages which showed that he was not content with what he saw. He looked for more reason and less impulse in religion, but knew that not much reason made its way into collective behavior. The social mechanisms of a commercial civilization "prevent the modern man from realizing that collective behavior is primarily impulsive, that its impulses are heedless and undirected and that will-to-live of every individual and social organism is easily transmuted into an imperial will-to-power." In that realm, "the dominance of reason over impulse is much more tentative and insecure than modern culture realizes." Hence, the dangers of pretension and pride in the collective life of the religious organization or the nation. The Pauline confession, "The good which I would do I do not:

but the evil which I would not, that I do," is *"perennially justified by human experience, particularly in collective human behavior"* (emphasis mine).[29]

Niebuhr himself did resist a simple determinism based on impulses and that will-to-power rooted in collective behavioral patterns. In his later years that resistance was reflected in a polemic against the behavioralism of B. F. Skinner, the psychologist author of *Walden Two*. At other times he reacted against a simple cultural relativism based on the observation of attitudes or customs, along with reductionist psychosocial explanations derived from Freudian and quasi-Freudian thought. He ranked Freudianism with Marxism in this respect, overlooking perhaps the degree to which Marxian economic determinisms tended to color his own often stereotypical views of behavior in American religion.[30]

That Niebuhr lacked a "doctrine of the Church" in a developed sense is obvious; that he outlined a complete sociology of the church is just as patent.[31] It is possible to trace almost every eventually developed view of the religious community in action back to his root experience in the Detroit parish. There he learned the limits of prophecy in the politics of the parish: "You can't rush into a congregation which has been fed from its very infancy on the individualistic ethic of Protestantism and which is immersed in a civilization where ethical individualism runs riot, and expect to develop a social conscience among the people in two weeks. Nor have you a right to insinuate that they are all hypocrites just because they don't see what you see."

In the parish he came to the conclusion that prophets almost have to be itinerants: "Critics of the church think we preachers are afraid to tell the truth because we are economically dependent upon the people of the church. There is something in that, but it does not quite get to the root of the matter. . . . I think the real clue to the tameness of a preacher is the difficulty one finds in telling unpleasant truths to people whom one has learned to love." In the introduction to the book that finds him reflecting on parish experience, there is a patient and tender note that disappeared when he became an itinerant prophet at Union Theological Seminary. As he looked back, he paid his tribute "to the [pastoral] calling, firm in the conviction that it offers greater opportunities for both moral adventure and social usefulness than any other calling if it is entered with open eyes and a consciousness of the hazards to virtue which lurk in it." Rarely later did he find open-eyed clerics. Most of them were wrapped in the illusions which he knew could come to people in contexts of mutual concern, responsibility, and love.[32]

Only rarely would he take pains to comment later on the intuitive and inherited wisdom and faithfulness of lay people, though he gave signs of an awareness of their qualities. In the *Christian Century* in 1934 he commented that "sometimes a healthy realism among laymen breaks through the illusions created by superficial moral preaching." Over against Christian idealists who "preach the law of love but forget that they . . . are involved in the violation of that law," he was "persuaded to thank God . . . that the common people maintain a degree of 'common sense,' that they preserve an uncorrupted ability to react against injustice and the cruelty of racial bigotry."[33] These compliments were rare, and they appeared almost exclusively when he wanted to make a point of lay realism over against clerical idealist folly.

Students of collective behavior in religion almost always preoccupy themselves with a study of ritual. Niebuhr was apparently only marginally interested in the esthetic and liturgical sides of religion, but he, too, did not underestimate the power of ritual. The editor of *Essays in Applied Christianity*, with compensatory vigor, reproduced eight essays on "The Weakness of Common Worship in American Protestantism." There Niebuhr commented on cathedral services, sermons and liturgy, and even architecture. His observer's eye was keen; most of what he saw in the Protestant churches reflected esthetic poverty, banality, and the separation of contemporaries from meaningful traditions: "There is a crying need for liturgical reform in American Protestantism." But that reform could not come if the evangelical churches merely aped the external estheticism of the liturgical churches. It would grow only out of a reevaluation of the whole meaning of worship. To make his case, Niebuhr discussed every nuance of typical church services.[34]

Burial rites play a major part in phenomenological treatments of religion; Niebuhr kept his eyes open. In Detroit he spoke well of the fact that Protestant funeral services took some cognizance of the "peculiar circumstances of a great sorrow" but were usually given to banalities and sentimentalities. "Religion is poetry. The truth in the poetry is vivified by adequate poetic symbols and is therefore more convincing than the poor prose with which the average preacher must attempt to grasp the ineffable." Both were superior to the generalized cultural burial rites parodied by Evelyn Waugh in *The Loved One*. Modern bourgeois culture's "effort to rob death of its sting by the perfection of appointments for coffin, grave and cemetery in funeral rites" was pathetic and perilous.[35]

Niebuhr often looked beyond the conventional churches; he knew that many of the churches went in "for vaudeville programs and . . . hip-hip-hooray" types of worship, with the "vulgarities of the stunt preacher." All this occurred in order for practitioners to compete for clienteles, especially among Methodists and Baptists, the large white denominations. He criticized Protestants who made churchgoing a matter of moral heroism, a positive duty. He could question the idea that "a formless service is more spontaneous and therefore more religious than a formal one." He was critical of some church leaders' need to rely on pomp, garb, and paraphernalia to create a sense of awe for their office, but he never lost interest in the question of symbolism and garb. It was natural that he would deal with these topics most when he was charged with leading worship, but as a regular preacher and worshiper he never lost interest. "Ivory tower"—if this means the academy away from the church—was never the locale for Niebuhr's ruminations.[36]

RELIGIOUS BEHAVIOR IN SOCIAL CLASSES

Niebuhr made clear, however, that ritual, worship, liturgy, devotionalism, and esthetics would no more be the fundamental tests of modern religion than would its intellectuality. The test would be ethical, and his behavioral observation concentrated massively on that sphere. There his disappointment and disgust showed more frequently. He knew that while many Americans would not join in denunciation of organized religion, "there are very many who ignore the church as a force for social amelioration."[37]

His observation was routinely and rigidly socioeconomic in outlook. Niebuhr, a man in quest of an American proletariat—who despaired of finding one or seeing it form[38]—devoted surprisingly little attention to the lower-class churches, the forces of the dispossessed. Richard Niebuhr had given two chapters of his book on *The Social Sources of Denominationalism* to "the churches of the disinherited";[39] Reinhold made only cursory reference to the social dynamics of these. He treated the black churches almost only in contexts where he was chastising whites for discrimination. The churches of the Appalachian poor, the white slum dwellers, the Roman Catholic bottom-rung immigrants—all these were treated with passing reference, little curiosity, and little detailed knowledge. The sectarian and immigrant churches were not made up of a proletariat but of a set of people on the way toward middle-class vulgarization.

Niebuhr was almost determinist and mechanistic on one point. He tended to see the American experience as one in which sooner or later almost everyone would be drawn as if by a magnet toward middle-class or bourgeois attitudes. It mattered little whether people came up from the ranks of the disinherited, from the late-arriving immigrant boats, or out of the segregated ex-slave churches. Somehow there would be eventual inevitable vulgarization and bourgeoisification, almost as if by a law of history. Here the determinist character of Niebuhr's observation was most patent. The "sect" churches he thought had been born honest, but in their conquest of the frontier they lost immediacy and mobility and became dominant, respectable, only vestigially charismatic. They secularized faith and let it lead to mere pursuit of worldly ends and sentimentality.[40]

The immigrant churches met similar fates. They became exclusive and guarded the immigrant against anomic urban culture. But what began as refuges from secular culture also served as a "resource for the uninhibited pursuits of essentially secular ends of life."[41] Churches became interesting to Niebuhr when they acquired middle-class semisecular status and were exposed to pluralist society.

THE CONSERVATIVE MIDDLE CLASSES

Niebuhr tended to classify middle-class religion—and here Protestantism interested him most consistently—along two lines. One was the semievangelical conservative religion of the American way of life, which was probably the majority pattern. Niebuhr needed the churches of this type for a discussion of normative American religion. They showed how pious citizens behave unless someone tampers with their patterns—as liberals were wont to do.

While his earlier works reflected an almost simplistic Marxian bias against the bourgeoisie, he softened criticism later and treated it ironically. In *The Irony of American History* he could even say that "the fluidity of the American class structure is . . . a gift of providence, being the consequence of a constantly expanding economy." This good fortune was sometimes "transmuted into social virtue" insofar as it left the worker free of social resentment and permitted the privileged classes to be less intransigent than had been their European counterparts in resistance to the rising classes. But when religious sanctions were combined with this way of life, Niebuhr was rarely so affirmative. In one case he did say that the middle class along with workers "have been significant bearers of justice in history" and "would have been, and would be, more perfect instruments of justice if they had not been tempted to regard themselves as the final judges and the final redeemers of history." In practice, he studied this messianism more than the bearing of justice.[42]

By 1950–51 he saw that "the alliance between Protestant pietism and political reaction" was achieving a new triumph. The middle-class religionists' churches used economic individualism to forge the religion of "the American way of life." Sectarian Christianity was thus vulgarized. "The problems of [these] sects are more important because they represent the dominant force in American Protestantism. Perhaps they are also intrinsically more important. The church lives in conscious compromise with the world. The vitiated sect lives in unconscious compromise with the world. The first attitude may lead to premature defeatism. The second leads to sentimentality and self-deception."[43] "Unconscious compromise" fell into the scope of Niebuhr as an observer of collective behavior.

If agrarian classes had been the stronghold of religion, "the life of the middle classes of the city" was becoming the new locus. The middle classes are religious, the young Niebuhr had written, "because they are comparatively unconscious of their responsibility for

society's sins and comparatively untouched by the evil consequences of an unethical civilization." So they may indulge hypocrit-
ically in a religion which creates respectability and self-respect.[44]

Niebuhr had least use for the fashionable bourgeois preachers,
the "false prophets of our day" who "speak of our bourgeois civilisation as a 'Christian' civilisation." Bourgeois churches transmuted
the idea of history into the Kingdom of God. The fashionable false
prophets would almost always win favor. "There are a large number
of eager young radical preachers in American Protestant churches
who are engaged in the business of trying to make proletarians out
of their middle-class church members." He knew American behavior. "It is a futile task." Surely "every common-sense realist, not to
speak of religious realists, must know that masses of men, even
when they are in Christian churches, move by interest" (1934). The
bourgeois church exists to "sanctify power and privilege as it exists
in the modern world."[45]

Despite its corruption, Niebuhr did not wish to see the middle-
class church abandoned. Indeed, the prophet should concentrate
there "because the church has the ear of these classes to a greater
degree than that of the disinherited" and also because change in
this class could be most significant.[46] In *Pious and Secular America*
Niebuhr took a synoptic view of the problem. He agreed with
Tocqueville, who a century earlier had noted the highly pragmatic
character of American evangelical preachers. They moved from
"eternal felicity" to the pursuit of worldly ends in their gospel. As a
result, "It becomes apparent that we are more religious and more
secular than any other nation, not by accident, but by the effect of
definitely ascertainable historic causes peculiar to the American experience." "Piety has not essentially challenged . . . [the] vulgarity
or futility." The result was "our gadget-filled paradise suspended in
a hell of international insecurity." Foreign visitors were confused to
find secular America "more religious in the devotion of a greater
percentage of the population to the religious institutions which,
contrary to expectation, grow rather than wither."[47]

Niebuhr knew that the sentimental and vulgarizing bond of religion and middle-class ideals was not wholly nonideological. In the
nineteenth century the "survival of the fittest" concepts of Social
Darwinism had served as an ideology when it was combined with

"moribund Calvinism." More recently bourgeoisified Christianity had been corrupted by its bond with conservative doctrines. "Religious conservatism and fundamentalism" played into the hands of social conservatism. The movement called Spiritual Mobilization, conducted by Dr. James Fifield of Los Angeles, was "one of the worst forms of religious rationalizations of a class viewpoint that we have had in American history." These formal ideological references were relatively rare in Niebuhr because they were unnecessary. Anyone with eyes could see: "There is not one church in a thousand where the moral problems of our industrial civilization are discussed with sufficient realism from the pulpit."[48]

Niebuhr's biblical realism, Puritan reminiscence, and critical Marxian viewpoint led him to blame individualism in economics for much of the corruption of this normative religious form. In practice, Americans were better than their individualist creed allowed in theory. Young men, "who have been assured that only the individual counts among us," had died for collective virtues on foreign battlefields. Here was "ironic refutation of our cherished creed" because the creed was too individualistic and optimistic. "It is necessary to be wiser than our creed if we would survive in the struggle against communism."[49]

Niebuhr contended that even middle-class churches could be better than their economic creed. Much of the popularity of the churches in the religious revival of the 1950s lay precisely in the fact that the individual could find his identity not over against an urban "crowd, gathered together by technics," but because some churches offered integral communities, where a person "lives in an environment of faith in which the vicissitudes of his existence are understood." Thus urbanness "has increased, rather than diminished, loyalty to the religious communities."[50] At the end of his career, Niebuhr even showed a rare awareness of the historical depths of this communitarian contribution that reached back to Jonathan Edwards in the eighteenth and Charles Grandison Finney in the nineteenth century. Both awakeners and awakenings "were productive of social as well as of individual creative commitments," and gave rise to antislavery and other social causes—even though people were eventually to lose heart in these causes.

5. *The Classic Public Theologian*

The faults of this evangelicalism lay in its individualism and perfectionism.[51] Observing behavior based on these commitments was a regular Niebuhrian preoccupation. "Protestant pietistic individualism" became a frequently used phrase in his later works just as observations of it had been common in his earliest. This individualism led religious leaders to focus on personal petty vices rather than on great social evils. His first book underscored this: "In America, Protestantism with its individualism became a kind of spiritual sanctification of the peculiar interests and prejudices of the races and classes which dominated the industrial and commercial expansion of Western civilization." Ministers were tempted in "our great urban churches" to "become again the simple priests and chaplains of this American idolatry."[52]

Niebuhr the prophet and theologian took his vision of bourgeois Christianity and called it to its biblical and, in the American instance, its Catholic and Puritan roots. "The social life of man" is "the source of common grace." To come to this understanding, "the adherent of religion must come to terms with the historic facts, that *in all collective behavior religious piety is likely to sanctify historical and contingent viewpoints*" (emphasis mine). Puritanism, he knew, worked both ways. Religiously it could bring the collective sphere into the orbit of God's judgment and common grace. Secularly it had transmuted a doctrine of providence and of the calling into economic individualism. Since New England days, "any grateful acceptance of God's uncovenanted mercies is easily corrupted from gratitude to self-congratulations if it is believed that providence represents not the grace of a divine power . . . but rather that it represents particular divine acts directly correlated to particular human and historical situations." To Niebuhr it was clear that Americans characteristically acted self-congratulatorily.[53]

"The whole non-Lutheran Protestant world," which meant the American non-Catholic majority, was "indoctrinated with [the] puritan spirit." This "puritanism is a religious sublimation of the life of the middle classes." For the heroic spirit of puritanism declined "in those classes which it had lifted to power," and was "reborn in the lower middle classes," which it helped turn into successful classes. "The puritan heritage of America . . . gives a clew to the paradox of our national life. It explains how we can be at the same time the most religious and the most materialistic of all modern nations."[54]

THE LIBERAL MIDDLE CLASSES

While the neo-orthodox Niebuhr was sometimes accused of being identified with conservative-pessimist Christianity because of his biblical concern and his restoration of the doctrine of original sin, no one ever accused him of being confused or bound up with pietist, individualist, evangelically orthodox, or fundamentalist churches. He showed that he was a prophet of biblical realism by turning most of his polemic attention against the churches in whose sphere he was located, the liberal minority in the essentially middle-class American context. He seemed to have despaired of fundamentalism; it was almost beyond redemption. The churches he served, the campuses he visited, the journals for which he wrote, the parties he advised, the seminarians he taught—all these were tinged with what he called liberalism. Their collective behavior patterns and their doctrines disturbed him most. He treated them nomothetically and stereotypically, rarely pointing to exceptions or citing individuals who transcended the boundaries he erected.

The first great work in which Niebuhr attacked the liberal middle-class churches was *An Interpretation of Christian Ethics*. He had repudiated that Social Gospel which had helped form him. The depression revealed the limits of the sentimental moral individualism and progressive optimism which had been the marks of the old liberal churches. Foreboding totalitarian powers in Europe further eluded their comprehensions. "The religion and ethics of the liberal church is dominated by the desire to prove to its generation that it does not share the anachronistic ethics or believe the incredible myths of orthodox religion." But, "in adjusting itself to the characteristic credos and prejudices of modernity, the liberal church has been in constant danger of obscuring what is distinctive in the Christian message and creative in Christian morality." Those lines pretty well delineate what might almost be called one of two separate churches in Niebuhr's observation. These churches cast a false aura of the absolute and transcendent ethic of Jesus around the "relative moral standards of a commercial age" and then capitulated to that age. They were too uncritically accommodated to modern culture, as the discrediting of that culture was progressively revealing.

Liberal Christianity was a religion of adjustment to the ethos of this age, a sacrifice of the Christian heritage through its destruction of "the sense of depth and the experience of tension" typical of profound religion. These churches also endorsed laissez-faire economic patterns until too late. By overstressing love and cooperation in place of conflict and coercion he removed the grounds for the socializing of life. The Federal Council of Churches (FCC), the endorsement of the League of Nations, the predilections for pacifism—which Niebuhr had been deserting—all showed how compromising liberalism in practice had become. These criticisms were constant in Niebuhr's later works and became so familiar that they hardly deserve citation here. Here it need only be noted that while Niebuhr brought ideological assumptions to his observations, he was, indeed, an observer—and a consistent one—of liberalism's behavioral regularities.[55]

Because of their blindness to tragedy in a warring world, he noted: "If the modern churches were to symbolize their true faith they would take the crucifix from their altars and substitute the three little monkeys who counsel men to 'speak no evil, hear no evil, see no evil.'" These churches close their eyes to suffering and "drug their conscience" so that they can make no significant distinctions between contending political forces. In order to make the point of the sentimental practice of liberal religion, Niebuhr even opened his mail for his readers and told of a parson who wanted to set "moral force" against Hitler's battalions. This was a "nice example of the sentimentalized form of Christianity which has engulfed our churches in America, and which has prompted them to dream of 'spiritualizing life' by abstracting spirit from matter, history, and life."[56]

The version of liberal Christianity that gave Niebuhr most problems was the Social Gospel. The embarrassment was evident when he was invited to give the Rauschenbusch lectures, dedicated to

115

the foremost advocate of the liberal Social Gospel. Niebuhr hoped that his lectures were "an extension and an application to our own day of both the social realism and the loyalty to the Christian faith" which characterized Walter Rauschenbusch, the brilliant founder and exponent of social Christianity. But throughout his career Niebuhr attacked the Social Gospel because its proponents "had . . . a faith which did not differ too grievously from the main outlines of the 'American dream.'" The Social Gospel displayed "a curious mixture of bourgeois prudence" with the pinnacle of grace, the message of the gospels.[57]

The final flaw in liberal religious practice was the almost consistent pacifism expressed in pre–World War II America. Liberal pacifism played into the hands of those who already had economic power, but it became more damaging when the demonic powers of Europe were underestimated by pacifists. Niebuhr's foils on this front were the FCC, where liberal churches were amassed, and the journal, *Christian Century*—with which he had been associated—which kept alive the progressive liberalism and optimism of the Social Gospel. Niebuhr's Christian realism needed a new outlet, and he helped form *Christianity and Crisis*. The FCC and the *Christian Century* were "completely divorced from all political realities" in their actions and attitudes toward Hitler. "Most of the neutrals of Europe to whose conscience the *Christian Century* pointed were destroyed while it was holding them up as glorious examples."[58]

While Niebuhr saw pacifism as an absolutist creed, he criticized it chiefly as a practical pattern born of a bad conscience over American hysteria in World War I and "the national fear of being involved in the war." The pacifists refused to look at the horrible consequences of tyranny. Here, as so often, Niebuhr looked at the behavior of the American and particularly the liberal churches. "The Christian Church in America has never been upon a lower level of spiritual insight and moral sensitivity than in this tragic age of world conflict. Living in a suffering world, with its ears assailed by the cries of the miserable victims of tyranny and conflict, it has chosen to identify the slogan Keep America out of the War with the Christian gospel."[59]

5. The Classic Public Theologian

THE CONDUCT OF NATION AND TRIBE

Niebuhr moved progressively away from seeing the churches as the repository of religious conviction and practice in America. He turned more and more to the need for seeing the nation itself in this role, though without denying the special custodial responsibilities of the Christian believing community. In this turn, Niebuhr began to combine in his person and vocation the once separate strands of past American public theology. We have seen Edwards, Bushnell, and Rauschenbusch typically using the covenanted religious community as a base for public action, while Franklin (or Jefferson), Lincoln, Wilson, and their kind were essentially public political figures who saw a kind of ecclesiastical dimension in national life. Niebuhr kept the tension between the two spheres, but also brought them dialectically into creative interplay and occasional fusion. He will be remembered more for his grasp of the irony of pious and secular American history than for any contributions to the sociology of religion.

While Niebuhr treated the church somewhat statically and stereotypically, he looked at the nation more dynamically. It seemed to be less of a finished product, more open to having its attitudes and practical patterns subjected to radical change. His later contacts were more with national than ecclesiastical figures: George Kennan, Dean Acheson, Arthur Schlesinger, Jr., Hans Morgenthau, Walter Lippmann, and James Reston make more of their debt to him than did ecumenical statesmen who, of course, also fell under his influence. Perhaps most revelatory of Niebuhr's final locale or situation was his designation of Abraham Lincoln and not a church leader as "America's greatest theologian."[60] His writings show a general agreement with the contention of his long-time colleague Paul Tillich that religion is the soul of culture and culture the form of religion, and he saw America as a problematic concretization of a spiritual reality.

Widely read in American sources, he operated basically out of pragmatic considerations and day-to-day observations. With his co-author, historian Alan Heimert, he opened a work on the American character with lines which summarize my essay: "The character of both nations and individuals may be defined as a pattern of consist-

117

ent behavior, created on the one hand by an original ethnic, geographic and cultural endowment, and on the other hand by the vicissitudes of history, which shape and reshape, purify, corrupt and transmute this endowment."[61] Niebuhr was aware of the particularity of this American history, but spoke critically of representatives of "our nominalistic culture" who were "intent upon finding specific causes for general tendencies" and who ascribed to American life certain universal human tendencies.[62]

The nation was not an autonomous generator of valid religious values; in the case of America, the Christian message had been especially determining. As had all the public theologians before him, Niebuhr wanted the churches to see "positively our task to present the Gospel of redemption in Christ to nations as well as to individuals." The church also had to "recognize that there are sensitive secular elements within modern nations, who, though they deny the reality of a divine judgment, are nevertheless frequently more aware of the perils of national pride than many members of the Church."[63]

As soon as Niebuhr mentioned national religiosity he would find it necessary to speak of the temptations of hubris and to idolatry. American citizens characteristically behaved idolatrously, and churches were little check against their tendency. "The god of American religion (the so-called 'American dream') is an American god." "Nowhere is the temptation to idolatry greater than in national life." "The idolatrous devotion to the 'American way of life' grows at a tremendous pace." Niebuhr used the business community and its devotion to the "free enterprise system" to demonstrate the point.[64]

How would idolatrous practices be countered? From two fronts. "There is no conceivable society in which the pride of the community and the arrogance of its oligarchs must not be resisted. It is possible to offer this resistance at times in the name of some minority interest." For example, religious, ethnic, and economic subcommunities "both enriched and imperiled the life of the community." "But the final resistance must come from the community which knows and worships a God, to whom all nations are subject."[65]

Americans acted not only idolatrously but also innocently, as if their nation were exempt from temptations of power and pride.

5. The Classic Public Theologian

Drawing on century-old observations of conduct by Tocqueville, Niebuhr commented that while every nation had an innocent and self-appreciative concept, "our version is that our nation turned its back upon the vices of Europe and made a new beginning." Because of the conflict between American ideals and realities, Niebuhr resorted to the basic category of irony to interpret national life. "Irony . . . prompts some laughter and a nod of comprehension beyond the laughter; for irony involves comic absurdities which cease to be altogether absurd when fully understood. Our age is involved in irony because so many dreams of our nation have been so cruelly refuted by history." For dealing with this irony not a churchman, but President Abraham Lincoln, was the model interpreter and theologian. "Lincoln's awareness of the element of pretense in the idealism of both sides was rooted in his confidence in an overarching providence whose purposes partly contradicted and were yet not irrelevant to the moral issues of the conflict."[66]

In *Beyond Tragedy* Niebuhr quoted Stephen Vincent Benet putting words into the mouth of Lincoln—words which underscored the concern for the churches' behavior patterns in American life:

They come to me and talk about God's will
In righteous deputations and platoons,
Day after day, laymen and ministers.
. . . God's will is those poor coloured fellows' will,
It is the will of the Chicago churches,
It is this man's and his worst enemy's.
But all of them are sure they know God's will.
I am the only man who does not know it.[67]

The nation stood as the powerful midpoint between the ethnic, religious, and economic subcommunities and the international community; for Niebuhr, it deserved most attention, but not in isolation. He was highly aware of region, of differences in North and South so far as race, religion, and nationalism were concerned. He even spoke of "the geography of morals," noting how different the church practices of similar denominations were in different regions.[68]

Niebuhr watched ethnic and racial subcommunities in action and was ambivalent. On one hand, their assertions of particularity could be a matter of tribal pride. "The chief source of man's inhumanity

119

to man seems to be the tribal limits of his sense of obligation to other men." "America, which has prided itself on being the 'melting pot' of many ethnic groups" was as late as the 1960s still trying to rid itself of tribalism that antedated the Civil War. Language, class, and religion joined race to create tribal distinctions. On the other hand, as dangerous as tribalism was, Niebuhr also saw virtues in subcommunities. In reference to the Jewish community he argued that the attempt to "solve the problem of the particularity of a race by a cultural or religious universalism" was false and destructive. He was critical of both "premature universalism" and a "conscious or unconscious ethnic imperialism." He had long been aware that integrationist models and tendencies toward universalism usually resulted from one's tendency "to make his own standards the final norms of existence and to judge others for failure to conform to them."[69]

The appreciation of the *plures* that interacted in the American *unum* resulted in part, he said, from the influence of his wife Ursula, who taught at Barnard College. She was "responsible for modifying my various forms of provincialism and homiletical polemics." Once again, his viewpoint was born of situation—or, at least, his wife's situation and circumstance. In his final retrospect he also credited Detroit Judaism for having made early and substantial contributions to his sense of justice born of particular subcommunities' witness. American Christians too often practiced "provisional tolerance" awaiting Jewish assimilation—and the end of Jewish identity and contribution. So awed was he by the realism and tenacity of America's Jews that he sometimes exempted them from the searching criticism he gave Christians. And Roman Catholics he eventually also viewed favorably from a distance, overestimating the degree to which their church temporarily spared them middle-class vulgarization and individual economic striving. Yet it was characteristic of him that he should train his eye and reserve his judgment for his own community. "Even in our nation, priding itself on its melting pot, the Protestant faith is undoubtedly an instrument of pride and cohesion for the North European or 'Nordic' groups, as distinguished from the Slavs and the Latins. Every Protestant denomination has some particular ethnic or historical particularity." This racial and even racist base of Protestant cohesion and conduct came to be reported on as commonplace in the 1970s, but was a rare observation in 1958 when Niebuhr made it. Even in his first book he could observe that "Orthodox Protestantism is intimately related to this day with Nordicism, with the racial arrogance of north European peoples."[70]

Nowhere did the problem of interpreting America as a spiritual reality present more problems for a synoptic thinker like Niebuhr than in the case of the majority's treatment of segregated blacks. Here, again, behavior was determining. "The churches, as Negro Christians long ago ruefully admitted, have been the most segregated communities in the . . . nation." This has been the negative by-product of one of the genuine achievements of the sectarian church in our nation: "the creation of integral communities on the level of local congregations," where "chumminess" invalidated the universal principle at the heart of the gospel.

Niebuhr's appreciation of Judaism and Catholicism was born of practical, and not dogmatic, awareness of their ability to transcend some of these circumstances. He even apologized to members of these religious groups, hoping they would "not be too shocked by the wholly pragmatic sources of my appreciations."[71]

Niebuhr's public theology not only related the nation to the tribe but also to supernation or internationalism. He was observant of the historical and not simply psychologically determining roots of national difference. The culturally relativist anthropologists lacked an "appreciation of the genuinely historical differences" between these national cultures. German problems could not be explained "as the consequence of defects in the toilet training."[72] One had to study the whole complex context of national conduct in historical lineages. It is not necessary here to detail Niebuhr's concepts of world community, the need for American expressions of responsibility, or his desire to see his nation purged of illusionistic idealism vis-à-vis other nations. At this point reference is in place only to his regard for national differences, so far as conduct and interest as well as ideology are concerned.

If Niebuhr was responsive to what some have come to call a civil religion, this awareness was born of his frustration over the limits of what particular churches could achieve. Never was it uncritical or short of prophetic; his every appreciation was tinged with irony

121

and marked by realism. And his national concerns had an ecumenical dimension: if God was somehow seen to be the transcendent reference for interpreting the life of the American people he was not less related to other nations and communities.

For all the limits in Niebuhr's observation and despite some hidden ideological biases and tendencies to stereotype, he joined in his person the two main approaches to public theology in America. He took the behavior of his people and, reflecting on it in the light of biblical, historical, and philosophical positions, offered the ensuing generation a paradigm for a public theology, a model which his successors have only begun to develop and realize.

Theology, however, only interprets experience. For a legally and, in ethos, often secular republic to retain religious pluralism, it must remain also religious. This means that its citizens themselves seek and claim religious experiences which, late in the twentieth century, more and more of them code-named a "spiritual search." Contrary to many expectations, they pursued things spiritual in a secular context, in the process converting some subcultures into quite religious expressions. They embarked, as we shall see, on what Ralph Waldo Emerson called "the spirit's holy errand."

6   *Spirituality: The Search in Its Secular Context*

In the religious revival of the 1950s and the social revolution of the 1960s, formal, theological, and ethical obsessions crowded out spiritual concerns. In the process, *spirituality* as a term was abandoned, especially by academic religionists.

During the 1950s, when people spoke of a "revival of religion," metropolitan newspapers enlarged their sections devoted to religion. For a decade, the press gave attention to the material expansion of institutions. It dutifully reported on the building of churches and synagogues and chronicled the growth of religious bodies and the rise in attendance at rites. By the end of the decade such reporting had begun to pall on both newspapermen and their readers. Few look back to the years of the purported revival as a time of spiritual increase in the United States.

Beginning in the middle of the 1960s, the media began to discover and portray a spiritual search, what came to be called a "religious journey" or "pilgrimage," often of a very private character. Leaving behind some of the programmatic and optimistic activism of the early 1960s and vying with the momentary radicalism of the latter part of the decade, this search came to dominate the religious scene in the 1970s and after. The secular paradigm itself came to be called into question. I prefer to say that ever since we have seen how in the "operative" sides of private and public life there are many secular expressions, while the religious shows up in the per-during "passional" aspects of personal and cultural life.

Urgent issues of theology, ethics, and the social forms of the church had so preoccupied the elite and the avant-garde of the religious communities that they tended to ignore "the spiritual dimension" of both individual and collective life. Paul Tillich, America's most prestigious theologian in these decades, spoke of "the almost forbidden word 'spirit'" and worked heroically to bring discussion of the term into sophisticated academic theology and philosophy: "Should and can the word 'spirit,' designating the particularly human dimension of life, be reinstated? There are strong arguments for trying to do so; and I shall attempt it." But even Tillich despaired of the attempt to resuscitate the adjective *spiritual;* it "is lost beyond hope."[1]

Despite the neglect or the despair of academic religionists, concern for the spiritual did not, however, disappear. It went underground and became the property of adherents of America's folk, lay, civic, or societal religion. With or without formal leadership, a search for a spiritual style in America went on.

EVIDENCE OF AN ONGOING SEARCH

When people detail their reasons for pursuing the religious quest, they usually speak of psychological and moral situations relating to what Tillich called the "unity of power and meaning" denoted by the term *spirit*. The same sociological surveys that find the majority of Americans professing belief in God and affiliating with church and synagogue find only a minority expressing any interest in theology or concurring with their church's major ethical positions. Although academic critics find the churches' theological quest earnest, and their ethical renewal reasonably impressive, they find missing any articulation of the profoundest features in "the particularly human dimensions of life."

During the period of institution building in the 1950s and activism in the 1960s, many religious leaders abdicated roles in spiritual development. The search became informal. Its signs in "high culture" included the popularity of spiritual books by Pope John XXIII, United Nations secretary-general Dag Hammarskjöld, Teilhard de Chardin in his mystical moments, and the monk Thomas Merton. These were only a few and, it must be said, elite signals of what was to come.

Late in the 1960s and for a period after, the spiritual search often took form in occult and cultic, African and Eastern and Ancient importations and transformations of religion. These extravagant versions drew media attention: this was an "occult explosion" or the "Age of Aquarius" or "The New Age." As it found its more or less secure place among the subcultures, it was matched by revitalizing spiritual movements in mainstream religious groups: the Jesus movement, Catholic charismatic groups, Hassidic and mystical Judaism, and any number of vivid spiritual searches.

After two decades of such striving, it may be hard to re-create the mood of the 1930s or the 1960s, when the only model presented for the human future by many educated Americans was secular. And with good reason. Many dimensions of life were presenting themselves with no window for transcendence, for the sacred, the spiritual. They have not gone away, but they are no longer simply privileged and must coexist with selectively powerful religious competitors.

DISAPPEARANCE OF THE TRANSCENDENT

Once, spiritual man was seen to be the one who stood before the *mysterium tremendum*. He maintained a direct or clearly mediated access to a transcendent order or being; he had some contact with the primal depths of a universe that both terrified him and pronounced perpetual benedictions on his doings. In modern times, this transcendent order became problematic in many humans' consciousness. New quests by persons who experienced the disappearance of transcendence had to take place in the empirical world that surrounded them. Their quest would eventuate from an affirmation by Merleau-Ponty to which we have alluded: "Because we are present to a world, we are condemned to meaning."[2] The spiritual person, in this case, would be the man who lives out the terms of condemnation creatively. Spirit, to quote Arnold Come's theological definition, is . . . man in the fullest possible actualization of what he is in his heart. Man as spirit is "the forceful and indeed purposeful individual," man at his most personal level, wherein the totality of all the dimensions and capacities and contents of his life (soul) are brought to conscious unity in realization.[3]

With this definition, discussion of spirit need not be restricted to certain formal religious objects or creedal propositions.

The advance guard of American theology approached sustained discussion of spirituality only in the context of the phrase *holy worldliness* (or its converse, *worldly holiness*), abstracted from Dietrich Bonhoeffer's attempt to find a nonreligious expression of the Christian faith. The phrase *holy worldliness* shocked an America accustomed to hearing preachers advocate the "holiness" of a realm set apart and associated with transcendence. The public had come to feel that religious leadership had deserted traditional theological, ethical, and spiritual beliefs. As the custodian of a kind of supernaturalist subculture, the clergy had been expected to summon rhetoric to advocate religiousness and a spirituality based on it. With their vested interest in transcendence and cosmic order, they could provide models for sainthood. They could stand for morals, law, and order.

For a time some theologians argued that Protestants, Catholics, and Jews must advance the cause of secularization. They must see that the world had come of age and must purge it of vestigial mythical traces. They could become God's "advance guard." Much of the clergy did briefly want to leave behind an approach that haunted their antecedents for several centuries. They were tired of being a rear guard who made grudging acquiescences to emerging worlds and world views. They wanted to seize initiative and rescue a few religious symbols, then to advance these. During this period, their opponents could exploit the vacancies they left on the spiritual landscape. It took these mainstream leaders some years to recover some of their roles.

THE NEW SETTING IN SECULAR AMERICA

Americans have consistently been considered a future-oriented people. They have often repudiated history, tradition, the Euro-

pean past. Pragmatic, optimistic, and now industrially or techno-
logically adept, they have chosen a secular mode of existence. In
their practical daily lives, "the world has become an entity rounded
off in itself, which is neither actually open at certain points where
it merges into God, nor [undergoing] at certain observable points
the causal impact (*ursächlichen Stoss*) of God."[4]

Practical godlessness does not presuppose a formal repudiation
of the old ways in theology, ethics, or spirituality. Norman Birnbaum has an insight into the mixed character of American life when
he observes that the typical American is a Calvinist who has neither
fear of hell nor hope of heaven. The Calvinism may be gradually
slipping away, but it symbolizes an element of the past that cannot
be shrugged off lightly. Sociologist J. Milton Yinger, as we noted,
saw the development of a "laymen's ecumenicalism, a folk effort,"
independent of religious professionals. The public redefines its religion "while disguising or obscuring the process by holding, somewhat superficially, to many of the earlier religious symbols."[5]

Americans are caught, then, between the "religious" and the
"secular," between the divergent directives from the religious institutions and leaders of the past and those of the present. Father John
Thomas, S.J., commenting on an extensive religious survey made
in 1952, admitted that the findings lent "considerable support to
the contention that the frame of reference within which modern
man defines the essential human dilemma has lost its transcendental referents," though roughly half the adult population "still regards the churches as representatives of a transcendental point of
view." Sociologist Gerhard Lenski also concluded that in general "a
transcendental faith is gradually being transformed into a cultural
faith."[6]

The "Calvinist" side of this new man, this American who has neither fear of hell nor hope of heaven, is nostalgic. This man looks
back, as his father before him looked back, to a society and a religious context in which spirituality grew out of an agreed-upon
frame of reference. He expects religious institutions today to propagate something of that earlier context's assumptions. He feels
cheated when religious leaders want to lead him away from those
assumptions.

THE SPIRIT'S HOLY ERRAND IN AMERICAN HISTORY

Ralph Waldo Emerson could hardly be seen as a spokesman of America's colonial orthodoxies, yet he was typically nostalgic about one feature of colonial life and was concerned about what would replace it.

> What a debt is ours to that old religion which, in the childhood of most of us, still dwelt like a sabbath morning in the country of New England, teaching privation, self-denial and sorrow! A man was born not for prosperity, but to suffer for the benefit of others, like the noble rock-maple which all around our villages bleeds for the service of man. Not praise, not man's acceptance of our doing, but the spirit's holy errand through us absorbed the thought. . . .
>
> And what is to replace for us the piety of that race? We cannot have theirs; it glides away from us day by day.[7]

Because of what he held in common with those who earlier had known "the spirit's holy errand," Emerson today sounds as archaic as they. His "piety," or spirituality, glides away too. Many today could more easily relate to the colonial covenant than they could to Emerson's transcendentalist Over-Soul. But in his time he was able to help give the contemporary "image of the free individual cosmic significance." If the "old Calvinism which in his youth hung like a benediction over New England, holding each man down to *his* place with the weight of the Universe," was gliding away, Emerson "pronounced the same benediction over his fellows."[8]

Most contemporary Americans are not, of course, direct spiritual heirs of colonial New England. The Roman Catholics, Jews, and Continental Protestants who immigrated after the middle of the nineteenth century would have found little congenial in New England village life. But consciously and unconsciously, by historical study and by osmosis, they share its general outline. More important, most of these later immigrants lived in subcommunities or enclaves that reproduced the essential feature in the life of the original covenanted community. Human personality and spirituality were still measured according to standards shaped by belief in a transcendent order. Beneath the sermons of oligarchical clerics or the constructs of the founding fathers, in the diaries and simple accounts of daily life, formal religious concerns seem less obsessive than they do today. Real infidels were rare, but disaffection was common; many were "nothingarians" in religion. One quiet dissenter addressed his clergyman:

> We have heard your animadversions upon our absence from Sabbath meetings, and humbly conceive if you wish our attendance there, you would make it worth our while to give it. To miss a sermon of the present growth, what is it but to miss of an opiate? And can the loss of a nap expose our souls to eternal perdition?[9]

But if disaffection was common and dissent widespread, it was easier then for people to be aware of what it was from which they were dissenting and how radically they desired to dissent. At the base was what verged on an ontocratic order, to use Arend van Leeuwen's thoughtful term. In it, man's spiritual life grew out of an understanding of the cosmos in the context of a total order of harmony between temporal and eternal, human and divine.

The sense of a quasi-metaphysical setting was pervasive. Late in the twentieth century a far higher percentage of the population was affiliated with religious institutions than at the end of the colonial era. All forms of society were given a sacral dimension. A theocratic foundation underlay or a theocratic penumbra surrounded these institutions. Toleration-minded pluralist colonies like Roger Williams's Rhode Island, or Catholic colonies like Maryland, hardly differed in this respect from the homogeneous and organismic society advocated by John Cotton in Massachusetts.

Oscar Handlin has written of this archetypal American experience:

> Every event had a deep meaning. The ministers were rationalists who had faith in the power of logic to resolve the most difficult theological problems; and the people had to think matters through for themselves when they could not depend on habit. . . .
>
> Indeed nothing that occurred in the world was simply a random event. Everything was the product of the intent of some mover. A tree did not fall; it was felled. When a monstrous child was born or a school of porpoises seen, that was a sign of something designed. Life was full of signs and portents which indicated the direction of events and the intentions of the forces at

work in the universe. . . . In the pilgrimage of life, man cautiously made his way, examining every incident for clues to his destiny.

. . . The second generation had not so much lost this sense as transformed it. . . .

They too, although in a different way, were moved by a conviction of the grandeur of their destiny.[10]

The quest was communal. As Yale president Ezra Stiles put it for a later generation: "We must become a holy people in reality, in order to exhibit the experiment, never yet fully made in this unhallowed part of the universe, whether such a people would be the happiest on earth."[11]

Not many in subsequent generations held to a pure Puritan vision in which people "could find cosmic issues in a sneeze."[12] But when they replaced this with their first formal "secular" experience, with what is often called the American Enlightenment, one constant remained. A sense of cosmic order and purpose still conditioned philosophy (not theology), laws, manners, character, "holiness." "The Heavenly City of the Eighteenth Century Philosophers" offered the spirit a new home. The deists maximized the sense of congruity between what was perceived in nature or reason and the ultimate order of things; they did not doubt that order's existence and meaning. They were confident about a Supreme Being or First Cause or Grand Architect of the Universe, the accountability of man, the assuredness of rewards and punishments. They shared with the theologues much of what had been implied in the term *Providence*, though they were beginning to translate it *Progress*. Thomas Jefferson and Thomas Paine, seen as the radicals of the later period, differed less than they thought from their orthodox opponents.

In the nineteenth century, Protestant evangelicals, the newly arriving Roman Catholics, and the romantic and transcendentalist spokesmen witnessed transformation, but a transformation that maintained continuity with the previous periods. They did not perceive a fundamental breach with the earlier order of things. This order could be perceived in Scripture, in creation, in Over-Soul. The westward movement in the early nineteenth century was marked by revivalist agitations. Yet during that era, when muscular Christianity seemed most appropriate, only belief in cosmic threat or salvation as the source and norm of spiritual values prompted revivalists' bold appeals for conversion. In the minds of many later Protestants, the evangelicalism of this frontier and early industrial period becomes fused with colonial religion and represents the mythical "good old days."

The Unitarians, in departing from and reacting against colonial Puritanism or their contemporaries' revivalism, did not depart from the sense that human spirit was in discourse with the Spirit. Foreign visitors like Tocqueville noticed with surprise the manifest spirituality of this materially successful egalitarian nation: "There is no country in the world where the Christian religion retains a greater influence over the souls of men than in America."[13] Neither denominational competition and entrepreneurial expertise revealed in the founding of new sects and movements nor the Civil War could break the fundamental unity of order and purpose. For later Americans, Abraham Lincoln stands as a representative of an American spirituality that could be nurtured outside the established denominations.

Ralph Henry Gabriel noted of these years that Americans affirmed "that beneath society, its customs and institutions, a law exists that men did not make. . . . For the individual it establishes the principles on which to found a beneficent and constructive life. For society it institutes an order within which persons may grow in understanding and virtue.[14]

Throughout the transformations of the nineteenth century—the replacement of Providence by Progress, and the general weakening of unity as America became conscious of her pluralism—something of this transcendent and unitive cosmic order survived. The nationalism of Manifest Destiny and the economic and religious creeds associated with Social Darwinism may have inverted much of the earlier value systems, but they were not fundamentally unsettling. The most radical modernistic theologies tended to be overt theistic systems; theologians were supremely self-confident concerning the order out of which spirituality grows.

THE LOSS OF THE COSMIC SENSE

What Protestant competition could not do to evangelicalism, what Roman Catholicism could not do to Protestantism, what Judaism could not do to Christianity during the peak periods of immigration, the onset of industrial life began to accomplish. Eventually, "instead of finding their democratic faith in supernatural religion, Americans . . . tended to find their religious faith in various forms of belief about their own existence."[15]

Only now are Americans becoming aware of the profound transformation of values that occurred during the nineteenth century. Perry Miller suggested that around 1815, when textile mills opened in New England, a business civilization came to be "the dominant theme of American history" at the expense of other value systems. Today a serious thinker like Clarence Ayres can contend that "it is [the] technological continuum which is the locus of truth and value."[16] Nineteenth-century prophets began to notice that the business community kept many of the old symbols and used them ideologically, but the business continuum had become the locus of truth and value. James Ward Smith was only a little overconfident in his writing of the obituary for the old:

> From 1620 to 1914 American thought was marked by a persistent optimism that courses of action can be justified by sweeping cosmic theories. Even our "pessimists," who deplored the actual course of events, retained the optimistic conviction that they understood ultimate truths which enabled them to judge and to condemn. . . . No single fact about American philosophical thought since 1914 is more important than the loss of confidence embodied in this "cosmic sense." . . . The cosmic sense of American philosophy was, while it lasted, universally religious in tone.[17]

According to Walter Lippmann, little survived the collapse of the single cosmic sense in personal, political, and philosophic life. But Lippmann did not stop talking about the spiritual; indeed, he called for a humanistic value system, "the religion of the spirit."

> In an age when custom is dissolved and authority is broken, the religion of the spirit is not merely a possible way of life. In principle it is the only way which transcends the difficulties. . . . The religion of the spirit does not depend upon creeds and cosmologies; it has no vested interest in any particular truth. It is concerned not with the organization of matter, but with the quality of human desire.[18]

6. The Search in Its Secular Context

Such an envisioned humanistic religion of the spirit shares space with creeds and cosmologies in America's mixed religious history. The search for a spiritual style continues.

PROFESSIONAL DISINTEREST AND SUSPICION

No doubt the informal search will continue to be met with some lack of interest and even suspicion on the part of some academic theologians, seekers of justice, leaders of religious institutions. They know how diverting and distorting the claims of the Spirit can be. As a category, it is notoriously evanescent. In 1888 Lord Bryce complained, "To convey some impression of the character and type which religion has taken in America, and to estimate its influence as a moral and spiritual force, is an infinitely harder task than to sketch the salient ecclesiastical phenomena of the country."[19]

What is more, as the academicians are well aware, resort to "the spiritual" can serve as escape from responsibility into narcissism, from community concern into self-seeking. Thus, John Dewey commented: "What is termed spiritual culture has usually been futile, with something rotten about it."[20] It is little wonder that the quest for a spiritual style goes on so informally, with few guides, or leaders, or norms.

In the best of circumstances, the effort is difficult and complicated. Questions come to mind: Is it legitimate to try to isolate American spirituality? Is the United States at present sufficiently homogeneous to support such an isolation? American ties to the history of spirituality in Europe, in the West, indeed, in Hebraic and Hellenic culture are fairly obvious. Yet, at the risk of seeing the quest perverted along nationalist lines, there are reasons to discern elements of uniqueness in America where the technological culture has developed most rapidly and where religious institutions have remained strong.

Although the search is complicated by many features of the American environment, few have as much import as the transition from rural to urban life, from a pre-industrial to a technological society. Authors of the manuals of spirituality have always tended to echo British bishop Samuel Wilberforce's father, who congratulated the son for turning down an urban see. Only in the country would he have been able to cultivate "devotional feelings and spirituality of mind."[21] Pastoral imagery haunts the counselors of piety; the monastic model of contemplation and withdrawal seems to remain normative in traditional texts on religion. But few Americans know such pastoral solitude. America has few contemplatives and does not know what to make of those it does have. Moreover, withdrawal is difficult in an activist, pluralist, interactive society paced by mass-media communications.

Critics of religion, both within and outside denominations, charge that American religion—voluntaryistic and competitive as it is and must be—is too political, too compromising, too institutionally self-seeking to provide room for spiritual development. The burdens of administration and the pressures on leadership are such that spiritual depth would be misunderstood and discouraged if not structurally ruled out. These familiar complaints further complicate the quest for spirit.

But most problematic of all features is the radical change in spiritual styles. "Humanist concerns now embrace the divine. Both speak the same language." The theologians have abolished the transcendent. Ernest Gellner writes:

> There is a sense in which the old conflict between religion and disbelief, profound though it seemed, was a parochial matter. The two sides often agreed on the kind of world they lived in: they just disagreed about one special feature of it. One side added an item—albeit an important one—to the cosmic inventory: the Deity. The other side refused to countenance this addition. One side considered the hypothesis of the Deity to be the best, or the only, or the obligatory hypothesis, required for the explanation of the other features of the world. The other side considered the same hypothesis to be inadequately supported or refutable, or objected morally to any hypothesis being made obligatory. But clearly, this disagreement presupposed a certain consensus about the world which was to be explained—and, in fact, there often was such agreement.
>
> That particular struggle is over—partly because we are told that the Deity has ceased to be an hypothesis at all. Just what It is instead is obscure and varies a good deal with intellectual fashion.[22]

Now, Gellner adds, more fundamental conflicts are before us. Divines and humanists form alliances for or against racial harmony, war, scientific understanding, or spiritual expression.

MODELS, EVENTS, FEATURES

Despite all these complications, Americans are beginning to make their way with some creativity in their quest for a spiritual approach without a cosmic reference. Such an approach needs personal models to fill the roles saints played in earlier pieties. Such models, in the form of a number of charismatic world citizens, have included Dorothy Day, Pope John, Thomas Merton, Martin Luther King, and some third world figures such as Mother Teresa, Dom Helder Camara, and Bishop Desmond Tutu. To these figures from conventional religions one could add any number from the flowering of unconventional, particularly Eastern ones. Events served functions similar to those of persons. The chaos and ceremony attending the celebrated assassinations of public figures, the recovery of hostages, or the disasters to a space shuttle provided paradigmatic events for the new spirituality. H. Richard Niebuhr speaks of revelatory activity as "an event that so captures the imagination of a community that it alters that community's way of looking at the totality of its experience. It is an event that strikes the community as illuminatory for understanding all other events."[23] In this case, the Kennedy death was revelatory in secular America: It enlarged the spiritual range and scope of both horror and ceremony as affirmation. American Jews, perhaps for generations to come, will see the experience of Auschwitz and other death camps as determinative for their spiritual value systems, though they may remain divided over the issues of relating Auschwitz to a Lord of history, a transcendent scheme or activity.

An interesting feature of the new search is the ability of its participants to live with pluralism. So much of the old spiritual style (Perry Miller's pre-1815 or James Ward Smith's pre-1914) depended upon homogeneity, upon assent to all details of a cosmic system. In the pluralist situation, many drew spiritual sustenance from titans in other religions, whose fundamental visions they could not fully share. Here was a syncretism or eclecticism born of necessity and developed into a virtue. Christian ecumenical and then interfaith movements helped, but soon seekers broke the bounds of merely Jewish and Christian repertories as they found spiritual models and leaders.

Certain substantive features in the new spiritual style are becoming apparent: a native *charisma* in the personal model of spirituality, coupled with a sacrificing life; an at-homeness in the world paired with a certain "otherness" or personality secret; a willingness to accept the terms of life "on the boundaries"—between epochs or value systems. Significantly, whether these heroes and models believe in a transcendent order or purported access to a transcendent being is considered irrelevant. Some of them are theists; some are not. Some have a clarified synthetic sense of cosmic purpose; others make their way existentially and in the face of the absurd—the example of Albert Camus's acceptability in American academic and religious circles comes to mind at once. Traditional American spirituality would have found the question of transcendence, metaphysics, and cosmic order all-important.

AN AGENDA FOR THE FUTURE

That traditional view was based on what Walter Lippmann called "The Great Scenario," inherited from the past and compounded of elements from the cosmic drama revealed and portrayed in the Bible. No such scenario is the common property of Westerners or of Americans in particular today. Lacking a scenario, Americans can still look ahead and envision certain determinants of the future of spirituality in secular America. What would help to give a more substantive plot to what is now an informal and vague quest?

The theologians would suggest that the public must first forego Emersonian nostalgia, not because they are ungrateful, but because they see the emotion to be uncreative. Many Americans consciously, deliberately, and consistently regarded the "secular," technological, problem-solving, pluralist life as liberating and life-enhancing. Should they wish to regress to the metaphysical, preindustrial, homogeneous religious and community life of their forefathers, they would have to pay prices they obviously are unprepared or unable to pay. In Bonhoeffer's terms, they would have to move mentally and spiritually from a kind of maturity to adolescence. If they borrow only a memory of the old piety without becoming aware of its detail, they are in danger of using it ideologically to the impoverishment of the spirit.

Purge of nostalgia need not imply destruction of tradition or jettisoning of history; rather, it helps introduce critical history. After examination of detail of the old piety, the "merits of borrowing" from it can be reexplored. In a famed address at Columbia's bicentenary some years ago, J. Robert Oppenheimer discussed spiritual malaise at a time when "orders disintegrate as well as bind. . . . Diversity, complexity, richness overwhelm the man of today." So? "Each . . . will have to cling to what is close to him, to what he knows, to what he can do, to his friends and his tradition and his love, lest he be dissolved in a universal confusion and know nothing and love nothing."[24] The "old piety" certainly lived on in many ways in Bonhoeffer, Pope John, and Tillich among the Christians, and in Buber and Rosenzweig among the Jews. Moreover, this did not inhibit them from being at home in the secular world.

Critical examination of tradition leads to a constructive exposition of a basis for life-style today. The public might legitimately expect theological leaders to clarify the implications of the widespread reluctance to discuss transcendence, the readiness to forget metaphysics, and the willingness to live with pluralism. Such clarity on the part of theological and ethical thinkers would necessitate radical change in the status and position of leaders in religious institutions. The reforms of Catholicism inaugurated by Vatican II and the pronounced ethical involvements of Protestants and Jews in current social issues may make many religious leaders unpopular, but they have also increased these leaders' credibility as sacrificial and spiritually compelling agents of change. In advocating "holy worldliness," theologians have suggested that material life and spiritual life are not incompatible. Religion means not withdrawal from but exposure to the world. Ecclesiastical leaders are trying to suggest that "the church as institution" and "the church as community of the spirit" are not mutually exclusive but rather represent polar functions. They will become persuasive to the degree that the institutions are seen to be reforming and self-sacrificing, and their leaders freed for authentic service and personal expression.

In the wild pluralism of American life, the search for a spiritual style appropriate to the secular setting will inevitably issue in wild experiment. At any moment such experiment may seem very "unspiritual" and plotless. Yet from it a new language of the spirit could evolve. Recently there were advocates of ESP, Psi-phenomena, and drug-induced religious experience. In search of the Spirit, people join prayer circles, seek to be "born again," crave the expression of "tongues speaking," build on Jungian archetypes, go to monastic retreats, read works of Oriental wisdom, see Jesus Christ as prototype of a new humanity, study phenomenology, or plunge themselves into action for others. Not a few go to synagogue and church, not only in exuberant or conservative churches but in mainstream institutions that have given a new priority to devotional and liturgical life.

THE ROLE OF PARTICULAR COMMUNITIES

Within this pluralism, the greatest responsibility will lodge for some time with the institutions serving the two-thirds of the American population that is formally affiliated with religious groups. These institutions have traditions, resources, personnel. They experience the most dramatic problems at a time of change. Living between old and new styles, they have shared the real benefits of neither. Until recently, they have been content to be repositories of safe cultural and civic religions. A measure of societal religion may be necessary for knitting a complex democratic society. But in taking refuge in compromise and utility, the churches often sacrifice their potential as agents of spiritual development. Some observers of this civic religion have compared it to the status of Antonine Roman religion as Gibbon described it:

> The various modes of worship which prevailed in the Roman world were all considered by the people as equally true; by the philosopher as equally false; and by the magistrate as equally useful. And thus toleration produced not only mutual indulgence, but even religious concord.[25]

Such concord is no small benediction in pluralist America. Its occasion, however, suggests the difficulty of developing spirituality out of civic religion. It is safe, compromising, bland, unembarrassing. Almost all the religious subcommunities in America have given evidence of their ability to share life in a free society—to accept its terms, to gain its ear. Many responsible religious leaders are concerned by the spiritual barrenness of individuals and the lethal measure of the culture as a whole. Out of traditions, their resources, their partly disciplined community life, they are trying to speak words of judgment, of the future, of hope.

These people may lose favor in certain quarters. They are trying to be taken seriously "by the philosopher" and not to be immediately useful to the magistrate. In the process, they may be able to extricate themselves from the web of cultural expectations. If they do, they can produce an exceptional model, moment, or thought as a contribution to the spiritual quest. Lippmann hoped the contributions that had once been "the possession of an aristocracy of the spirit" could be seen as a possibility for all people. Profound spirituality is rare. It belongs to exceptional individuals. But all can profit from clarification of the context out of which "spirit" grows— the human in the fullest possible actualization of what she or he is in the heart. Seen in this light, spirituality would contribute to— but need not compete with—the deserving searches for meaning and the ethical on the part of responsible Americans.

The Spirit gives life, while the letter killeth. According to the Christian Gospels, Jesus posed such a contrast. Yet Jesus also advocated or at least described a searching of letters, scripts, and scriptures, and his and other religious stories come enscriptured, on papyri or pages. Americans have chosen to draw guidance for their spiritual search and much of their civic culture from one book, the Bible. It, too, demands attention as a unifying book in a pluralist culture, or a book of plural meanings and uses that can be disruptive in a coherence-seeking culture. For reasons that we are about to see, it became and remains an icon in the Republic.

7 Scripturality: The Bible as Icon
in the Republic

"We are all critics, I trust, and higher critics too." Thus Angus Crawford, without spelling out the details of who "we" were, rushed to judgment from the Theological Seminary of Virginia during a debate at the Episcopal Church Congress in 1896.[1]

The public, be it churchgoing or in the general culture, did not share those conclusions. Four years before Crawford spoke, during critic Charles A. Briggs's heresy trial in New York, newspapers nationally covered the subject. Most of them pointed to the growing gap between the scholars and the public. One could choose from scores of sources, but this comment from the Savannah, Georgia, *News* is typical:

> The great majority of Christians regard the Bible as the inspired work of God, and therefore, cannot contain errors. An admission that it does contain errors opens the door to doubts, and when doubts are once entertained, it is a difficult matter to place a limit upon them. Professor Briggs's doctrines may be entirely satisfactory to those who clearly understood them, but it is about impossible to make them understood by the masses. To the average mind the whole Bible is true, or it is not the inspired work of God.[2]

Events during the first two decades of American biblical criticism before the turn of the century set the mold for controversy that has not ended at the end of a century of such scholarship. Crawford's word, "we are all critics, I trust, and higher critics too," is true of scholars at Jewish, Roman Catholic, nondenominational, mainline Protestant, secular graduate, and—their enemies would have it— some of the flagship evangelical schools. Wherever people in the humanities teach others how to analyze the historical, formal, and structural elements of texts and wherever there are no vested interests in fending off ecclesiastical resistance to the critical, the critical methods and outlooks prevail. Yet the Savannah *News* report could be written even today about much of the churchgoing outlook and, if polls are a measure, also about much of unchurched America. The public still connects criticism with the spotting of errors and the planting of doubts. A century of biblical criticism, however presented to the public it may be, has produced little difference.

Gallup polls find that 42 percent of the general public finds the whole Bible to be inerrant. We must presume that at least that many are therefore resistant to critical scholarship. Gallup found 48 percent of the self-named Protestants in his sample and 41 percent of the Roman Catholics to be on the anticritical side.[3] This side is powerful beyond its numbers because its leadership has effectively mobilized sentiment. Anticritical forces have been outspoken in intradenominational warfare and in the 1980s are being heard in public school board rooms, where battles in defense of biblical creationism are being waged as intensely as they were in 1925 at the time of the Scopes trial in Tennessee.

In this division between camps and the opposition to critical study something is going on that reaches beyond the merely cognitive, beyond the critical-analytic method. The resistance to critical understanding, I propose, has its root in what Suzanne Langer would say lies "much deeper than any conscious purpose, . . . in that substratum of the mind, the realm of fundamental ideas."[4]

It is time to revisit the already explicated notion about such fundamental ideas, which José Ortega y Gasset calls *creencias;* they are ideas so deep that we do not even know we hold them. They are not the ideas that we "have" but the ideas that we "are." And these *creencias* hook up with certain *vigencias,* binding customs of a culture, customs that have a hold much stronger than that which law itself can impose.[5] Anthropologist George Boas showed his at-homeness with such notions when he urged students to pursue the locations of profound ideas: "When an idea is adopted by a group and put into practice, as in a church or a state, its rate of change will be slow."[6] An idea that the American churches and in some ways the society have adopted and put into practice is the uncritical acceptance of the Bible's worth. Thus Perry Miller observed of the role of the Old Testament in historic American society: it was "so truly omnipresent in the American culture of 1800 or 1820 that historians have as much difficulty taking cognizance of it as of the air people breathed."[7] Jacob Burckhardt said that the most important things in life do not get written about by historians simply because they are *too* close to people, too taken for granted. This may account for the absence of good histories dealing with American attitudes toward the Bible.

An example of the way anticritical attitudes were locked in to the mainline culture appears in an often quoted trio of sentences by a great American average mind and exemplar of its day-to-day and less than Lincolnesque civil religion, President Grover Cleveland. We have already heard him averring that he wanted the plain old Bible book without criticisms or cross-references, which were unnecessary and confusing.[8] He spoke for an American consensus that sometimes might vie for extensive support with the one we overheard Groucho Marx voicing: "Take care of me. I'm the only one I've got."[9] If this is "a nation with a soul of a church,"[10] that soul is fed by documents, in addition to the Declaration of Independence and the United States Constitution, enshrined in its archival heart. The Bible is also there.

Nothing is supposed to be, say very sober historians. They find America seeing itself as an aniconic nation, one that lacks images or icons. In a brilliant epigraphic choice to illustrate the main theme of his book *The Genius of American Politics,* Daniel Boorstin, now the Librarian of Congress and thus keeper of the archive, compared the American aniconic intention to a scene in Heinrich Graetz's *History of the Jews:* "Pompey then penetrated into the Sanctuary, in order to satisfy his curiosity as to the nature of the Judaean worship, about which the most contradictory reports prevailed. The Roman general was not a little astonished at finding within the sacred recesses of the Holy of Holies, neither an ass's head nor, indeed, images of any sort."[11] A refusal to fill our sanctuary with ideological images characterizes American life, say historians like Boorstin. Yet if they stayed around and took a little longer look in that shrine they would not find it empty. In the corner, under a layer of dust, there is a leather-bound, gilt-edged, India-papered object, a Bible, revered *as* object, *as* icon, not only in Protestant churches but in much of the public congregation as well.

Such an observation can be fighting words in a self-described aniconic culture or set of churches. Yet if we use our terms with conceptual propriety and great care and are willing to take some risks, this insight—if it holds up—can illumine the history of response to biblical criticism in America. It can help explain why so many found it possible to ignore or to resist the main line of biblical scholarship for a century.

Five risks come to mind at once. First, to use such a vivid image as "image" is to risk confusing instead of clarifying. A notable and notably difficult Catholic philosopher once made a distinction between types of abstractions that could apply here to types of images, metaphors, or similes. At a Catholic philosophers' convention he was comparing notes with his peer. They were discussing how many of their reviewers commented on the level of abstraction with which they both operated. "Yes," said the friend, "but there is a difference. I use enriching abstractions and you use impoverishing ones." Some might say that they use clarifying images and I may be using a confusing one.

Second, the image employed may be inappropriate because it is too arcane. The icon, for example, is at home in an Eastern Orthodox Christian culture, where it congenially reposes among its connotations, but one may do violence by snatching it away from those connotations and resituating it on the more bare spiritual landscape of America.

At midpoint during our risk assessment we should mention that to some the image of the icon is so obvious, so lacking in subtlety, that to use it adds nothing but banality. "My love is like a rose." Of course, everyone knows my love is like a rose—to me. Americans use the Bible, even as a physical object, as an icon. Of course . . .

A fourth risk has to do with emotional connotations. The image can be so vivid that it diverts from inquiry. In the 1950s an opponent of the World Council of Churches who made his living staging protests against it, found that he scored the strongest points when he pointed to one of its constituencies: "the bearded Orthodox icon-kissers." Being bearded and kissing icons called to mind something so overpowering that it swept away all the more ordinary functions and images. Thus to say that America treats the Bible iconically will, in the minds of pure prophets, connote paganism and thus something bad. I can only urge that we must also keep in mind ordinary functions of the Bible. Sometimes an image *does* carry people away. One thinks of a moment when the late philosopher Herbert Marcuse said something humorous; that was a noteworthy event, because he usually, figuratively, lumbered steatopygically across the stage in efforts at being humorous. But, once: "Yes, yes, I know that the jet airplane is a phallic symbol. But it can also get you from London to Brussels." Yes, yes. I know that the Bible is an icon, but its contents can also be read, marked, learned, and inwardly digested, and lived by.

A final risk is the notion of *pars pro toto*. One can concentrate on a subculture, Protestant conservatism, which guards the shrine and fights for the iconic object, without noticing that today the shrine itself is often neglected. Or if not neglected it is surrounded by other objects and symbols until it recedes from center stage, no longer informs, or is lost in a diffusion and confusion of symbols.

These risks notwithstanding, I believe there are values in using the image of the icon as an effort to lead beyond merely rational analysis to the root emotions of people in a culture. Only then can we assess the power situation, which has little to do with the *content* of ancient scriptures but much to do with the *form* of modern American life.

First we must establish the place of the Bible among the other fonts and sources of culture. The Bible is a book. The molecules that make it up constitute paper and ink. The ink is shaped in the form of letters whose agglomerations in the form of words, sentences, chapters sign something; they signify, they impart ideas, they at least potentially disclose meanings. Thus people gain access to other minds or learn something about their own. Since the meanings come from the past, they may study their history or analyze them structurally, with special interest in the cast of contemporary mind. So one would expect that the same Gallup poll that showed Americans believing the Bible to be beyond criticism, without error, would also find it being used and find it informing life.

Strangely, significantly fewer people who consider the Bible to be the errorless book of God consult it first when in trouble. Forty percent turn to it, 27 percent to the Holy Spirit, 11 percent to the church, and 22 percent to "Other." So far, so good; the Bible out-ranks the other sources of wisdom or consolation. But, writes Walter A. Elwell in his comment on the disuse of the book, "It is apparently one thing to *believe* that the Bible is God's word [as 72 percent of the polled public simply does] and quite another to read it." The general public average daily readership is 12 percent, with the Protestant average being 18 percent and the Roman Catholic 4 percent. Who reads the Bible less than once a month? Fifty-two percent of the general public, 41 percent of Protestants, and 67 percent of Roman Catholics. As for knowledge of the content as opposed to claimed reading of the book, the figures are even lower. Asked to name the Ten Commandments, perhaps the most familiar part of both "testaments," 45 percent of the public could come up with four or fewer; this public found 49 percent of the Protestants and 44 percent of the Catholics able to do so. Elwell adds: "Belief in God is not much affected by how often people read the Bible."[12] The public resists critical analysis of its revered object, calls this object the Word of God. A minority claims to consult it first in trouble; yet few read it regularly and not many know its basic contents. This anomaly occasions an examination of the iconic hold this book exercises.

Let me draw on a frequent experience of Marxian scholars when they visit Marxist societies. They lecture on articulated and filiated aspects of *Das Kapital*. They assume that assenting communists, be they university students or peasants, would be conversant with many dimensions of the writings of Marx. They report on responses that range from incomprehension through bemusement to disdain. As one told a friend of mine, "You are not communicating well. You know too much Marx. You know where his ideas came from and how he put them together and how they relate and what they mean. We don't need all that Hegelian metaphysical stuff. We only need the basic Marxian notion as a trigger to get our revolution going." A proletarian or a peasant might not articulate it so well. What the people need is the awareness that somewhere there *is* an authority and perhaps an elite that regards it as, shall we say, inerrant? The society draws security from the knowledge that an enclosure or a support exists, one that transcends mundane and practical living.

So it is with the use of the Bible as an image in a society like that of pluralist America. In a brilliant passage on icon and image, Rosemary Gordon has written that "every man walks around in the world enveloped in a carapace of his own images. Their presence enables him to structure and to organize the multiplicity of the objects and the stimuli which throng him."[13] A zoological carapace is "a hard bony or chitinous outer covering, such as the fused dorsal plates of a turtle, or the portion of the exoskeleton covering the head and thorax of a crustacean." But the dictionary goes on to refer to it as "any similar protective covering." Here we are speaking of the protective covering, the sort of cocoon that individuals, subcultures, and in their own way societies need for the structuring of experience.

Far from using the iconic image disdainfully, then, I am trying to suggest that it has a value of great anthropological and psychic significance; without such carapaces people would likely go mad. Relate this to the observation of Talcott Parsons that "good fortune and suffering must always, to cultural man, be endowed with meaning. They cannot, except in limiting cases, be accepted as something that 'just happens.'"[14] The Bible, in American history and in much of present-day culture, provided and provides as an object a basic element in the carapace of images, and its presumed contents, that for which one would consult it if one did consult it, remove the "just happening" dimension from human existence.

A reach beyond churchly into public culture demonstrates this kind of location for the Bible as icon. Benjamin Franklin, back when he chartered and called for "the Necessity of a *Publick Religion*," took pains to speak well of the Bible, whose contents he did not regard as supernatural at all but whose form he regularly printed and published. When asked to join John Adams and Thomas Jefferson on July 4, 1776, to prepare a great seal of the United States, this Franklin reached for biblical imagery (of Moses and the Red Sea), though the design was later compromised.[15]

7. *The Bible as Icon in the Republic*

Under the carapace of organizing images for the Republic, the "founding father" of his country has a central place. So it is that George Washington is associated with the Bible, even though the most notable scholar of Washington's religion says he made "astonishingly few references" to it in his many volumes of literary remains. While he accepted a gift of Bibles as "an important present to the brave fellows" in the military during the Revolution, only one letter in his corpus has a reference to his own reading of the book. There are few biblical allusions in his writings, and they are in settings as near to the jocular as Washington ever came. Yet Washington was a Freemason, and the Masons regarded the Bible as their key icon, even though they did not regard it as supernatural. Observers took pains to notice the precedent at the Washington inaugural, when the first president brought along his Masonic Bible; "the president kissed the Bible after taking the oath of office." In 1789 he was thus an unbearded icon-kisser. Later presidents would upset the images under the carapace were they to neglect or despise the role of the Bible in their oath—even though the Constitution is silent on the subject.[16]

Thomas Jefferson did upset the images by taking the content of the Bible seriously. He appeared to be the great iconoclast among the fathers. Yet he read the book. We know of 271 religious titles in the Jeffersonian library. He collected editions of the Bible: two Greek Septuagints, ten Vulgates, ten Greek New Testaments, one French and six English versions, with four Apocrypha. "For a man with a reputation for being irreligious he had an amazing number," writes an analyst of that library. And Jefferson was not a collector but a student. We have already visited him as he pieced together his "wee-little book," "The Jefferson Bible," which began as a moonlighting project in the White House. There he pasted together the nonsupernatural elements of the Gospels, clipped from English, French, Latin, and Greek versions, into *The Life and Morals of Jesus of Nazareth*. For this he came to be thought of as an infidel, and his place in the American evangelical pantheon was less secure than was that of owners-but-not-readers like Washington, who probably had the same hermeneutical principles as Jefferson but did not put them to use.[17]

Abraham Lincoln, the center of American public faith and its greatest theologian, illustrates the positive role of the iconic use of the Bible. In the library at Fisk University there reposes a Bible given Lincoln on July 4, 1864, by the "Loyal Colored People" of Baltimore. Lincoln responded: "In regard to this Great book, I have but to say, it is the best gift God has given to man. . . . All the good Savior gave to the world was communicated through this book. . . . To you I return my most sincere thanks for *the elegant copy of the great Book of God* which you present" (emphasis mine). It was noted that Lincoln regularly read the Bible in the White House and that it was the old Lincoln family Bible, a version from the Society for Promotion of Christian Knowledge (S.P.C.K.) dated 1799—such details always mattered. While Jefferson was a church member but an infidel for his iconoclasm, Lincoln was well received by the churches, though he is the only president ever who was not a church member. He had the right attitudes toward the Bible, whose cadences entered his very speech.[18]

One could further survey the central figures who have sacerdotal roles in the public religion and hence in guarding the sanctuary. We have already heard Grover Cleveland, the first president to be vocal after critical views of the Bible reached America. Years later another priestly president, the well-informed historian Woodrow Wilson, made iconic use of the Bible. John Mulder says of him that "Wilson showed no awareness of problems in the Bible or controversies surrounding interpretation of its passages." The Bible was the standard for the culture, and it spoke to Wilson and the nation more in terms of law than of grace.[19] Wilson effectively mounted military crusades using biblical imagery.

One candidate for the presidency did more than any American scholar or cleric to harden public sentiment against biblical criticism. William Jennings Bryan was always a populist about religious knowledge. He spoke critically against the scholarly elite who wanted to make a different use of the arcanum. "A religion that didn't appeal to any but college graduates would be over the head or under the feet of 99 per cent of our people." Bryan, of course was not everyone's chosen keeper of the sanctuary, and many in his time and ever since repudiated him or even saw his latter-day opposition to criticism to be a mark of senility. Yet Bryan gained a broad following, and showed both an iconic and an unreflective use of the Bible in many exchanges during the Scopes trial, which had to do with biblical literalism. Asked by his antagonist Clarence Darrow about certain calculations of historical biblical accounts of The Deluge, Bryan replied:

> I never made a calculation.
> *Darrow:* What do you think?
> *Bryan:* I do not think about things I don't think about.
> *Darrow:* Do you think about things you do think about?
> *Bryan:* Well, sometimes.

Liberal America scorned Bryan for his literalism and was sure that his fundamentalist outlook, soon a mark of disgrace, would disappear from the scene. It happened, however, that many to Bryan's right felt that he let them down because there were moments in the trial when he allowed cracks in their carapace. He was not perfectly literal about the biblical accounts at all times. Bryan never deserted or changed his boyhood biblical faith, which gave him security for political contingencies and defeats. "Give the modernist three words, 'allegorical,' 'poetical,' and 'symbolically,'" said Bryan in 1923, "and he can suck the meaning out of every vital doctrine of the Christian Church and every passage in the Bible to which he objects."[20] Darrow slew his thousands, but in pious America, Bryan slew his ten thousands.

This attitude in moderate form continued. Thus President Jimmy Carter did what he could to evade questions that might draw him away from defense of biblical literalism. Whatever Americans thought of him politically, the polls found them admiring his moral construct based on reverence for the Bible. And his successor, Ronald Reagan, was not out of character or tradition when during a presidential campaign he pointed to the icon and said with an emphasis few evangelical clerics would be bold enough to use: "It is an incontrovertible fact that *all* the complex and horrendous questions confronting us at home and worldwide have their answer in that single book" (emphasis mine).[21]

Perhaps I have dwelt too long on presidential candidates, but vote-getters in their public expressions are custodians of the national carapace and the images under it. One could as well point to the role of the Bible as an object in legislative halls or, more vividly, to the part the Bible plays in judicial history in the context of "the nine high priests in their black robes" in the Supreme Court. It is in the courts that all but a few dissenting individuals take their oath on the Bible so consistently that in colloquial America one swears on "a stack of Bibles," to prove one's seriousness. The Supreme Court has been seen as the great iconoclastic desecrator because it "took the Bible out of the schools," when it limited not the pedagogical but the devotional use of the book in public institutions.

The Court did no such thing. The public had "taken the Bible out of the schools," but, significantly for my thesis, it did not know or does not even now know that it did this. What mattered under the carapace of images in the national mind was that the Bible belonged in classroom devotion. Yet a year or two before the Supreme Court decisions of 1962 and 1963—according to social scientist Richard Dierenfeld, who took pains to take a survey—not many were reading the Bible in schools. Even "without comment," as one should read it if it is an icon beyond interpretation, few read it. About 42 percent of the respondents were still reading it, thanks to the heritage of the older parts of the country. The putatively profane East found almost 68 percent of its classrooms in public schools still using the Bible, and over 75 percent of the Southern districts reported such use. But in the other half of the Bible Belt, the Midwest, only about 18 percent did. And in the West, including California, whence came so many protests to the Court against "taking the Bible out of the schools," only 11 percent kept the practice. (By the way, where the Bible was used, 70 percent chose the King James Version, which until the 1950s was almost universally the iconic version.) But if the Bible survived *devotionally,* which usage underscores our point, its contents were not subjects of analysis. Are there Bible *classes* of any sort in your schools? Now *one-tenth* as many polled districts, 4.51 percent nationally, replied in the affirmative. In the South 9 percent, in the East barely 1 percent, in the Midwest 4 percent, and in the West fewer than 9 percent of the districts looked at the contents.[22]

The Bible worked its way into the schools as icon because in sectarian America it was seen as "nonsectarian," and the "not commented upon" aspect was to assure objectivity in its use. Horace Mann, a Unitarian cleric, as much as anyone else, helped establish this use of the Bible in schools. His form of comment or interpretation would have been abhorrent in most of the Protestant then-dominant culture of his own day. After World War II the follower of John Dewey and an advocate of a postbiblical nonsectarian religion of democracy, Chaplain J. Paul Williams, commented critically on this iconic use: "This belief in the efficacy of spending a few minutes daily in reading the Bible grew up in a time when it was almost universally believed by Protestants that there was some kind of magic in the Bible to which one needed but to be exposed in order for it to have a very great influence on life."[23]

In the unofficial but privileged mainstream American literary culture there was an almost immediate acceptance of biblical critical outlooks, a fact that gave this culture a marginal status in what today we would call "Middle America." Already in his sermon of 1841 on "The Transient and Permanent in Christianity," Theodore Parker showed his awareness: "Modern criticism is fast breaking to pieces this idol which men have made out of the scriptures." Parker helped import radical German criticism, such as De Wette's *Einleitung*.[24] Others were iconoclastic enough to point to iconodulism among Bible-believers who were, they thought, not Bible-readers or Bible-followers. Thus Henry David Thoreau: "It is remarkable that, notwithstanding the universal favor with which the New Testament is outwardly received, and even the bigotry with which it is defended, there is no hospitality shown to, there is no appreciation of, the order of truth with which it deals. I know of no book that has so few readers."[25] This was still in the period before critical study was widespread.

A towering mainstream literary figure of the generation in which knowledge of biblical criticism reached the public was Oliver Wendell Holmes. In 1869 he wrote Frederic H. Hedge:

> The truth is staring the Christian world in the face, that the stories of the old Hebrew books cannot be taken as literal statements of fact. But the property of the church is so large and so mixed up with its vested beliefs, that it is hopeless to expect anything like honest avowal of the convictions which there can be little doubt intelligent church men of many denominations, if at all, entertain. It is best, I suppose, it should be so, for take idolatry and bibliolatry out of the world all at once as the magnetic mountain drew the nails and bolts of Sinbad's ship, and the vessel that floats much of the best of our humanity would resolve itself in a floating ruin of planks and timbers.[26]

We do not need to accept Holme's conspiracy theory about ecclesiasticism to agree with his understanding, one that under different images matches our own, that a carapace of images is necessary in order for individuals and society to function cognitively or morally.

As in public religion or literary culture, so in popular social behavior there are evidences on all hands of the iconic use of the Bible in America. These may be losing out in many elements of "post-biblical" pluralist America, and the recent distancing from the Bible may be part of the presumed chaos, malaise, or anomie of such a culture. People suffer from what Robert Jay Lifton calls "*historical, or psychohistorical* dislocation," which he saw to be the "break in the sense of connection men have long felt with vital and nourishing symbols of their cultural traditions—symbols revolving around . . . religion." This breach in tradition is accompanied by a "*flooding of imagery* because of mass communications networks."[27] Some of the contemporary political polemics from the American right results from reaction against this breach, this flooding.

Only some of the rejection was thoughtless, thanks to the passing of time. At least in the years of the rejective counterculture or wherever "now" people advocated historical amnesia as liberating, it is the biblical culture that serves as a foil. But the rejection has not been successful or complete, so locked into the corners of the carapace of images have been awarenesses of the Bible. Culture critic Eugene Goodheart rose up at the height of such rejection to speak with historical sense and sanity about the moment. He referred more to the content of the traditions than I am in the present instance, but the point is still in place:

> The *tabula rasa* is a presumption of innocence. It is not the result of genuine discovery, for instance, that the Christian and classical traditions are no longer part of us. The enactments of our personality and character are involuntary, often compulsive. We are not free to choose what we are or even what we will do. We cannot simply wish away traditions that we have grown to dislike. The very dislike may be conditioned by the fact that they still possess us, if we do not possess them. If Judeo-Christian and classical traditions are still alive in all of us (and I suspect they are), despite attempts to deny them, then an education that fails to address itself to these traditions (I do not speak of arguing for or against them) would fail according to the ideal of relevance. The

mere repudiation of these traditions does not have the effect of exorcism.[28]

Here and now it would be easy to show at great length the ways in which the Bible as the object that embodies the center of Goodheart's "Judeo-Christian" religion endures iconically. Instead of documenting I shall only point, to stimulate the vision and imagination of professional biblical scholars concerning their context and environment. Some pointings:

Americans have an adjectival use of the noun *Bible* as one indicator: Bible belt, Bible camp, Bible believer, Bible Sunday, Bible week, Bible school, Bible institute, Bible college, Bible battle, Bible bookstore, Bible puzzles and crosswords and quizzes, Gideon Bible in airplane and hospital and hotel room (enhanced in the Mormon Marriott by a Book of Mormon). There are tours to Bible lands, and Bibles brought back with covers made of wood from the Mount of Olives. The Bible is a gift at rites of passage, to new mothers, in Sunday school, at confirmation, in white covers for marriages, at graduations, for *bon voyage*. Protestants who always found the Catholic practice of burying grandmothers with an object like a rosary repulsive characteristically buried grandmother with a black Bible. The family Bible is also the place between whose testaments one is always going to fill out the family tree, as ancestors once did.

Bibles are as ubiquitous in hotel rooms as wire coat hangers. Have any of us ever seen an old one, a used one, a spinecracked version? What happens to them? A Second City comic would have it that one does not know either where wire coat hangers come from. They are absent when one checks in but still mysteriously proliferating by the time one checks out. Could the Gideon Bible be a wire coat hanger in its larval or pupal stages? No one has seen an old Bible in the garbage. Nor are Bibles burned, except when defenders of the iconic King James attacked the National Council of Churches' desecrating Revised Standard Version as "Stalin's Bible." When that RSV was issued, an iconodule figured out that the first edition consumed twenty million square inches of twenty-three-carat gold leaf, enough to make a twenty-four-foot-wide sheet one mile long, and that the Bibles of that first year's edition, all of which soon were sold, could be stacked high enough to equal one hundred Empire State Buildings. In 1954 *Catholic Digest* estimated that two hundred million Bibles were in circulation, far more than one per citizen of all ages—and probably a low figure, were one to add all the atticked and betrunked versions in semicirculation.[29]

The Bible legitimates other expressions. Cecil B. De Mille learned that he could serve up magic and miracle and sex as long as the main images were sanctified by reference to the Bible. A few biblical lines about Bathsheba or Delilah were enough to keep Susan Hayward or Gina Lolabrigida in motion on screen for an hour and a half, before a public that was not then yet free to watch in clear conscience similar unclad secular imagery.

Even in those parts of Protestant culture that do not favor magic, superstition, or relics, the Bible is allowed a special role. The stories of soldiers whose lives were spared because they had a bullet-proof covered New Testament in their breast pocket are so frequent that one almost pictures an army with people tilting by the weight of the book to their left sides. In frontier folklore there were stories of infidels and deists who on death beds faced the horror of hell because they had "burned all the Bibles they could get." A Methodist itinerant, it was said, faced off a robber in Chillicothe, Ohio, who let him go when he saw the Bible. The victim was "more than thankful for my Bible, which had served me better than a revolver. This was a new kind of weapon, the merits of which he appeared to have no desire to contest." The wife of a circuit rider needed money for provisions while her husband was on the road and she was ill. She asked for a Bible, "intending to seek comfort from its holy counsels, opened it, found a five dollar bill."[30] These stories have not disappeared from the culture of television evangelism, where miracles associated with the physical object of the Bible continue.

So much for the Protestant/Enlightenment–formed general culture. The case is little different in Judaism, which in America has been forced to be "more biblical than it is." Jewish scholars constantly point to the transformations of Judaism and its texts during the past twenty-seven centuries, showing that the Bible is only a part of their tradition. But just as rabbis, who are lay people in Europe, have to be clerics in American culture to round out the priest-minister-rabbi tri-faith triad, so Jews have had to be "people of *the* book" in America in a special normative sense. Literalist understandings of the Bible among premillennial fundamentalists in America have blunted anti-Semitism and led to surprising coalescences between Jews and evangelicals who must keep respect for Jews because of Jewish reverence for the Hebrew Scriptures.

Solomon Schechter, dedicating the Jewish Theological Seminary in New York in 1903, summarized the case for America and Judaism:

> If there is a feature in American religious life more prominent than any other it is in its conservative tendency. . . . This country is, as everybody knows, a creation of the Bible, particularly the Old Testament, and the Bible is still holding its own, exercising enormous influence as a real spiritual power in spite of all the destructive tendencies, mostly of foreign make. . . . The bulk of the real American people have, in matters of religion, retained their sobriety and loyal adherence to the Scripture, as their Puritan forefathers did. America thus stands for wideness of scope and for conservatism.[31]

The iconic case is weakest in the instance of Roman Catholicism, as Gallup polls and cultural evidences show. In the liturgy the priest kisses the Gospel. Catholic conservatives point to *Providentissimus Deus* of 1893 to certify their at-homeness with Protestant doctrines of inerrancy. But Catholicism was not under the carapace in the nineteenth century. It was the fact that Catholics had other icons, talismans, relics, amulets, and sacramentals that kept them in part from being seen as "true Americans" by the others. The Nativist battles of the 1840s make this clear. In October of 1842 an overfervent priest in Carbeau, New York, angry because the King James Version was being distributed in his parish, burned some Bibles. Bishop John Hughes, "Dagger John," spoke up: "To burn or otherwise destroy a spurious or corrupt copy of the Bible, whose circulation would tend to disseminate erroneous principles of faith or morals, we hold to be an act not only justifiable but praiseworthy." A wave of Bible burnings was said to ensue, and this was followed by larger waves of nativist anti-Catholic sentiment.[32]

Yet even if the Catholic case for faith did not depend only on the Bible but also on "the tradition," Catholics were also wary of anything that touched this icon. Cardinal William O'Connell, later archbishop of Boston, remembered how in the 1880s at the American College in Rome students had discussed higher criticism, which had its source "mostly in Germany, from a group of clever agnostics whose plain purpose was to destroy completely the fundamentals of the Christian faith by a well-planned attack upon the whole system of divine revelation."[33] To Catholics as to others, higher criticism was un-American, foreign, alien. The Americanist and modernist controversies found the few early Catholic critics undercut and displaced. And today, as Catholics link up with conservatives in many causes, the polemical columnists—one thinks of the weekly efforts in the *National Catholic Register*—consistently attack biblical criticism as a desecration of the book that—according to Gallup—few Catholics read.

The case for seeing the Bible as America's iconic book is both most important and most startling in the instance of Protestantism—most important in that today it is hard to picture how dominant was Protestantism for three centuries, while the *creencias* and *vigencias*, the root ideas and the binding customs, of the culture were being programed and set. Yet in the British colonies that made up the original United States, non-Protestant religious expression was almost nonexistent outside Maryland, southern Pennsylvania, and on occasion Rhode Island and New York City. Not until the great continental Catholic migrations to America in the 1840s and the Jewish influx after the 1880s did other religious voices begin to gain power and privilege.

If important, it was also startling that the Bible became an icon, for Protestantism for the most part—except in its liturgically high wings—has seen itself as aniconic and even iconoclastic. C. G. Jung wrote from a psychological point of view about a stereotype cherished in many disciplines:

> The history of the development of Protestantism is one of chronic iconoclasm. One wall after another fell. And the work of destruction was not too difficult, either, when once the authority of the church had been shattered. We all know how, in large things as in small, in general as well as in particular, piece after piece collapsed, and how the alarming impoverishment of symbolism that is now the condition of life came about. The power of the church has gone with that loss of symbolism, too.[34]

Protestants were nervous because, while images also represent other things, they *could* displace unseen realities and thus lead to the worship of created objects or, in short, to idolatry. Protestants failed to discriminate between reverence for icons and worship of images. Albert C. Moore draws the distinction finely, and I quote him because this is crucial for my theme, which is *not* a charge that America worships the Bible as an idol. "When the icon is treated with reverence in the context of worship, this attitude can be described as 'iconolatry', veneration of the icon. This term should be used in preference to the term 'idolatry' which has so many censorious and pejorative associations in Western usage."

Are the objections raised against idolatry applicable to the use of images? At the very least one must ask what is the source of the information concerning alleged idolators; was it, asks Moore, from biased observers?

> For instance, at the Reformation both Catholics and Protestants agreed that idolatry was forbidden to Christians by the Bible; but they disagreed over the question as to when an image became idolatrous: "At no time was it possible to prove that idolatry was taking place, since the worship of a created thing in place of God occurs in the mind of the worshipper rather than in the image addressed."[35]

In other words, were some Protestants and other Americans "Bibliolators," as beleaguered biblical critics sometimes cried out in counterattack? They may have *acted* like idolators. But, following Moore, how do we know if they were? It is far fairer to say that they were iconodules or iconolatrous people, so long as this observation does not include an implied theological denunciation. It means taking believers at their word and watching them at their work.

If I may condense more of Moore's argument to explain why Americans of Protestant stripe could reverence the Bible as an icon, there are five points to stress. First, an image evokes the experience of the numinous. Second, it captures a religious experience that is valued as a continuing reality, so that each confrontation of the image allows for repetition of the experience even if in "frozen" form. Third, the image embodies a manifestation of sacred power and presence that is then celebrated in myth and ritual, in sacred space and time. Thus the Bible is the book of worship as well. Fourth, the image offers the worshiper an ideal archetype or sacred model for the sake of regular transformation. One "grows into" the plot of the Bible, and in the child's imagination its land-

scape and characters are as familiar as is the view out the window.
Finally, the image enables one to be related to the cosmos, for it is
a microcosm with which one can identify. One almost needs a physical object for gathering images under the individual and collective
psychic carapace.[36]

Ordinarily the books on religious iconography include images
taken from the Bible, but they rarely if ever notice the Bible itself
as icon. Yet on soil where other icons were prohibited, the same
five needs or roles that Moore cited remained operative, and Prot-
estant-minded America took to the use of the Bible to fill them.

On American Protestant soil, the Quakers come nearest to being
aniconic people, at least in relation to the Bible, though not a few
prophets in their midst accused their fellow believers of "lapsing"
in this respect. And latter-day (but by no means early) Unitarian-
Universalism may have moved far enough from biblical norms to
have put the book aside. Beyond that, it survives. In colonial Puritanism where there was to be no adornment or distraction in the
beautifully simple meeting house, the Bible was allowed to be
oversize far beyond the function. Certainly not all the buildings
were so dark or the preachers' eyes so weak that such enormous
print in such huge volumes was necessary. The leather binding,
the high placement on reading desk or pulpit, the focus of eyes on
the Book—all these enhanced the iconic aspect of worship and the
Bible. In paintings of pilgrims heading for worship in colonial New
England, the gun and the Bible are the standard images.

On the frontier, the circuit rider had to be a light traveler. A bit
of rum under the saddlebags (until temperance made its way), a
few personal necessities, perhaps a Book of Discipline—these were
all that went along with the evangelist on the trail. Except for the
Bible. Even Quakers used the Bible as a "civilizing" instrument in
their work among the Indians.

As for blacks, what Hylan Lewis said about "Kent" applies
widely: "References to the Bible—which are frequent—are verbal
props used to prove, document, underscore, or just to display a
kind of erudition. 'The Bible says . . .' is an expression used by
even the most profane and secular when occasion demands."[37] The
slaves were not permitted the Bible, but every chronicler reports
their love for it and on the way the book itself became a symbol of

liberation. Carter G. Woodson says that "Negroes . . . almost worshiped the Bible, and their anxiety to read it was their greatest incentive to learn." Reports of fugitive slaves liked to stress that they carried "a big Bible," hardly a useful object in the precarious passage on the underground railway. Of course, the content of the Bible, its message of hope and liberation, meant much to people denied the book as object or literacy as access, but they regarded the book numinously as did their white brothers and sisters.[38]

As for recent times, Protestant America by mid-century was taking on the attitudes the Gallup survey found to be extant in 1980. In a *Catholic Digest* survey, 83 percent of the Protestants regarded the Bible as the revealed word of God, but 40 percent of the Protestants read it "never or hardly ever."[39] In a survey of a very Protestant county in Bible-believing mid-America, Victor Obenhaus found that 63 percent of churchgoing Protestants could not designate any differences between the Old and New Testaments, few knew a single thing about the prophets, few could apply the story of the Good Samaritan to life, and biblical materials as such were "only slightly comprehended,"[40] despite weekly access to these themes in church. I have often suggested that this same population cohort could spend one evening of three hours in a community college on the Bhagavad-Gita and know more of it than they gain by way of knowledge of the Bible through a lifetime. Yet all reverence the book; they might join in denominational warfare against critics who might challenge its literal truth or in political conflict against courts that would "take it out of the schools." The knowledge that the Bible is cherished, is a supreme authority, and is available to experts like preachers who can consult it is more important than exploration of the contents. Bible classes seem most popular where the contents of the Bible are least critically examined, whereas when the Bible is an object of scrutiny and study the iconic sense disappears and the crowds dwindle.

In the political realm, iconoclasts have learned to keep their distance from the Protestants on the subject of the Bible if they wish to win any causes. In the 1890s radical feminists began to prepare a *Women's Bible* in order to counteract what they felt were antiwoman passages and emphases in the use of the Bible. But in 1895 Susan B. Anthony showed political savvy when she wrote Elizabeth

Cady Stanton: "*No*—I don't want my name on that Bible Committee—*You* fight that battle—and leave me to fight the secular—the political fellows. . . . I simply don't want the enemy to be diverted from my practical ballot fight—to that of scoring me for belief one way or the other about the Bible." Stanton went ahead, and lost power. She had no idea about the level of denunciation she would receive, including from Protestant male clerics who supported both the Bible and the rights of women. She made the mistake of saying, "We have made a fetich [*sic*] of the Bible long enough. The time has come to read it as we do all other books." Even nonreaders who were supporters of the Bible were not ready to hear that.[41]

It is natural to want to hear out the founders of biblical studies in the American academy. The last thing any of them wanted to be was a destroyer of the Bible. They were virtually unanimous in their theme that biblical criticism, historical and structural and analytic in character alike, would enhance faith in an age of science. To this day biblical scholars in the ecclesiastical community are frustrated when given no chance to show their fellow believers among the laity how much more exciting is one's pursuit of the "acts of God" through the environmental and contextual studies they cherish or the formal inquiries that lay bare so many dimensions of a text. They have fused critical scholarship and faith, and wonder why others are not allowed to share their enthusiasm. Yet in most denominations they know that partisans of anticritical outlooks can always exploit the iconic sense of people and go on to suggest that there will be less, not more, Bible as well as less, not more, faith, once one enters the mental furnished apartment in which the critic has no choice but to live.

In the beginning, when critical scholarship had its first pre–Civil War hearings, Edward Robinson was the patriarch, the only American to gain an international hearing. Robinson set the theme: "It has ever been the glory of the Protestant Faith, that it has placed the Scriptures where they ought to be, above every human name, above every human authority. THE BIBLE IS THE ONLY AND SUFFICIENT RULE OF FAITH AND PRACTICE."[42]

In the first critical generation, the celebrity preachers, the ones Winthrop Hudson called "Princes of the Pulpit,"[43] almost to a person—T. DeWitt Talmadge was the exception—accepted biblical criticism as an advancement of the Protestant principle and an enhancement of faith in a scientific age. Only a few critics who were spoiling for a fight made their case less plausible by doing violence to the iconic sense of the Bible or the iconolatry of their attackers. Thus Charles Briggs was sarcastic about the "Bibliolatry" that treated the Bible magically instead of as "paper, print, and binding." Yet even such iconoclasts felt that they were helping the Bible in the public arena: "We have forced our way through the obstructions; let us remove them from the face of the earth, that no man hereafter may be kept from the Bible."[44] Briggs and other early critics regularly defended themselves by saying that no scholars would give a lifetime to the study of a book in which they did not believe. That, however, was not a telling point among conservatives who were fed a diet of stories that told how infidels from the Enlightenment to Robert Ingersoll studied the Bible in order to destroy it.

William Rainey Harper is an ideal type of the reverent biblical critic who did expend his energies sharing the critical outlook for the purpose of extending and deepening faith also among the laity, and for half a generation it worked. In 1892 he gave a speech on "The Rational and the Rationalistic Higher Criticism" at Chautauqua. First, the iconic regard:

> Can we, in the multiformity of the work which lies before us during the few weeks of our sojourn together, find anything in which we possess a common interest? At first thought it would seem impossible to name a subject related directly or indirectly to the work of all of us; but if we think again, if we recall the place occupied among us by the Bible, a place fundamental in all thought and life; if we recall the conflict of opinion which to-day rages on every side about the Bible, a conflict in which most vital interests are concerned; if we remember that in this conflict the principles at stake are principles of universal character and application—if we think of all this, I fancy we shall agree that the question of the higher criticism of the Bible is one in which we have a common interest, and one, the consideration of which at this time and place will not be inappropriate.

In other words: only the Bible would bring them together, and only biblical criticism would quicken their inquiries. Harper recognized that "criticism" conveys "to some minds an unpleasant

161

idea, but the right usage of the word carries with it nothing of this kind. . . . Do you ask what criticism is in its technical sense? I answer in a single word, 'inquiry.' The whole business of a critic is to make inquiry." Then Harper went on to criticize the rationalism of both the conservative scholastic defenders of the Bible and the rationalists themselves. He wanted a scientific not a "scientifistic" view of the Bible.

Then came the pastoral and faith-building sense of the critic:

> Great care, therefore, must be exercised, lest the learner, whether a professional student or a casual listener, be led to give up old positions before new positions have been formulated. The proper spirit is the building spirit, but the more natural spirit and the more easily developed is the destructive spirit.

Harper was confident, as were most of the other pioneers, that if the reverently critical approach were to be adopted, "the man who has believed without knowing why will have an intelligent basis for his faith," but Harper did not recognize that "believing without knowing why" better satisfied the wishes and wants of people whose view of the Bible as icon did not need another base. The critical approach would further remove grounds of hostility and skepticism. And the large class of people who had been coolly indifferent would learn "that this Book is what it purports to be, the word of God. . . . It will become to them a thing of life, not because it has changed—it has always been alive—but because they have changed toward it." To a "destructive" or "objective" critic, of course, Harper would have been dismissed as an iconolatrous believer programed by his Sunday school faith in childhood with presuppositions that would not let him read the Bible as he would "any other book."

As Harper heard it, "the cry of our times is for the application of scientific methods to the study of the Bible," but he heard the cries of University of Chicago students and the lay elite, while Grover Cleveland probably spoke for louder cries when he wanted an uncommented-upon Book. "If," Harper continued, "the methods of the last century continue to hold exclusive sway, the time will come when intelligent men of all classes will say, 'If this is your Bible we will have none of it.'" And Harper wrote an epitaph for himself that he could have applied to most of his contemporaries in the critical circle: "He has done what he could to build up not only an interest in the study of the Scriptures, but a faith in their divine origin."[45]

For half a generation, Harper and the Chautauquans, the university extension propagators, and some of the lay elite or princes of the pulpit made some progress, but in the end it was not the scientific outlook that drew the masses but the pre- or anticritical views of the Dwight L. Moodys and Billy Sundays that prevailed. There is some pathos in the attempt of Harper and the "scientists," one that I am reminded of in the similar courting principles of a modern young subject of a limerick:

A free-living damsel named Hall
Once went to a birth control ball.
   She took an appliance
   To make love with science;
But nobody asked her at all.

Harry Emerson Fosdick from the twenties through the forties of this century was the last "prince of the pulpit," the last celebrity cleric, who effectively propagated the biblical critical view as an enhancement of faith to huge audiences and readerships. Since then we have seen a "collapse of the middle" between the world of the scholars on one hand and the lay and sometimes the preaching public on the other.

Believing critics have seldom gotten much help in the larger culture. The press, beginning early in this century, knew it could always create sensation by dwelling on the iconic regard for the Bible and then "exposing" the iconoclasm of critical elitists. The *Cosmopolitan* magazine turned loose a writer named Harold Bolce, who month after month toured the major campuses and spread shocking news of how the scholars treated the Bible as a great spiritual book but not as the unique book of God.[46]

Through the twenties of this century humanists like H. L. Mencken, Ben Hecht, Clarence Darrow, Joseph Wood Krutch, Walter Lippmann, and others found it convenient, however historically inaccurate it was, to treat fundamentalist biblicism as normative Christianity from which modern biblical critics were falling. In fact, this spirit lived on into the 1970s in the hands of Princeton philosopher Walter Kaufmann, who accused anyone of a developmental view of "gerrymandering" theology. The biblical critic has therefore progressively withdrawn into the company of other professionals and has become inept when denominational politics or cultural assault see him or her as an iconoclast.

Where does this history leave us? I shall set forth a few summary remarks, each of which could merit further development by scholars.

1. The critical approach in the course of the century established itself in the academy. Opponents on their turf seem apologetic and defensive, knowing that their battle for scholarship that would repeal "the crisis of historical consciousness" or would move people out of the mental furnished apartments characterized by the critical outlook is an uphill task.

2. Biblical scholars in the *academy* are expected to reflect only humanistic (humanities-based) concerns, employing critical methods on the Bible just as they find their colleagues using them on the *Iliad* or Shakespeare. They are not to claim special privileges for their work or their texts. And like all other humanists, they can expect the respect and curiosity of a small circle of colleagues.

3. Biblical scholars in the context of *religious* communities, in church-related colleges, theological schools, church and synagogue, or the proreligious but nonpracticing public have no such luxury. They deal with texts that are engendered by a community and that engender community and, though some complain of this situation, it is from such communities that they gain a kind of power. But they have reason to complain when political forces in those communities keep them from gaining a fair hearing.

4. About half the Protestant community, some of the Jewish community, and an indeterminate number in the Catholic community have *ignored or resisted* the century of scholarship. The critic is in a position not unlike that of the poet in Dylan Thomas's vision, whose "craft and sullen art" concern the lovers who lie abed, unheeding. The believing public, for reasons of preoccupation, faith, or whatever, pays little notice.

5. I have argued that the main reason for ignoring or resisting critical scholarship has been the iconic regard for the Bible as an object in the national shrine, whether read or not, whether observed or not: it is seen as being basic to national and religious communities' existence. They hold it in awe and give *latreia* to it.

6. This iconic sense puts critical scholars at a disadvantage because they will also appear to be *iconoclastic* by the mere fact that they engage in inquiry. The media show that one can always be controversial if treating the Bible in any way other than iconically.

7. Biblical *scholars* for the most part are aware of this situation because the vast majority of them—can we get surveys to confirm or refute the impression?—were nurtured in childhood in "Jerusalem," not "Athens." Few come to critical study of the Bible through a random search for texts in the context of humanities. Most come through the passages of faith and life inspired by childhood experience of the Bible as icon in mind, home, church, and culture. Since the critical sense has enlivened their adult lives, they are often mystified about why everyone else does not make their passage. This seventh point has to be based more on personal observation than extensive defensible empirical inquiry, and I can only invite the community of scholars to begin to test it on each other.

8. As for the future, it may be that our secular-pluralist culture is becoming so differentiated, its norms so diffuse, that each generation will see the Bible surrounded by an increasing number of icons, until it *loses centrality.* It is not likely that in foreseeable futures there will be no icons in the subcommunities of national life, for under the carapace of individual and social existence it remains necessary to have a framework for organizing effects and impressions. That the Bible has held such a position for such a significant number of Americans has been good for biblical scholars, who cannot help being curious about the future and who are not likely to be on the sidelines as that future unfolds.

The Bible is prime, but it is not alone. Already in the second chapter of this volume we were paying attention to John Robinson's words to the Pilgrims, that "the Lord hath more truth and light yet to break forth out of his Holy Word." To have seen Spirit and then Letter in sequence, poises us to see how Americans have fared with an endeavor that we and others before us have linked with their biblical reverence and outlook: the experimental spirit. To discern it, we shall listen to foreign visitors as they tried to make sense of a pluralist nation, with wisdom that still speaks to our day.

8 Experiment: The Perceptions of Visitors

Students of American religious history have long debated whether they should speak of "American religion" or only of "religion in America." Has the nation's environment left some sort of stamp on its varied religious forces or do they merely pursue their inherited ways in America, sharing little more than locale? What has American religion or religion in America been "about"? It would be futile to look for unique features, elements that are shared by all spiritual agencies and religious organizations in the United States but unshared by all others elsewhere in the world. But it is at least legitimate and possible to look for distinctive characteristics that serve to color America's religious expressions.

Experiment and experimentalism as forces in national life have on occasion been proposed as the unifying theme, and I believe them to be fundamental for understanding the whole of American spirituality. One might mistrust the introduction of a novel category, one that could somehow have been wholly overlooked by the thousands of observers and analysts of the American past. At decisive turns in this history, notable articulators have converged on the terms. In early colonial times, Baptist Dr. John Clarke pleaded for the idea that "a flourishing civill State may stand, yea, and best be maintain'd . . . with a full liberty in religious concernmts," and called such a situation "a lively experiment." At the moment of the epochal turn toward "separation of church and state," Thomas Jefferson pleaded for religion "without any establishment at all," an experiment that had been "new and doubtful." Now: "Let us . . . give this experiment fair play."

In the middle of the nineteenth century, when it could be shown that religious groups had made a creative adjustment to the new circumstance, the nation's foremost church historian, Philip Schaff, could say that "in America the most interesting experiments in church-history are now made." And while Benjamin Franklin back in what he called "the age of experiments," the Enlightenment period, spoke up for "the Necessity of a *Publick Religion*," in the twentieth century an unhappy critic of its development, England's Roman Catholic visitor to America poet Hilaire Belloc, again referred to it as an experiment. Speaking of what some were later to call America's "civic religion," he wrote:

> I must close with this suggestion, putting it so that it shall be as inoffensive as possible, though I fear there must always be some note of offence in it. The new and separate spirit which has made America, which creates a spiritual condition peculiar to that Continent, may produce, perhaps will soon produce, at any rate tends to produce, some quite unique experiment in the field of religion.
>
> We have had islands, as it were, of such experiment in more than one case; but seeing the way in which great waves spread suddenly over that field of a six score millions, seeing the rapid intensity and unity of their action, I cannot but think that the future holds some rapid, and to us of Europe startling new, American growth; a new body and organization of the domain of religion. Not an isolated, fractional experiment, but a great national or cultural invention. A new Religion.[1]

It may be argued that the application of the term *experiment* to the four great turns in the shaping of religion in the Americal *polis,* the political city, need not necessarily lead to its use as a designation for the many other dimensions of spiritual life. But both advocates and observers from the first have with considerable consistency used the word or its cognates to describe the temper, character, efforts, and achievements of American religionists in many areas of life. The lively or fair experiment was, in a sense, both the product of the temper and the efforts and a matrix for the development of more character and achievements.

If the term was so frequently noted by participants in the activity, it also did not go overlooked by the scholars. Lest any reader receive the impression that I consider myself the inventor or discoverer of the motif, let me point out that in my particular tradition at the University of Chicago all four historians who have set the terms for my profession have converged on the experimental theme—a fact that does not necessarily make them correct, but one that at least gives me the confidence born of having company and precedent. In the beginning and in the hands of the first two such scholars, Peter Mode and William Warren Sweet, the experimental sense was often stated in environmental terms, terms that remain in widespread use. Thus Mode, referring to the physical feature that most frequently served as the context or corollary for experimentalism, the frontier, noted that "for more than one hundred and fifty years the almost inexhaustible resources of our plains and mountain areas have been keeping American society in a state of constant fluidity," so that the character of successive generations . . . has been undergoing a transformation." Mode spoke of "Americanization," which "thus far in our history resolves itself largely into *frontierization*." This was a part of a gigantic "enterprise"—another favorite term—which had as its result an Americanized Christianity that had "been *frontierized*."

After Mode's brief career, his successor, Sweet, took up the frontierizing and Americanizing theme with a vengeance and then made explicit use of the experimental theme. Thus, in the opening pages to *The Story of Religion in America*, the book that encapsulated his lifework, Sweet spoke of the religious radicalism of American colonials as something that provided a motif that endured. These settlers would have found that, had they "remained in Europe, their radical tendencies would doubtless have been somewhat held in check by tradition, by the presence of high church and civil officials . . . [by] conservative forces and influences." But in America "these restraining forces were not present, 'and men moved forward rapidly, even recklessly on the path of . . . experiment.'"

That Sweet's successor, Sidney E. Mead, made the sense of experiment his main theme should be clear from his quotation of John Clarke and Thomas Jefferson on "the lively experiment" and "the fair experiment," and by the whole argument of his major book with its Clarkean title, *The Lively Experiment*, and its somewhat inaccurate subtitle, *The Shaping of Christianity in America*. (More properly, the book might have been named "The Shaping of American Religion," for this was Mead's actual framework for discourse.)

Here it is valid to revisit and elaborate upon a theme of Mead's successor and my teacher and later colleague, Jerald C. Brauer. In his *Protestantism in America* Brauer might as well have spoken for all American religion when he set his theme or drew his conclusion. But because he added a biblical concentration and because his topic was only Protestantism, America's majority faith, he was more modest: "It is not easy to characterize Protestantism in America, but two characteristics seem to mark it. One is a constant free experimentation and search for a fuller manifestation of God's truth and will, and the other is a sustained effort to avoid going beyond the truth and light already known in the Bible and codified in certain basic beliefs and confessions. Thus Protestantism in America can be characterized in terms of a full, free experimentation and an enduring Biblicism."[2]

Emboldened by the publicists and scholars whose observation of "full, free experimentation" has shaped a tradition, it remains for me to test the theme by reference to the conclusions drawn by two centuries of visitors to America from Europe. Most of them tried to "see America whole," to imagine America in cosmic terms. Virtually unanimously they spoke in the language of "American religion" and not merely "religion in America." Whether they employed the term or not, "full, free experimentation" in most dimensions of religiosity made the greatest impression on them. There is one important exception, one area that some observers considered to be static and safe: the intrusion of clerical voices into the public sphere beyond the security of the institutions they were eager to serve. That exception will receive separate attention later.

Before launching on a review of their conclusions, it is well to remind ourselves of the variety of these hundreds of visitors, only a score of whose diaries or records can here be cited. From 1776 to 1976 they have come to make a brief pit stop or to linger long, some to react positively and others negatively. There were male and female, religious and nonreligious, Protestant and Catholic, crabby and smiling, profound and superficial, hasty and cautious, obscure and well-known types alike. It would be dangerous to make a homogeneous family of such a group. That is all the more reason why their convergence on the experimental theme is so remarkable.

The fact that they all came from Europe may have made this convergence somewhat less remarkable. The Europe that most of them knew still struck them as having a kind of religious fixity or rigidity that seemed to them to have been associated with religion from time immemorial. While they were not all informed about Eastern religion, African religion, "primitive religion," and ancient religion, each of these is often marked by a sense of heavy and all-determining fate, the weight of givenness. Mortals are supposed to order their times and places in relation to the ways they apprehend sacred forces, to adhere to predetermined plans, and to cohere around preset myths, symbols, and rituals. The prophetic note of the Hebrew Scriptures and the messianism of Christianity introduced developmental and, in a sense, experimental themes. But the experience of Christendom, the formal establishment of Christianity by law in European empires East and West, coupled with long canonical and dogmatic traditions and stable polities, led most of the Europeans to be surprised and startled at the freedom with which their American heirs and fellow believers tampered with arrangements that these observers would have regarded as ontological, the settled products of divine revelation, or the issues of untouchable traditions. Even more surprising was the way in which Americans, so ready to resort to "Plan B" whenever "Plan A" failed, were eager to justify their acts in the name of an unchanging Bible and what Brauer called a codification "in certain basic beliefs and confessions."

What the visitors were noting correlates with an observation of sociologist J. Milton Yinger that we have already cited. He noted that "religious change is usually a latent process, carried on beneath symbols of nonchange." "Changes are . . . obscured by the continuity of symbols."[3] Especially in a society rich in pluralism and confusion has it been necessary for experimenters and innovators to disguise or rationalize their changes with "symbols of nonchange . . . and continuity of symbols." This natural process and the toleration for ambiguity that went with it have puzzled the European visitors and led to expressions of dismay from many Americans who would have looked for more neatness in the peoples' adjustments.

8. *The Perceptions of Visitors*

Some recent students of European and American styles have tried to account for the different vantages and visions by reference to the distinctive kinds of sociology of religion that developed on the two continents. In a provocative essay, Hugh Dalziel Duncan contrasted "the European tradition" and its "systems of knowledge (how we 'apprehend' the world)" with "American . . . systems of action (how we 'act' in the world)." Duncan cited Jacob Burckhardt, Ernst Cassirer, Wilhelm Dilthey, Pitirim Sorokin, Max Weber, and, in other passages, Émile Durkheim among those who used the European mode of noticing how we apprehend the world. In America William James, G. H. Mead, John Dewey, Robert E. Park, Charles Cooley, and Kenneth Burke expressed "the tradition of the 'act,'" which is more congenial to the experimental manner. In another context Duncan related these two ways to historical tenses, again with implications for our current topic. In the process the enthusiastic sociologist located himself in the American experimental tradition:

> I, and here of course I am typically American, would rather have acts determined by a future than a past—especially when it is assumed that knowledge of the past is blessed as "real" while our knowledge of the future is damned as "subjective" and "imaginary." The past may be pregnant with the present, and even with the future, as Tönnies, Spencer, Maine, Sumner, and the social theories of the "organic" schools would have us believe. But if this is so, there have been far too many monsters born of these "irrevocable pasts" (as in Italy, Russia, and Germany) to take much comfort in this depressing doctrine. Like Ward, Dewey, Mead, and Cooley in American sociology, I hold to the future because the future can be treated purely as an image or an "idea" and is, therefore, open to criticism. Plans for the future are not always considered "sacred" or "inexorable."[4]

It would be hazardous if not foolish to associate oneself with all the things Duncan did with his observation and commitment. But the basic distinction does go a long way to describe not only two kinds of scholarly tools but also what it is that possessors of these tools consequently noticed. Duncan was particularly perturbed by the imperialism with which European analysts have confused "social integration with religious integration," using sociology of primitive religion as the encompassing approach to American "acts." That concern need not disturb us as we set out to isolate the religious motif in the American past. Duncan was in some respects simply translating the theological theme that Brauer and other documenters of the experimental theme hear in the sermon with which the Reverend Mr. John Robinson bade farewell to *The Speedwell* on July 21, 1620. "Let us be certain, brethren, that the Lord hath more truth and light yet to break forth out of his holy Word."[5] Even though predestination and predeterminism were factors in the very "holy Word" with which Robinson's people and their kind were to struggle for 150 years of colonial history, these themes did not distract from the sense that people were free to make changes. Edward W. Chester, seeing "Religion on Trial" in a chapter of his synthetic work, *Europe Views America,* quite accurately concludes: "Significantly, there are few European commentators who label the American state of mind as fatalistic, since fatalism is a form of predestination which usually involves passive resignation before future events," a fatalism that would have meant death for the experimental spirit.[6]

An English Methodist clergyman, James Dixon, who visited Pittsburgh in 1848, referred to both place ("soil") and history ("institutions") as factors that made possible Americans' religious experiments, including their lively and fair one: "It can be no matter of surprise that the American people, being favoured with the opportunity, the soil being clear, and no old institutions standing in the way, should be disposed to adopt a new principle, and, discarding all authoritative church-organization, try the effect of Christianity, itself, in its own native grandeur and divine simplicity. This they have done." Dixon spoke of this way being "tried," of a process that has "been tested." The language of experimentalism is consistent. But since both trying and testing imply religious change, not all Europeans were able to regard them favorably. Some distortions of vision occur as a result of the visitors' sense of absolutism or unchangeability in religion.

Even the best known and most influential of all the visitors, Alexis de Tocqueville, had to wrestle constantly with the question American pluralism and developmentalism posed: "Should religion change?" Joachim Wach quotes Tocqueville: "A religion must be absolutely true or false. How can it make progress?" But unless progress is in mind, why "try" or "test" something? Wach notes that

Tocqueville coped with the features of change that he enjoyed—
and he enjoyed many in *Democracy in America*—by conceding
"that there may be progress in [religion's] application, if not in its
dogma." American Protestant biblicists, Catholic confessionalists,
and most of their codifying counterparts would have agreed that
this was precisely the mode of their own experimentalisms. Dixon
noted this, while overstressing the ties between Christianity and
the American state:

> We have seen that the people is the state; and the state, in this
> sense, namely, through the people, has, with the exception of the
> infidels amongst them, adopted Christianity; only, instead of
> being an hierarchical government, it is that of the holy Scrip-
> tures—the Bible itself being the governing light, the decisive
> authority, the court of final appeal. All the interests of society
> converge to this point; religion is its life, its power, its beauty. It
> is like the *substrata* of the world, on which all the soils whence
> the vegetable productions spring repose in security.[7]

With those words Dixon located the civil and social base for much
American religious experimentalism. From these roots the people
drew security to try, to test, to engage in process, to change, by
blending their canon and its spirit ("the holy Bible . . . being the
governing light") with their environment, ("the *substrata* of the
world . . . [and] the soils"). With experiment, then, we associate
the corollary theme: Americans, also in the eyes of these European
visitors, *have regarded their environment as being itself somehow
redemptive and revelatory*. The divine forces, the power of the sacred, God himself or itself, were perceived as speaking through the
strata and soil, the history and the people. Citizens had to cope
with and transform wilderness and frontier, make use of natural and
popular resources, and make sense of their common life in such a
setting.

At its worst this understanding can lead and has led to tribalism
and chauvinism. As British visitor James Lord Bryce once observed—without specific reference to American worship of place—
that to tribes "religion appeared . . . a matter purely local; and as
there were gods of the hills and gods of the valleys, of the land and
of the sea, so each tribe rejoiced in its peculiar deities, looking on
the natives of other countries who worshipped other gods as Gen-

tiles, natural foes, unclean beings." But transcendence of both local tribes (e.g., denominations) and of national exclusivism ("chosenness") has also occurred along with that construing of "the *Publick Religion*" that I have elsewhere spoken of as "public theology." We have developed public theology in this book in respect to Reinhold Niebuhr (chap. 5).

Public theology is the interpretation of "the nation's religious experience, practice, and behavior in the light of some sort of transcendent reference." It has been practiced in the churches by, among others, Jonathan Edwards, the towering religious figure, who would charter "a body of divinity in an entirely new method, being thrown into the form of a history," one that culminated in his own place and time. In the civil realm it was best articulated by Abraham Lincoln, who gave the people the sense of chosenness and then compromised their temptations to hubris by qualifying it when he spoke of Americans as God's "almost chosen people."[8]

Not everyone has seen the natural and historical environment in these openly congenial terms. Many fundamentalistic religious groups and others claimed not to see it thus. Yet, in the eyes of foreign observers and many of their domestic counterparts, the celebration of the milieu has been consistent across the spectrum from the doctrinally intransigent or biblically conservative groups to the religiously and civilly liberal ones. Perspectivalism and circumstantiality marked the national religious expression. In the eyes of their voyeurs and guests, Ortega y Gasset's sweeping claim was often true of Americans in the scope of world religion: "Tell me the landscape in which you live, and I will tell you who you are."[9] Because of this impress of landscape, the observers were free to sweep with generalizations. Thus Tocqueville: "I have seen no country in which Christianity is clothed with fewer forms, figures, and observances than in the United States; or where it presents more distinct, more simple, or more general notions to the mind. Although the Christians of America are divided into a multitude of sects, they all look upon their religion in the same light."[10] American Jews, without forgetting their prayer, "Next year in Jerusalem," and without seeing later Zionism as a compromising element, came to speak of America as "our Zion." Ludwig Kempert, the German poet, urged: "It is to America that our longing goes forth. . . . In your adopted fatherland . . . a man is worth what he is, and he is what he does. Before all else, be free—and go to America." Blacks in America have frequently resorted to language similar to that of W. E. B. Du Bois, who spoke of a "doubleness," the reality of "two souls in one dark body," because they could continue to use Africa as a symbolic reference point but it was America that became their land of promise, their Zion. Roman Catholics could never understand how and why the Protestant majority thought of them as anything but completely at home in the environment; they were hypernationalists and felt no complicating pulls from Roman authority.[11] And the Protestant majority gloried in the environment whose history they felt they themselves had made.[12]

In the opinion of America's more audacious religious thinkers, the idea of situating people in the national environment did not necessarily mean that God dealt only with them there. When they spoke of God's "latter-day glory" unfolding in America—as Jonathan Edwards and millennialists in his train regularly did—they saw a cosmic significance in such divine acts. Reviewing the work of these thinkers, historian William A. Clebsch has argued with good warrant that they even "tried to divert American spirituality from its natural spillover into moralism by translating the religious impulse into being at home in the universe. . . . The religious experience of Americans has been emphatically more voluntary than organic, more diverse than standard, more personal than institutional, more practical than visionary or (in that sense) mystical. . . . Certain great exemplars of American religious thought . . . shaped a recognizably American spirituality to changing times and needs." Using the concept of Americanness to determine who such exemplars might be, Clebsch said that "foreign observers like Alexis de Tocqueville and Frederika Bremer do not count." Jonathan Edwards, Ralph Waldo Emerson, and William James do.[13]

On some terms, the foreign observers do indeed not count, for they did not all discern the main theological impulse in American experimentalism and environmentalism. Yet even where they could not comprehend it the visitors helped document its presence simply by the surprise they evinced or the dullness of their observation. How could Tocqueville fully discern the central meaning of the American religious endeavor, given his own view of religion as fated, static, given? His contrast between the religious or moral world and the political is revealing: "in the moral world everything is classified, systematized, foreseen, and decided beforehand; in the political world everything is agitated, disputed, and uncertain. In the one is a passive though a voluntary obedience; in the other, an independence scornful of experience, and jealous of all authority. These two tendencies, apparently so discrepant, are far from conflicting; they advance together and support each other."

This attitude suggests what Duncan meant when he spoke of a typically European way of apprehending the universe in religion, rather than acting upon it. In this context Tocqueville saw the New Englanders as "ardent sectarians and daring innovators." By "sectarians" he meant that they were not free to improvise in religious thought, while the term "innovators" pointed to the fact that "under their hand, political principles, laws, and human institutions seem malleable, capable of being shaped and combined at will." At the edge of the political world, "the human spirit stops of itself; in fear it relinquishes the need of exploration; it even abstains from lifting the veil of the sanctuary; it bows with respect before truth which it accepts without discussion."[14] Yet the historical record of Americans in both colonies and nation finds them in a religious world that was also "agitated, disputed, and uncertain . . . malleable, capable of being shaped and combined at will."

What sense can be made otherwise of a catalog of religious experiments in an environment evidenced by the following sample: The first Virginians came with a theology designed for explorers seeking a northwest passage, but they developed one that legitimated planting and settlement. To all the colonies came people who made their claim before God on missionary terms. Yet they found theological grounds soon for evicting or killing the "salvages" they had come to convert. In New England they brought a metaphysical rationale for pilgrim's failures and quickly transformed it into a set of divine explanations for settlers' successes. Most colonists came to perpetuate theocracies and to exclude outsiders. They then produced or came to find theories that made possible recognition of dissent and an eventual pluralist or secular society. Most came to assure that there be a union of the civil and religious realms on their favored terms and then, when they "separated church and state," these old foes of such separation turned around and convinced the world that separation was what God had had in mind as the only way for them all along.

They further invented the denominational system and devised biblical arguments for the churchly divisions that Saint Paul had explicitly condemned in his First Letter to the Corinthians. They fabricated new denominations when the theoretical frameworks and revelations of the old ones failed to satisfy all; some of these, like Mormonism, were explicitly designed to make people at home in the American universe. They nurtured theologies to support both slavery and emancipation, racism and liberation, on the basis of the same scripture. They converged on the theme of innocence in the natural world and then embraced an urban-industrial order, later invoking symbols of "the new creation as metropolis" and "the secular city" on biblical grounds. They began by arguing that God in his providence had shielded the American environment from Western eyes until the Protestant Reformation could occur and then, after building a Protestant empire, devised theologies for pluralism. Obsessed with the divine grounding of government, they provided numerous ways of "making things come out right" in defense of their national constitution, one that intended to bracket metaphysical commitments. Theologians, pastors, lay leaders in the churches, joined political theorists or practitioners in regarding "the veil of the sanctuary" and what it symbolized to be "capable of being shaped" at will. Yet—and this is the great exception to a generally wise comprehension of which we spoke earlier—Tocqueville and many other observers consistently argued that Americans were *not* theologically enterprising and that their experimentalism was restricted to a small and tight sphere!

Politically astute denominational leaders quite wisely disguised their innovations. They effected religious change under the symbols of nonchange, by resort to biblical defense, by contentment with traditional dogma, or neglect of the formal doctrinal lore. It was their inability to construct or their lack of interest in generating such formal intellectual patterns that threw the observers off the trail at many crucial turns. While one would not expect most of them to be theologians or experts at discovering distinctive patterns of political thought in America, even the professional theologians among them often came equipped only with European models and paradigms. These prepared them to call that thought alone religious which was "classified, systematized, foreseen, and decided beforehand."

Contemporary theologian Herbert Richardson's complaint about even a gifted modern like Dietrich Bonhoeffer applies as well to many another European theologian who might visit these shores:

> Bonhoeffer [pronounced] the ethnocentric judgment that "God has granted American Christianity no Reformation."

> Bonhoeffer's judgment is ethnocentric because he uses different criteria in comparing religion in America with European Christianity. He explains American religion *sociologically* but he explains his own German religion *theologically*. . . . Suppose, however, we were to utilize Bonhoeffer's technique and simply reverse the criteria, interpreting the European Reformation *sociologically* and American Christianity *theologically*. Then we might see that the Reformation was not primarily a religious event, but was merely the accidental result of social and psychological circumstances. . . . But . . . God carried His new Israel to these shores, a free and democratic people whose trust in divine providence and whose theocratic hope are evidences that the true Church of Jesus Christ has been reestablished here.

Richardson himself calls this an "obviously fallacious comparison" which he used simply to show the inadequacy of Bonhoeffer's style of observation and his devices. He cites Ernst Benz's complaint that two prejudices govern European judgments regarding American Christianity: "The first prejudice is: *Americana non leguntur*—'one does not read American literature,' in this case, theological literature. The second prejudice is: 'There is no independent American theology.'" Therefore for Bonhoeffer the "only 'real' theologians . . . in America are those who are reiterating European doctrine. All else is, at best, a pagan humanism, and at worst an eclectic and inconsistent conglomeration of sectarian oddities and spiritualistic wrong-headedness."[15]

This concept of American theology came to its most bizarre and gauche moment when a German theologian in the 1960s, encircled and befuddled by a group of American hermeneuticians, dismissed them as pathetic exemplars of a nation that just never could think deep theological thoughts—but that had showed Christian love by sending Germans relief after the Second World War!

One should not fault Tocqueville and his kith for not finding a high premium on dogma or the articulation of inherited theological ideas in conventional styles. French nobleman turned Floridian, Achille Murat, was not inaccurate when in 1832, nine years after his arrival, he reported that he desired not to expound the dogma of the 1,001 sects which divide the people of the United States: "Merely to enumerate them would be impossible, for they change every day, appear, disappear, unite, separate, and evince nothing stable but their instability. . . . Among this variety of religions, everybody may indulge his inclination, change it whenever he pleases, or remain neuter, and follow none. Yet . . . there is no country in which the people are so religious as in the United States; to the eyes of a foreigner they even appear to be too much so."[16] But pluralistic bewilderment was not the only reason for dismissing the dogmatic enterprise. In the churches, as Tocqueville noted, the language was too frequently restricted to morality, while of dogma he heard not a word. Most observers simply regarded the Americans as being incapable of philosophical extrapolations of their revelation and experience. Henry Sienkiewicz, author of *Quo Vadis*, visited American Catholicism from Poland late in the nineteenth century and confided to his letters his impressions:

> The American people are extraordinarily matter-of-fact. No one troubles himself about things which have no connection with reality of material benefits or which cannot be grasped and calculated. Such questions as the origins of the universe, the existence of the Creator, the immortality of the soul, all of which are agitating the minds of European youth, professors, philosophers, and the intelligentsia—these ideas, which so often lead first to philosophical bankruptcy and then to widespread doubt among the people, here carry no weight at all. No other people are less capable of philosophical reflection than Americans.[17]

Only at the left borders did some analysts discern such reflection. In 1862 Camille Ferri-Pisani, a French-Corsican, remarked that after 1830 some Hegelian philosophy did begin to cross the Atlantic to a nation "not very open to the novelties of transcendental philosophy," there to find refuge in the bosom of Unitarianism. The Unitarians and "most men who no longer believe in the supernatural or the letter of any revelation" but who "still [feel] the spur of the religious spirit and of a divine curiosity no longer satisfied . . . consider all religions, from the most primitive fetishism to the most refined Christianism, as developments of the divine idea."[18] He stopped short of finding such transcendentalism still further to the left, among the transcendentalists, or such developmentalism present among the more orthodox. A reading of the postmillennial tradition beginning with Jonathan Edwards and moving through Horace Bushnell to Walter Rauschenbusch might convince skeptics that the Protestant mainliners themselves were quite experimental and innovative in their theological searchings. Similarly, a reading of the political or literary figures who consistently expounded "the *Publick Religion*," the Enlightened Founding Fathers, the Emersons and Whitmans, the Hawthornes and Melvilles, the Abraham Lincolns and Walter Lippmanns, would give evidence of the emergence of a public theology that was overlooked by most conventional foreign observers.

For the rest, these visitors were often richer in insight. Most of them thought that the environment and its opportunities had led to the transformation of their American cousins' very human nature, seeing the emergence of a new being, of an American character. Tocqueville could not allow himself to see this character in religion, where "every principle of the moral world is fixed and determinate," but it was true that the "political world is abandoned to the debates and the experiments of men." For him, because of religious restraints, "the imagination of the Americans, even in its greatest flights, is circumspect and undecided; its impulses are checked, and its works unfinished."[19] Other visitors did extend the observation of religious experience more broadly. Philip Schaff found his new fellow citizens in country and church to be part of "a land of the future," thanks to the Providence of God, which made America as yet an unripe youth, not seldom wanton and adventurous, but fresh, vigorous, and promising. Little wonder that Schaff could find the people to be "of the boldest enterprise and untiring progress—Restlessness and Agitation personified. Even when seated, they push themselves to and fro in their rocking chairs; they live in a state of perpetual excitement in their business, their politics, and their religion."[20]

8. *The Perceptions of Visitors*

I know no better way to reinforce the present theme than to quote in more detail a passage from the twentieth-century French Catholic philosopher Jacques Maritain, a passage already cited in a different context. I thought enough of its perception to use it as an epigraph for a book and to draw from it the book title, *Pilgrims in Their Own Land*. Its point here is clear. From such a staid observer one might have expected a gruff dismissal. Yet Jacques Maritain saw in Americans the embodiment of Hegel's concept of the "infinite elasticity" of the spirit, of resilience and versatility. Americans "prefer to change things and situations. They prefer to find a new arrangement, new equipment, a new gadget, a new line of social activity. . . . There is no stagnation. . . . At the origin of this *fluidity* there is the activity of the mind at work in the people, in the humble ways of daily life."

> Americans seem to be in their own land as pilgrims, prodded by a dream. They are always on the move—available for new tasks, prepared for the possible loss of what they have. They are not *settled, installed* (I would say, in French, *"installés"*—a word which carries a strong moral connotation). . . . This sense of becoming, this sense of the flux of time and the dominion of time over everything here below, can be interpreted, of course, in merely pragmatist terms. It can turn into a worship of becoming and change. It can develop a cast of mind which, in the intellectual field, would mean a horror of any tradition, the denial of any lasting and supra-temporal value. But such a cast of mind is but a degeneration of the inner mood of which I am speaking. . . . In this sense of becoming and impermanence one may discern a feeling of evangelical origin which has been projected into temporal activity.[21]

In America, said Lord Bryce while pointing out contrasts to the English situation, "there is rather less conventionalism or constraint in speaking of religious experience."[22]

Decades later another Englishman, D. W. Brogan, touched on that spirit in the American character and found experimentalism to be based not in optimism but in the idea of progress. America had known no Dark Ages in its past; its people believed in the possibilities of human effort. "The American historical experience . . . has been the product of profound faith in man's possibilities and of repeated historical justification for that faith." It was true that "the religious tradition imported from Europe by the earlier settlers . . .

had its ingredient of Christian humility and pessimism." But Americans always came up with "Plan B" in the new environments: "Even in early New England, as Perry Miller has shown, optimism about the destiny of man and society was always breaking in. . . . The American experience fought against the orthodox doctrine of Protestant Europe. . . . American religion was committed, more and more, to an optimistic view of God's purpose in the world and to an identification of that purpose with the purpose of man, especially American man. Religion more and more lost its supernatural and other-world character."

While he acknowledged tragic or pessimistic vision in Henry David Thoreau and Abraham Lincoln and in "the excessive gloom of current American letters, . . . the American religious mind to Brogan was made ready for the acceptance of the optimistic deism of Franklin and Jefferson." Even the evangelicals shared "more of their views than they suspected and were further removed from the views of old orthodox Christianity than they realized," to the point of linking evangelicalism itself with competition, acquisitiveness, and the aspiration for success seen as a virtue.[23]

Few observers thought that this kind of character was restricted to Protestants, even if the evangelicals had done more to shape the environment. The environment worked its effect on Catholics, who reshaped their life to help them fit in—while retaining fidelity to traditional Catholic dogma and order. Congregationalist visitors from England, Andrew Reed and James Matheson, in the mid-1830s announced to their English sponsors that "the *principle of adaptation*" and "pliancy" marked the whole American voluntary system.[24] Roman Catholics adapted with a vengeance. Brogan reminded his readers of the obvious: "The United States is a Protestant country; this seems a platitude but it is much more than that." Protestantism was in "the historical background, the historical traditions, the folkways, the whole national idea of the 'right thing' is deeply and almost exclusively Protestant. . . . In practically every part of the United States, the Catholics are newcomers, what Charles Maurras used to call '*métèques*,'" and thus they are expected to "Americanize." Writing in 1950 just before the new ecumenical age, Brogan was not yet able to foresee Protestant-Catholic concord and entente.[25] But the Americanizing and adaptationist spirit of Catholics in their Protestant environment had not been hidden from observers during the century before Brogan.

The notable American philosopher George Santayana in 1912 had noticed how adapted and at home in the American universe Catholics had become. Catholicism "is ancient, metaphysical, poetic, elaborate, ascetic, autocratic, and intolerant. . . . Everything in American life is at the antipodes to such a system. Yet the American Catholic is entirely at peace. His tone in everything, even in religion, is cheerfully American." The irascible and orthodox Catholic novelist Evelyn Waugh, writing after a visit in 1949, found Catholic "fermentation everywhere." "Catholicism is part of the American spirit." "'Americanism' is the complex of what all Americans consider the good life and . . . in this complex Christianity, and pre-eminently Catholicism, is the redeeming part. . . . The lay American Catholic insists more emphatically on his 'Americanism' than do Protestants or atheists of, perhaps, longer American ancestry. There is a purely American 'way of life' led by every good American Christian that is point-for-point opposed to the publicized and largely fictitious 'way of life' dreaded in Europe and Asia."[26]

British socialist Harold Laski thought that Catholics were able to get along so well chiefly because they had retired to a ghetto, where their improvisations were shielded from view. "It is interesting to observe how little in one way, and how much in others, the Roman Catholic Church has been influenced by the environment of America." The fact that Catholicism is "an *imperium in imperio*," a citadel, kept it from consistent Americanist fusion. But the Catholicism is not only "in America, but it is an American church," though in a different sense from that of any other denomination. Ministering though it did to the laboring classes dear to him, Laski still found Catholicism to be a conservative force, even though it had produced some notable progressive giants like Orestes Brownson, Father Isaac Hecker ("The American Vincent de Paul"), Monsignor John Ryan, and other social philosophers.[27]

To say that American Catholicism was conservative did not mean that it was not experimental. One of the most conservative of visitors, Eric von Kuehnelt-Leddihn, in 1950 pointed to "the real achievement of American Catholics. . . . Again and again I was cheered by the American [Catholic] readiness and freshness in tackling organizational problems; the old pioneering spirit is far from dead." It was in the realm of dogma that von Kuehnelt-Leddihn would not have welcomed pioneering.[28]

The summary position on this subject was best stated by André Siegfried, another French visitor who both in 1927 and 1955 published observations about the Protestant environment in America. American Catholicism, ever since "great prelates such as Monsignor Ireland or Monsignor Gibbons," had been busy helping Catholicism become "Americanized" and assimilated or integrated. "It is already a Church that has adapted itself to the national environment." The priests' "contribution to the religious thought of the world is negligible," but Catholic action, while "it belongs to the national environment," and "though essentially American, . . . has its own particular moral and religious aspect." And Siegfried was ready to say that Catholicism bore witness to transcendence, "a more strictly religious concept of religion," and a liturgical sense. Catholic thought has nevertheless exercised its influence in the very heart of the Protestant world."[29] To the Catholic, too, the new environment was seen to be in some way or other a redemptive and revelatory part of God's plan.

All these experimental elements in the American character and in its group life came to focus in the *Ur*-experiment, the normative and decisive turn taken in "the lively experiment" of religious freedom and "the fair experiment" that resulted in separation of church and state and the rise of the voluntary system. Here the European visitors were virtually unanimous in their awe for the seismic shift and cosmic adjustment that American practice *and* thought had worked in the history of Western if not of all religious life.

It would be wearying to the reader and might seem almost unnecessary to document this generalization; the reports of virtually any visitor find voluntaryism and its accompanying innovations to be the center of the American experience and experiment. Everything else seems to lead up to it and flow from it; other temperings and tamperings in religious life are corollaries of this, or they are made possible by it. The canonical version of this observation is from Lord Bryce:

It is accepted as an axiom by all Americans that the civil power ought to be not only neutral and impartial as between different forms of faith, but ought to leave these matters entirely on one side, regarding them no more than it regards the artistic or literary pursuits of the citizens. There seem to be no two opinions on this subject in the United States.

Of all the differences between the Old World and the New this is perhaps the most salient. . . . All religious bodies are absolutely equal before the law and unrecognized by law, except as voluntary associations of private citizens.[30]

Harriet Martineau, no friend of the fruits of the voluntary principle in America, chiefly because she saw the competitive clergy reduced to a position of servility toward their clienteles and thus too meek in the social realm, at least thought that the fair experiment represented "higher ground" than that of European establishments. It was this nonestablished or voluntary system that had to produce its own criteria for Americans' self-judgment or self-evaluation.[31]

Camille Ferri-Pisani took a far more positive view of the churchly effects of the system. While he was too timid personally to raise the question as to whether European nations should effect disestablishment, "It is a question of an unmeasurable gravity," and "America is the only country in the world where they have put the voluntary system into practice (complete separation of church and state) and there was not a single voice that did not proclaim the excellence of this system." Ferri-Pisani did not take his testimonies merely from the enemies of religion—as Jefferson was—or simply the indifferent, but from "the scrupulous and fervent consciences" who had originally "accepted it in the past as a fateful necessity" but who were now "enlightened by experience" and saw that the experiment was the greatest boon to religion that they could have wished.[32]

William McLoughlin has recently reminded us that "it is a misreading of American history to see voluntaryism as a theory of religious laissez-faire, at least as voluntaryism worked out in and after the Revolution."[33] The Europeans friendly to religion consistently stressed the completeness of separation of church and state and then went on to show how religious and civil realms were actually and positively fused or interactive, to the benefit of both. Philip Schaff would "by no means vindicate this separation of church and state as the perfect and final relation between the two," because "the kingdom of Christ is to penetrate and transform like leaven, all the relations of individual and national life." But

> we much prefer this separation, however, to the territorial system . . . and we regard it as adapted to the present wants of America and favourable to her religious interests. For it is by no means to be thought that the separation of church and state there is a renunciation of Christianity by the nation. . . . It is not an annihilation of one factor, but only an amicable separation of the two in their spheres of outward operation. . . . Under such circumstances, Christianity, as the free expression of personal conviction and of the national character, has even greater power over the mind, than when enjoined by civil laws and upheld by police regulations.[34]

Such a Christianity was to become ever more divided, and non-Christian and nonreligious groups were to be constitutionally free to assert themselves in an increasingly complex pattern of pluralism. This pluralism could breed indifferentism or mere toleration-ism. In 1819 the Italian Jesuit who for five years had been president of Georgetown College, Giovanni Antonio Grassi, complained of the improvisatory character of Americans who produced too many sects and, with them, an attitude of ignorance on the part of believers of each other's beliefs and a failure to take on themselves the expression of their own. "Many, when asked, do not answer, 'I believe,' but simply, 'I was brought up in such a persuasion.'"[35]

Sometimes voluntaryism was seen to be simply erosive of distinctiveness; the pluralism of the American experiment produced only a blur. Here again the best-known observer, Tocqueville, may be a bit misleading because his predispositions led him to stress only homogeneities in the American religious experience. Max Lerner appropriately comments of him:

> despite his stress on religion in America, [there is not] a vivid sense of the religious pluralism, nor of that fusion of religion, ethnic origin, region, speech, and even occupational diversity that were to form so many pockets to relieve the standardized flatness of the larger society. Curiously Tocqueville, who himself noted that democratic peoples have a way of personalizing the

formless movements of mankind, did exactly that with the movements of opinion in American democracy. The American "majority" is usually a cluster of minorities whose diverse motivations happen to result in a similar stance. . . . [He] turned what is pluralistic into something monolithic. . . . As a political sociologist he overdid the simplicity of his "model" of American society, making it less complex in order to make it more compassable.[36]

Certainly there *was* something monolithic about the Americans' adaptations to their own fair experiment, but another side was also evident to European observers who imposed a less static view of religion on the new scene. The most careful among them admitted to some perplexity over the Americans' paradoxes and over their ability to tolerate ambiguity in such a decisive sphere. Where in the world did intersectarian rivalry find more expression and yet where were there more fusions? Gustave de Beaumont, Tocqueville's traveling companion, we have seen, was simply bewildered by the improvisations, the apparent indifference to religious sectarianism on one hand and the profound attachment to one's own sect on the other. He thought the stance issued from superficiality.[37]

Or could it not be that then as now the scholar and critical analyst look for distinctions and discriminations that the larger population would not welcome, need, or know how to define? It could be that peoples' ability to live with particularism and universalism, with a love for the *plures* and the *unum*, may be one of the most impressive if confusing results of the American experiment.

In any case, few visitors could overlook the competition between churches that resulted. This competition led to claims by various groups that each of them better than others could both offer people transcendence of the present universe and at-homeness in the current environment, that they were both most traditional or biblical and most experimental and progressive. The primitive or restorationist churches of the nineteenth century, the Churches of Christ, the Disciples of Christ, and in an extreme way the Mormons, were sure that they were repristinating a pure faith that had been tainted by the European centuries. Yet they were not themselves free from the dialogue with the environment and turned out, in the eyes of many, to be the most "at home" American churches of all.

Competition did lead to its own experiments. Scottish physician Alexander Hamilton visited in 1744 and observed, to use the words of a modern show tune, that "you gotta have a gimmick," and that the sects' ceremonies served for this:

> All sorts and sects whatever made a kind of trade of religion, contriving how to make it turn out to their own gain and profit. . . . Men of sense of every perswasion whatsoever are sensible of the emptiness and nonsense of the mere ceremonial part of religion but, att the same time, allow it to be in some degree necessary and useful, because the ignorant vulgar are to be dealt with in this point as we manage children by showing them toys in order to perswade them to do that which all the good reasoning of the world never would.[38]

Similarly, Achille Murat also saw the rise of the new religious societies to be "truly surprising; there are some of them for every thing. . . . There is no end to them. . . . This explains a little how it is that the vineyard of the Lord is so flourishing." The enterprising religious young man, "if he have an aptitude for business . . . invents some new society."[39]

Not all the observers of this inventive spirit saw the clergy as being so guileful or venial; more frequently, even when they were put off by the competitive spirit, the visitors respected the intentions of the entrepreneurs to give some voice to divine visions of moral reform. They could not resist pointing to the utilitarian spirit, to the "joint stock company" character of the churches, to the fact that people supported the clergy "to the degree of their usefulness," as Francis Grund put it,[40] so that the clergy became, as Tocqueville and Martineau complained, too much the servants of their customers, too timid a class in society. The clergy, said Martineau, "belong to the apprehensive party," fearing that they might alienate actual or potential clienteles. Absolved "from the common clerical vices of ambition and cupidity, it remains to be seen whether they are free also from that of the idolatry of opinion."[41]

To the socially conscious Martineau, the clergy seemed to draw a line in society and did their experimenting within the safe circle. This was precisely the division that Tocqueville also observed and popularized. His observation is not fully accurate, but there is enough truth to it to merit its reproduction:

I have shown elsewhere how the American clergy stand aloof from secular affairs. This is the most obvious, but it is not the only, example of their self-restraint. In America religion is a distinct sphere, in which the priest is sovereign, but out of which he takes care never to go. Within its limits he is the master of the mind; beyond them, he leaves men to themselves, and surrenders them to the independence and instability which belong to their nature and their age.

All the American clergy know and respect the intellectual supremacy exercised by the majority; they never sustain any but necessary conflicts with it. They take no share in the altercations of parties, but they readily adopt the general opinions of their country and their age. . . . Public opinion is therefore never hostile to them. [42]

This is not the whole story, for the history of American religion, not restricted to the role of professional clergy in institutional churches, is full of religious influence and experiment in many zones of life. But Tocqueville was correct: the clergy were engaging in a new experiment, adapting as they were to modernity, settling for a sphere apart from the whole. So successful were they that a century later it was those clergy who had withdrawn to minister to personal, familial, residential, and leisured aspects of life who were regarded as bearers of "the old-time religion," while the ones who resorted to tradition and tried to reintrude in the spheres of political, social, economic, or cultural life were seen to be meddlers.

Only a book-length study would permit analysis of all the observations of experimentalism in the American religious environment. Every visitor from the First Great Awakening down to Billy Graham has been obliged or invited to attend the revivals or other means of helping people "get religion." These observers faithfully documented the experiments with which the evangelists became expert at the phenomenology of conversion, the sociology of collective religious behavior, the philosophy that had to do with "the religious affections." Others concerned themselves with the apparent conformity and the covert experimentalism of the black churches. Frederika Bremer, one of the most patient and gifted of the observers of black religion, spoke of "that talent of improvisation, and of strikingly applying theoretical truths to the occurrences of daily life, which I have often admired among the negroes." [43]

Hilaire Belloc's suggestion that America is on the verge of devising a "new religion" as its next experiment remains to haunt us. He thought that citizens would solve the issues of particularism and pluralism eventually only by developing "a *Publick Religion*" that would see the nation itself as a kind of church. His friend and contemporary G. K. Chesterton looked back on the "dogmatic lucidity" of the American creed as it had been stated in some lines of the Declaration of Independence and then spoke of the United States as "the nation with the soul of a church." Belloc was full of concern for Catholicism in the future of such a nation: "The chief political problem presented by religion has, then, still to be solved in the New World. What the result will be certainly no foreigner could attempt to predict. . . . But presented the problem certainly will be, and in one or other of the many fashions, stable or unstable, more or less tragic, it will have to be solved." Belloc's gloom rose from his vision of a kind of *Publick Religion* housed in the nation's legal tradition, a tradition with sacred sanctions behind it as it calls for Catholics (or others) to act against conscience. What will happen if and when the state calls for the removal of incapable and imbecile human beings? A Catholic would call this murder. What if marital laws go against Catholic conscience? What if children be compelled to attend a public school, wherein the established civic religion is practiced? "The State here affirms the doctrine and practice that a certain religious atmosphere is, or should be, universal to the human race; or, at any rate, to all its citizens; which religious atmosphere is other than the Catholic." There will be inevitable clash.[44]

Belloc's vision was prophetic. After America came to understand the extent of its pluralism in the middle of the twentieth century, calls for the development of a "civil religion" or of "the religion of the Republic" became urgent. Most of them were issued at the expense of particular church religion. Sidney Mead, who has spoken up for such a republican religion, says that from the viewpoint of the "theology behind the legal structure of America" for which he speaks, "it is religious particularity, Protestant or otherwise, that is heretical and schismatic—even un-American!" Phillip E. Hammond has persuasively argued that Americans now see "Legal Institutions as Religion:

8. The Perceptions of Visitors

A new rhetoric is still in developing stages. Were this new religion—this new moral architecture—fully mature, it would be very much a part of the common culture. . . . Public schools are the new "Sunday schools," it might be said, whereas courts are the new pulpits. . . . The emerging theology of the legal system is . . . more clearly seen in America's "civil religion," where its sacred literature, shrines, and saints are already institutionalized. Far from being merely the cheap patriotism of ignorant people, it is a vibrant ideology. . . . Moreover, commitment to it does not preclude self-identification as religious in other, older ways as well. What is not so clear yet are the connections between the civil religion as theology and the parallel civil religion as moral architecture.[45]

These are words of domestic disputants, though Bellah has been influenced by Rousseau, Mead by Chesterton, and Hammond by Durkheim. The foreign visitors themselves have tended to concur in their observation of this newest stage of the American experiment. While the visitors of Tocqueville's generation could clearly see religion to be the integrator and cohesive element in a denominational society, our contemporaries find present stronger impulses for a national religion supported by, but independent of, church religion. Commenting on civil religion, the redoubtable D. W. Brogan saw it to be a derivative of the old Protestant sense of chosenness. "The new God of the highly diversified people is a vaguely Protestant God. . . . The civic religion has its rituals. There are many, but one is unknown in the other 'Christian' countries which I know at first hand. It is the ritual of flag worship. . . . The ritual of the flag—the rabbinical rules about raising it and lowering it—is unknown in Britain, where most people neither know nor care. . . . This is only one instance among many of the public rituals of the American civic religion." Brogan turned with hope to the Catholic faith, "an older or, at any rate, a different religion, which denies the omnipotence of Caesar." Speaking of Catholic criticism of America's "just war" in Vietnam, he concluded: "If such dangerous thought spread, the civic religion may have to fight for the things that are Caesar's against more and more men and women concerned with the things that are God's—a God who may condemn the American nation as, so the Bible tells us, he has condemned other nations just as confident of his favor."[46]

The American experiment had been believed by many visitors or new settlers to be one that would produce what J. Hector St. John Crèvecoeur calls "the American, this new man . . . who acts upon new principles; [who] must therefore entertain new ideas and form new opinions."[47] Philip Schaff, who came to remain with a European perspective, typically thought that America represented a racial, ethnic, cultural, and religious "digestive power [which] is really astonishing." "America is the *grave of all European* nationalities; but a *Phenix grave,* from which they shall rise to new life and new activity." He added: "in a new and essentially Anglo-Germanic form." It was hard to leave provincialism behind! "America seems destined to be the Phenix grave . . . also of all European churches and sects, of Protestantism and Romanism. . . . Out of . . . mutual conflict of all something wholly new will gradually arise."[48] Such an expectation has been pervasive among the foreign observers who thought that assimilation would lead to human and religious transformation.

America is now rejoining the world, its mission more obscure and its moral pattern more uncertain than before, after events condensed in the code words *Vietnam* and *Watergate*. Experiment may have led to transformation but not to the perfection many had hoped for. The American experiment has turned out to be partly exportable, for along with its missionary technology there has gone some of the experience of its pluralism, while the example of its constitutionalism has shaped the style of constitutions elsewhere. No longer do experiments of these sorts occur only in what Belloc called "islands." Meanwhile both private or particular and civil or *Publick Religion* are now going through what Robert Bellah calls "a time of trial."[49] Whether the next stage of the experiment will accent the *plures* or the *unum* of civil-religious society, few who continue to visit America have believed that the experiments themselves will come to an end or that the environment, natural and human, will cease to be regarded as integral to religious development. If the consistent witness of visitors over more than two centuries is to be heeded, it is possible, with an eye on experiment in environment, to speak with confidence of more than "religion in America," and, indeed, to recognize despite sectarianism and pluralism the presence of "American religion."

8. The Perceptions of Visitors

This American religion is not disembodied, not an idea in intellectual history. It is embodied in individuals and groups. The American pluralist experience cannot be understood unless one grasps something of the "peoplehood" of the Republic. In part 3 we shall see how peoples have come to crowd each other on landscape and cityscape and yet to retain ethnoreligious identity. It will be important to see social forms they have devised, ghettos whose walls could not contain them. To get some sense of the "thickness" of pluralism, we shall then visit three sets of people who, according to keepers of the core culture, did not quite fit in it, but who recently are complicating pluralist existence. To make sense of them all, though, we begin by visiting them, by grasping something of their quasi-religious attachment to this place, this country, this landscape, this land.

THE PEOPLES' REPUBLIC

9   Land and City: Space and Conflict

"Tell me the landscape in which you live, and I will tell you who you are."[1]

"*Tierra! Tierra!* Land! Land! . . . you *have* found land!"

The reported cry of Rodrigo de Triana aboard the *Pinta* at 2:00 A.M. on October 12, 1492, and Christopher Columbus's words when sight of land was verified begin the American epic. They set the theme for much of what follows, just as the words "In the beginning God created the heaven and the earth" precast Genesis or "Midway upon the journey of our life I found myself in a dark wood" anticipates the rest of Dante's great work. For almost five hundred years the land itself has served as the unifying theme of the American epic, not least of all in its religious dimensions. If a person stammers when asked what is American about American religion, he or she can attempt a first word by pointing to the obvious and banal: the adjective *American* points to a place, a land, a landscape, an environment that shapes and then is shaped by the people in it. So pervasive, so constant has this theme been that it has often been overlooked.

Overlooked? The historian of American religion should not complain about any slighting of the concept of space or of place in a field that has already seen innumerable studies of nationalism, sectionalism, regionalism, and localism. The attention that the scholarly community has paid to one man's "frontier thesis" alone would fill a small library. But most of these studies of place have to do with episodes and not with the whole sweep. Frederick Jackson Turner's frontier thesis[2] is appropriate for one aspect of one era, the theme of democratization during the one century out of five characterized by the movement West across the continent. Sectionalism, meanwhile, has to do chiefly with issues related to the War between the States.

Were it not for the efforts of Edwin Scott Gaustad,[3] the geography of religion would be virtually neglected in recent America. Even less systematic notice has been paid to "the ecology of faith." While there have been many studies of religious conflict, few have explored primal conflicts over land and place themselves. Literary studies of the wilderness and the virgin land have rarely been matched in studies of religious history.[4] The neglect may well have come about because of American religionists' often noted obsession with time over space, or, more likely, because the word *land* itself seemed to become chiefly a metaphor after 1890 and the "closing of the frontier," the exhaustion of public lands. That date marks the symbolic turn for the transforming of landscape to cityscape, land dominance to urban dominance. Ever since, it is said, Americans are nothing but victims or celebrators of a rich and wild pluralism, a jumbled together people, being only rootless and mobile, unmindful of land and place.

A survey of the contemporary religious map, however, suggests that anything but this is the case. It is no less true in the later 1980s than it was in the 1930s, and no less surprising to many, that regionalism persists most notably in denominational life. Harlan Paul Douglass, a scholar sensitive to the environment of religion,[5] summarized it in 1934:

> Geographically considered, the outstanding fact about American denominations is that, for the most part, they are strongly regional. Many of them occupy territory which is almost mutually exclusive. All but some half-dozen are characterized by limited areas of extreme concentration of memberships. Time has thus identified their natural habitats in contrast with other areas of their occupancy where they are substantially "out of bounds." In any extensive area of the United States not more than six denominations would include a strong majority of the Protestant Chris-

tians of the area. . . . The most obvious principle of territorial distribution is sectional. In very large measure organized Christianity is divided into southern or northern or western churches, rather than national ones. Were there to be an inclusive church covering the whole nation, these sectional habitats of strong denominations might require recognition as geographical provinces within the whole.

A map from 1971[6] shows little change in this situation. There are five religious Americas, five regions of single-denominational dominances. Utah is overwhelmingly a Mormon kingdom; the entire South is a Southern Baptist empire; the upper Midwest and near Northwest is a Lutheran bastion; Methodists are relatively strongest in the mid-South belt all the way west to Kansas. Roman Catholics predominate in the Northeast, the Great Lakes area, and the West Coast.

Habits connect with habitats. Southern Baptists steadily and steadfastly refused in convention to change their name from "Southern." The Missouri Synod Lutheran leadership described its problems as having arisen because of the synod's postwar expansion too far from Missouri, to the "peripheries" of the nation. Indian religion is certainly "located" on reservations. Black religion belongs chiefly to rural South and urban North. Eastern Orthodoxy is pocketed in several cities. To say "Jew" is almost to say urban Northeast or even New York. Half the nation's Jews live in five counties of New York and eight of New Jersey and one-third live in New York City alone.[7] The western states of Alaska, Hawaii, the West Coast, Montana, and Colorado are especially regionalized concentrations of the unchurched, while California is both the symbolic and actual center of most of the "new religions," the Asian and occult and therapeutic flowerings of recent years. Moravians are Pennsylvanians and Dutch Reformed are Michiganders. Mennonites are in Pennsylvania or Indiana or Kansas and the Churches of Christ are southwestern plains outposts. Unitarians used to be in "the neighborhood of Boston" and are still highly localized and concentrated. Only the colonial "big three," the Episcopal, Presbyterian, and Congregational (United Church of Christ) are truly diffused without many special power bases. Most of the others have a place on the map of the American land and have difficulty understanding people from landscapes other than their own.

As with the map, so with the silhouette. It is hard to hide $100 billion worth of real property in a nation:[8]

> The spires of churches in Christian lands are only a single element linking evidently diverse landscapes whose molding forces have been technological and ecological rather than spiritual. But through such indices as the varying ratio of unit cult structures to population, the landscape may tell something about the relative intensity of religious expression at different times and in different places.

When the landscape turned into cityscape, the spires were dwarfed but they have not disappeared. Huge churches were subsequently squatted on suburban acreages, and storefront houses of God proliferate in the ghetto cityscape.

The land as a scene of conflict and the landscape as a scene have long histories, reaching back to de Triana's shout almost five hundred years ago. It is a story that divides quite neatly in two. Land was a dominating reality from 1492 until the 1730s and 1740s in the religious scheme. After that period, the concept of land as territory was supplemented by the idea of land as nation. "God bless our native land." Then it became proper to speak of a religious concern for the city and cityscape, first in the sense of the city as "the body of citizens, the community" and later, just as the dictionary does, of the city as related to the *urbs*, the physical town or place occupied by the community. Therefore, *city* first implied civility, discourse, interaction, pluralism, nation-building; after 1890 it designated the brute facts of the urban condition.

TEN STROPHES

Let me condense the plot of the American religious environmental story into ten strophes, a digest of a thousand pages as it were, to serve as background to the question *why* "place" plays such a great part in the religion of a people who are usually said to be preoccupied with time, not space.

Land and Landscape

The 1500s were given over to *finding the land* and *dividing the lands*. The first half century belonged to Catholic Spain, which clashed at once with the Indians who had different concepts of land use than did the Spaniards. The second half saw France and England beginning to explore with an eye to the settlement of the land, neither of them accepting the papal division of the New World into Spanish and Portuguese domains.

The 1600s knew both the *settling of the land* and then almost at once the *unsettling of the land* after Spain was joined in the first half century by English Episcopalians, Separatists, Puritans, and Catholics and Dutch Protestants, each of whom wanted an exclusive place. New England was then unsettled by dissenters whom the established Protestants had to banish from their lands; Quakers arrived with a disturbing nonexclusivist policy; New Spain and New France threatened to link up in the West and cut off the English colonies; New Englanders spoke of declension in the face of dissent and religious variety brought on by experimenters and merchants alike.

The 1700s saw a dual revolution, the first half century's being specifically and narrowly religious. It spelled the beginning of the end of religious territorialism in the legal sense in America. The Great Awakening sent people *itinerating in the land,* upsetting the settled clergy and church monopolies, intruding, invading, vagabonding, being vagrant—all the terms were used—as they set out to convert people and make religion voluntary.

City and Cityscape

The second half of the century found religious America involved in *building the nation* (as "our land" came to mean "our nation") through independence, revolution, and religious freedom, all of them assaults on the vestiges of territorialism. The new "City" (*civitas*) was being founded.

The 1800s did not by any means see the end of the land theme; *occupying the land* dominated the religious plot in frontier days, the era of curcuit-riding, Mormon treks, evangelization, and mass immigration—all of which stimulated a competition and indeed even a race to church vast America and denominationally to stamp its way of life. But by the century's end the great new fact was the cityification of the landscape (*urbs*) as religion was being trans-

201

formed by the urban-industrial America it sought to address. Jews and Catholics "Americanized," blacks were segregated, Indians "removed."

The 1900s found the "nation of nations" *rejoining the nations.* Some citizens resisted modernizing influences deriving from Europe but none escaped the meaning of involvements in two world wars, or failed to confront the many models for transforming the world. But in recent decades the blur of pluralism and lost identity had become so much the plot of religious life that being *lost in one's own land* was the obsessive theme. Some sought recovery through the dream of a Christian America, through tri-faith identifications with "the American Way of Life." Blacks still looked for the promised city and Indians tried to recover sacred lands. New religions flowered, some of them attempts to see "a new heaven and new earth" in the American setting.

Throughout, what united the majority of the pious was something we stressed before and cannot accent too often: they "*have regarded their environment as being itself somehow redemptive and revelatory.*"[9] The divine forces, the power of the sacred, God himself or itself, were perceived as speaking through the strata and soil, the history and the people. Citizens had to cope with and transform wilderness and frontier, make use of natural and popular resources, and make sense of their common life in such a setting. That they were spatialists as well as temporalists becomes increasingly clear against this giant map or canvas. Competing visions led to constant conflict; this is the central vivifying theme in the story of America's ever-changing cast of religious "winners" and "losers."

That American religious groups were and are in conflict over land and city space is clear from the documents. *Why* they were is a more difficult issue, given the fact that so many of them were committed to religious and civil creeds that encourage cooperation, interaction, and the enjoyment of pluralism. To be content with the "what" without addressing the "why" does a disservice to the story. British historian E. H. Carr properly points out:

> No document can tell us more than what the author of the document thought—what he thought had happened, what he thought ought to happen or would happen, or perhaps only what he

wanted others to think he thought, or even only what he himself thought he thought.[10]

For this reason, as Robert F. Berkhofer, Jr., urges, the historian "is forced to fall back upon implicit or explicit hypotheses in order to discover the actual behavior" of the people he or she studies,[11] especially when dealing with the motivations, intentions, and the "supposed internal states" that presumably produced them. The debates over "consensus" and "conflict" in American history do not appear to be of much help at this point except insofar as the defense of space relates to the property, the point at which class-conscious Marxist historians come into action.[12]

Human motivation in a story on this grand scale is far too complex to be reduced to a single theory or explanation. The Marxist resort to a conflict theory does not do justice to the manifest fact that, after the first permanent settlement in North America in 1565, there have been very few dead bodies as a result of religious warfare; nor does it do much to account for the many kinds of consensus and cooperation developing between religious groups that occupied competing territories, regions, or city spaces. The cynic can say that denominations themselves were an ingenious, if unconscious, American invention designed to drain off conflict into harmless channels. This approach also leaves room for the suggestion that religion matters chiefly as an epiphenomenon, something tagged on to real history as in the case of the nation's real fratricides like the Civil War. It does not do justice to the depth of commitment people express for their religious groups, commitment which elsewhere—in India, Lebanon, the Arab-Israeli Middle East, Northern Ireland, and the like—lead to millions of recent deaths in what Harold R. Isaacs calls "tribal/racial/ethnic/religious/national" group conflicts.[13] In America processes developed that permitted people to remain deeply involved with particular religions without deserting universalistic ideals or shared life across religious boundaries.

The story of land and place in American religion suggests a variety of hypotheses or theories of human behavior, approaches that vary greatly in the degree of human volition for change that each allows. Some have to do with instinct and nature; others with culture and nurture. I have gathered numbers of these into four categories, the existential, the evolutionary, the psychosocial, and the religious accountings of behavior.

FOUR CATEGORIES OF HUMAN BEHAVIOR

The Existential

The *existential* understanding refers here not to a formal philosophy of existentialism but to something much more matter-of-fact: the experiental, evidential history with which most historians deal when they simply tell the story of human behavior, particularly in moments of crisis or at turning points in a people's life. In the present story, such turns came with "the discovery," "the settling and colonizing," "the revolution and nation-building," "the occupation," "urbanization," and the like. At such moments the historian at least begins with some trust in the documents as these reveal patent human actions. At least three dimensions are present in this existential mode as they relate religion to the American land: the practical, those having to do with mission, and the esthetic.

The Practical. Practically, religious groups claimed, settled, fought for, and enjoyed the land out of simple necessity. Their members had to eat. Spanish Catholics claimed the land for the gold that might be under it as well as the faith they might spread on it. Protestant colonizers and refugees stayed to plant and banished outsiders, out of a mixture of motives that included conversion of the natives but gave due attention to the need to draw upon the soil to keep body and soul together. Hutterites in South Dakota kept others at a distance to preserve their group values but they also farmed industriously in order to survive and prosper. This reality is so obvious that it needs no theory, and is basic in all American group life. In the history of American religion it becomes interesting only when the practical use of the environment is given a religious rationale, as it almost always has been.

Mission. So far as mission is concerned, while the historian may want to examine motivation and the gap between peoples' declared intentions and actual expressions, there is no question but that sincere believers regularly staked out a place on the land because they believed that God sent them there to subdue it, to convert natives and each other and their children and strangers in their midst. They ordinarily believed that they could fulfill this destiny most efficiently if they had a solid regional or territorial base for mission, a context in which they could nurture their values without being subject to predators carrying other values, and a distance between them and such invaders or threats. Enough of them made great sacrifices to carry on this mission and so manifestly lived in congruence with their own stated intentions that there are few reasons to be suspicious of them. They loved the land because it was a good place for their errands and manifest destinies.

The Esthetic. The third existential and evident realm is the *esthetic*. The religious colonists believed that the place they found and occupied was beautiful, and that God had given that beauty for their enjoyment. Any accounting of American religion that does not do justice to the love of landscape and cityscape as gifts of divine favor overlooks one of the most important facts of life. Some literary and theological critics point to the grim purposefulness in much of American spiritual life, the love of mere production and the absence of romantic environmentalism or nature-mysticism. But there are many ways to enjoy an environment, whether natural or humanly made, other than through romanticism or mysticism. The early colonizers, eager to promote the new shores in order to attract others, lavishly described the beauty of coast and mountain and forest. Small-town churchgoers relished the order and symmetry of their sanctuaries. Folk expressions address this well; in the unlikeliest and apparently least attractive landscapes one hears throughout history the strenuous and sometimes awesome boast that this is or that area is "God's country!" True, there were terror of the forbidding wilderness and lonesomeness on the unvarying plains. But pioneers on the old landscape and lovers of parish neighborhoods in the new cityscape more often than not matched the enthusiasm Elder Wolford Woodruff attributed to Mormon leader Brigham Young when he pronounced in Utah that "This is the right place." Also more often than not they spoke of their "right place" the way Elder Orson Pratt did when he first glimpsed the

Great Salt Lake as it "glistened in the sunbeams" of the Salt Lake Valley skies:

> We could not refrain from a shout of joy, which almost involuntarily escaped from our lips the moment this grand and lovely scenery was within our view.[14]

A scale that runs from the instinctive to the volitional, from the difficult to change to the easy to change is apparent in these various approaches. Thus, one can do little to change people's commitment to a divine mandate for land insofar as their sustenance depends upon it. Until the gold or the soil give out or become inferior to the promise of other available places, whether these be on frontiers or in suburbs, they are likely to be intransigent in their understanding of the divine claim they have on a place. Mission, however, is a much more malleable and alterable concept and can be changed constantly. Almost all the Europeans who came to the thirteen colonies professedly did so in order to convert the natives, but they soon replaced this idea not with *no* mission but with *other* missions. America, we noted, has always been so rich in promise and problems that it regularly elicited "Plan B" where "Plan A" gave out for religious groups, and these groups have been richly experimental. The esthetic has been the most malleable and alterable of all spheres. Humans can create new environments and find them attractive to the eye. Remarkably, many retiring Iowa farmers can leave behind the simple beauty of a white country chapel and find something pleasing in a jerry-built suburban church on the asphalted parking lot landscape of southern California, or can enjoy the leveling of meadows for housing developments that offer new environments for their formerly urban churches.

Historical accountings of American religion will normally focus chiefly on these obvious explanations of why citizens have enjoyed and defended a place on the landscape or the cityscape for the working out of their purposes. But other accountings have also been given, and some of them at least will help suggest why religious groups behaved as they did.

The Evolutionary

The second field of theories about the understanding of place and the use of land and landscape, city and cityscape in American religion can be called *evolutionary* and includes the most instinctual or deterministic of all popular hypotheses about behavior. I refer to what is usually called "territorialism" and, with it, "instinctive aggression." The historian who observes Spanish Catholics killing French Huguenots at the first settlements in Florida in 1565 is tempted to begin looking for a simply predatory version of history. And if such a transplantation of European religious warfare to America was unprofitable and almost instantly abandoned, territorialism seemed to live on. On these grounds the New Englanders banished Anne Hutchinson and Roger Williams from the land. They were not allowed to share territory with the homogeneous and protective Puritans who dominated that place. Territorial instincts could be discerned in the impulse of nineteenth-century communal leaders to remove themselves physically from contact with others, in Mennonite and Amish practices of "shunning" waverers in their midst, in settled ministers' rejection of itinerants and invaders on their spiritual turf, and in the scramble of post–World War II church extension experts for suburban space and their rejection of comity plans for cooperative churching.

The ideological territorialist immediately reaches for the most extravagant explanation of such behavior, employing theories that date back only to the work of English ornithologist H. E. Howard in 1920. Edward T. Hall defines the approach:

> Territoriality, a basic concept in the study of animal behavior, is usually defined as behavior by which an organism characteristically lays claim to an area and defends it against members of its own species.

Territoriality serves also to imprison a species even as it insures the propagation of a species by regulating density. It contributes to understanding personal and social functions and is associated with status. Hall wrote:

> Man, too, has territoriality and he has invented many ways of defending what he considers his own land, turf, or spread. The removal of boundary markers and trespass upon the property of another man are punishable acts in much of the Western world.[15]

The territorialist accounting is highly deterministic. Its great popularizer, Robert Ardrey, says that "the territorial nature of man is genetic and ineradicable." He writes:

The territorial imperative is as blind as a cave fish, as consuming as a furnace, and it commands beyond logic, opposes all reason, suborns all moralities, strives for no goal more sublime than survival.[16]

His peer, Desmond Morris, says that

unhappily, where matters as basic as territorial defence are concerned, our higher brain centres are all too susceptible to the urgings of our lower ones. Intellectual control can help us just so far, but no farther. In the last resort, it is unreliable, and a single, unreasoned, emotional act can undo all the good it has achieved.[17]

Such a view may seem to help account for Salem's witch-burnings, but does little to describe the benefits of the Declaration of Independence or the First Amendment to the United States Constitution, the religious humanitarian ventures that have characterized American history, and some forms of ecumenical endeavor.

To the territorialists, religion is always epiphenomenal and ideological, the sanctifier of killer instincts in the name of God. The white slaveholder or segregationist, for example, rather consistently found biblical justification for his endeavor to keep black members of the same species and even of the same faith at a social and physical distance. What really matters, say some ethologists, is what has been inherited from a particularly violent or, as Konrad Lorenz would have it, aggressive prehuman species.[18] Everything depends upon biology, inheritance, instinct, and evolution. Against such forces, advocates of civil religion, creative pluralism, interfaith understanding, and ecumenists are doomed from the first. In that case an all-purpose a priori account of *Why Conservative Churches are Growing* is available before inquiry begins.[19]

The territorialists have a ready explanation for the rejection of Catholic or Jewish or black in-migrants to new territories throughout American history. They in effect also say that not much can be done to change the pattern. John Rowan Wilson, an English physicist who favorably reviewed Ardrey's *Territorial Imperative*, summarized this case:

If Ardrey is right, the assimilation of immigrants, particularly those of a noticeably different culture and physical appearance, is a more fundamental problem than we have previously believed. Racial prejudice may not simply be a matter of ignorance, which a more progressive policy will eliminate in time. Distrust of the foreigner may be an inevitable accompaniment of the group cohesion which holds our own society together. Perhaps we should stop aiming at the impossible task of trying to love and understand our neighbours. It might well be better if we kept ourselves to ourselves, barking across our fences now and then, and baring our fangs in ritualized aggression, but never going so far as to engage in open conflict.[20]

That last sentence may summarize the bloodless but still violent history of older American denominationalism, but it is questionable whether the territorial hypothesis is necessary to explain that history. On purely empirical historical grounds, the theory can be dismissed: too many events and processes deny simple territorial imperatives and aggression. The whole controversial proposal is being examined and refuted by numerous schools of inquiry. Anthropologist Clifford Geertz[21] summarizes much of the case against the "animal behavior" school of human conduct:

Recent research in anthropology suggests that the prevailing view that the mental dispositions of man are genetically prior to culture and that his actual capabilities represent the amplification or extension of these preexistent dispositions by cultural means is incorrect. The apparent fact that the final stages of the biological evolution of man occurred after the initial stages of the growth of culture implies that "basic," "pure," or "unconditioned" human nature, in the sense of the innate constitution of man, is so functionally incomplete as to be unworkable. Tools, hunting, family organization, and, later, art, religion, and "science" molded man somatically; and they are, therefore, necessary not merely to his survival but to his existential realization. It is true that without men there would be no cultural forms; but it is also true that without cultural forms there would be no men.

The most that can be said for territorialism in discussing American religion on the land and in the cityscape is that it prepares one emotionally for the most violent features of the history; but it remains utterly inadequate to account for the many levels of concord and consensus that have regularly appeared.

Cultural Evolution

A more moderate, more malleable, less deterministic reading of evolution in the American religious story is the cluster of theories that can be associated with the concept of "cultural evolution," an idea which for a long period was regarded by many American anthropologists as "the most inane, sterile, and pernicious theory in the whole theory of science." Such an endorsement is hardly encouraging to the historian, whose training is likely to lead him to side against "laws of history" and for history as William James[22] describes it in his attack on

> the evolutionary view of history, [which] when it denies the vital importance of individual initiative, is, then, an utterly vague and unscientific conception, a lapse from modern scientific determinism into the most ancient oriental fatalism. [It is] a metaphysical creed, and nothing else . . . the mood of fatalistic pantheism.

Despite the wariness, historians' researches do show great regularity in a pattern of dominance in cultural-religious groups in American history, beginning with the displacement of the native American Indian, and the suppression of the blacks, continuing through the Catholic and Jewish immigrants who were coming to dominance in the city, and living on in the triumphalist expansionism of contemporary evangelicals who masterfully meet people's desires for authority and the thrill of immediate religious experience.

Both the evolutionary readings strike most historians as being too deterministic, too mechanical, too patterned. But the second or cultural evolutionist version allows for much more freedom than does the instinctual or territorially aggressive one. Translated to simplest language all this means in part that the religious system that can best create a sense of or discern specific human needs in a given environment and then address these will have satisfied customers or clients—and thus fulfill the law of life in competitive American denominationalism.[23]

Theologian Paul Tillich described the absence of creative contact between the cultures in the language of cultural evolutionists. There can be little cross-fertilization of cultures, said Tillich "in the case where the strangeness of the foreign effects its repulsion; and . . . where the weakness of the foreign effects its eradication."

The latter is the case whenever a highly developed group conquers a group which has no cultural development or strength. The greatest example of this is the European immigration into this country and the complete lack of cross-fertilization with the American Indians, at least in North America.[24]

And David Kaplan says:

> From the standpoint of Euroamerican culture, the Indians' exploitation of the continent's rich resources was deemed to be highly inefficient and there was no question but that they had to go. Consequently, the Indian societies were exterminated or driven off and the remainder gathered together and placed on reservations.[25]

The white dominant culture subsequently spread so fast that it is reaching "to just about every ecological nook and cranny of the planet." This language of Tillich and Kaplan is not sentimental or searching. An environmentalist would question the statements about Indian "inefficiency," but that is not the issue here. We are presently accounting for the dominance by more complex and more "efficient" groups, forces that come with stronger weapons and religious ideologies to motivate their conquest.

The earliest English colonizers reproduced Spanish and French patterns and set the terms for whatever followed. The Reverend Robert Gray blessed the Virginia colony in 1609, facing "the first objection," which was

> by what right or warrant we can enter into the land of these Savages, take away their rightful inheritance from them, and plant ourselves in their places, being unwronged or unprovoked by them.

He used the Old Testament concept of God sending his children into an already occupied but misunderstood land of promise. As long before as 1583 Sir George Peckham in *True Reporte of the Late Discoveries* referred to a "Law of Nations" by which the English needed only small concessions to plant on the lightly settled, limitless land whose resources the unresourceful Indian did not know how to develop. How could whites let God's riches go to waste as they now were? And, Peckham reasoned, if English Protestant whites would not take over, Catholic Spain or France would, and then the Indians would know more cruelty and worse religion. "If after these good and fayre means used," the Indians respond "barbarously," "I holde it no breach of equitie for the Christians to . . . resist violence with violence." The decision not to abandon the Indian converts to a "return to their horrible idolatrie" was a Christian move.[26] The threat of weapons aside, the language differs not much from that used by post–World War II Southern Baptist Convention legitimators of their plantation of northern churches, or fundamentalist and evangelical announcements that they will invade the turf where mainline and ecumenical churches inefficiently address the spiritual needs of an otherwise lost America.

The Psychosocial

The third cluster, which we may call the *psychosocial,* would include the whole bewildering range of approaches associated with psychological and social sciences, from which we shall have to select only three or four overlapping ones. Together they help suggest why American religious groups have behaved as they did in reference to land and city, scape and space. The first of these approaches is akin to the territorial instinct, though it allows for some cultural shaping and does not rely simply on biological inheritance. I refer to a loosely defined school of thought that propounder Edward T. Hall calls "proxemics,"—"the interrelated observations and theories of man's use of space as a specialized elaboration of culture." In this view, *"man and his environment participate in molding each other,"* as they manifestly have done in American religion. The wilderness and unbroken plains greeted colonists in what they endowed with meaning as a "land of promise," and they were given a charter in Genesis to "have dominion over the earth and subdue it." The heirs of the colonizer also created a surrounding culture, one of whose basic components has always been religion. "Man is now in the position of actually creating the total world in which he lives." "In creating this world he is actually determining *what kind of an organism* he will be," is Hall's apotheosis of the process that I have described as the transformation of landscape into cityscape, the creation of a new environment in which spatial uses, proximities, and distances between individual groups change but do not disappear as a field of observation and inquiry.

The persistent communal impulse in religion is summarized in Hall's obvious observation: "Social animals need to stay in touch with each other." These "social animals" used to have to do this by occupying space near each other and far from predators or invaders. But in the cityscape, "social distance in man has been extended by telephone, TV, and the walkie-talkie," and religion on the consumers' market can become a mail-order, televised affair that builds a kind of *ad hoc* community through what William Stephenson calls "convergent selectivity." On these terms the subscribers or dial-twisters who follow a particular yogi or evangelist when they do come together, distance themselves from those who follow other gurus or heroes. In another illustration, parish boundaries mean little in the cityscape, but groups like the Jehovah's Witnesses practically create and enjoy a social distance from other groups no less effective than that which is insisted upon by Doukhobors in the remote parts of the Canadian landscape. "Social distance" often replaces physical distance in the religion cityscape but it is most effective for providing a "place" or base for predation or proselytizing. The Jehovah's Witnesses attack "up close" in one's "castle" or living room. Such tight groups are held together by shared perceptions and language; witness the bonding effect of glossolalia, which demarcates Pentecostal groups in an urban and pluralist or ecumenical environment. Hall quotes Antoine de St. Exupéry on this function of language:

> What is distance? I know that nothing which truly concerns man is calculable, weighable, measurable. True distance is not the concern of the eye; it is granted only to the spirit. Its value is the value of language, for it is language which binds things together.[27]

Significantly, this is the poetry of a man in the airplane, in the age of radio, television, and electronic leaping of physical distance. Much of the modern psychosocial theory about social distance arose precisely in the crowded, urban world where such a theory became necessary. When the landscape itself provided the protection of distance for religious groups, they did not have to concern themselves so strenuously with the language of bonding and community. Their members would not regularly confront alien languages. The arrival of the itinerating evangelist with his unsettling language about settled ministers was a revolutionary moment in American religion. This is one reason why the Awakening of the 1730s and 1740s was "Great" in its effects. As Erving Goffman has put it, "A region may be defined as any place that is bounded to some degree by barriers to perception." New England Congregationalism, Pennsylvania Moravianism, Maryland Catholicism, Carolina Anglicanism enjoyed perceptual boundaries created by physical distance on the landscape. The circuit-rider or evangelizer who rode into town from a distance enlarged and threatened the boundaries, creating a new situation. The crowding of the pluralist city environment forced even more pressure on groups to retain strength by creating boundaries of language and perception. The "proxemics" people make much of the physical and psychic distance humans as individuals do create and must create for themselves. By associating different distances between different ethnic, cultural, and religious groups—as Hall does in discussions of the German, English, French, Japanese, and Arab senses of crowding and social behavior—he shows how far from mere instinct and thus how malleable and open to experiment and change this approach is.[28] But proxemics, or whatever one chooses to call this study, is not the only available approach to studying many religious groups' frequent and consistent choice of physical and social distance from others.

A second address to the urban and technological cityscape is the set of psychological theories typified by the work of Robert Jay Lifton and other discerners of "boundaries." Lifton's short essays in *Boundaries: Psychological Man in Revolution* seem at first glance to deal not with social groups but with individuals—but the implications for group life, including religious group life, are immediately apparent. Lifton, as already noted, describes people who experienced a threat to necessary boundaries or liberation from inhibiting boundaries. He accounts for the emergence of fluid "Protean man," on two grounds. Both have much to do with change in American religion in the move from landscape to cityscape:

> The first of these is the world-wide sense of what I call *historical*, or *psychohistorical* dislocation, the break in the sense of connection men have long felt with vital and nourishing symbols of their cultural traditions—symbols revolving around family, idea systems, religions, and the life cycle in general. . . .
>
> The second large historical tendency is the *flooding of imagery* produced by the extraordinary flow of post-modern cultural influences over mass communication networks. . . . The images [the mass media] convey cross over all boundaries, local and national,

and permit each individual everywhere to be touched by everything, but at the same time often cause him to be overwhelmed.

Such persons are in a vastly different circumstance than the Swedish Lutheran in isolated nineteenth-century rural Minnesota settings, or the rural black Baptist in Mississippi just before World War II. Boundaries are now disappearing. But, says Lifton, this change causes some to develop "the opposite of the Protean style," a

> closing off of identity, the constriction of self-process, . . . a straight-and-narrow specialization in psychological as well as in intellectual life, and a reluctance to let in any extraneous influence.[29]

Such a constrictive process was socially assured by ecclesiastical territorialism in the colonial days of established churches or regionalism in the national period; but it has to be worked at in the time of metropolitanism and mass media. This basic change accounts for some of the understandings of space and place, or boundary-settings and wall-buildings by the Unification church or the Children of God, the more militantly closed-off fundamentalist groups. Persons may or may not be genetically programmed to be "open" or "closed" types and to have the problems associated with either psychological style. In any case, one can create differing environmental circumstances so that the protean types can reacquire some psychic boundaries. This process is visible in at least mild recent retreats from ecumenical back to denominational models, from integrative to tribal and ethnic patterns in exposed sectors of American religious life, and in the occasional crossing or lowering of boundaries among once rigid groups.

The classic statement about groups that corresponds in many respects to the psychological studies of boundaries is the sociology of Georg Simmel, whose studies of group conflict can illumine American religious history. Parallels to Simmel's understanding appear in many sociologies of religious belonging. Simmel was always sensitive to environment and scape in his studies of perception and bonding. He could thus speak of

> one's always living in the same landscape and thus never suspecting the problem of influence by scenery—a problem which im-

presses us, however, as soon as we change our surroundings, and a different life-feeling calls our attention to the causative role of the scenic milieu generally.[30]

Those lines point to the subtle but still dramatic role of environment in American religion. But Simmel was more interested in conflict between groups that share a landscape or intrude upon each other whenever strangers, migrants, or invaders arrive, and when people must fend off such intrusions, as American religionists have characteristically done.

Simmel and similar social thinkers elevated the concept of conflict to positive status. Thus, Charles H. Cooley:

> Conflict, of some sort, is the life of society, and progress emerges from a struggle in which individual, class, or institution seeks to realize its own idea of good.

Max Weber thought that "conflict cannot be excluded from social life."

> "Peace" is nothing more than a change in the form of conflict or in the antagonists or in the objects of the conflict, or finally in the chances of selection.

Kurt Lewin:

> On whatever unit of group life we focus, whether we think of nations and international politics; of economic life, . . . of race and religious groups, of the factory and the relations between top management and the worker, . . . we find a complicated network of . . . conflicting interests.

Simmel himself saw conflict as a "form of socialization." In his writing on *Conflict*, Simmel pointed to the "group-binding functions of conflict."

> A certain amount of discord, inner divergence, and outer controversy, is organically tied up with the very elements that ultimately hold the group together.

Antagonism has a "positive and integrating role." Conflict establishes identities and boundary lines of societies and groups. Not all conflict is focused on a necessary subject, but it is necessarily focused on a subject. Lewis Coser, an interpreter of Simmel, quotes

Else Frenkel-Brunswick on the "ethnocentric personality" that shows up so often in our American religious history: "Even his hate is mobile and can be directed from one object to another."

The American Protestants who vehemently hated the French in 1758, lauded them in 1776, and hated them again in the revolutionary "infidelity" of 1794, may have been moved in part by practical interests; but they also found it important to overstress first the Catholicism and then the "infidelity" or atheism of France during the hate periods, in order to help define their own Protestant republicanism.

Much American anti-Semitism, as Coser points out, is of this character in various periods of history. Simmel even goes so far as to say that hate is not always natural. "It is *expedient* to hate the adversary with whom one fights, just as it is expedient to love a person whom one is tied to." Such expediency was frequently expressed in interreligious conflict in America.

In order to understand hostility in primary groups, one must go a step further, with Bronislaw Malinowski:

> Aggression like charity begins at home. . . . Indeed the smaller the group engaged in cooperation, united by some common interests, and living day by day with one another, the easier it is for them to be mutually irritated and to flare up in anger.

The denominations of small size that share confining space experience the most traumatic internecine warfare. Civil conflict in Catholicism is less bruising than in the Black Muslims in the ghetto or in a back-country peace church.

The heretic, deserter, or renegade is the most hated person of all. Anne Hutchinson and Roger Williams were more despised in New England than was the religiously slothful dweller who never knew the experience of covenantal living. The renegade cannot go back, and so is most intensely loyal to his new group, a fact that makes him more dangerous to the old group. He will be tempted, as Max Scheler suggests, to "engage in a continuous chain of acts of revenge on his spiritual past," a tendency that is another common theme in a nation where denominational switching is easy. At the same time, conflict with an out-group increases internal cohesion, observes Coser. Says Simmel,

A state of conflict . . . pulls the members so tightly together and subjects them to such uniform impulse that they either must get completely along with, or completely repel, one another.

To illustrate this theme: as modern evangelicals find mainline ecumenical organizations to be increasingly less vulnerable targets, they have also begun to see their own cohesion disappear, and they experience the luxury or necessity of some fragmentation. Protestants found one style of ecumenical activity easier when they were in conflict with Catholicism than after they affirmed Catholicism. The retreat from ecumenism on the part of groups (more than individuals), and the ensuing problems for the ecumenical movement as opposed to the ecumenical spirit, has something to do with the question of bonding, cohesiveness, and boundary-setting. Thus Simmel:[31]

Groups, and especially minorities, which live in conflict and persecution, often reject approaches or tolerance from the other side. The closed nature of their opposition without which they cannot fight on would be blurred. . . . A group's victory over its enemies is thus not always fortunate. . . . Victory lowers the energy which guarantees the unity of the group; and the dissolving forces, which are always at work, gain hold. . . . Within certain groups, it may even be a piece of political wisdom to see to it that there be some enemies in order for the unity of the members to remain effective and for the group to remain conscious of this unity as its vital interest.

American Christians persistently exaggerated the role of the infidel in order to stimulate their own group cohesion, creating enemies to faith where there were few. Jews were often accused of exaggerating the scope of Christian anti-Semitism in America to stimulate group bonding. But for all this, the concept of conflict as an element in religious cohesion is not as confining as are theories of territoriality and proxemics, since it has to do with learned behavior and is open to much fluidity and change.[32]

We may also borrow a term from Ashley Montagu and speak of "the philosophies of real estate," a catch-all term for all the ways groups associate their life with territory without resort to explanation based on instincts biologically transmitted from a prehuman hunting ancestor. These include the linkage of religion with patriotism, ownership, and property. Montagu comments on one of these as an illustration, the one most patently connected with the "publick religion" that Benjamin Franklin sought, down through the "common faith" of John Dewey to the civil religious rites of the Knights of Columbus:

> The human emotional attachment which human beings develop for their "homeland" is customarily reinforced by the institution-alization of private and public allegiances to the "land of one's birth, loyalty to the community, and the equivalents of such mod-ern institutional devices as flag-waving, pledges of allegiance to the flag, "my country, right or wrong," and all the other shibbol-eths of patriotism. "Fatherlands," "Motherlands," or "Home-lands" become emotional involvements endowed with all the complexity and beliefs that the tribalist zealously brings to the support of such emotions. All such sentiments are identified with a particular territory . . . the attachment to the homeland will remain something woven into the fabric of one's being all the days of one's life. The weaving is done out of the elements of the individual's experience; it is culturally conditioned by the train-ing received from all those social, political, religious, secular and educational sources that work upon the members of the tribe. These are all cultural forces and have nothing whatever to do with biological imperatives. [33]

Peter H. Klopfer, in a work on "A Study of the Use of Space by Animals," concludes with a chapter on "extrapolations to man." He makes the point that whatever the origins of defense of property in human beings are, it is not very likely that they would relate to primordial and unalterable habits that resulted from inherited ani-mal traits.

> As for territoriality, it probably represents not a single adaptation by a host of different adaptations serving different purposes for various animals. This fact alone precludes a facile extrapolation to man and a biological justification of property rights. [34]

The philosophy of real estate was strong in all the nine colonies where religion was established by law and citizens were taxed in support of its holdings; in the land-holdings of later communal and rural sect groups; in the Mormon "quest for empire" or kingdom; in the desire of suburban churches to possess land for vistas around their buildings. The early Americans who fenced off property that Indians had left open were sanctioned in this practice by their religious groups; their heirs became subjects of Marxist scorn. Thus, Georgy Valentinovich Plekhanov,[35] in *The Development of the Monist View of History:*

> The founder of civil society, and consequently the grave-digger of primitive equality, was the man who first fenced off a piece of land and said, "It belongs to me." In other words, the foundation of civil society is property, which arouses so many disputes among men, evokes in them so much greed, so spoils their morality.

The religious defense of private property, especially in the form of land, did not inspire aggressive behavior so much as it did aversive behavior. Wallace Craig noted that "Even when an animal does fight he aims not to destroy the enemy but only to get rid of his presence and interference." Often in such encounters there has been more noise than bloodshed. Montagu quotes John H. Crook:[36]

> Much of the aggression in territorial defense consists of threatening display or ritualized fighting whereby spacing is achieved with little damage done to the protagonists.

White or black Protestants, Catholics, or Jews made much noise and put on ritual displays of antagonism, but there was never much they could do by way of aggression to keep each other away. They could best accomplish their purposes through aversive expressions.

A modern illustration of religious groups' "philosophy of real estate" was the failure of the comity movement. H. Paul Douglass and his colleagues gave much attention to the endeavor to space new churches scientifically and judiciously. For new urban and suburban moves this policy was advocated by the least aggressive and aversive Protestant groups. Thus, Harry Emerson Fosdick's liberal Park Avenue Baptist Church in New York was lauded by Douglass for reestablishing itself only after "it first made a careful survey of the city to find a strategic site, where it would not directly compete with any other organized church."[37] But more rigorous denominationalists and fundamentalists repudiated and destroyed the relatively noncompetitive system, even as they customarily rejected offers of free space in multipurpose buildings by builders of high-rise high-density apartments, preferring "a plot of ground of our own" at the edge of the development. Machiavelli contended that avarice for property exceeded all other loves and aspirations in man.[38] Combine the love of homeland in patriotism, the desire to fence property for religious purposes, and the impulse for religious institutions to have a place apart, and a whole additional set of understandings of the impulse for land and conflict appears.

The Religious

Finally, there are important specifically religious understandings of why Americans have so relished the landscape and so frequently been in conflict over the land and their place in it. One of these understandings carries with it a measure of irresistibility, a defense of space and place, and fate. The "history of religion" schools like to stress how strong is the drive to locate the sacred in relation to the soil and special places. In his study of *The Idols of the Tribe* Harold Isaacs summarizes the case:

> The physical characteristics that bear on group identity extend in critical ways to the place, the land, the soil to which the group is attached, literally, historically, mythically. We are not as far as we may think we are from the myths to which, as Mircea Eliade has shown, we keep eternally returning, and these myths have heavily to do with the places with which we identify ourselves.

Isaacs cites Octavio Paz who sees in human solitude a "nostalgic longing for the body from which we were cast out, but also for the place from which the body came or to which in death it will return," a center of the world, a navel of the universe, a Rome, Jerusalem, or Mecca. Because Americans other than Indians did not begin with a mythic past, it has been more difficult for them than for other peoples to have such a natural sense of identification. Their use of the Hebrew Scriptures to identify America as the "promised land" was largely metaphorical, connected to future time more than past myth, and thus it was unlike Zionists' desire to develop "the physical link with the land" of Israel, as Martin Buber put it.[39]

Vine Deloria, Jr., speaks out of the communities of native Americans in a discussion of "Thinking in Time and Space." He argues that the American Indians "hold their lands—places—as having the highest possible meaning," while the European immigrants overvalued time. This is the kind of overdrawn distinction that can

221

confuse as well as guide—much like the distinctions between "Hebrew thought compared with Greek" or "the prophetic versus the priestly," and the like. Deloria points to an important distinction, but the Europeans did not fail to think in terms of space. Anything but that; the clash came because they thought and think of space in different ways than did Indians. What he says about the Indian outlook merits hearing, however. In spatial contexts,

> a revelation is not so much the period of time in which it occurs as the place it may occur. Revelation becomes a particular experience at a particular place, no universal truth emerging but an awareness arising that certain places have a qualitative holiness over and above other places.

Europeans in America, Deloria argued, seldom endowed a site or saw one endowed with such a special holiness. Few in America identified their revelation with a place, as the Mormons did with Hill Cumorah in New York. There have even been a few approved shrines marking visitations by the Virgin Mary north of Guadalupe. But there are certainly concepts of "this hallowed ground," of places sanctioned by special associations and regarded as sources of solace, solitude, or strength. Deloria sees the later impulse toward recovery of Indian attitudes and the acceptance of Eastern religion as drives toward developing a new world view to replace the compulsive, preachy, time-oriented messianisms of European faith.[40]

Mircea Eliade makes much of "Sacred Space and Making the World Sacred" in the field of the history of religion. "There is . . . a sacred space, and hence a strong, significant space." There are remembrances of American colonization of a wilderness in his description of how

> an unknown, foreign, and unoccupied territory (which often means, "unoccupied by our people") still shares in the fluid and larval modality of chaos. By occupying it and, above all, by settling in it, man symbolically transforms it into a cosmos through a ritual repetition of the cosmogony.

"Our world" must thus be "created," the creation of the universe by the god being the paradigm. Hence, the naming of the new land in the light of biblical references. "The Spanish and Portuguese conquistadores, discovering and conquering territories, took possession of them in the name of Jesus Christ. The raising of the Cross was equivalent to consecrating the country, hence in some sort to a 'new birth.'" Their northern Protestant successors were less ready to use vivid symbolism, but their acts were similar. "To settle in a territory is, in the last analysis, equivalent to consecrating it."[41]

Over against such a more or less fated view of space there has been posed a dialectical view of prophetic religion that allows for more change and rearrangement in human affairs. It allows for the love of hallowed ground and homeland but also calls for exodus and exile to a land of promise. The great exponent of this view in recent times was Paul Tillich, who saw the double motif in his own autobiography. In a self-portrait written by the German exile in America, Tillich saw both "destiny" and "freedom."

> The boundary between native land and alien country is not merely an external boundary marked off by nature or by history. It is also the boundary between two inner forces, two possibilities of human existence, whose classic formulation is the command to Abraham: "Go from your home . . . to the land that I will show you." He is bidden to leave his native soil, the community of his family and cult, his people and state, for the sake of a promise that he does not understand. The God who demands obedience of him is the God of an alien country, a God not bound to the local soil, as are pagan deities, but the God of history, who means to bless all the races of the earth.

Whoever was responsible to this biblical call "must ever leave his own country and enter into a land that will be shown to him." The leaving of the homeland may mean actual migration or it may mean "to break with ruling authorities and prevailing social and political patterns." In Nietzsche's words, it means moving into "the land of our children" and out of "the land of our fathers and mothers." Tillich said that his own attachment to his native land "in terms of landscape, language, tradition, and mutuality of historical destiny" was so instinctive that it did not even deserve special attention. Those who make too much of the instinct, may be expressing insecurity. Of more importance, he thought, was the crossing of boundaries in the form of migration.[42]

In an obscure piece written for the consecration of a home Tillich reflected on the polarity of man's spaces. Space supports existence and is its soil, possessing its own house-gods. James Luther Adams summarized the theme:[43]

> But not only is one's own house the locus of the delimitation of space. So also are the . . . city in which the house stands, the landscape, the nation and its soil. And all of these share in the sacredness of the space which supports our existence.

But such an approach can also lead to a demonic exaltation of blood and soil—as was the case with National Socialism. On the other hand, humans with their space-creating power can go beyond limits, thought Tillich, and transform the earth into a unified dwelling place of humanity. "In doing so it detaches itself from every special soil." Space remains but—and here Deloria's perceptions are correct—time becomes powerful over space in the form of propheticism, in the myth of Abraham and the detachment from any particular soil. "Man must again and again leave the space that surrounds him. He does so for the sake of time, for the sake of the future," beginning from the womb.

> It is symbolic . . . of the spiritual and social struggles of our time, for today the deepest cause of struggle is the fact that the gods, the powers of limited spaces, resist being uprooted to grow into a more encompassing space, into a space for humanity and into a future in which human existence may fulfill itself anew. This struggle of our day seems to have awakened and irritated the demons of the soil, and they show a terrible, a savage energy of resistance.

What Tillich saw as operative is the power of any social group applied especially to territorialism and regionalism in American religion.

> Coercion is used in settling and defending the space which is the given or chosen place of this group, space not only in the geographical sense but also in the sense of social and cultural traditions of ideas and hopes.

On these terms Tillich, ordinarily a friend of Jews and Israel, feared "a new spatial bondage" in Zionism,

> a spatial bondage that will then manifest itself as nationalistic, polytheistic, and against which the full power of prophecy will have to be brought to bear.

At the same time he listened to the word of Zionists who said that "a being in time is no being," that "space and time are bound up together." Tillich concludes: "The tension between these two elements has always been, and is today more than ever, *the* problem of Judaism and also of Christianity." He also saw something valid in Protestant protest against spatial bondage by Catholics to the place of Rome and even feared lest Geneva might become the Protestants' new "place"! In his protestant and prophetic attacks on American nationalism Tillich also pointed to a kind of spatial bondage for which Protestants were most responsible. The religious groups in America and the nation's "publick religion" itself frequently generated such prophetic voices—one thinks of Abraham Lincoln preeminently—to counter idolization of tribe and shrine.

SUMMARY

To summarize, then, American religionists loved their place and were in conflict for land or space for a variety of reasons. They needed it for living, felt called to work in it, enjoyed its landscape. They may, say some, have been giving expression to territorialism and were finding new ways to exploit environmental energy resources. They needed social distance and boundaries for the sake of cohesion and identity and sought sanction for their real estate. They expressed impulses to sacralize their settlements and shrines, and even when impelled toward exile or disengagement, could not leave behind any sense of homeland. The fact that the first permanent settlement was also the last site of an explicit religious war was a mark of America's need to find a new way to relate religion to place. The mid-nineteenth-century Mormon Mountain Meadows' Massacre or the mob burning of convents at Charlestown and Philadelphia were events notable chiefly for their exceptionality.

Accounting for the universalism, the tolerance, and the ability to live with pluralism is a complex task. Some of them may have been occasioned because of the sheer numbers of American competitors over space. It is easier, said James Madison, to have civil peace in the face of a "multiplicity of sects" than if there is only an establishment that owns the soil and a dissent that would share it. Indifference, apathy, and casual secularity may also be instruments of future peace. Conscious formulators of policies that made for consensus or conversation from Thomas Jefferson to John Courtney Murray also made their contribution. The assimilating and erosive processes of a nation of mobile people were and remain counter forces. But envisioning a future of simple blurring, homogeneity, or the loss of religious regionalism and localism in a secular age would be to deny the evidence of almost five centuries. Most American immigrants with religious interests came in groups that might have sung Psalm 137:4: "How shall we sing the Lord's song in a foreign land?" and answered their own question by transforming it into what they considered to be the Lord's land, God's country.

10   Peoples: The Thickness of Pluralism

"The story of the peopling of America has not yet been written. We do not understand ourselves," complained Frederick Jackson Turner in 1891.[1] Subsequent immigration history contributed to national self-understanding. Without ever completely abandoning Turner's frontier thesis, which historians used as far as it went, they added other preoccupations. A century after Turner, historians were busier with a second chapter in the half-told tale of the peopling of America. They have concentrated on the story of the regrouping of citizens along racial, ethnic and religious lines, and of their relations to each other in movements of what have come to be called "peoplehood."[2]

PEOPLEHOOD AND TRIBALISM

First, the realities of black power, black religion, black theology and black churchmanship inspired historians of religion in the 1960s to explore hitherto neglected elements in the makeup of spiritual America. The murder of integrationist leader Martin Luther King and the publication of separationist Albert Cleage, Jr.'s *The Black Messiah* in 1968 were signs of a developing sense of "peoplehood" among blacks as well as of what was called the "religiocification" of a black revolution. Ties to the African religious past and to other spiritual forces outside America were regularly stressed: "We must seek out our brothers in all of Asia and Africa."[3]

The black revolution triggered or was concurrent with other expressions of peoplehood. The American Indian frequently stated his case in religious terms and even provided a metaphor for understanding all the movements: people came to speak of the presence of "a new tribalism."[4] Meanwhile, many Jews resisted being blended into the American mixture. They reinterpreted their community around two particular historical events, the Holocaust and the formation of modern Israel; their new self-consciousness resulted in "the retribalization of the Jew."[5] This change was accompanied in America by some retreat from interfaith conversation on the part of Jews and some questioning as to whether the common "Judeo-Christian tradition" was anything more than a contrivance.[6] The ghetto walls had largely fallen, but the suburban Jew had not fully resolved his questions of identity and mission.

"Peoplehood" movements brought to view the 15 million Americans of Spanish descent, including the newly assertive Chicanos, chiefly in the Southwest. "Chicano describes a beautiful people. Chicano has a power of its own. Chicano is a unique confluence of histories, cultures, languages, and traditions. . . . Chicano is a unique people. Chicano is a prophecy of a new day and a new world."[7] In the Northeast, particularly in New York City, almost a million Puerto Ricans, representing the first airborne migration of a people, stamped their distinctive claims on the consciousness of a nation.[8]

Americans of Eastern Orthodox descent made moves to recover their heritages. Orientals in San Francisco protested school busing because integration might threaten their people's heritage. Chinese and Japanese all across the country became subjects of curiosity by their non-Oriental contemporaries who showed interest in Eastern religion, in Yoga or Zen. Nationalist separatist groups in Quebec gathered around French culture and Catholic faith in neighboring Canada and provided local examples of a worldwide neo-nationalism.

The racial and ethnic self-consciousness of what had been called the "minority groups" led to a new sense of peoplehood among the two groups which together made up the American majority. One of these clusters came to be called "white ethnic," its members, "ethnics." They took on new group power at a moment when paradoxically, as students of *The Real Majority* pointed out, "ethnics are dying out in America and becoming a smaller percentage of the total population."[9] The actual decline was from 26 percent of the population ("foreign stock") in 1940 down to an estimated 15 percent in 1970. Austrians, "Baltics," Czechoslovakians, German Catholics, Hungarians, Italians, Poles and other heirs of earlier immigration from Europe were often led to see a common destiny despite their past histories of separation and often of mutual suspicion or hostility. Most of them were of Roman Catholic backgrounds, members of a church which in its Second Vatican Council taught its adherents to think of themselves in the image of "The New People of God."[10] In America they wanted also to be a people with identity, a people of power.

Finally, there is "One of America's greatest and most colorful minority groups."

> They came here on crowded ships, were resented by the natives and had to struggle mightily for every advance they made against a hostile environment. Despite these handicaps, despite even a skin color different from the native Americans, this hardy group prospered and, in prospering, helped build the nation. They fought in her wars, guided her commerce, developed her transportation, built her buildings. The debt that the country owes to this particular group of immigrants can never be over-estimated. In short, like most American minority groups, they made good citizens.

"The only thing different about the group is that it is the one traditionally viewed as the 'American majority.'" The minority group just described by Ben J. Wattenberg and Richard M. Scammon is "White Anglo-Saxon Protestant," further qualified today as "native-born of native parentage."[11] The acronym and designation WASP-NN in the 1960s represented only about 30 percent of the population. It was divided into 60 percent urban and 40 percent rural, 35 percent southern and 65 percent nonsouthern communities and included great inner variety. But its critics tended to lump all WASPs together, and increasing numbers of Americans accepted membership in this "people." Among them are large numbers "who happen to be both Anglo-Saxon and white, but whom none would think to describe in terms of WASP power structures. For these particular

Protestants (in rural Appalachia, for example) also happen to be exploitable and as invisible as any of America's other dispossessed minorities," and are sometimes themselves referred to as a separate people."[12]

Despite internal variety, at least as late as the 1960s, "the white, Anglo-Saxon Protestant remains the typical American, the model to which other Americans are expected and encouraged to conform."[13] One of the most significant events in the recent study of the peopling of America has been the growing sense, however, that WASPs are a minority themselves. They have at least lost statistical bases for providing a national norm for ethnic self-understanding.

RACE, ETHNICITY, AND RELIGIOUS HISTORY

These good years for peoplehood have given rise to whole new historical and social inquiries concerning *ethnicity*. The term ('obs., rare') once meant "heathendom," "heathen superstition."[14] Today it is coming to refer to participation in "an ethnic group—racial, religious, or national" in origin.[15] In this essay, *racial* is a species of the genus *ethnic*. People may have authentic or only imaginary ties to a common place of origin, as Max Weber noted.[16] Thus when a nonchurchgoing American of Swedish descent is listed as a WASP and accepts that designation, his part in an "Anglo-Saxon" people relates only to an imagined common origin with some Englishmen.[17] Two American Italians who share actual ties to common birthplaces in Europe present a more obvious case for membership in an ethnic group. Yet in practical life and in the world of the politicians or analysts the Swedish WASP and the Italian will tend to be treated as equally legitimate participants in the lives of their people.

The new movements of peoplehood and the expressions of ethnic and racial consciousness—almost all of them marked by claims of "chosenness"—caught many Americans off guard. I shall argue that professional students of religion in America for the most part had become committed after the middle of the twentieth century to theories of interpretation, models and paradigms of inquiry which led them to neglect, gloss over, or deliberately obscure the durable sense of peoplehood in the larger American community. This also left many members of the fraternity ill prepared to tell the stories of those who shared new styles of ethnic consciousness.

If that argument can be established, we may properly speak of ethnicity as the skeleton of religion in America. In a plea for historically informed ethnic studies and in an account of the history of the neglect of ethnic groups, Rudolph J. Vecoli says: "Ethnicity in American historiography has remained something of a family scandal, to be kept a dark secret or explained away."[18] This suggests two dictionary images. One is that of "a skeleton in the closet," which is "a secret source of shame or pain to a family or person." The other is that of "a skeleton at the banquet," a "reminder of serious or saddening things in the midst of enjoyment." Equally seriously, ethnicity is the skeleton of religion in America because it provides "the supporting framework," "the bare outlines or main features," of American religion.

When the new particularism was first asserted in the 1960s, students had been enjoying their realization that consensus-minded America no longer seemed to be "tribal." (Tribes, to repeat Lord Bryce's observation, possessed distinctive and localized religions. "Religion appeared to them a matter purely local; and as there were gods of the hills and gods of the valleys, of the land and of the sea, so each tribe rejoiced in its peculiar deities, looking on the natives of other countries who worshipped other gods as Gentiles, natural foes, unclean beings.")[19] In the midst of the enjoyment, tribalism reappeared. Black messiahs, black madonnas, the black Jesus, "the Great Spirit," the Jewish identification with the land and soil of Israel and charges that white Gentile America had been worshiping a localized self-created deity suddenly disturbed the peace. The issues of ethnicity and racism began to serve as the new occasions for a reexamination of the assumptions and often hidden biases of students of American religion.

OBSERVERS AND ADVOCATES OF A COMMON RELIGION

For the sake of convenience, these students can be divided into two broadly defined schools. Members of the first seek some sort of spiritual "sameness," if not for the whole human family, then at least for the whole American people. In the Protestant historical community this search is a kind of enlargement of the nineteenth-century evangelical vision typified by the words of Lyman Beecher in 1820:

> The integrity of the Union demands special exertions to produce in the nation a more homogeneous character and bind us together with firmer bonds. . . . Schools, and academies, and colleges, and habits, and institutions of homogeneous influence . . . would produce a *sameness* of views, and feelings, and interests, which would lay the foundation of our empire upon a rock. Religion is the central attraction which must supply the deficiency of political affinity and interest.[20] (Emphasis mine)

Another spokesman of this tradition was theologian Charles Hodge, who in 1829 claimed that Americans were overcoming Europe's problem of disunity by becoming one people, "having one language, one literature, essentially one religion, and one common soul."[21]

In the course of time that vision had to be enlarged so that it could accommodate other Americans though many of these others have regularly complained ever since that Protestant views of "sameness" and "essentially one religion, and one common soul" were superimposed on non-Protestants. Many Roman Catholics, on a somewhat different set of terms, also affirmed a religious nationalism that transcended their particular creed.[22]

Historian Philip Schaff, the reader may recall, in 1855 observed continuing immigration and thought that a national amalgamation was going on. It would blend all European nationalities into a "Phoenix grave," as he called it. From it they would rise to new life and new activity. Yet he still followed ethnocentric lines: this blending would be "in a new and essentially Anglo-Germanic form."[23] Later, Frederick Jackson Turner, the historian who had wanted the "peopling of America" to be studied for the purposes of national self-understanding, chose to concentrate on the frontier. He argued that "in the crucible of the frontier the immigrants were Americanized, liberated, and fused into a mixed race, English in neither nationality or characteristics."[24] His successors came to expect that a spiritual fusion would accompany the amalgamation of peoples.

Through the years the seekers of spiritual sameness or oneness and ethnic fusion or assimilation had to include the physical presence and spiritual strivings of ever more varied peoples. Those who advocated what John Dewey in 1934 had called *A Common Faith*[25] made little secret of their desire to overcome particularisms of religion, race and class. For some this desire may have been born of weariness over all tribal-religious warfare; for others, it grew out of conscious philosophical choices about reality, religion and nation.

In this spirit at the beginning of this period sociologist Robin M. Williams, Jr., wrote during 1951 that "Every functioning society has, to an important degree, a *common* religion. The possession of a common set of ideas, rituals, and symbols can supply an overarching sense of unity even in a society riddled with conflict."[26] A year later, at the end of a long book on denominational varieties in American religion, J. Paul Williams moved beyond Robin Williams in the quest for a common national faith. He spoke of it as a "societal religion." Williams favored teaching democracy as a religious ultimate, mildly criticized men like Walter Lippmann for having been content to describe it merely as a "public philosophy" when it ought to have been termed a religion, and called moreover for "spiritual integration."[27]

The dean of American church historians throughout this period, Sidney E. Mead, gave a generally positive interpretation of "the religion of the democratic society and nation" (over against "the religion of the denominations"). While he clearly retained a Lincolnian sense of judgment over against idolization of the nation, he also agreed with G. K. Chesterton's observation that America is the "nation with the soul of a church," and that it was "protected by religious and not racial selection."[28] The question of racial or ethnic selection played only a very small part in Mead's thought. He was critical of those who stressed religious and theological particularity at the expense of the idea of the nation's "spiritual core." Mead promoted Ronald Osborn's suggestion that "a common type of faith and life . . . common convictions, a common sense of mission . . . could and should be the goal for Americans."[29]

One did not have to be a promoter of the search for "sameness," "oneness," or a "common faith" or religion in order to point to their development after mid-century. Mead singled out Winthrop Hudson, Will Herberg and myself as three definers of societal religion who withheld consent from it because of interests in religious and theological particularity. It was true that during the Eisenhower, Nixon, and later the Reagan eras, many had been critical about priestly and nationalist forms of civil religion. This religion may have been sanctioned by a national majority,[30] but many members of the liberal academic community rejected it.

Most of the intellectuals' affirmations of a generalized American religion came during and shortly after the brief era when John F. Kennedy seemed to be portraying a new spiritual style for America. It was in this mood and at this moment that Robert N. Bellah in 1967 attracted a latter-day market for the term "Civil Religion in America." This was "at its best a genuine apprehension of universal and transcendent religious reality as seen in or, one could almost say, as revealed through the experience of the American people."[31]

The defenses of the common vision as against the particular contention were based on historical observations of good moments in past American expressions of religious "sameness." They also revealed philosophical commitments toward the higher unity. Most of the defenders overlooked ethnic and racial factors because these usually reinforced senses of difference. Rudolph J. Vecoli believes that "the prevailing ideology of the academic profession" which has been the "prime article of the American creed" has been a "profound confidence in the power of the New World to transform human nature." Vecoli related this to Hector St. John Crèvecoeur's eighteenth-century discernment of a "new race of men," a "new man," this American, who, "leaving behind him all his ancient prejudices and manners, receives new ones from the new mode of life he has embraced, the new government he obeys, and the new rank he holds. Here individuals of all nations are melted into a new race of men." The result of this faith has been an "assimilationist ideology."[32] In the nineteenth century Ralph Waldo Emerson, among others, kept this faith alive. Let immigrants come: "The energy of Irish, Germans, Swedes, Poles, and Cossacks, and all the European tribes—and of the Africans, and of the Polynesians,—will construct a new race, a *new religion,* a new state, a new literature."[33] Regularly throughout American history, those who failed to be assimilated or who stressed separate racial, ethnic, or religious identities were embarrassments. Ethnicity became the skeleton in the closet and had to be prematurely pushed aside and hidden from view.

THE ANALYSTS AND DEFENDERS OF PARTICULARITY

The other line of interpretation has been dedicated to the love of what the philosopher Gottfried Wilhelm Leibnitz and the historian Marc Bloch spoke of as "singular things."[34] Some representatives of this approach may have shared a concern for or belief in ultimate unity, but at least they recognized that pluralist terms for life in the civil order must be found. Against this background in 1958 Father John Courtney Murray, S.J., made his profound comments about religious pluralism being the human condition, the script of history, the troubler of the human city.[35]

The historians and analysts who dealt more critically with "sameness," "oneness," and "common" religion in America after mid-century ordinarily devoted themselves to the religious shape of this pluralism. Only as the result of the racial upheavals and the new ethnic consciousnesses which were manifested during the 1960s did some of them begin to perceive again that ethnicity has been the skeleton, "the supporting framework" of American religion. These historians and other observers have seen that racial, ethnic, class, partisan, religious and ideological conflicts in America have countered or qualified the homogenizing ideals that earlier held together the "consensus" schools of history. Some of them began to try to cope specifically with the ethnic pluralism that is also part of "the human condition."

Some spokespersons for ethnic or racial pluralism and separatism have attached ideological commitments to their observations. Out of myriad possibilities the word of Thomas H. Clancy can be regarded as representative. Clancy quoted Daniel Patrick Moynihan, who was one of the first to speak of the failure of assimilationist or "melting pot" theories to explain the American situation. Wrote Moynihan: "The sense of general community is eroding, and with it the authority of existing relationships, while, simultaneously, a powerful quest for specific community is emerging in the form of ever more intensive assertions of racial and ethnic identities." Adds Clancy: "Black nationalism caused the white ethnics to remember what they had been taught to forget, their own origins." Thus came his own theology of "unlikeness":

> The year 1970 is the date when the drive for group rights became more important than the struggle for individual rights. (In the demonstrations and rallies of the future, most signs will bear an ethnic adjective.). . . For a long time now we have been exhorted to love all men. We have finally realized that for sinful man this is an unrealistic goal. The saints and heroes among us will still face the challenge in a spirit of unyielding despair. The rest of us will try first to love our own kind. This is the year when 'brother' and 'sister' began to have *a less universal and hence truer meaning*.[36] (Emphasis mine)

Of course not all historians who tried to make sense of racial and ethnic particularism have shared this creed, but it is the common affirmation of many spokesmen for "differences" over against "sameness" in civil and religious life.

The two general approaches just described can be best studied by reference to several prevailing models—many of them defined by sociologists—which are regularly used for historical explorations and contemporary analyses of the shape of American religion.

SAMENESS THROUGH COMMON SECULARITY

First, some advocates of "sameness" have chosen a *secular* interpretation of American religious life. In this view the belief is expressed that there will be progressively less religion in society. Secular people will unite on the basis of some sort of emergent godless, homogenizing, technological and political scheme. The result will be a global village marked by nonreligious synthesis for world integration.[37] The "secular theologians" of the 1960s shared this creed, as did many working historians.[38] In the view of British sociologist Bryan Wilson, participation in American church life could itself be called secularization, because on the legal basis of the nation's formal secularity "religious commitment and Church allegiance *have become* elements in the American value system." Wilson presupposed or observed that "the common values" embodied in religious institutions and the secular American Way of Life were rather simply congruent with each other.[39]

10. The Thickness of Pluralism

Seymour Martin Lipset, also writing in this frame of mind, dealt in passing with racial and ethnic groups and explained their continuing appearance in terms of cultural lag: "American religious denominations, like ethnic groups, have experienced collective upward mobility." On these terms, contemporary

> Negro religious behavior resembles that of the nineteenth-century lower status migrant white population. The Catholics have taken on the coloration of a fundamentalist orthodox religion comparable in tone and style, if not in theology, to the nineteenth-century evangelical Protestant sects.[40]

Because distinctive religious symbols have been connected with almost all the recently recovered movements of peoplehood, racial and ethnic, their spokesmen would not have been content to see themselves on Lipset's escalator. They would resist and stress their distinctive symbols (*Afro-American, Amerindian, Chicano*, and the like) rather than accommodate themselves to the secular trend of "the common values" of American life or simply be an element in the scheme of "upward collective mobility."

CIVIL UNITY, RELIGIOUS PRIVACY

A second line of interpretation is close to the secular one. It simply says that a person's beliefs are *private* affairs and thus have little common or civic consequence. Ideological support for this view is deep in the American tradition. While Thomas Jefferson supported the idea that those moral precepts "in which all religions agree" could be supportive of civil order, he believed differing private religions to be a societal luxury: "It does me no injury for my neighbor to say that there are twenty gods, or no God."[41] One could be for sameness and for a common faith independent of private religious opinions. Religion, said philosopher Alfred North Whitehead in 1926, is "what the individual does with his own solitariness."[42] Religion, for William James in 1903, had meant "*the feelings, acts, and experiences of individual men in their solitude.*"[43]

These views find support in the conditions of modern urban and industrial life, says social theorist Thomas Luckmann. He claims that "the most revolutionary trait of modern society" is the fact that "personal identity becomes, essentially, a private phenomenon." Religion, now housed in specialized institutions and religious opinions, has become "a private affair." Each person selects a world of significance from a variety of choices. "The selection is based on consumer preference, which is determined by the social biography of the individual, and similar social biographies will result in similar choices." "Individual religiosity in modern society receives no massive support and confirmation from the primary institutions."[44] Families, sect participation and the like are of some help, but cannot provide much support for community. Luckmann, unfortunately, does not dwell on ethnicity or race as religious factors in this context.

The new advocates of peoplehood, however, would contradict these pictures. "The new tribalism" accuses the American majority of having forced people to lose their identities by throwing all into the private sphere. One Indian summed it up long ago: "You are each a one-man tribe." Another said: "The question is not how you can Americanize us but how we can Americanize you."[45] Whether or not they succeed in the effort, the new ethnic and racial recoveries are designed to supplant the private interpretation of identity and religion, and historians at the very least have to explore these claims at a time when, as Luckmann and others point out, denominational and sectarian involvement supply little of either.

RELIGIOUS, NOT ETHNIC, PLURALISM

The third model for religion in America, the *pluralist*, moves the discussion to the center of the debate over "sameness" versus "unlikeness" on national versus ethnic-racial and religious lines.

The religious pluralist interpretation was born in the face of the problem of identity and power which increased as ethnic origins of Americans became progressively more remote and vague. In a sense, it served to push the skeleton of ethnicity into the closet. Thus Gerhard Lenski in 1961 condensed the thought of Will Herberg, the best-known representative of this view at mid-century:

Earlier in American history ethnic groups [provided community and identity] and individuals were able to enjoy this sense of communal identification and participation as members of the German,

10. The Thickness of Pluralism

Polish, Italian, and other ethnic colonies established in this country. Today such groups have largely disintegrated, but many of the needs they served continue to be felt. In this situation, Herberg argues. Americans are turning increasingly to their religious groups, especially the three major faiths, for the satisfaction of their need for communal identification and belongingness.[46]

Herberg himself in 1955 had deplored the "sameness" or "common religion" schools, but he recognized the presence of a common faith in the "American Way of Life" as the ultimate. Identification with Protestant, Catholic, or Jewish religions were paths for reaching it.[47] E. Digby Baltzell, a student of the WASP establishment, observed in 1964 that "religious pluralism is replacing the ethnic pluralism of the earlier era."[48] Historian Arthur Mann, ten years earlier, had seen that in the matter of pluralism and a single religion of democracy "American Catholicism, American Protestantism, and American Judaism appear like parallel shoots on a common stock."[49] John Cogley, after hosting a tri-faith conference on pluralism in relation to common religion in 1958, reported with favor on the response of one participant. This man had learned "that the free society of America means more than an agreement to disagree; it is posited, rather, on the idea that Americans will disagree in order to agree."[50]

Ethnic and racial pluralism, however, did not go away just because religious pluralism was able to serve some social purposes during the religious revival of the 1950s. Religionists themselves could not agree on the three-faith interpretation. Thus, Orthodox theologian John Meyendorff overstated the case somewhat when he said in 1960 that the Orthodox had later come to be recognized as a fourth "official" American faith.[51] Lenski, who asked no ethnic questions when he studied Detroit religion, did find that Herberg's single "Protestantism" had had to be divided and understood on black/white lines, at least. The religious revival eventually waned, and many people in a new generation no longer found it possible or desirable to define themselves in terms of one of three religions. Most of all, ethnic and racial reassertion did provide identification and community for the "different," who were dissenters against a common faith for all Americans.

239

MANY DENOMINATIONS, ONE RELIGION

The fourth interpretation has to be taken more seriously because of its obvious appropriateness on so many levels. This is an application to the whole of American Christianity by others of Sidney E. Mead's classic statement that *denominationalism* is the shape of Protestantism in America. "Denominationalism is the new American way in Christianity," wrote Karl Hertz.[52] Catholicism is also regarded as a denomination by historians. Judaism, too, is formally denominationalized.

At first glance it may seem to make little sense to say that the denominational interpretation tended to be favored by those who looked for a common religion. After all, denominations had been invented in order that they might protect peoples' differing ways of looking at religious ultimates without permitting society to disintegrate. It turns out that they seem to have been clever but almost accidental inventions. They served to channel potential conflict out of possibly violent racial or ethnic spheres into harmless and irrelevant religious areas. Where are the dead bodies as the result of persistent denominational conflict?

In effect, argue the viewers of a single American community, denominationalism works just the opposite way. Two illustrations, one from a man who favors a secular and the other a religious scheme for seeing America, in that order, will serve. British sociologist Bryan Wilson, as we noted above, posited "secularization as the experience of Christianity" in America. In a long chapter he then discussed "Denominationalism and Secularization." Denominationalism is "an aspect of secularization." Using an interpretation which stressed class distinctions, Wilson saw "the diversity of denominations . . . as the successive stages in the accommodation of life-practice and ethos of new social classes as they emerged in the national life." And denominational diversity "has in itself promoted a process of secularization." The religious choices offered people effectively cancel out each other. Denominations exist and even thrive, but when people accept the ground rules of denominational civility they telegraph to others that society's ultimate values are being bartered outside the sects, if anywhere.[53]

Sidney Mead's religious interpretation works to similar effect.

10. The Thickness of Pluralism

While the churches accepted denominationalism as a pattern which would guarantee their own integrity and relevance, in practice the opposite has happened. The competitive element in sectarian life has worked against the truth claims and the plausibility of the denominations. Those who seek religious affiliation of any sort cannot avoid denominations, though it is true that they need not necessarily repose their ultimate concerns in denominational formulations. In this context Mead includes one of his rare references to nationality and racial backgrounds:

> [There has been] a general erosion of interest in the historical distinction and definable theological differences between the religious sects. Increasingly the competition among them seems to stem from such non-theological concerns as nationality or racial background, social status, and convenient accessibility of a local church. Finally what appears to be emerging as of primary distinctive importance in the pluralistic culture is the general traditional ethos of the large families. Protestant, Roman Catholic, and Jewish. If this trend continues, the competition inherent in the system of church and state separation, which served to divide the religious groups in the first place, may work eventually to their greater unity.[54]

By the end of the paragraph, then, the ethnic skeleton has been placed back in the closet, and trends toward higher unity prevail in Mead's world.

The matter was not resolved so easily, however. Denominational distinctiveness remained durable, as Charles Y. Glock in 1965 showed in an essay on "The New Denominationalism."[55] Glock, basing his assertions on his findings of a population sample in California, disagreed with both Will Herberg on the theme of a "common religion" and with Robert Lee on there being a "common core Protestantism." Glock is probably correct: great numbers of Americans *do* want to be loyal to their denominations. The interdenominational Consultation on Church Union, which would cluster and merge denominations, attracts little support. Non- and inter- and para- and counter-denominational, ecumenical ventures do not prosper. Despite this, it would be easy to overstress the importance of denominational pluralism.

For one thing, the denominations are divided down the center in a kind of two-party system. The differences on vital issues (such as

241

racial and ethnic matters) are expressed within and not between denominations, as Jeffrey Hadden demonstrated in 1969.[56] What is more, on matters of deepest significance, even where denominational names have been useful, denominational designations reveal little. For example, black religion was denominationalized, but sectarian bonds have meant almost nothing across racial lines. Millions of southern blacks have been Baptist, but there was until recently almost no contact between them and Southern Baptists, the largest white Protestant group in America. The racist has looked at the Negro as a black, not as a Methodist or a Protestant. The black American has had little choice between church bodies when he wished to look for differences in attitudes among them. "Denomination mattered little, for support of the racist creed ran the gamut from urban Episcopalians to country Baptists," wrote David Reimers concerning the late-nineteenth-century situation.[57]

Even among whites, ethnic lines usually undercut denominational interests. WASPs, for instance, once established a line-crossing mission to "Catholic Immigrants." Theodore Abel wrote in 1933 that "in general the work among Catholic immigrants is carried on with the aim of promoting Americanization and breaking down the isolation of immigrants from American society by bringing them into the fellowship of the Protestant Church." In the fifty years before 1933 between fifty and one hundred million dollars had been spent on the cause. But

> The mission enterprise has failed to realize the main purpose for which it was instituted. It has failed to accomplish to any significant degree the evangelization of Catholic immigrants and their descendants, and it has not achieved the control that it sought of directing the process of their adaptation to American life. No movement toward Protestantism has taken place as a result of these missionary efforts.[58]

That report dealt with a half century during which Protestants had been notably missionary, expansionist and devoted toward transforming remote churches. But at home, ethnic factors served to frustrate such motives or achievements. Black, Indian, Chicano, white ethnic and other movements of peoplehood found neither the denominational shape nor the nation's soul to be as effective for promoting identity and power as they found race or ethnicity, which was still—or again—the skeleton or supporting framework for their religion.

A COMMON RELIGION

The fifth major line of interpretation has been implied throughout. In it "sameness," "oneness," and a "common faith" found their home in a societal or civil religion that informed, infused and inspired virtually the whole population. How does it fare in a time of new peoplehood or "new tribalism"? Its expression is complicated and compromised. At the very least it must be said that the racial or ethnic group "refracts the national cultural patterns of behavior and values through the prism of its own cultural heritage," as Milton Gordon put it.[59] The black child in the ghetto or the Amerindian youngster may engage in ceremonies of civil religion. But they may think of something quite different from the world of the white child's Pilgrims or Founders when they sing of a "land where my fathers died." This is the land where their fathers were enslaved or killed. The symbols of societal religion can be used in more ways than one by separate groups.

Most of the movements of racial and ethnic consciousness have found it important to oppose militantly the symbols of civil religion. Historian Vincent Harding in 1968 defined Black Power itself as "a repudiation of the American culture-religion that helped to create it and a quest for a religious reality more faithful to our own experience."[60] An Indian does not want the white man's religion. The Chicano detects the Protestant work ethic in the calls for his participation in a common civil religion. The white ethnic at his American Legion hall relates to civil religious symbols in a different way than does the Jewish member of the Americans for Democratic Action. The young WASP countercultural devotee rejects all American civil religion. The delineations of civil religion themselves are never universal in origin, content, ethos, or scope; they are informed by the experience of the delineators' own ethnic subcommunities. Robert N. Bellah's and Sidney E. Mead's views are unexplainable except as expressions of particular WASP traditions. Orientals, Africans, Latin Americans ordinarily would neither bring Bellah's and Mead's kinds of questions nor find their kinds of answers in civil religion. As British observer Denis Brogan wrote concerning Bellah's essay, "The emblems, the metaphors, the 'note' (as Newman might have put it) of public civil religion is Protestant, even when those symbols are used by Catholics, Jews, Greek Orthodox."[61] It is precisely this feature that has led to attempts at rejection of civil religion and "common faith" on the part of so many ethnic and racial groups.

In summary, it would appear that the five main models for interpreting American religious "sameness"—the secular, the private, the pluralist, the denominational, and the common-religious—apply appropriately only to the white and largely generalized Protestant academic circles where they originated. Other ethnic-racial-religious complexes can be only occasionally and partially interpreted through these.

ETHNIC AND RACIAL THEMES REINTRODUCED

To suggest that ethnic and racial themes have to be reintegrated into the schemes for posing historians' questions was not to say that these should displace the others. The secular tendencies in America will probably not be successfully countered by the new religious practices of minority groups. Many people can find identity in the private sphere without explicit reference to ethnic and racial religious motifs. Protestantism, Catholicism, Judaism may long serve to identify practitioners of a common American religion. Denominationalism may indeed be the shape, and civil religion the soul, of American religion—just as ethnicity is its skeleton or supporting framework. But as the most neglected theme until recently, racial and ethnic particularity deserves compensatory interest and inquiry.

Numerous benefits could result from such an effort. Concentration on religious dimensions of peoplehood could lead to a more accurate portraying of the way things have been—that is always the first goal of the historian. Historians in the once-majority traditions, WASP and white ethnic combined, can re-explore their own assumptions and may be able to discern the ethnic aspects in what they had earlier regarded as their universal points of view. The theories seeking "sameness" and "oneness" tended to be based on a kind of optimistic and voluntaryistic spirit. Ethnic-racial recovery should help historians deal more adequately with the faded, pre-destined, tragic and even violent elements in religion in America.

WASP HISTORIES AS ETHNIC EXPRESSIONS

In any case, WASP and white ethnic American historians would be able critically to revisit their own older traditions, traditions which were once racially and ethnically self-conscious, for better and for worse. When WASP is seen not as the norm but as an ethnic minority among minorities, the racial special pleading of the fathers appears in a different light. Robert Baird, whom many regard as the first historian of American religion, in 1843 insisted that "our national character is that of the Anglo-Saxon race," and he ranked other ethnic groups downward from Anglo-Saxon.[62] Baird began his history with reference to the differences of Indian, Negro and other non-Anglo-Saxon peoples and kept them in mind consistently as he measured them in the light of his own racial norm.

Not only WASPs were particularists. Baird's counterpart, John Gilmary Shea, the father of American Catholic historiography, was a spokesman for the Irish minority, and Catholic history has been consistently marked by ethnic distinctives.[63] Philip Schaff, a Continental "outsider," had to invent artificial ways to blend his German-Swiss background with the Anglo-American dominant strain. Daniel Dorchester in 1890 criticized the German and Irish influx as people of "low habits and ideas, retaining supreme allegiance to a foreign pontiff, or controlled by radical, rationalistic, materialistic, or communistic theories. . . . Can Old World subjects be transformed into New World citizens?"[64] Even Leonard Woolsey Bacon, a man of ecumenical temperament and a devotee of religious "sameness," spoke during 1898 in terms of "masterful races" in American white Protestantism.[65]

Josiah Strong—shall the historians claim him?—was explicitly racist in his accounting of American religion in the 1880s and 1890s. For Strong, the Anglo-Saxon's religion was "more vigorous, more spiritual, more Christian than that of any other." It was destined to "dispossess many weaker races, assimilate others, and mold the remainder, until, in a very true and important sense, it has Anglo-Saxonized mankind."

> If I do not read amiss, this powerful race will move down into Mexico, down upon Central and South America, out upon the island of the sea, over upon Africa and beyond. And can anyone doubt that the result of this competition will be the 'survival of the fittest'?[66]

The themes of WASP ethnicity and superiority which had been explicit in the nineteenth century became implicit and taken for granted in the twentieth. The assimilationist ideal took over. In 1923 Peter Mode could write that "American Christianity has . . . no racial coloring and its Americanization as yet has been a process void of racialism," a suggestion about America that would be incomprehensible to most of the world. Instead, said Mode, American Christianity has taken its character by having been "frontierized."[67] Joining the frontierizing-sameness school was William Warren Sweet, who dealt at length with slavery, but most of whose energies were devoted to the white Protestant mainline churches as normal and normative. Sidney E. Mead changed the topic to denominationalism and a common national religion without picking up much interest in non-WASP religion.

On the other hand, Robert Handy's *A Christian America: Protestant Hopes and Historical Realities*[68] is one of the first important attempts by a WASP to come to terms with the WASP particularism which once had paraded itself as universalism. Handy stresses ethnic, racial and other conflict-inducing questions over against the interpretations which derived from the mid-century "sameness" and "oneness" schools.

THE FUTURE OF TRIBAL CONFEDERATION

Even though the future is not the historian's province, it is sometimes asked whether it is worth scholars' efforts to retool so that they can henceforth include the ethnic and racial questions. The assimilating, blending, melting processes do remain and are accelerating. Yet ever new immigrations—Asian, Islamic, Hispanic—come to complicate the visions of "sameness" with which some would cope with pluralism. It would seem as if the plot will thin and thicken at the same time. While "ethnicity" can be a periodic fad, the attempt to understand the bonds of religion and people-hood should continue to quicken anyone who would address issues of American pluralism, past and present. As the ethnic factor remains strong, certainly there will be times of crisis when a sort of "tribal confederation" will be instinctively and informally convoked so various peoples can get together and affirm their common, not their separate, symbols. The historians can then stand ready to interpret both the past interplay between conflicting particularities and homogenizing concordant elements in national life and the considerable assets and liabilities of each.

Whatever happens, however, it seems clear that not all human needs can be met by secular interpretation and private faith, by trifaith or conventional denominational life, or by a common national religion. New particularisms will no doubt continue to arise, to embody the hopes of this "people of peoples." Meanwhile, when representatives of the oldest of American peoples, the American Indian, assert that they wish to Americanize the rest of the nation and that they would like to teach their fellow citizens the merits of life in tribes, these other citizens could appropriately reply: "In some senses, we never left home."

11   Locations: At Home in the Ghettos

TWO IMAGES IN AMERICAN HISTORY

"I am in the final agonies of getting out a belated paper." Since the paper in question was due only two days later, Frederick Jackson Turner with those words was expressing what may be the one universal trait of historians: panic over deadlines. Turner wrote them in a letter from a dormitory at the new University of Chicago while his wife and friends toured the World's Columbian Exposition. On the afternoon of July 12, 1893, two days having passed after he drafted the letter, he again closed himself off while his friends attended Buffalo Bill's Wild West Show. That hot evening, after five dull and deadly papers, he read to a dozing crowd and indifferent press his renowned paper on "The Significance of the Frontier in American History." Turner had pondered the thesis already for several years. His paper stamped the image of the frontier on historians' minds as the most vivid and controversial in American historiography.[1]

No biographer has yet told us how Father John Tracy Ellis spent his days toward mid-May of 1955. But on May 14, 1955, at Maryville College in St. Louis, Ellis produced the most vivid and controversial image in American Catholic historical writing. With his speech on "American Catholics and the Intellectual Life," Ellis confronted the Catholic Commission on Intellectual and Cultural Affairs. Not until thirty-four journal pages and who knows how many minutes of oral presentation had passed did Ellis almost casually introduce a spatial image to match Turner's. American Catholics, he said, had experienced "a pervading spirit of separatism from their fellow citizens of other religious faiths. They have suffered from the timidity that characterizes minority groups, from the effects of a ghetto they themselves fostered." Historian Ellis charged that Catholic scholarly defects resulted from "their frequently self-imposed ghetto mentality which prevents them from mingling as they should with their non-Catholic colleagues."[2]

THE GHETTO CONTROVERSY

Popular historian Robert Leckie chose a sonic image to describe the Ellis effect, especially after *Thought* disseminated the paper in its Autumn 1955 issue. "Ellis's manifesto, as it came to be called," Leckie wrote, "rocked the American Catholic community in an unprecedented earthquake of controversy."[3] Ellis himself seems to have made less use of the image in later writings than did many other Catholics. In his revised general history called *American Catholicism* in 1969 he only casually and generically treated the "respective ghettos" of earlier American peoples, and then moved on.[4]

What is a ghetto? In 1933 the canonical *Oxford English Dictionary* gave it only fourteen words: "The quarter in a city, chiefly in Italy, to which the Jews were restricted." At that time only one *Oxford English Dictionary* literary citation, dated 1897, was metaphoric. It referred to "the veriest Ghetto of bookland." But the dictionary's supplement volume in 1972 reckoned with the increasingly frequent generic uses and added the definition: "an isolated or segregated group, community, or area." The citations now included reference to the suburb as a ghetto (1961), to Harvard and M.I.T. as intellectual ghettos (1968), and twice, once from America (1968) and once from England (1969), to "the Catholic ghetto" and the Catholic "ghetto mentality." Father Ellis, with whom the best-known use is identified but who may not have originated the notion, receives no credit. He is probably happy not to be credited with the now-licit but inelegant verbal forms in the *O.E.D.*, "to ghetto," "ghettoed," "ghettoize."

The "unprecedented earthquake of controversy" after Ellis included the charge by English professor Donald B. King in *The Catholic World* a year later that the "vague and imprecise" terms *ghetto complex* and *ghetto mentality* were terms of "obvious opprobrium." Ghetto, thought King, was in such cases "in fact, an exceptionally nasty smear word, and like most smear words is a slothful substitute for detailed and reasoned argument." It implied that "the segregation and isolation from the rest of the community must often have caused in the inhabitants of a ghetto an ignorance and lack of concern about many of the problems of the community as a whole."[5]

Four months earlier in *America*, Father Thurston N. Davis was more jocular and then more helpful.

> If there is any truth in the charge that American Catholics are living in a ghetto, they have at least made up their minds to get out of it. True, a recent advertisement in a diocesan newspaper read: "WHY NOT HAVE A CATHOLIC DO YOUR TERMITE WORK?" But most U.S. Catholics, I believe, smile at this sort of thing. . . .

> Here and there in this broad land there may be a catsup-eater who prefers to live with his termites until he can locate a Catholic exterminator, but by and large we have no hankering after the ghetto. In fact, the idea of a Catholic ghetto strikes us as being just about as funny as Lutheran toothpaste or Baptist bourbon.

Davis also quoted with favor a comment by sociologist Father Albert S. Foley in *The McAuley Lectures* of 1955:

> The old walls of the immigrant ghettos of the last century have come tumbling down. Their dual buttresses—on the one side the repelling of the foreign-sounding immigrant by the nativists, and on the other, the ethnocentric withdrawal into group-preserving but narrow circles—are losing the remnants of their support. The strong Catholic of the present day is seeking to rise to the challenge of life in the real world of the community.[6]

While Ellis restricted his image to American Catholic intellectual life, it soon was applied to social behavior. Thus in a popular paperback Don Brophy and Edythe Westenhaver could take the ghetto image for granted and subhead a chapter "The Ghetto Collapses." In their *The Story of Catholics in America* (1978), the ghetto was "the walled city that symbolized the experience of Catholic life in

America." They noted that the metaphor "applies both to the Catholic mentality and the way Catholics actually lived their lives."[7]

Daniel Callahan stressed this feature:

> In [the Catholic ghettos, the immigrant] could find those who spoke his language, shared his religion, ate the same foods, and were, like him, struggling to better their economic lot. While these ghettos did have the advantage of helping him make the transition from the old country to the new, they also kept him tied to his old culture for a far longer time than if he had been thrown immediately into the strange life of a growing America. . . . and, once established within a sheltering ghetto, it was psychologically difficult [for immigrants] to uproot themselves once more to start a new life again on the American frontier.[8]

Whether or not Pope Pius XII, who lived near the original and classic ghettos, had the American controversy in mind, he did reflect on *mis*uses of the notion of shelter in his Christmas address in 1957: "There are some even who hint that it is Christian prudence to return to the so-called modest ambitions of the period of the catacombs"; this notion he opposed.[9]

The history of the ghetto image in Catholic usage tells much about the changes of mood in Catholic life during the past quarter century. When apologists for Catholic behavior and critics of the encircling WASP cultures wanted to reinforce and legitimate Catholic group-bonding, they accented the ways in which ghetto life was imposed on minorities. This Ellis did only briefly, when he said that the "aloof and unfriendly" American intellectual climate had discouraged Catholics, led them to slacken their efforts, and prompted this "minority to withdraw into itself and to assume the attitude of defenders of a besieged fortress."[10]

At other times during the domestic *aggiornamento* that followed the Second Vatican Council, however, a self-deprecating, indeed sometimes almost masochistic view of the tradition prevailed. Then the ghetto was seen not as imposed from without but self-imposed from within. Angry James Colaianni typically wrote that "Ghettoism suffocates. It is just another jail man builds for himself to keep from becoming free."[11] Some such critics were romantic about the surrounding glories of the secular city, naive in their neglect of the role of intimate community in human life, and scornful of ancestors whose ways they could never understand or emulate.

Garry Wills graphically summarized the ghetto way in a time and with a tone that allowed for more nostalgia and empathy:

> Bingo, large families, fish on Friday, novenas . . . , clouds of incense . . . , car blessings . . . , *Dies Irae* on All Souls . . . , the sign of the cross before a foul shot . . . , food-chiseling in Lent . . . , tribal rites, superstitions, . . . and, all of them, insignia of a community. These marks and rites were not so much altered, refined, elevated, reformed, transfigured as—overnight— erased. This was a ghetto that had no one to say 'Catholic is Beautiful' over it. Men rose up to change this world who did not love it—demented teachers, ready to improve a student's mind by destroying his body. Do we need a culture? Only if we need a community, however imperfect. Only if we need each other.[12]

Whatever view they held of it, most historians joined David O'Brien in assuming that "events of the 1960s shattered forever the social and psychological bases of 'ghetto Catholicism.'"[13] With him, they and many colleagues in Catholic faith have engaged in acts of selective retrieval from the ghetto ruins, in a time when tradition once again receives more attention than it did early after the Council.

THE "THE" CULTURE AND THE GHETTOS

What shall we make of the ghetto image today? Lest there be confusion about my premises, I could come up with a match for the bumper sticker which reads, "I SUPPORT THE FRONTIER THESIS," and say that "I SUPPORT THE GHETTO THESIS." The claim that it existed and the fact that it was both imposed and self-imposed seems incontrovertible. Now to go beyond mere support of the thesis, it is important to say first that ghetto existence is not the only thing to observe. American Catholicism was *American* already in impressive ways during the very years when the ghetto took shape before the turn of the century and it was *Catholic* in ways that never permitted believers in the United States to close themselves off entirely from the world church. If Catholicism was more than a ghetto, it was also less than a ghetto. American Catholic life was broken into numberless subghettos along national, regional, and ideological lines at the turn of the century. All these are deserving of notice on other days and in other forums.

11. At Home in the Ghettos

My thesis is that while Catholicism often did nurture ghetto existence, it was by no means unique in its relative isolation from a putative Protestant-secular world which I shall henceforth call "*The* Culture." Surrounding the Catholic version were so many other religious, national, and ideological ghettos that they cast the Catholic ghetto in a less distinctive light. Their presence forces us to reconsider whether the *The* Culture was not in many ways a larger and more expansive ghetto itself.

The discovery of "all the other ghettos" is not new. In one of the more systematic treatments of the subject, a chapter on "The Ghetto Culture," John Cogley noted that Catholicism was only "the best organized and most powerful of the nation's subcultures," in the face of "unchallenged Protestant dominance" and "liberal secular establishments." But even his cautious presentation contributes to the picture of the Catholic ghetto as especially problematic for its inhabitants and heirs.[14]

This picture of the Catholic ghetto among all the other ghettos runs counter, then, to the idea that there was a simple, inclusive, majority form of *The* Culture which grudgingly tolerated and sometimes oppressed a minority subculture or two. In his address at St. Louis in 1955 John Tracy Ellis did not develop this theme. He merely and casually referred to "the American intellectual climate." At least once he was more specific and referred to the reputedly cosmopolitan culture, using the image of "the green wood of New England Protestantism" in contrast to "the dry in the small and despised community of American Catholicism." The "green wood" culture in his address included the world from which the Brownsons and Heckers had come as converts; it was the world of Henry Adams, Harvard and Chicago and Yale, the business elites and the population (only 3.8 percent Catholic in 1927) of *Who's Who in America*, and the world of scientists in which Catholics were almost unrepresented.[15]

Of course there was a set of population cohorts from which the non-Catholic 96.2 percent in *Who's Who* came. But when one begins to walk into that mentioned "green wood," it is clear that it shrouds from view and houses many other ghettos—now we probably should call them shtetls—and that to many in non-Catholic subcultures, ghettos, or shtetls, that green wood *The* culture did not at all serve as the dominator or integrator of life. To them it would have been also one more ghetto or set of ghettos among the ghettos.

CONFLICT WITHIN THE GHETTOS

The majority culture, as Ellis and others conceived it, was itself no single entity. Insofar as it was made up of what someone called "the brain-working families of the northeast," it was usually busier contending with contention in its own ranks than with outsiders in remote ghettos. In the *The* Culture the Adamses fought the Jameses or, better, the Adamses fought the Adamses and the Jameses fought the Jameses, just as the Polish Catholics fought the Irish or German Catholics in their Wisconsin ghettos, or, better, just as the Polish Catholics fought the Polish Catholics there. William James in the lofty Cambridge culture often appreciated what he knew of Catholic existence and only rarely scorned a Protestant subculture like that of the Salvation Army. He saved his disdain for the up-close Boston Unitarians at Harvard or the modernizing Anglo-Saxon liberal clergy that were so close to home. In all these respects, the *The* Culture and the subcultures bore the marks of what anthropologist Bronislaw Malinowski once observed and we have noted, that aggression like charity begins at home and that the smaller the co-operating group, the more intense the conflicts, the more easily the flare-ups occur.[16]

Historians of intergroup relations who have concentrated on the anti-Semitism of some Populists or Henry Adams, or on the anti-Catholicism of the nativist American Protective Association at the turn of the century, do have virulent and potent topics on their hands. But they often miss the dynamics of ghetto existence. One sees more vitriol and hears more vituperation, for example, in conflicts between Catholic Americanists and anti-Americanists, Ukrainian Uniates and Ukrainian Orthodox, Czech Catholics and Czech freethinkers, Catholic traditionalists and Catholic modernists, within their ghettos, than between any and all of them, and, say, the American Protective Association. Sociologist Georg Simmel seems to have been right, at least in the American historical instance: "People who have many common features often do one another worse or 'worser' wrong then complete strangers do."[17]

Of course, people in many ways transcend ghetto mentalities and existence. American Catholics, as patriotic Americans, united massively in support of even a dubious war against "Catholic" peoples in 1898 and, even if they were German Catholics, against Germans in 1917. And sometimes the Catholic ghetto was held together by the threat of the outsider. Simmel had a word for that process, too, even if Ellis did not make it the prime feature in forging ghetto solidarity.

> The group in a state of peace can permit antagonistic members within it to live with one another in an undecided situation because each of them can go his own way and can avoid collisions. A state of conflict, however, pulls the members so tightly together and subjects them to such uniform impulse that they either must get completely along with, or completely repel, one another. This is the reason why war with the outside is sometimes the last chance for a state ridden with inner antagonisms, or else to break up definitely.[18]

It may well be that those responsible for the almost instant demise of the neo-nativist American Protective Association in the 1890s did the Catholic ghetto a disservice. More recently, the ineffectiveness of Protestants and Other Americans United for Separation of Church and State to thwart the presidential candidacy of John F. Kennedy and the general decline of anti-Catholicism in the *The* Culture may have done as much as the internal changes occasioned by the Second Vatican Council to cause Catholic ghetto walls to crumble.

COSMOPOLITANISM AND GHETTOS

The two decades before and after the turn of the century provide the best occasion for observing the Catholic ghetto alongside "all the other ghettos." Non-Anglo-Saxon, often Catholic, peoples had arrived in force by 1880 but kept coming with new forces through World War I, until the exclusionary legislation of 1924. These were the decades when it was natural for peoples to feel the ghetto walls imposed around them and to choose their self-imposition—to the point that residents of each ghetto tended to overlook the presence of so many others.

Thus in 1893, in the same building—now the Chicago Art Institute—where at another congress Frederick Jackson Turner had delivered his address on the frontier thesis, avant-garde, ecumenical, and interreligious representatives of many communities held the World's Parliament of Religions. In the hyperbole that goes with World's Fairs, Alfred W. Momerie of London announced in advance that the cosmopolitan Parliament was "the greatest event so far in the history of the world, and it has been held on American soil." The most notable scholar of religion at the time, Max Müller, stayed in England, but observed only slightly less awefully that it was "one of the most memorable events in the history of the world."[19] On that occasion swamis, gurus, rabbis, bishops, a cardinal, laypeople, bureaucrats, and scholars all came out of their ghettos to participate in a kind of interghetto, interreligious interchange. Alongside some representatives of 49 million Protestants was James Cardinal Gibbons of Baltimore, the best-known Catholic hierarch of the day, friend of U.S. presidents, and hardly a denizen of a ghetto. On the stage at Chicago such leaders modeled images of American life that transcended the ghetto. But back home and in back woods, back waters, and back precincts, there was less interaction and there was also more chaos.

This disparity became clear in the paper of H. K. Carroll, "In Charge of the Division of Churches, Eleventh [U.S.] Census." In the mood of the day, Carroll tried to be ecumenical, universalizing, cosmopolitan, synthetic, and homogenizing. Yet the ghetto existence lurked behind his every observation.

> There are so many religious bodies in America that it is desirable, if we would get a comprehensive idea of them, to arrange them, first, in grand divisions: secondly, in classes; and thirdly, in families. I would specify three grand divisions: 1. The Christian. 2. The Jewish. 3. Miscellaneous.

"Miscellaneous" turns out to be a series of ghettos, self-contained if not geographically isolated worlds. "Under the last head come the Chinese Buddhists, the Theosophists, the Ethical Culturists, some communistic societies and Pagan Indians."

All of these groups, of course, had nothing in common with each other. The Buddhists were chiefly on the West Coast, the communistic societies spatially segregated themselves, and the Pagan Indians, three years after Wounded Knee, were almost all on remote reservations. Carroll also made life in Judaism sound too simple. "The Jewish division embraces simply the Orthodox and Reformed Jews." And the Christians included "Catholics, Protestants, Latter Day Saints—all bodies not Jewish, Pagan or anti-Christian."

Carroll found 143 Protestant denominations, but noted, in the spirit of Simmel and Malinowsi, "No denomination of Protestantism has thus far proved to be too small for division." He was "reluctantly compelled to exclude one with twenty-one members" in his census reckoning.

> It is the little bodies . . . that give religion in the United States such a divided aspect. If most of them were blotted out we should lose little that is very valuable, but much that is queer in belief and practice.

His homogenizing impulse was patent when he claimed that of the 14,037,417 Protestant members "all but 128,568 are evangelical" and thus, in a way, like-minded; "over ninety-nine per cent of Protestant communicants belong to evangelical denominations." No wonder that Catholics of the day did and Catholic historians now often do look on the Protestant culture as a *The* Culture. In their eyes it was united and interactive, able to put constant pressure on Catholics to stay in the ghetto. But the statistician's view, which Carroll's was, tends to miss the flavor and feel of life in ghettos.[20]

FOUR TRUE OUTSIDERS

Carroll's book-length expansion of the Parliament address got somewhat closer, but a ghetto's eye view changes its aspect somewhat. Decency and terminological propriety compel one to begin a review of the other subcultures with the communities that best laid claim on the word *ghetto*, the Jews. In *The Religious Forces of the United States* Carroll accounted for 130,496 Jews in 533 organizations. His two subcommunities, Orthodox and Reformed, sound neat, but were not. Thus for Carroll, "In some cases the departure from orthodoxy is slight, as in worshiping with the hat off, the mingling of the sexes in the synagogue or temple, and the introduction of the organ and female choir." Yet those "slight" differences pointed to utterly different worlds.[21]

Reform Judaism, for example, had as a spokesman Kaufmann Kohler, a rabbi who despised the ghetto and believed in an economic trickle-down view of ecumenism. "Religion is, at the outset, always exclusive and isolating. Commerce unites and broadens humanity." His attack on the ghetto continued: "Too long, indeed, have Chinese walls, reared by nations and sects, kept man from his brother, to rend humanity asunder." Therefore, for "establishing the unity of mankind, trade has as large a share as religion." To Orthodox and more moderate but more religious rabbis, Kaufmann Kohler lived in a ghetto of assimilated Jews.[22]

More defensive was Reform rabbi Joseph Silverman. When ghetto Jews were accused of "exclusiveness and clannishness, with having only tribal aspirations," this was not because of contempt for the world around but the result of social barriers others imposed and, more positively, of the "utter abandon to the charm of home."[23] Josephine Lazarus was more assertive: "When we are attacked as Jews, we do not strike back angrily, but we coil up in our shell of Judaism and entrench ourselves more strongly than before." As an Enlightenment Jew, she added, "Away then with all the Ghettos and with spiritual isolation in any form."[24]

When there were intrusions on the New York ghettos, these were rarely of an intellectual kind. Joseph Hoffman Cohn, boy evangelist, distributed proselytizing tracts in tenements, beginning on the first floor and working up. By the time he was back down, the speed-reading Jews pelted him from above with hot soup and bombarded him with pots, pans, and garbage. "Thus I learned that the next time I went into a tenement I must start on the top floor and work down." The Chicago Moody Bible Institute "gospel wagon" that invaded ghettos was met with "an avalanche of watermelon rind, banana peelings, overripe tomatoes, and other edible fruit." When Rabbi Jacob Joseph died, the procession took his body through Irish turf toward the Grand Street ferry. There it was ghetto versus ghetto, as Irish toughs, eschewing banana peelings and hot soup, went at the Jews with iron materials; two hundred were injured.[25]

Gentiles did keep pushing Jews back into their ghettos. Naturalist John Burroughs, in response to a query by a Jewish magazine, wrote, "the Jew will be a Jew; he will not fuse or amalgamate with the other races." And *Harper's Weekly* complained that "The Jews don't want to merge. They prefer to be a part, belonging to the whole, but not merged into it."[26] This was the language of assimilation which Catholics in ghettos kept hearing. But it came from other Jewish ghettos as well. The best-known Reform rabbi of those decades, Isaac Mayer Wise, attacked the Orthodox and other new Eastern European immigrants to Lower East Side New York ghettos: "We are Americans and they are not. . . . We are Israelites of the nineteenth century and a free country, and they gnaw the dead bones of past centuries."[27] Any Orthodox Jew who wasted time fighting back against Anglo-Saxon anti-Semites when given such a target within Judaism would have been simply beside the point.

Alongside Catholic *and* Jewish ghettos, there were other sets of people in even more exclusive enclaves, most notably among these the original Americans, the Indians. Carroll had to dismiss them within parentheses: "(The pagan Indians are not included in the census, and no account is made of them here.)"[28] The reservation was an absolute demarcator for these people who were not even citizens. In his years there were people like Richard Henry Pratt who protested the reservation model which "prolongs the massing, inactive, herding systems" and "continues to lead to destruction and death" through "this whole segregating and reservating process." Some outsiders did want to break up the reservation ghettos. One agent knew that religion bonded the Native Americans: "As long as Indians live in villages they will retain many of their old and injurious habits. Frequent feasts, heathen ceremonies and dances, constant visiting—these will continue as long as people live together in close neighborhoods and villages."[29]

So there were assimilators, like agent Thomas Jefferson Morgan, who wanted Indians to graduate from the schools thoroughly Americanized, safely out of their reservation ghettos, "speaking the same language . . . loving the same institutions, loyal to the same flag, proud of the same history, and acknowledging the one God the maker of us all." Since Morgan did not think residents of the Catholic ghetto were capable of taking part in this sameness, he, incidentally, became a notorious anti-Catholic.[30]

It almost goes without saying that the Native Americans therefore made up another large kind of ghetto. A man who was to become a president of the United States, Theodore Roosevelt, put his seal on their status back in 1888 when he wrote,

I suppose I should be ashamed to say that I take the Western view of the Indian. I don't go so far as to think that the only good Indians are the dead Indians, but I believe nine out of every ten are. . . . I shouldn't inquire too closely into the case of the tenth.[31]

Roosevelt in 1905 did just once host a commuter between a fourth ghetto and the *The* Culture when he invited the docile Booker T. Washington to lunch in the White House and drew criticism for it. Washington was acceptable because he knew his place, which was in the ghetto of rural southland and, increasingly, urban America. The years when the Catholic ghetto took decisive shape were also the years around 1896, the *Plessy v. Ferguson* case, when "separate but equal" facilities for blacks and whites gave legal sanction to the enforced ghetto approach.

The Chicago Methodist *Northwestern Christian Advocate* might bemoan the ghetto trend, because "separate sections in our cities, separate churches, and in some instances separate schools for separate nationalities or races, exist at the behest of race prejudice." But this was a minority voice as the North in the decades at the turn of the century adopted the southern Reconstruction patterns of imposed segregation. At the same time, the pariah blacks in their churches were imposing segregation on themselves. The southern churches were almost in unanimous support of this policy. Thus the *Christian Index* in 1892 spoke for the ghetto, "Let each know his place, stay in it, and do his duty there, and we shall have no trouble, otherwise, there will be conflict, bloodshed, extinction." The *Alabama Baptist* in 1900 urged that the black, also in religion, "stay absolutely in his own sphere, and let us manfully, religiously and patriotically maintain our dignity, supremacy and social status in our own sphere." And in 1908 the *Christian Advocate* quoted Methodist pastor S. A. Steele, "We will keep the Negro in his place if we have to dig his grave."[32] H. K. Carroll accounted for the numbers of Baptists and Methodists who were black and in black churches, but conveyed not a hint of the segregation burden. Nor could he tell the now familiar story of intraghetto warfare as the church leaders fought over the meager spoils within segregated black Methodist and Baptist church life.

Numerically no match for the other three truly excluded sets of people, the Jews, Indians, and blacks, were the Asians in their "Chinatowns," ghettos if there ever were any in America. Carroll counted 107,475 Chinese in the United States in the 1890 census, of whom 72,472 were in California. He puzzled over the statistics of temple participation and blandly told of temple worship. But the census now showed no awareness of the way Asiatics were forced into spatial and social segregation, or of the murders, massacres, fires, and harassments that were worked upon them or that they inflicted on each other. Together they were no part of a *The* Culture that could work negative effects on Catholics. As California State Controller John S. Chambers said after the Japanese "invasion" of his state, "As these people stay apart socially, industrially, politically, so do they religiously."[33] With good reason.

CATHOLIC GHETTOS AND THE CATHOLIC GHETTO

Further assault on the notion that Catholics nurtured a ghetto mentality in isolation from the rest of an interactive America comes from the understanding of enclave life among other peoples whom Carroll also called Catholic. When the Census of 1890 was taken, there were too few for anyone to hold Carroll accountable for them. He did find 10,850 Uniates, 13,504 Russian Orthodox, 100 Greek Orthodox, 335 Armenians, hardly enough to make up a corner of a ghetto.[34] But by the end of the period of ghetto formation these peoples numbered in the many hundreds of thousands. They were distinctive as the only Christian groups that began with a West Coast presence, in Alaska and then Washington, Oregon, and California, before they were at home in the eastern cities and mining areas. They had no Cardinal Gibbons to represent them, no base for transaction with other Americans, and remained—and to many, remain—an arcane presence in residual ghettos more durable than Roman Catholic ones. Carroll knew little of them, just as most non–Eastern Orthodox people do not nine decades later.

The Eastern and Orthodox complex was a ghetto of ghettos, each divided, each a self-contained world of recipes, language, memory, and hope. Thus one observer noted that "each Serbian Church community made its own regulations, hiring and firing the parish priest at will. . . . There were no laws with which to regulate Serbian ecclesiastical life." In the spirit of Malinowski and Simmel, they knew how to put their aggressive tendencies to work in intraghetto, not interghetto exchanges. Thus among Cleveland Romanians, six Farcas brothers, all bartenders, were able to create a schism. What a charming glimpse within the ghetto one gets to observe as the new priest, Ioan Podea, wrote regulations for his parish. They included one which insisted that no bartenders would be admitted to church membership.[35]

Even within Roman Catholicism a scrutiny of this period makes it difficult to speak of the Irish-German-Polish-Italian nexus as *the* Catholic ghetto which generated a Catholic mentality or ghetto complex. During the turn-of-the-century decades, for example, not the ghetto but the barrio prevailed in the Southwest. There "illegal aliens" made their way back to soil where Spanish people had the non-Indian monopoly a couple of centuries earlier.

In Santa Barbara a Pueblo Viejo served as the barrio form of ghetto. There, too, aggression began at home—not in defense against the Anglos but over the sparse resources of the barrio. The battle lines were between Catholic *cholos*, newly arrived Mexicans, and *phocos*, the American-born Mexicans. Both lived with these terms of derision. In 1916 a new immigrant said, "There was not much contact" between the two sets, despite their cramped-together existence. The *phocos* "were a very standoffish people. They were very proud. . . . We didn't like each other." And a native-born Santa Barbaran in turn said, "You had two classes of people . . . Mexicans never wanted anything to do with the 'phocos'!"[36]

By World War I El Paso, Texas, was a half-Mexican city of 80,000, an Ellis Island for Mexican immigrants. They gathered around St. Ignatius, St. Rosalie, Sacred Heart Church, and others. During the Mexican Revolution they learned what ghetto dwellers often did: that to look and be more American, whatever that meant, was advantageous. So they transcended the ghetto walls that they had earlier chosen or found imposed on them. J. A. Escajeda, who trained a sort of army of patrol officers to keep order said, "We are Americans; born and brought up under the Stars and Stripes and as loyal to it as any other American." And in war, he said, his people were "ready to shoulder a rifle and march in the ranks with the American soldier who is of Anglo-Saxon or Celtic origin."[37]

It is tempting to visit each Catholic subghetto to explore the ways the people spent their energies fighting each other more than fending off the outsider. Let one headline from an 1885 Milwaukee *Sentinel* speak its volumes for the kind of conflict that went on within ghettos Protestant, Catholic, and Jewish. After a dispute over the capabilities and contract of an organist who also taught school at St. Hedwig's Parish, the headline read: "Poles up in Arms, A Catholic Priest Gets into Hot Water. His House stormed by An Angry Congregation. Bloody Fracas Resulting in Smashed Heads, Destruction of Furniture and Many Arrests." Yes, there was a ghetto mentality and complex.[38]

PROTESTANT GHETTOS

A critic might well say that one hardly enlarges the case as he points out that other marginal people, nonwhite, non-Protestant, shared ghetto existence and thus took away from the exclusivity of Catholic exclusivism. But various forms of ghetto existence characterized Protestant cultures and kept them from forming a simple *The* Culture of intellectual cosmopolitanism. That nationality had as much to do with exclusion as religion is clear from the isolation and self-segregation of non-English-speaking church groups, or heirs of continental immigrants. The largest of these clusters was the Lutherans, of whom Carroll in the 1890 census found 1,188,119. They grew to twice that number of communicants by the time of immigrant exclusions in 1924. Carroll found sixteen Lutheran groups. While he and the World's Parliament of Religions people met a few of the more public kinds of Lutherans they could hardly have understood not only how isolated most Lutheranism was from its neighboring culture, but how remote from each other the various Lutheran ghettos were.[39]

In 1914 Pastor George H. Gerberding boasted about the varieties that Lutheranism "is the most polyglot Protestant church in America. We like to boast that the Gospel is preached in Lutheran pulpits in more languages than were heard on the day of Pentecost," he wrote. Then he went on to show how these tongues were a burden for those who sought a common Lutheran identity or an American presence. German Lutherans did suffer much in the period because of their ghetto status. The Evangelical Lutheran Synod of Missouri, Ohio, and Other States, almost hermetically enclosed in its ghetto and sustaining almost no formal ties to other Lutherans or non-Lutheran Christians, shunned the public order. Two exceptions occurred, first when they had to engage in self-defense during the time of the Bennett Laws in Wisconsin. Then they linked with German Catholics to fight for repeal of laws prohibiting German in the parochial schools. Second, they sent legates to Washington in efforts to prevent an American alliance with the Allies after 1914, against Germany. What the *The* Culture advocates thought of their agent, Dr. Friedrich Bente, was clear after Senator Henry Cabot Lodge, from the "green wood" New England Protestant culture, heard him testify: "Some of us are not hyphenates—we are just plain Americans—and the wrath of the members of the Committee, Democrats and Republicans, was pleasing to witness." Lodge wrote Theodore Roosevelt that Bente's accent was "so strong you could stumble over it."[40]

Danes fought Danes and both fought Swedes and Norwegians and all fought Germans in the skirmishing within upper Midwest Lutheran ghettos. They argued over fine points of doctrine, a field in which the Missourians were preeminent wall-builders. A Wisconsin Synod paper wrote admiringly of Missouri, "Never has the pure doctrine of God's Word been in uninterrupted control of one and the same church body for so long a time." And Missouri theologian Friedrich Bente, commanding the ghetto gate, insisted that the Synod could never change nor could its teachings be criticized, for "that would be to accuse God Himself, indeed, to mock God, who has commanded that these very doctrines be taught."[41]

Such language has to deal with the cognitive and intellectual sides of religious ghetto existence, but the behavioral ones received full attention as well. On that score, the Norwegian pietists from their rural ghettos scorned the heavy-drinking members of the Missouri Synod, which one recent historian called "the most thoroughly wet denomination in America, or in the world."[42] In 1903 at the Synod's Concordia Seminary in St. Louis students protested noisy beer parties. The school in response engaged in an act of discipline not against the topers but against a student who persisted in protesting their guzzling. The Missourians, fighting to protect their parochial schools, also wanted to keep Sunday schools out of their ghetto. An advocate argued that "a house divided against itself will not stand. This nation will not remain half slave and half free." Missouri, if half schooled, half Sunday schooled, could not stand or remain.[43]

All this ghetto activity was far removed from the Finnish Lutheranism which was isolated in the iron and copper country of northern Michigan. The inhabitants there paid no attention to Missourian doctrinal disputes. Each of their towns was torn between people with loyalties to the Lutheran church versus devotees of Marxist union hall, Lutheran paper and Communist paper, preacher and union organizer. Intraghetto contention there led to bloodshed and a Christmas Eve catastrophe that caused the death of seventy-four people.[44] These Lutherans were probably anti-Catholic, if someone asked them. They would have felt pressed upon by the secular-Protestant culture at large, if they knew about it. But they had issues of defense and aggression within their walls with which to deal. Seldom would they be aware of an issue like evolution, which agitated green wood Protestantism, and never with the writings of a William Dean Howells or an Edith Wharton. They came from another ghetto, far from view or influence.

English-speaking Protestants were segregated from interaction in the *The* Culture on religious lines, especially if they were in the new religious groups. Utah was a vast ghetto for Mormons; Battle Creek, Takoma Park, and Loma Linda became self-contained worlds for Seventh-Day Adventists. Jehovah's Witnesses on creedal grounds cut themselves out of American society's legitimation as a whole. Christian Science, born in the green wood of New England Protestantism, may not have been spatially segregated. But its followers used language that befuddled more people than Mark Twain, even if their words were in English.

More conventionally, there were stirrings within the orthodox Anglo-Saxon Protestant bodies which meant an erosion of denominational walls and the erection of "movement" ghettos. If Mormons, Adventists, Christian Scientists, and Jehovah's Witnesses, of common Anglo-Saxon, racial, national, and earlier religious stock, knew and cared little about the inner life of each other's people, the same came to be true of huge minorities in Baptist, Methodist, Congregational, Presbyterian, and similar mainstream church groups.

Three movements illustrate this. Their ghettos were not of a physical or spatial sort. They were not segregated even in a religious Solid South or Bible Belt, or in the lower middle class from which so many came. But they were cut off by private religious language and concerns from the rest of Protestantism. I can only point to them now: Pentecostalism, born around 1900–1906 in Kansas and in Los Angeles on Azusa Street; dispensationalism and premillennialism with their language of "rapture" and "tribulation" and a whole way of life that pointed to Christ's early return; fundamentalism, which began to acquire a name and was coming to be a party by 1925.

Each provided cradle-to-grave, morning-to-night, shelter in the form of words, meanings, values, and gestures. These kept fundamentalist Presbyterians in a ghetto apart from moderate Presbyterians, Pentecostal Wesleyans from mainstream Wesleyan Methodists, or premillennial Baptists from every other kind of Baptist. Each had its own set of celebrities and scholars, mentors and images. Not only could secular, Jewish, or Catholic Americans not find any of them comprehensible. Fellow denominational members not of their own party knew nothing of their language or rationale—nor did they visit each other's ghettos with much frequency or in any spirit of congeniality. By 1894 the bishops of the Methodist Episcopal church were able to point to an adjective that anticipated the Pentecostal-holiness ghetto: "there has sprung up among us [Methodists] a party with holiness as a watchword; they have holiness associations, holiness meetings, holiness preachers, holiness evangelists, and holiness property."[45] All outsiders were less holy or unholy.

One could extend the list to show how a southern Protestant ghetto defined itself very sharply against green wood Protestantism. To its leaders, the agents of the presumed *The* Culture on Protestant soil were a ghetto of snobbish, compromising, modernizers. Let them unite in 1908 in a Federal Council of Churches or any other ecumenical agency that would try to overcome the ghetto life of Protestant sects—they would only erect a larger ecumenical ghetto. The liberals met resistance from conservative Southern Baptists, Anglo-Saxons all. What goings-on in a Catholic ghetto could attract notice of or comparable hysteria from someone as agitated about Protestant ghetto life as was the secretary of the Arkansas state Baptist convention, who wrote: "The colossal Union Movement is a colossal blunder, but it threatens us Baptists unmistakably. . . . Smite, smite, hip and thigh, the 'bastard' Union movement, dear preachers of God's Book, by calling every Baptist soul under the reach of your prophetic voice to toe the denominational line and then show his faith by his fruits."[46]

ARE MAINLINE PROTESTANTS IN A GHETTO?

What about the agents of Protestantism in the *The* Culture with its appearances of green wood at Harvard and Chicago? To the millions who followed evangelist Dwight L. Moody, these thousands held no privileged claim on the word *Protestant* or *American*. Their evolutionary optimism, progressivist metaphysics, and Christocentric universalism helped them form an enclave which had its own mentality and complex. Few of its celebrities were taken seriously by their secular counterparts. Not one of them had a mind to match the intellects of the new shapers of culture, people named William James, John Dewey, George Santayana, Charles S. Peirce, and the like. Today it is easier, in a more tribal time, to describe the plausibility of Pentecostalism than it is to get a young person back inside the world view of the modernist Protestants early in this century. The Social Gospel Protestants were evidently public figures, but actually inhabitants of a ghetto that was not fully recognized by true socialists or other preachers of the Gospel. Feminism and antifeminism in the early years of the century also made up similar separate worlds.

To speak of America on the model of a nation of nations, a people of peoples, or a ghetto of ghettos is not to exhaust its history or promise. Of course, there were interactions and causes other than the wars of 1898 and 1917 which pulled people toward common

action. Of course, people in the privileged heritages of Protestantism and the Enlightenment dominated in many respects. In a time
when many who express nostalgia for the ghetto are aware of tribal
solipsisms around the world, it is refreshing to recall the already
cited words of William Clancy, the Catholic lay leader, who in 1953
expressed a hope. "We may not, all of us, have grown used to the
hazards of living within a pluralist culture," we heard him say. But
he hoped that, beyond nostalgia and with maturity, people would
learn to lower voices and demands and raise their sense of vocations
in the American time and place.[47]

I have tried to show that there was a Catholic ghetto made up of
Catholic ghettos; that it was imposed *and* self-imposed; that it is
best understood not in isolation from the *The* Culture but as being
surrounded by other subcultures in similar ghetto forms; that
ghetto existence does not explain everything about Catholicism or
all the other ghettos. We know that selective retrieval of ghetto
details belongs to what philosopher Ernest Gellner calls the "decor"
of life more than to its substance, for intellectuals and the middle
class. There are on the other hand reasons for alarm when the ghet-
toes of denominations, peoples, or doctrines are overcherished, as
in some of the New Christian Right movements in our time. One
side of the lives of most Americans *is* open to cosmopolitan images
from commerce, entertainment, athletics, mass media, and higher
education. The ghetto walls have crumbled considerably. But they
still do obscure the views of the outsiders and they still do help
provide coziness for the insiders. The hinges may creak, rust, and
be loosening, but they are still there on gates which may no longer
confine but which do still swing shut.

Just as American Catholic and other minds were in the ghetto,
thus forming a ghetto mentality, so it may be said that something of
the ghetto remains in the mind. I am aware that in a corner of my
own, after describing America's ghettoed life, a major intellectual
issue remains for another day. That agenda is a call to explore, after
this reconnaissance of subcultural ghettos, whether there really was
a *The* Culture. If so, in what ways did it bear some marks of the
ghetto, though now with leakier walls and wider gates?

It may be best to leave that thought in question form. Other
forms of religiously based solidarity beckon. No one associates the

word *ghetto* with them. For some the walls have to do with region, for some with ethos, for some with ideal. Three examples are evangelicals, fundamentalists, and Mormons. They wrestle with modernity and with historicity in vivid ways that inform the life of many and threaten the ethos and practices of more in our pluralist society. It is time to wrestle with them, their claims, their place.

12　Old-Time Religion: The New Face of Southern Evangelicalism

The American Sunbelt has available a wide choice of pasts, so far as religion is concerned. Understanding most of them is urgent for anyone who wishes to deal with the American present.

The first of the religious pasts derives from the sixteenth century, when Spanish missionaries made their presence felt in Florida and today's Arizona, New Mexico, and southern California. Their power was to wane in the course of time, but in the Southwest at least, natives and tourists find plenty of evidences of this Catholic presence. Those who thought that Hispanic America was something antique, nothing but a museum piece, were unprepared for the great *Völkerwanderung*, the migration of peoples which we are seeing in our own time. Today's Hispanic peoples may not feel themselves in direct continuity with the pioneers, but they come from the same religious background, share something of its ethos, and give new motives for studying that past.

A second available past was Establishment religion, which in the seventeenth-century South meant Episcopalianism. Supported by law throughout the colonial era, this form of Christianity has also left its stamp on a part of the country, belongs to its antique shops, and rouses the curiosity of visitors to Virginia and the Carolinas. The Bruton Parish churches and their kind are among the prime monuments of the colonial past.

12. *New Face of Southern Evangelicalism*

Episcopalianism was overwhelmed by revivalist churches after the Revolution, and today dominates nowhere in the South. It was disestablished at about the same time that it lost ground. But its churches are still prominent in many southern cities. They offer alternatives to the more fervent evangelicalisms. Most of all, they remind Americans of the ways in which, by law or custom, someone or other comes to dominate a region. In many a southern city of today a fashionable Baptist church plays the role Episcopalianism once did. Establishment never quite dies.

Through those two centuries, the seventeenth and eighteenth, black religion in America, the third of the Southern pasts, got its start. Slave owners often grudgingly but later willingly began to share aspects of Christianity with their plantation hands, who later took their own nurture into their own agendas. Most of the blacks were members of churches that by genre belonged to the evangelical type. They borrowed freely from white churches and contributed more to the latter than these whites recognized. Today many of the great-great-grandchildren of those pioneers have moved to northern cities, but they dominate in much of the rural South. Many have begun to return with Sunbelt job markets to the prosperous cities. In any case, one would not pretend to understand the South or American religion without knowing the black churches. Their presence also forms a context for white Evangelicalisms.

A fourth available past to the South was the religion of the Enlightenment, which issued as much from Virginia as from anywhere. George Washington, Thomas Jefferson, James Madison, and their contemporaries ordinarily belonged to established Anglican churches and did their rounds of duty as vestrymen. Most of them, Jefferson sometimes excepted, spoke respectfully of Christianity, and believed in God. But this God took on the outlines of deism's Supreme Being more than of Christianity's involved Father, and Jesus Christ was an exemplar of the divine more than a Savior. The Bible was a good book of conduct, but not of revelation. This form of religion is stamped into the legal tradition and many institutions of America, even though it was swamped and overwhelmed by the revivalists of the nineteenth century. It provided a foil for evangelicals, who also profited from some of its contributions to religious freedom. It remains more than a monument from the past, and some of its arguments come back when evangelicals argue for prayer in public schools. They derive the arguments for opposing "secular humanism" from founding fathers whose outlook today would be branded "secular humanism." That past is present.

This is not the place to exhaust the pasts: there are Mennonite and Lutheran pasts; there is a Jewish presence that dates far back to nineteenth-century times. But these four samples show that evangelicalism did not have the turf to itself; its triumph was not taken for granted. When the earliest Baptist and Methodist pioneers and circuit riders came to the scene where the other white establishments were already present, they were greeted about as warmly as a Unification church or Hare Krishna recruiter would be on the premises of First Baptist Church in Dallas.

Yet they won their way, the hearts of the people, and the dominant position in southern religion. For the better part of a century and a half they tended to be looked down upon by the rest of the United States and Western European Christendom. They were written off as redneck by bluenose, as dirtpoor by landrich, as merely illiterate by Christians who were selectively illiterate (which means they could read but did not read religious texts), and/ or as prejudiced by those who were prejudiced against them.

Ever since the 1730s, partisans of evangelical revivalism in American Protestantism have spoken of its appearance in terms of surprise. Jonathan Edwards set the pattern with his *A Faithful Narrative of the Surprising Work of God etc.*, with its reports on awakenings in Northampton and nearby towns in Massachusetts. In this pattern, advocates insist that no social scientist may reduce the understanding of their religious movement to the idea of "nothing but"; it is never to be seen as "nothing but" a psychological eruption, a sociological freak, a mere anthropological manifestation. "The beginning of the late work of God in this place was so circumstanced that I could not but look upon it as a remarkable testimony of God's approbation of the doctrine of justification by faith alone," wrote Edwards in a preface to his published series of sermons.[1]

From that "surprising" motif, moderns should draw two reminders. First, the caution against reductionism is still in place. Attempts to provide critical historical accountings of a movement need not exhaust all its meanings nor deprive it of rich spiritual and theological understandings. Second, the repeated presences of evangelicalism based on revivals tend to take the form of surprising reappearances after times of decline and repeated prophecies of its permanent end. It surprises the skeptics and sometimes also its advocates by its durability.

To take but one example, William G. McLoughlin has both looked ahead to and back on the most recent previous period of high morale for evangelicalism. The Brown University professor is by common if not universal consent among informed observers regarded as the best-equipped and most persistent chronicler of revivalism among those who write from an "outsider's" point of view in the American academy. In a position that he fashioned in the mid-sixties but did not publish until 1967, McLoughlin appraised the claim that evangelicalism, growing out of revivals, might make up a new "third force" in Christendom alongside Catholicism and traditional Protestantism. He then dismissed this claim, choosing to see the religious resurgence of that period to be too pluralistic for such a picture. In any case, the new evangelicalism was, he thought, too tied to the political right wing to survive its own new setback. "Probably the high-tide of this neo-evangelical 'third force' was the selection of Barry Goldwater as the Republican candidate for the Presidency in 1964." Everyone knew what happened to Goldwater and, hence, to his evangelical kissing kin. They had little future.[2]

Between 1967 and the present, the various evangelicalisms instead turned out to be the most aggressive and vital forces in American religion. Catholicism suffered after Vatican II and traditional or mainline Protestantism was dispirited and slipped statistically. But evangelicalism, its hard-line counterpart in fundamentalism, and its soft-line partner Pentecostalism knew prosperity. Yet McLoughlin in 1978 remained unconvinced that all of those made up a new "surprising work of God." A pluralistic revival of religion was indeed prospering, but it would not come to permanent focus in the evangelical subculture. As we have earlier suggested, considerable ideology revealed itself in McLoughlin's view of the future: that in the 1990s it will be likely for a new consensus to emerge, one that will produce a fresh kind of political or civil religion and that will alter the structure of American life insofar as that structure has been dependent upon Protestant evangelical awakenings. "Such a reorientation will most likely include a new sense of the mystical unity of all mankind and of the vital power of harmony between man and nature."

Over against a new kind of public pantheism McLoughlin posed the authoritarian and obscurantist fundamentalist leavings in the new Evangelicalism. "The current popularity of neo-Evangelicalism has led to the claim that 50 million born-again Christians are the avant-garde of the Fourth Great Awakening. This is hard to sustain." McLoughlin found evangelical Bible-centered faith to be attractive to millions of Americans, but evangelicalism was too escapist, individualist, soul-centered, and unworldly to serve as the basis for a universal set of values for the culture.[3] He tended to reduce the surprising revival to the status of a social subculture, explicable in patent cultural terms.

Our task is not to play the game of who or what will win in the long run, nor are we called to put the new evangelicalism in its place, as many secular historians do, or yield it the whole future, as do many of its advocates. We are to attempt to locate its place and power in ever-changing American society, especially in the context of the American South. Though I have an eye on the present and future, my accounting is historical and rests on this thesis: *Because evangelicalism is the characteristic Protestant* (and, eventually and by indirection, Christian) *way of relating to modernity, it has recently experienced a revitalization concurrent with the development of a new stage of modernity.* This does not mean that evangelicalism is epiphenomenal in relation to modernity, or that the modern condition predestines the outcome for passive religious adherents. Evangelicalism has been too inventive and assertive to make such an understanding look plausible. But there has been a symbiosis between unfolding modernity and developing evangelicalism.

My one-sentence thesis demands and deserves unpacking, since inevitably one must employ terms in contexts that are not at first equally accessible to all. It includes at least four words that need some sort of definition.

By *evangelical,* I mean a Jesus-centered form of Protestantism that emerged during the last quarter millennium largely on Anglo-American soil. It is generated through the call for a turning from the old self and world, in a conversion through an intense experience of Jesus Christ by the power of the Holy Spirit. This conversion it reinforces with a fresh resort to biblical authority supported by high claims for the literal accuracy of the Bible. Evangelicalism then issues in a plea for ordered moral behavior and efforts to witness to and share the faith in the form of evangelism.

The reference to *Protestant* (and Christian) does not grant on any a priori basis to Evangelicalism its claim to be simply the whole of the faith once delivered to the saints. Even on a statistical basis, Evangelicalism is small compared to the Roman-Orthodox-Anglican-Lutheran complex. Temporarily, it made little if any mark in recognizable cultural and theological forms in most of the Christian centuries, when conversion was not so obvious a necessity for the survival of Christian community. Instead, historically it grew up on the soil of continental pietism and Moravianism and then emerged in Puritan, Methodist, and specialized "evangelical" and primitive movements in Anglo-America and, henceforth, "in all the world." When referring to its indirect role in larger Christianity, I imply the fact that Roman Catholicism in a voluntary society both instinctively and by borrowing adopted much of the evangelical style and some of its content. This derivative evangelical Catholicism was apparent in nineteenth-century Catholic revivalism, whose story is only now being told,[4] and in twentieth-century Catholic Pentecostalism.[5]

Third, *revitalization* refers to a construct that, with McLoughlin, I borrow from anthropologist Anthony F. C. Wallace, and carry over from "primitive" society into complex ones like our own. Revitalizations grow out of widespread understandings of individual stress, periods of cultural distortion when the old ways no longer work, followed by nativist or traditionalist movements within the culture to restore its beliefs, values, and behavior patterns. Then comes the development of new world views or "mazeways" by which individuals and finally the culture find their way toward new syntheses. More than McLoughlin, however, I see innovative power in appeals to traditional forms. Reworked, they can revitalize a culture and need not lead to cultural Byzantinism or ossification.

Because McLoughlin looks for revitalization of the *whole* culture on
an almost unitary model, he has to see evangelicalism as but part of
one wave, a passing stage toward a larger and more creative whole.
Because I see modern societies like America more as a cluster of
subcultures in search of but not necessarily finding a postpluralist
integrative culture, awakenings in subcultures—some of them perhaps forty or fifty million citizens strong—are more impressive to
me. I do share with McLoughlin more sense of the limits of evangelical scope than do triumphalists in the evangelical movements.[6]

The reference, fourth, to new stages of *modernity* is to post–
World War II America with its culture dominated increasingly by
electronic communication, rapid transportation, mobile and kinetic
styles of living, affluence, and a sense of entitlement in large pub-
lics. All of these factors place new demands on traditional religion,
which has shown marvelous abilities to adapt. Sometimes the adaptation is evolutionary, in continuity with the content of old symbols; at times it is revolutionary, wrenching as it does utterly new
meanings from old symbols. To take but one illustration: when
evangelicalism was the voice of dissent or of the disaffected, its call
to conversion in Christ meant a call to turn one's back on the world.
In the recent surge, prosperous evangelicalism still uses the language of a call to turn one's back on the world. But it now serves as
a means of providing ritual process for applicants to the approved
world, in a day when the president of the United States, business
leaders, celebrities, athletes and beauty queens, and civic figures
attribute their worldly success to the fruits of conversion.[7] The symbols "world" and "convert" remain constant but their content has
been drastically changed by an improvising set of leaders and respondents.

Now, it may seem quirkish to see evangelicalism, "the old-time
religion," as the most adaptive and inventive new ("modern") faith,
but maybe we should not be so surprised at this. Through the years
of the first evangelical stirrings, its parties received names like New
Light, New Side, and New School, even if at times the opponents
of these parties—one thinks of proto-Unitarians like Charles
Chauncy and Jonathan Mayhew in Massachusetts—were enlightened rationalists of a sort, "moderns" in the eyes of intellectual historians. Here it is important to make a distinction on one hand

between the modern*ism* of the Chauncys and their nineteenth-century counterparts who received the name The Modernists, and, on the other, these evangelical exemplifiers of modern*ity*. Modernism was at heart a movement that called for open adaptation to the new worlds of science, nature, and reason; it called for a synthesis of Christ and culture even to the point that Christianity lost its own initiatives. If modernity is different than modernism, what is it?

Modernity exemplifies at least three characteristics in this context. First, in colloquial-sounding language, it refers to the *"chopping up"* of life, and of the functions and understandings of religion in life. Historians are wary of deterministic sociological schemes of religious evolution, so we shall use them with care. Yet it is fair to picture "premodern" existence as characterized by more nearly wholistic approaches to life. Lines between sacred and profane developed, but there was evidently less confidence that the profane or secular had true independent or autonomous standing beyond the realm of the unseen spirits who dominated all of life. Rather than attempt to trace the whole development of modernity, let me repeat in this context the pithy condensation of some of its processes, a formula with which we became familiar in chapter 1, and which is implicit in many subsequent analyses in this book. John Murray Cuddihy spoke of differentiation, which I sometimes call "chopping up":

> differentiation of home from job; the differentiation of political economy (Marx) into politics and economy; differentiation of the culture system from the personality and social systems; differentiation of economy from society (Weber and Parsons and Smelser); differentiation of fact from value, of theory from praxis; differentiation of art from belief.
>
> Differentiation is the cutting edge of the modernization process, sundering cruelly what tradition had joined. It separates church from state (the Catholic trauma); it produces the 'separated' or liberal state, a limited state that knows its 'place,' differentiated from society. Differentiation slices through ancient primordial ties and identities, leaving crisis and 'wholeness-hunger' in its wake.[8]

Evangelicalism ministers to the hunger for wholeness, but is itself based on the differentiation model. It relishes separation of church and state, in the main has argued that religion should not meddle in politics and should abandon the social sphere, and has concentrated on the private dimensions of life in a voluntaryistic church mold.

Not that evangelicalist triumphalism has no desires to smuggle Catholic understandings in the back door behind its "separationist" facade. Thus some Baptists who argue for the separation of church and state might be the strongest advocates for prayer in the public school, as if a universal base for prayer could be found in society. They know that with "majority rule" in evangelical communities the faith of the civic institution would be evangelicalism. But this reveals a cultural inconsistency born of nostalgia for the pre-evangelicalism world or for the cultures of evangelical dominance. Who does not like to have power and monopoly? In practice, evangelicalism was born at the moment when the understanding that religion passed through the genes or came with the territory—the old model of Christendom—was disintegrating. With genius it chose to specialize by differentiating portions of life. Evangelicalism concentrated in private vices and virtues, saving souls even at the expense of care for the whole life of humans, seeing the ecclesiastical sphere as one of special concentration on private, leisured, familial, and personal life no matter what happened to political, social, or cultural meanings.

Alongside this sense of "chopped-upness," modernity produced and evangelicalism creatively exploited and exploits voluntaryism or *choice*. David Apter, who sees the roots of modernity especially in economic choice, has spelled this out. Let us cite him a second time:

> The dynamic aspect of modernization . . . can be expressed in the general proposition that modernization is a process of increasing complexity in human affairs within which the polity must act. . . . Personal meaning and social meaning; the rhythm and pace of social activity; the roles of the misfit and the innovator; the hierarchy of power and prestige; concern with interpersonal associations, political ideology, religion—each of these implies a different pattern of desire, motive, and choice. . . . Modernization as the process leading to the state of modernity, begins when man tries to solve the allocation problem. . . . Self-conscious concern with choice has led to an attitude of experiment and invention that has changed man's entire outlook. . . .

Hence, in these times, more than ever before, it is not only interesting but also important to recognize this characteristic of modernity: Choice.[9]

The evangelicals of 1734 and ever after discerned this feature of modernity while established religion in the earlier period and adapted religion in the later one did not. The National Council of Churches through its social engagements in recent decades has acted as if it is an established church, entrenched and inescapable as a moral voice in the society. Evangelicalism took pains to recruit people, to ask them to make a choice, and even to find "the church of their choice," which became a locale for a new kind of power, albeit a specialized form.

From the First Great Awakening to recent evangelicalism the impulse to choose has been strong. Billy Graham most successfully calls for decisions for Christ by voluntary agents and characteristically calls his magazine *Decision*. Christendom (and Judaism) did not call for "decision"; religion was passed through the genes, through the loins of godly parents.[10] It did "come with the territory." Theologians, of course, may discern behind the language of grace in evangelical Protestantism some of the old Pelagian nuances of merit and achievement. One thinks of the "I Found It!" bumper stickers as the direct opposite of Protestant evangelical understandings of divine initiative. But the initiated knew how to translate this symbol of successful choice and integrate it into their grace system.

In this view, it was not mere coincidence that evangelicals came along at the beginning of the modern period of economics. Adam Smith was also an eighteenth-century person. There were good reasons for it to emerge during the rise of the voluntary political system of which antievangelical Thomas Jefferson was an agent, or of the early industrial capitalist period where the choices Apter describes became urgent. Alfred North Whitehead was correct when he saw evangelicals as people of genius when they made direct intuitive appeals to the hearts of new industrial classes in England and frontier people in America.[11] The evangelicals are the pioneer religious moderns, with their pietist *ecclesiola in ecclesia*—the chosen little church inside the given great big surrounding one—as a model. They still remain in the avant-garde in the electronic age as they adopt the most rigorous secular advertising and entertainment styles for the gathering of television clienteles, the final development of "chosen" religion.

The third feature of modernity in religion is *intensity*. Moderns who are to be attracted at all want their religion to be "hot." If it is to be portable and personal, it cannot trade on footnotes in libraries or rely on scholarly elites. It must be accessible and instantly open to experience and interpretation by common people in the industrial city, on the frontier, or in the suburb. While liberal religion has lived off the capital earlier generations invested in the realm of experience, evangelicalism insists that the immediate experience of the prophets and saints and mystics can come to the object of revivals. Thus was born what Perry Miller calls "the rhetoric of sensation,"[12] calculated to give the "hot" experience. Then followed the contrived "means" of the era of Charles Grandison Finney.

As with experience, so with authority: for chopped up and chosen religious life there must be intense or "hot" understandings, usually in the form of an infallible and unambiguous Bible. Here appear no nuances of ecclesiastical hierarchy, no subtleties of scholarship, but, far more than in the original Reformation, there are insistences that a clear and unerring God must speak clearly, unerringly, and without contradiction or ambiguity in the code book of his revelation, the Bible. With this hot understanding came other assets necessary for moderns: the ability to maintain boundaries, something which cannot easily be done on the basis of ambiguous or controverted understandings of scripture. All must be deposited, secure, closed in, yet accessible to ordered and repentant minds. In modern crisis, this set of understandings originally prospers at the expense of more reserved and restrained ones, and thus in times of identity diffusion such as recent decades have produced, evangelicalism saw new openings.

Modernization in these terms is not a simple, one-way process without counteractions or trends. Cuddihy can speak of "demodernization" or "dedifferentiation" through ideology and force, as in the case of Marx and Mao. They ministered to "wholeness-hunger" by developing an encompassing outlook that overcame the chopping up of the realms of life and minimized if they did not remove all choice.[13] Similarly, there can be episodes in history in which spiritual forces give special attention to new problems and opportunities posed by developing modernity. It is possible to speak of the older evangelicalism developing against the background of "Modernity A" and after a pause, the new one emerging in the midst of "Modernity B."

Modernity A was the period of the industrial, capitalist, and democratic revolutions of the eighteenth century. John Wesley, George Whitefield, and Jonathan Edwards and their aftermath, of course, were not pondering religious solutions to the problem of alienation in the era of factories. Edwards' Northampton was a quiet little town and Whitefield had successes on the back roads. But their style, in most cases itinerant, and the claim by Wesley that "the world is my parish," were posed over against the older notion that "my parish is the world," as it was in territorial Christendom. Evangelicals thus revealed their ability to minister to new spiritual needs. Where there was not itineracy and where the parish remained "the world," it was necessary to intensify the experience of Jesus Christ so that people knew conversion while staying in their immediate context.

Yet the first response was moderated by several factors. "Chopping up" of life was not fully developed at once because of the relative homogeneity of the population in Protestant, and especially white Protestant, American or British provenance. Southern white civilization remained especially homogeneous through the nineteenth century. The element of "choice" was not so drastic in a day when relatively similar evangelical forces competed for a common market; they crowded the center theologically. When an Evangelical Alliance was formed, Continentals and Britishers were attracted to it, but not a few visitors observed that Americans did not take to the Alliance because they did not need one. They were already allied, were strangely similar across church lines. And the matter of "hot" or intense experience, while it stirred great controversy, still drew less notice than it would in an era which prophets had denominated secular or cool about religious stirrings.

The First and Second Great Awakenings and even the 1857–58 lay revivals in American cities were part of this moderated modernity. Strains, however, came during the century after the lay revival. Between it and 1908, when the Federal Council of Churches was formed, American Protestantism developed a two-party system on matters social, with the more conservative evangelicals tending to deal more with the private dimensions of faith. They had "chopped up" life and were so settled in this new pattern that they made the more liberal factions look like innovators for simply trying to regress to wholistic medieval models. Meanwhile, the challenges by biological evolution and higher criticism to the Protestant theological synthesis, accompanied by the rise of an adaptive modernist party, led a large element of evangelicalism to turn to hard-line resistance in the movement called fundamentalism, which crested and was apparently defeated around 1925. After that date the more intransigent versions of evangelicalism were supposed to have retreated in disgrace, to become fossilized or at least to remain on cultural bypaths. Instead some of the children of fundamentalism regrouped, learned some new civility, and came to fresh understandings of the modern assaults and opportunities. And the old strain of evangelicals who had never even been in the frontline fight against modernism and who therefore could keep a more open and flexible style, began to reemerge in the 1940s as organized "neo-evangelical" parties. The 1950s saw Billy Graham relate to a new stage of modernity, and soon ethical leaders and intellectuals emerged to give new definition.

During the interlude between 1925 and the mid-fifties, a number of threats posed themselves to evangelicalism. Some thought it might wane and virtually disappear. Thus British evangelicals of the Clapham Sect sort had been followed by generations of ever-declining church involvement and the rejection by their own young. Individuals could also commute between value systems. They might retain their minute membership in evangelicalism but "pass" in the larger culture. Third, they might institutionalize themselves in new denominations, Bible schools, publishing and broadcasting enterprises, and the like. Or, fourth, they might sustain themselves and wait for revitalization in congregations and in the mainline denominational underground. All four of these happened between 1925 and, say, 1952.

Evangelicalism in many minds came to be lumped with fundamentalism, and was mentally located in the Bible Belt of the South. In what others saw as cultural backwaters it prospered, but few thought it could erupt from there until Billy Graham and his kind brought new respectability. In short, evangelicalism endured.

Then, just before its most ambitious flowering, it encountered cultural shock of many sorts in the 1960s. Activists stole the media limelight. An era of the prophets of a new secularity emerged; heirs of the late Dietrich Bonhoeffer or Teilhard de Chardin, they pictured the demise of the symbol systems that evangelicals cherished, rich as these were in miracle and metaphysics, mysticism and meditation. "God is dead" did not promise much for the evangelical cause!

Far-seeing thinkers then made desperate attempts to "demodernize." Thus Sidney E. Mead and Robert Bellah led the ranks of those who looked for wholistic civil or republican faiths which might help people transcend the "chopped up" life of the denominations.[14] Interfaith, ecumenical, and semisecular thinkers, by celebrating this civil sphere or the religions of world integration, set out to minimize choice, albeit without necessarily trying to impose coercion in their utopias. And intensity seemed out of fashion as Harvey Cox asked for a moratorium on God-talk, in the spirit of Bonhoeffer who had called for diffidence in speaking about religious experience.[15] Clearly the emergence of such a "nonreligious" religion bode ill for evangelicalism, but it also did not satisfy the religious needs and interests of people as they faced Modernity B.

Modernity B posed new needs. First among these was for personal identity in a time of diffusion, of confusion over social location, of bewilderment over the questions Who am I? and To whom do I belong?[16] Evangelicalism, by forming a new community and using its code words about conversion and biblical authority, helped provide boundaries for the psyche.

Second, the new modernity called for fresh interpretations of the world of Americans whose system—witness Vietnam and Watergate—seemed no longer to be full of promise. Millennial language now reappeared, and believers looked for the promise of personal rewards in a society they could not change on any large scale. Over against the impersonal administrative styles of management in state and commerce and church, there rose a generation of people who enjoyed immediate experiences. Some of them chose mind-expanding drugs or fashionable therapies; many "turned East." But the largest wave of experiencers were in traditional forms of Judaism, Catholicism, and most of all in Protestant evangelicalism.

What issued from the encounter with Modernity B is what I

would call an "ultramodern" adaptation, in which evangelicals are again the avant-garde, the "old-time religion" being the most modern and new of all. Thomas Luckmann's *The Invisible Religion*[17] has described the structure of this period. Religion now became a matter of final "chopping up" into utter differentiation and a world in which mediating structures play little part. There came to be as many religions as there were people. The electronic church ministers to this situation, since it generates no tangible congregation, only clienteles of people who converge on a set of signals.

Ultramodernity further enhances choice, for the clienteles are not content with even the maze of denominational inheritances. Each denomination is chopped in two and one must choose this party or that. That division is only the beginning. Each must also choose a caucus, a cause, a movement, a celebrity, until these all come to compete with the congregations and denominations. The ultramodern solution certainly generates intensity, "hot" experiences. One is "into" Pentecostalism or the Jesus movement, an evangelical commune or a charismatic healing group, each of which has its passwords and argot, its rules of behavior and sectarian sets of meanings. Mainline Christianity has been puzzled by the new demands made on faith in the ultramodern world, but fundamentalists, Pentecostals, and evangelicals thrive on them and in their midst.

The question of *communitas*, profound community and social control, is left over in the newest adaptation. What is ahead? Once again, there may be large-scale dropouts and wanings, as there were after British evangelicalism's prime in Modernity A. There may be more commutation than before between worlds, as some mainliners acquire evangelical traits and various evangelical groups go looking for "catholic roots." In the circulation of elites, many evangelicals may become so adapted as to turn mainline; it is hard to be marginal when one of your own is president of the United States and all the worldly celebrities are in your camp. Or the movement may represent a longer-scale revitalization if it is well anchored in the congregations.

What does all this have to do with the southern religious theme?

Historically, southern evangelicalism matches this two-stage or two-episode approach. It is shaped during Modernity A, a period which saw the established Episcopal church lose ground. Blacks and whites together in the Second Great Awakening found evangelicalism most to their liking. During the interlude period, southern evangelicals were not asleep. They had succeeded in stamping southern faith with the outlooks and behavior patterns of the older evangelicalism and took as their foil not only European radical Christian thought but even the more moderate novelties of northern American "brain-working" families and scholars.

But Modernity B has seen sudden new prosperity for the evangelical cause. The South is the new center of mobility and affluence, of electronic and technological hunger and capability in the aerospace age. Demographic trends favor southern evangelicalism over all comers and the face of new comers. At this time of drastic social change, the people of transition did what pioneers have often done: they looked backward, taking symbols from the past to legitimate and inform the cultural moves they make. They are vulnerable to the charge that they are turning success-minded and worldly.

Those of us who share many of the assumptions of the evangelical world but are listed as being on its margins, and those of us who by accident of birth and vocation do not live in the South, are watching southern evangelicalism in the face of Modernity B with special interest. Let the media deal with the more exotic and esoteric Eastern-based occult and cultic movements; the real power and the greater share in American destiny will probably emerge from the course southern evangelicals take. If they should regress, as it were, to intransigent forms during the *Battle for the Bible,* they are likely to become very strong in a defined subculture. If they should consolidate some of their gains made along the lines of ultramodern appeals, by converting them to stronger communal and congregational life—as they do in many locales—it is likely that the subculture will be less well defined but more potent.

It was clear that by the 1980s these forms of evangelicalism had burst the bounds of southern subculture—had left *its* ghetto, if you will, as Catholics had long left theirs—and crowded the old mainstream. In the process of adapting to the larger culture, evangelicalism may have changed more than America did. Many of its leaders projected images of attachment to worldly success, to the cults

of athletics and entertainment and celebrity. Others reacted by calling for new critical and prophetic efforts. There is always the danger in popular religious movements that they will gain much of the
whole world while losing something of their collective soul. There
is also always the possibility that, in the present case, as they learn
their place and way in a pluralistic society, they might, some of
them, indeed be seeking the kingdom of God. And all kinds of
things can be added as surprising benefits along the way.

13 New-Time Religion: The Old Face of Fundamentalism Lifted

Evangelicalism north and south has a more rigid partner which in the 1920s acquired the name fundamentalism. For decades it was seen to be the religion of individuals who kept some distance from the public world. They were a set of people with private interests, aloof from and hostile to a pluralistic culture. In the course of recent decades they have remained hostile to many elements and aspects of pluralism, but they are less aloof. And, far from being seen as a passive, remote, private force, their movement suddenly came to be seen as a social thrust in United States society.

Fundamentalism, involving as it does some ten to twenty million Americans,[1] is obviously a social phenomenon and demands interpretation as such. But the observer who isolates the social dimension has to take special care to be fair-minded, to give something of the participants' point of view. To descend on fundamentalism from the outside with too many presuppositions about social movements may mean to lose the necessary sense of what animates the movement and inspires loyalty to it.

INDIVIDUAL RELIGIOSITY

Fundamentalists for the most part would not see themselves as members of a "social phenomenon." Almost all observers have agreed with participants that fundamentalism is in many respects a highly individualized version of Christian faith. The fundamentalists for the most part are church members, but they are not "churchly" in a sacramental sense. They make little of an ontological reality that calls them to communal existence, a church that exists in the mind of God or the structure of things before it manifests itself as voluntary local associations.

To the fundamentalist, participation means being saved. It begins with a separation from the world in the form of being "born again," though there are fundamentalists in, say, the Presbyterian tradition who find that term less congenial than do the majority in the Baptist traditions. From this separation follows a deeper desire to be separated also from sin and from half-faithful or even apostate people who call themselves Christians but who waver on certain fundamentals. The believer wants to be with Jesus in the Rapture, the millennial reign, and finally in the new heavens. The terms for the eschaton vary somewhat, but no one should ever forget the otherworldly or next-worldly dimension in this faith.

So it comes down to an individual search and a personal reception of grace. To take fundamentalists seriously and to see their faith as a matter of integrity, we must, in any fair analysis of the social phenomenon, listen to the participants' description. In the deepest sense of the term, people who are religious cannot help but be religious. They cannot be beguiled out of their vision, distracted from their passion, diverted from what consumes them. Members of lackadaisical mainline churches who have to be cajoled into the pew and seduced toward the tithe may forget the power of such engrossing religious appeals. But the fundamentalist does not forget. He or she is out to "get saved," and little else matters.

VOLUNTARY ASSOCIATION

Holding constantly to that understanding, however, the observer moves on. Fundamentalism, like all modern faiths—and this one is nothing if not modern, born in the face and challenge of modernity and taking advantage of its mixed technical offerings—involves the possibility that the believer will keep religion a "private affair."[2] Yet one will notice that the majority of the saved do form social organizations. The most powerful of these, of course, is the local church, which in the technical sense is the only church fundamentalism knows. However, there are voluntary extensions of this local reality. These take the form of clienteles for religious radio and television; power movements within moderate denominations like the Southern Baptist Convention; constituencies that support Bible institutes, crusades, and publishing ventures.

A SPACE IN THE SOCIAL WORLD

By this point of organization the individual fundamentalist can no longer hide from the awareness that a social phenomenon has developed. Even as an ecclesial reality of a nominalist sort, fundamentalist church life takes institutional form and thus takes up space in the world. Wary of receiving government aid for their churchly enterprises, fundamentalists long insisted on separation of church and state. This insistence has become muted and compromised in recent times as many began to project a sort of theocratic Christian America model. Yet despite these moves, most of them keep insisting that they are truly independent of and separated from involvement of church in state and state in church. Yet by accepting tax exemption of church properties, they are involved. This exemption may be seen as a right, or good policy, or public benefit. It is in any case a fiscal boon to American churches that far exceeds the subsidy established churches receive in Europe. And as tax-exempt by the public, which thus helps pay for them, the churches willy-nilly enter the public realm.

The move from individuals' "being saved" to their being part of a social phenomenon goes far beyond the physical space of fundamentalist properties and the indirect public support through tax exemption. Fundamentalism wants to win converts, and this means moving door to door in public communities, passing out tracts in pluralist settings, and using air waves that are conceived as "belonging" to everyone. In this sense, in many parts of the country at least, nonfundamentalists become aware of the social dimensions of a voluntaryist religious vision.

THE POLITICAL DIMENSION

A third stage of presence, however, moves fundamentalism further in the public eye as a social phenomenon. This is its political aspiration. Most fundamentalists do not see themselves as political, and their own witness about themselves has to be taken seriously. Through most of their history, most members have tended to be passive about connecting religion and politics. Their social class, often upper-lower or lower-middle, had kept them from the kinds of colleges, support funding, or aspiring that brings people to Congress or executive mansions. Intensely patriotic, they would vote or accept the call to military service, since fundamentalist pacifism is extremely rare. They paid their taxes and probably had a lower crime and delinquency rate than the general public or some more relaxed religious forces could boast.

Fundamentalism as a social phenomenon has often been hard to isolate on the political level because voting tends to follow partisan and regional lines. Most fundamentalists insist that they do not wish to organize political parties. Although many analysts see ties between theological and political "conservatism," that term itself is problematic when dealing with fundamentalism. When the movement was born, it did not "conserve" much of what Roman Catholic, Eastern Orthodox, and mainline Protestant churches—which must make up nine-tenths of Christendom—would have regarded as the tradition worth preserving. It was quite radical in its primitivism, insisting that it was reproducing biblical-era belief and organization. More than it knew, the movement did draw on traditional thirteenth- and seventeenth-century scholasticism, Catholic and Protestant. Often in its more open Calvinist forms, it also paid respects to the sixteenth-century Protestant Reformation. But the movement makes no sense except as a very modern reaction to modernism,[3] a highly selective selection of the "fundamentals" of faith, a fresh patterning of the presumed "essences" of Christianity, one that makes little sense to the sacramental churches, whose "essentials" seldom come up. Fundamentalism in many senses, including the best ones, was not "conservative" but radical.

Yet the public and liberal religionists type the movement as theologically conservative and assume that this conservatism carries over symptomatically into politics. Certainly there are predispositions of this sort; yet examinations of voting records often show that fundamentalists of the South and the Plains states allied themselves with populist movements that were anything but conservative. In the 1930s true political conservatives often thought of the Tennessee Valley Authority as socialistic or communistic. Appalachian fundamentalists who wanted their farms electrified voted for such a program, whatever socialist images it carried. It would be a mistake to picture all fundamentalists as political reactionaries at all times.

DEFENSE AND AGGRESSION

Sometimes fundamentalism as a social phenomenon shows up politically in a defensive way. Before the Democratic Convention of 1960, fundamentalists and other Protestant conservatives sometimes made ephemeral common cause with the Protestant liberals to raise criticisms of Catholicism in American life in connection with the candidacy of John F. Kennedy.[4] They regularly hurry to Washington with the best of liberals to protect themselves from real or presumed intrusive threats on the part of the Internal Revenue Service or the Federal Communications Commission.[5] They may not see these defensive gestures as being political, bringing them into the zone of "social phenomena," but in the process of building coalitions and making alliances, testifying in Congress, lobbying, or seeking votes on specific issues, they have to be seen as far removed from individualist, nonpolitical life.

Beyond automatic participation in social life and defensiveness, much fundamentalism has moved into more aggressive endeavors to be a social phenomenal presence. This occurs whenever its leaders, backed by visible followers, assert themselves in efforts to reshape social life in America. This is almost always done in the name of "morality" in putative distinction from or even opposition to "politics." Fundamentalists have cared deeply, as is their right, about gambling, alcoholic intemperance, and accessible pornography. These are, of course, moral issues: they are issues congenial to that strain of Protestantism that had long before become expert at dealing with individual "virtue" and "vice," as opposed to social and structural reworking of society.

The problem with keeping fundamentalism an individual religiosity as opposed to a social phenomenon is that one cannot move far beyond simple personal voluntaryism without bumping into contravening political forces that have their own interests. The bumper sticker that says "Against Abortion?—Don't Have One!" illustrates an approach that would allow fundamentalism to remain withdrawn from the political order and to be seen less as a social phenomenon. Studies in the summer of 1981 that revealed fundamentalists to be represented almost as regularly in audiences of sexy-and-violent TV shows as was the general public might have inspired another set of bumper stickers: "Don't Like 'Em? Shut Them Off!" "Don't like intemperance? Don't drink." Let us take in good faith the fundamentalist claims that members do restrain themselves in the matters of abortion, pornography, and alcohol. They thus make a contribution to a moral America on their terms.

LEGISLATED MORALITY

Fundamentalists would not be satisfied, however, with only that measure of contribution. Nine-tenths of America is not fundamentalist, and if it continues in immoral practices, America will still not be "moral." So a moralist vision does and must move into politics again, let us keep insisting, in a process that is fully legitimate. Fundamentalism has its rights. It is at this point, however, that a blind spot develops, one that matches the blinders liberals wear when *they* sometimes say that fundamentalists should not enter the political arena. To the fundamentalist, religious liberal support of the civil rights or antiwar movements a dozen years ago and more was political, not moral. Liberal opposition to capital punishment is political; fundamentalist support of it is moral. Saving lives through poverty programs in the public sector is a political act; saving fetal life by prohibiting abortions is a moral venture. This distinction has not been compelling to any nonfundamentalist.

Fundamentalist leaders in 1980 and 1981 began to see the anomaly, indeed the bad faith, implied in this distinction. The best known of them, evangelist Jerry Falwell, very frankly and openly admitted that he had been "wrong" when he previously inerrantly followed his inerrant Bible in opposing clerical involvement in the politics of civil rights. He spoke with some measure of repentance for his old stand—perhaps prudently, possibly with deep conviction after a "conversion" and some measure of admiration for people like Martin Luther King, Jr.; perhaps it was a ploy, but here we should also grant the possibility of good faith, as a latter-day recognition of King's effort for human good. In either case, Falwell made no secret of his having led part of fundamentalism overtly into that moral-political realm.

To work for constitutional amendments, to seek passage of certain specific legislation, to attempt to prevent this or that international treaty—all these are marks not of individualist religiosity but of a social phenomenon of considerable power. The leaders justify their about-face on the grounds that America has grown so immoral that they must engage in a "teleological suspension of the ethical." Intemperance was and abortion is such a gross immorality in the sight of God and such a hazard to the civil order that one must take extraordinary means to address them as problems. Then one can lapse back into political passivity. This would mean that fundamentalism is only *sometimes* a social phenomenon.

A POWER AMONG POWERS

Once the policy of separation, passivity, and even withdrawal is broken, however, much else follows. Today's fundamentalist leadership has spotted a power vacuum and has enjoyed beginning to fill it. "How're ya goin' to keep 'em down on the farm after they've seen Paree?" How are you going to keep fundamentalists off in individual religiosity after they have seen how easily they can effect some parts of their social vision? To seek power is not necessarily an evil: without power one cannot achieve good. But to seek power on present terms is to recognize that fundamentalism, whatever its historic voice, today overtly seeks to be a social phenomenon with political dimensions.

If political fundamentalism inconveniences other people, people who support the Panama Canal Treaty, abortion clinics, the Department of Education, or cocktail lounges, it has to understand that its jostling of the social fabric will inspire criticism and counterorganization. Legitimately wounded by a few unfair attacks on their rights as they intruded into the political order, some of the leaders overstepped or showed naïveté by creating the suggestion that the idea of counteraction, even if only in the form of criticism, was always out of line. But there are no exempt spaces for people who enter the political order. Politics, however unready fundamentalists may be to recognize it, is an order that involves conflict and compromise.[6] It is an assertion of power amidst other powers, an attempt to make moves that step on the toes of others who, thus alerted, stop wincing and start marching or arming or organizing. The social phenomenal character of fundamentalism, then, has become patent. Attempts to disguise it are to be short-lived. Efforts to hold out against the move on the part of fundamentalist minorities are not likely to protect the movement as a whole from a public perception that sees its social presence.

Fundamentalism, then, has become a political force among the forces. Politicians reckon with it as they do with labor unions and senior citizens' action agencies. Television critics regard it as a social phenomenon for its presence in "the electronic church." *Publishers' Weekly* gives an accounting of its book sales. There is no place to hide, and the majority of fundamentalist leadership does not wish to. Far, far removed seem the days when the individual search for salvation was the encompassing feature of fundamentalism.

A TWO-PARTY SYSTEM CHANGING?

Seeing fundamentalism as a social phenomenon today makes most sense when viewed against the past. Some years ago, in *Righteous Empire*, I made a distinction within Protestantism.[7] It had a "two-party" system, one termed "public" and the other "private." In 1857–58, at the time of the "laymen's revivals," whose social consequences Timothy Smith has so well chronicled in *Revivalism and Social Reform*,[8] one could view revivalists also as social movement leaders for reform, welfare, and political purposes. Before them Charles Grandison Finney's generation of revivalists engaged themselves with issues that ranged from dueling to slavery.[9] But by 1908, when the old Federal Council of Churches was born, it was organized chiefly around certain more liberal social purposes and had left evangelism pretty well behind. By then, also, evangelists in the train of Dwight L. Moody through Billy Sunday, for all their casual and even sometimes forceful social comments, were seen as specialists in soul-saving, rescuing people from a world of shipwreck into salvationist lifeboats, to use Moody's celebrated metaphor.

POLITICAL NOT PUBLIC

Has the picture now changed? In some respects, yes. Fundamentalism allows for development, indeed development of doctrine, if one listens to the Falwell apologia, and what was once wrong can now become right, on biblical grounds—the only grounds fundamentalists will finally admit to taking seriously. But I believe that public/private distinction remains appropriate for the most part, at least with respect to the evangelistic-evangelical tradition. The fundamentalist move into politics in the 1980s is of a somewhat different character. Not to put too fine a point on it, its theological assumptions are now "political" but not "public." A public theology, as numbers of us have set out to define it, allows for the integrity of movements that are not conservative Protestant, Christian, or Jewish-Christian at all. God can work his "order" through the godless, in secular-pluralism. A public theology allows for a positive interpretation of that secular-pluralist order with its religious admixtures, even as it recognizes all the while the way the demonic pervades the orders of existence. The political theology of privatist fundamentalism does not do so. It is born of separatists who do not regard nonfundamentalists with any positive ecumenical feelings. The fundamentalist political scope may recognize Catholics and Jews or "traditional theists" as belonging in the civil order, but then insists that nontheists are outsiders, to be tolerated at best. Let it also be said that not all fundamentalists have made the overt political move, and not all conservative Protestantism is fundamentalist.

This public/political distinction is not a hard and fast one, and its nuances, now apparently fine, may easily elude us. Yet through the years we shall need some handle to separate the two, for there are vastly different consequences in civil life. Admittedly, one can approach the subject in Humpty-Dumpty's way: "When I use a word, it means just what I choose it to mean—neither more nor less." And when one comes to study *public* in the *Oxford English Dictionary*, there is a growing sense of elusiveness: "The varieties of sense are numerous and pass into each other by many intermediate shades of meaning. The exact shade often depends upon the substantive qualified." Yet in thirty and more *OED* definitions, the word *political* never appears to explain public. The first definition of *political* does need the word *public*, however, which suggests that *political* in some ways can be a species of a genus called *public*.

In the sense that I here use the word *political*, it refers to the activity by which interests—in this case, the fundamentalists—seek their way, though they must finally compromise (or retreat) and be conciliated by receiving a share in power in proportion to their weight in the political community. While politics is not exhausted by self-interest, it is moved chiefly by it. In the present case, the interest group seeks to protect its turf, to extend its mission, and to have its way at the expense of other ways.

On the other hand, the public is pre-, para-, and postpolitical. It allows to other interests a full integrity. In its sphere strangers meet and overcome their fears; conflict occurs and is to be resolved; life is given color, texture, drama, a festive air; mutual responsibility becomes evident, opinions are heard and countered; visions are tested. Crucial again in this second sense: religionists in the public sphere have a theological accounting of the validity of those who do not share their final outlook. Politically minded church bodies need have a positive explanation of only their own and their allies' causes; all the rest may be neutral or negative. Thus it is that one can seek one's own way in politics without taking on a public mien, guise, or intention.[10]

EVANGELISM AND PENTECOSTALISM

The evangelists from Moody through Graham tried to "work" the private realm. When Billy Graham moved beyond it, as he did frequently in the 1950s through the 1970s, he saw this as casual extrusion from his evangelist calling or part of his responsibility as a citizen, without connecting the activity to his evangelist movement. Many evangelists are even less expressive than he was about positive political points. Their evangelism makes up a social phenomenon to them, but of a largely ecclesiastical character. That is, it takes up social space, but in the modern division of labor that space is sequestered in the bloc called "religion," not "culture comment" or "social impact" or "political pressure."

It is similar with Pentecostalists, who are also often confused with fundamentalists. Taking rise early in this century concurrently with fundamentalism, this Pentecostalism could make common cause with the scholastic-minded intransigents over against modernism. But the two made an uneasy partnership because not all Pentecostalists accepted fundamentalist-scholastic views of biblical inerrancy, and the Pentecostal claims of a kind of "enthusiasm" in connection with Spirit-baptism and speaking in tongues threatened many fundamentalist dogmatists. Pentecostals may often have been populists, and they did their voting. But it has always been more difficult to get them into focus, not as a social phenomenon but as a social movement with discernible political bents.

One could add other groups that are conservative but not part of the fundamentalist social phenomena: black Protestant, whether Methodist or Baptist or Pentecostal; the Southern Baptist Convention, which has a fundamentalist wing but also has a quite separate history and existence; conservative Reformed and Lutheran movements like the Christian Reformed Church and the Missouri Synod. These are examples of groups whose social-political careers differ widely from that of fundamentalism.

A LONG POLITICAL TENDENCY

Fundamentalism almost from the beginning, then, was more ready to be overtly political than were these cohort groups at the side. If we see fundamentalism as a conservative Protestant force born of reaction to liberal modernism that fused premillennialism with (Princeton-style arguments for) inerrancy, began to make a proto-statement in *The Fundamentals,* got named in 1920, and was the aggressor in efforts to sway major denominations in the mid-twenties, we must realize that even in the first generation fundamentalism had a political posture. This was focused chiefly on the issues of Zionism. There were Protestant fundamentalist Zionists in America before Jewish Zionism took hold. This derived from the peculiar reading of biblical prophecy which was popularized in the *Scofield Reference Bible* and which in a series of prophetic biblical conferences led to a virtual takeover of protofundamentalism by dispensational premillennialists. Thus, as early as 1891, the tireless agitator William E. Blackstone gathered the names of over four hundred prominent Americans and presented to President Harrison a petition asserting the political right of Jews to rebuild the nation of Israel.[11]

In the second generation fundamentalism was an organized force in the political realm, as was evident from its participation in the most celebrated religious event of the 1920s, the Scopes trial. This had to do with antievolution legislation and school book policy and was thus overtly political. Through the thirties the fundamentalists were busy rebuilding their institutions after the denominational defeats around 1925. They did this very effectively through the war years, as various fundamentalist fronts were organized around 1942.[12]

Then in the fifties, during the Cold War era, fundamentalists like Carl McIntire and Billy James Hargis and any number of anti-Communist crusaders began their program for a fortress America. Then as now, part of their chauvinism grew from the conviction that Falwell still announces. Even if the Second Coming is imminent, Christians are to "occupy until Christ comes." And they are to see America as a new Zion, its people as a chosen people. America must remain free, through fundamentalist efforts, since it is the last training ground for evangelists who will rescue individuals elsewhere before the Rapture. This is far from a developed "public theology," but it is certainly a nationalist-political one.[13]

So the New Christian Right, which has fundamentalism at its core even as it picks up some Pentecostalists, evangelicals, Southern Baptists, and conservative Protestants from confessional denominations, has precedent chiefly in the scholastic-millennial "hardline" tradition that took shape almost a century ago and was formally organized in the 1920s. What had been latent is now patent; the covert became overt, but there has been less switching and more "development" than spokesmen like Falwell allow for in their apologiae.

13. Old Face of Fundamentalism Lifted

WHY SOCIAL-POLITICAL *NOW?*

If fundamentalism is a social phenomenon with a political cast, and if it has been so in some ways from the beginning, it remains only to ask why it has become so visible, explicit, and belligerent *now.* The answer is too complex to be reduced to a few paragraphs, but several main features of a response to the question will throw light on the phenomenon today.

First, there is a worldwide reaction against many of the mixed offerings of modernity.[14] Fundamentalism, as part of it, both ministers to the victims of modernization and exploits them. Iran is the prototype. Technology and affluence swept the scene there, but the benefits were for the few. The shah's family, the Iranian elites who studied in America, and the oil sheiks reaped the benefits. The rest of the population did not have its physical circumstances improved and only saw its traditions threatened. In reaction, ayatollahs preached the old scriptures, women returned to wearing the chador, and there was a fundamentalist-based religious revolution. Something similar is going on in numbers of underdeveloped nations. American fundamentalism cannot be dismissed as a lower-class-aspirant economic cohort, though some dimensions of social class are apparent in its movement. But it is clearly a force of resentment against "intellectuals," "elites," "the media," and the like, people who are at home with modernization and care little for the presumed traditions.

Second, there is a worldwide movement, which we might call "tribalism," that is obvious in African nations, Israel, Iran, Lebanon, Ireland, the Asian subcontinent, and elsewhere.[15] In this movement people retreat from modernity by withdrawing into their ethno-religio-cultural-tribal bonds. This retreat was easier to begin in Lebanon, where there are spatial separations between such groups, than in America, where there is more intermixing. But in America too, one might see fundamentalism as the latest in the two-decade movement of groups, be they black, Chicano, Jewish, Catholic ethnic, homosexual, young, feminist, or whatever, to find and assert symbols. These, then, are designed to assure a group's power, place, and pride—over against the real or presumed threats of others. For example, there are not many blacks in formal fundamentalism, though most blacks would be typed as belonging in the conservative revivalist tradition. Fundamentalists are visible as a social phenomenon because they are now getting their tribe together and finding ways to be assertive about their place.

Third, there was an ecological niche or cranny to be filled, a void that had room for a new growth. There has been, no one can deny, some sort of "values crisis" in America, a shift in understandings and practices having to do with family life, sexuality, and expression. Those who are devotees of pluralism and who believe that transmittable values can emerge from public debate and conflict somehow tolerate ambiguity and pick their way through the confusions of the decades. The fundamentalists, however, can appeal to the impatient. Theirs is an almost Manichean world of black/white, God/Satan, Christ/Antichrist, Christian/"secular humanist." On these terms it is easy to invent and expose "conspiracies" of the forces against good—good America, good fundamentalists. People who seek authoritarian solutions are likely to follow charismatic fundamentalist leaders in such a time.

Finally, fundamentalists, though they may lack a positive view of certain scientific and technological processes, are uninhibited in their use of the products. Radio, television, computers, direct-mail technology—all of which remain practically mysterious and inaccessible to mainline Christianity—seem made for the world of fundamentalist splinter groups. Speakers on radio and television can portray clear choices with great simplicity. They have found ways to raise paracongregational funds to make possible opinion-surveying and pressure-grouping. They have "borrowed" the technology of modernization with all its bewilderments and used it substantially to promote nostalgic and simplistic visions of the past as models for the future.

THE FUTURE

Will they win? The fundamentalist message and pattern of meanings appeals to a rather definite class and personality type. Leadership has to content itself with making the most of its market potential within conservative Protestantism. America is not "turning fundamentalist." It has become aware of fundamentalism, and fundamentalists have seen a great growth in morale and visibility. They will not soon slink away. But their interpretations, grounded in one kind of biblical inerrancy and premillennialism, are not the choice of the many.

This means that fundamentalists have to build some coalitions, as they have done on the abortion front. It is also likely that some leadership will adapt and modify itself to become more smooth, ingratiating, and palatable. It has begun to do this and, in the process, has already alienated huge sections of "nonpolitical" fundamentalism on one hand and "hyperfundamentalism" on the other. But the American *Danegeld* is too rich for these leaders not to be bought off, and the political lures are too strong for them to resist. Fundamentalist clienteles will also become ever more pluralistic. Their interests have to be met. Hence, for example, the exclusion of deadly tobacco from its usual place alongside deadly alcohol in the program. Leaders admit that they cannot make an antitobacco plank part of a crusade because too many followers smoke or make their living off raising and treating tobacco. Such waverings make fundamentalism more compromising, more assimilable, more capable of being conceived as one more element in the Republic.

Only if the "formal system" should break down and the economic order collapse would it be likely that fundamentalists could break out of their current cohort in the competitive market. If there has to be a whole new social contract some day, it is likely that there must be in it a state religion, compulsory in character, authoritarian in tone, "traditional" in outlook. America would be "socialized" not in the name of Marx but of Jesus, not in the name of communism but of Christian republicanism.[16] To mention all this is not to hint at a self-fulfilling prophecy but to sketch the terms by which fundamentalism could ever "win America" as a social phenomenon. Until then it must pick its shots, build alliances, and make skillful use of the edges that technology and dedication give it in close American elections. Until then, fundamentalists have to rely on the evocative power their often inaccurate images induce whenever they talk about the Jewish-Christian stipulations of "Enlightened" founding fathers, or the "traditional theism" of once-Unitarian deist public schools, as transmitters of the founding fathers' values.[17] Until then, they can also do their best service by making nonfundamentalists think about values and their transmission, pluralism and its problems, American public faith and individual religiosity, in their always changing conjunctions.

14 History: The Case of the Mormons, a Special People

What we have described as the "thickness of pluralism," the particularities of American peoples in their religious groupings, shows up most vividly in a multimillion-member movement called Mormon. It is made up of chiefly WASP populations, yet they acquired as distinctive a character in the larger public as Judaism possesses. Often overlooked in assessments of American religious demography, this "new religious tradition" increasingly demands separate analysis. A most striking feature is that while "differentiation" is an aspect of modernity that challenges other sets of people, the Mormon crisis has to do with the challenge of modern historical consciousness and criticism. Such a burden of history assaults all fundamentalisms and conservatisms, but it confronts Mormons most directly, for reasons that we shall shortly point out.

Mormon thought is experiencing a crisis comparable to but more profound than that which Roman Catholicism recognized around the time of the Second Vatican Council (1962–65). Whatever other changes were occurring in the Catholic church, there was a dramatic, sometimes traumatic shift in ways of regarding the tradition. One of the conventional ways of speaking of this shift comes from the observation of philosopher Bernard Lonergan. He and others in his train argued that Catholicism was moving from a "classic" view of dogma to a thoroughly "historical" view of faith.

In the classic view, Catholic teaching had come intact, as it were, protected from contingency, from a revealing God. Deposited in Scripture, church tradition, and especially dogma, it was protected from anything but ordinary or trivial historical accidents. In the new vision, this classic understanding gave place to an approach which saw Catholic events, thought, and experience as being at all points and in every way colored by the contingencies and accidents of history. God was revealed in the midst of this history.

Mormonism never was constituted around anything so formal and, it was believed by Catholics, uncontingent as dogma. From the beginning this faith was always characterized by its thoroughly historical mode and mold. Yet almost inevitably this understanding after a century took on what we might call an "historically classical" form. Today, in what some might regard as a dramatic and traumatic shift among Mormon intellectuals, there is a move so expansive and sudden that it hardly needs chronicling. While tautology might sound cute, one could say this shift is from an "historically classic" to an "historically historical" understanding. A focus on this issue can serve for reexamination of the historian's vocation—whether this be of the believing "insider" or the non- or other-believing and "outsider" version. At the same time, the inquiry can point to some of the limits of historical contributions to issues of faith and certitude.

HISTORY AND THE HISTORIAN

Whatever else historians do, there are at least two components in their work. They deal with the past and they tell stories. As G. J. Renier[1] reminds us, their subject is the human social past (in contrast to, say, "natural history"). And while today various structuralisms and "cliometric" statistical approaches may obscure the story character, yet over all the historical mode is one of narrative, of story. Stories have subjects. Here things begin to get interesting.

We may not know exactly why anyone else follows the vocation of the historian. When one is an historian, it is also hard to account for the choice of subject. Some people who are Mormon will choose to write on other than Mormon history: roofing technology in Virginia, dairy farming in Wisconsin, or the middle years of Michael the Drunkard may be compelling subjects to some. Others will inquire about the past of their own people. Meanwhile some people who are *not* Mormon will abandon other subjects and find themselves drawn to the history of the Saints. Historians cannot all avoid the story of the social past of a movement of up to five million people. It would be inconceivable that they escape the notice of non-Mormons, Gentiles. At once, two sets of people set out on similar topics. This often has produced clashes.

The ethics of the profession calls historians to do careful research, not to hide evidence, to be suspicious when handling sources, and then to be fair. People used to say they should be "objective," but objectivity seems to be a dream denied. This means that historians have to be reasonably aware of their assumptions, the viewpoints they bring, the thought worlds of the people they are representing at second hand. What results, all thoughtful historians agree, is not a reproduction of reality, which cannot even be grasped by people on the scene during events, but "a social construction of reality." The historian invents.

Historical construction or invention is more delicate when the subject is the experience of the sacred in the life of people, of a people. The sacred, Rudolf Otto's *mysterium tremendum et fascinans*, appears in the midst of the mundane and ordinary world with an Otherness which sometimes threatens, often eludes, forever beguiles the historian who comes in range of it. Because people who respond to the sacred stake their arrangement of life and their eternal hopes on this experience, they bring to it a passion which often leads them to want to be protected from historians and other social scientists. "Our" sacred, "our" Otherness, we think, is different— pure, uncontingent, protected from accident, beyond the scope of inquiring historians, be they insiders or outsiders.

Most of the time both those internal to the history of a people and a faith as well as those external to it can go about their business without creating suspicion or arousing a defensive spirit. So long as the life of the people proceeds routinely, they may not pay much attention to what historians discover and publish. It is when people are in a period of crisis that they notice the historians. Renier has a charming passage on how historians, used to obscurity, become suddenly relevant when people "stop to think." They are especially

on the spot when what they discover and publish *causes* the people
to "stop to think." They have successfully done so, from within and
without, in the case of Mormons in recent times.

STOPPING TO THINK ABOUT HISTORICITY
AND RELIGION

The Mormon ferment of today, like the Catholic analogue during
and after Vatican II, is a species of a genus we might call "the crisis
of historical consciousness." This crisis cut to the marrow in the
Protestant body of thoughtful scholars in Western Europe in the
nineteenth century and continues, though it has been lived with in
various ways and thus seems more domesticated, in the late twentieth. Before the Enlightenment and the rise of a critical history
focused on Christianity, professional historians were ordinarily cast
as story-tellers who were defenders of the faith. A few learned to
direct their suspicions against forgeries and frauds like the Dona-
tion of Constantine. Most were called, if they were Catholic, to
summon events from the past to certify the truth of Catholicism
over against Protestantism. Needless to say, vice versa.

This meant that the ordinary historian was much like other believers in respect to the people's past. It is useful here to introduce
Paul Ricoeur's concept of "primitive naïveté,"[2] by which he means
nothing pejorative or condescending, merely something which designates. Children have such a naïveté: they receive and accept
more or less without question a world, a world view, and views,
from parents and nurses and teachers. Tribal people can sustain a
similar naïveté: they know other tribes with other ways only from a
distance, at best. Or they find no threat in these because they see
no lure: other ways belong to the enemy. Isolated people, whether
in a valley or an urban ghetto in a pluralist society, even in the age
of mass media, can sustain the naïveté. So can people in massive
isolations of the sort which bind together every fifth human, religions like Islam. Most places where it is strong it has a monopoly,
and the Muslim never knows and need never consider alternative
ways of being or believing.

The primitive naïveté of Catholic Europe, protected by space
from the Muslim and contrived space in the form of ghetto walls

from the Jews, was challenged with the introduction of variety by the Protestant Reformation on Western soil. Yet it waited for the Enlightenment to introduce the full-fledged asssault on this naïveté. The Enlightenment brought other religions close to home: one thinks of Lessing's *Nathan der Weise* as a typical attempt to see rough parity between Christianity, Judaism, and Islam. The Enlightenment went further: while beginning to relativize Christian distinctives in the face of other ways, it also used critical tools on Christian texts and traces from the past.

In the nineteenth century, the age of modern critical history, the crisis of historical consciousness became intense and drastic. Now no events, experiences, traces, or texts were exempt from scrutiny by historians who believed they could be value-free, dispassionate. Today, of course, no one sees them as being successful in their search. They were tainted by radical Hegelian dialectics, neo-Kantian rigorisms, or the biases of a positivism that thought it could be unbiased. We may see these critical historians as naïve in this respect. Otherwise they were highly successful at destroying the primitive naïveté among those who read them seriously. The responses could vary among these readers. Some lost faith while others shored it up with defensive fundamentalisms which focused on papal infallibility or biblical inerrancy. Most adapted their way of looking at faith and lived with it in transformed ways. Whatever else happened, however, the believer who made the passage beyond primitive naïveté was very busy picking and choosing responsive attitudes.

THE CHRISTIAN CRISIS OF HISTORICAL CONSCIOUSNESS

Protestantism, like Catholicism, had a "classical" aspect through its own dogmatic structure. All Christians then, like the Saints now, had much at stake because their faith was so thoroughly historical in character. It lived by reference to events like the creation, the call of Israel through its exodus and exile, the happening of Jesus Christ and especially his death and resurrection within calendrical history, and the calling into being of an historical people, the Church. To see these events as shaped by historical forces, their traces and texts unexempt from critical examination, altered responses of faith and practice.

The clash between classic and historical views was stated classically by Lessing (1729–1781), the Lutheran minister's son who became an Enlightenment philosopher. He argued what has since become a commonplace: an historical truth was not capable of logical demonstration. Reported miracles, from creation through the signs and wonders which accompany biblical accounts of Israel and Jesus and through the visions which led to the vocations of prophets and apostles down to the resurrection of Christ could never thus demonstrate the truth of Christianity. "Accidental truths of history can never become the necessary truths of reason." Lessing called the gulf between the truths of history and the truths of reason "the ugly broad ditch which I cannot get across, however often and however earnestly I have tried to make the leap."[3]

Henceforth whoever believed in God and the integrity of God's people while aware of what Lessing and his successors posed, clearly had to believe in a different way—Ricoeur would say through a second naïveté. After criticism, people believe not in spite of but through interpretation. Much of educated catholic (Catholic and Protestant) Christianity is made up of people who thus believe. They would not call themselves "literalists" about history and would even question whether self-styled literalists are really literal or whether these do not select which events to protect from scrutiny under the leaky canopy of historical contingency.

The transit to the second mode of being and believing was not easy; a little garland of testimonies should suffice to recall it. John Viscount Lord Morley[4] spoke of the subsequently developed "triumph of the principle of relativity in historic judgment," the "substitution of *becoming* for *being*, the relative for the absolute, dynamic movement for dogmatic immobility."

The result was what historian Friedrich Meinecke called "one of the greatest spiritual revolutions which western thought has experienced." Ernst Troeltsch, a great Christian scholar, personalized it in a way that speaks to and for many. He had come with a solid belief in the events and the demonstrability of events which made up the Christian story, protected from and within the rest of history. Like others, he personally had felt the "demand of the religious consciousness for certainty, for unity, and for peace." But:

14. The Case of the Mormons

I soon discovered that the historical studies which had so largely formed me, and the theology and philosophy in which I was now immersed, stood in sharp opposition, indeed even in conflict, with one another. I was confronted, upon the one hand, with the perpetual flux of the historian's data, and the distrustful attitude of the historical critic towards conventional traditions.

So Christianity was henceforth "a purely historical, individual, relative phenomenon." Further, the inference from all this was "that a religion, in the several forms assumed by it, always depends upon the intellectual, social, and national conditions among which it exists." Gone for him was "the absolute validity of Christianity."

Not all scholars took Troeltsch's course. Critical historians who are Christian believers abound in most Catholic and Protestant communions. Yet the testimony of a profound and empathic figure like Troeltsch has led them not to be disdainful of people who take "literalistic" or "fundamentalistic" ways of responding to the crisis— just as they have to hope for sympathy and understanding from those who resist and, in resisting, show the depth of "the crisis of historical consciousness."

Where "primitive naïveté" is simply no longer possible but the desire for faith is matched by the presence of faith and participation in the life of a people, it is clear that people who live with and pass through the crisis of historical consciousness may have the same "object" of faith, but believe in different ways. We must at least entertain the possibility that there can be integrity in the response of believers who believe after criticism, through interpretation.

THE SAINTS' CRISIS OF HISTORICAL CONSCIOUSNESS

From the earliest years there have been Mormons who left the faith because their view of the historical events which gave shape to it no longer permitted them to sustain it. Others remained with the Mormon people but were uneasy and made their own adjustment. We may safely assume that all thoughtful people must have some struggles with elements of a complex history. Faith attached to or mediated through historical events has always had some dimensions of an "offense" or "scandal" to the insider just as it has been *only* that to the outsider who despises. Awareness of pettinesses and peccadillos among leaders or injustices in the record of a

309

people—one thinks of the Christian Crusades and Inquisition or papal corruption in many ages—has to be some sort of threat to the clarity of faith's vision, though it clearly has not meant the loss of faith or abandonment of peoplehood on the part of so many who are aware. Those more familiar than I with Mormon history can point and have pointed to questioners within the historical profession through the years.

As far as the profession as a whole and the intellectual community at large are concerned, however, the crisis has been noticeable only in the past two decades, and urgent only in very recent years. The hostility of the Gentile world, geographical remoteness from alien forces, and the necessarily defensive agenda of the Mormon churches and people long protected the Saints. Serene in their grasp of Mormon faith, the historians could busy themselves marshaling evidences to defend the integrity of the people. More often they simply chronicled the story of the amazing formation, trek, colonization, and expansion of a people—subjects that have to stir the hearts of either insiders or outsiders who have a musical ear for human drama.

Someday the crisis had to come. Few others of the 20,870 separate denominations listed in the most recent encyclopedia of Christianity have as much at stake so far as "historicness" is concerned as do Mormons. The character of their shaping events takes on a different nature in that these occurred so recently, on familiar soil, in check-outable times and places, *after* historical "science" had become developed. The shaping events of classic Christianity, whose story Mormons share, are accessible almost entirely through insider Christian sources alone. The Romans ignored them. Mormon events, meanwhile, occur inside a history chronicled by smalltown newspaper editors, diarists, hostile letter writers, contemporary historians. The beginnings are not so shrouded in obscurity as are Christian beginnings which were recorded especially in the New Testament. People now alive in their nineties who talked as little children to people then in their eighties have "memories" which link them to the years of Mormon beginnings. There is no place to hide. What can be sequestered in Mormon archives and put beyond the range of historians can often be approached by sources outside them. While Mormon iconography developed impressively early in its history, the images of Mormon beginnings are not yet haloed or sanctioned the way Christian beginnings are by their reflection in stained glass, their inspiration in centuries of classical music. There is little protection for Mormon sacredness.

Whoever knows how Christian faith survives and can survive knowledge of all the evidences of fallibility and scandal that occurred through history will understand why the outsider historian finds trivial the question of whether the faith is threatened by the revelation of human shortcomings in the later administration of the Mormon churches. Of course, for public relations reasons, one likes to portray one's heroes and Saints as saints. Lives of quality and character and policies of justice and fairness enhance one's identification with them and the people at large. Yet intellectually these are not of much interest. One can cut through all the peripheral issues and see that most of the writing on Mormon history which poses the issue of the crisis of historical consciousness focuses finally on Joseph Smith's First Vision, often capitalized to set it apart, and then, many agree, more importantly on the later vision which led to a second capitalization, the Book of Mormon.

Let me clear the air with a stark, almost crude, but still lighthearted and well-intended analogy.

> When Cardinal de Polignac told Madame du Deffand that the martyr St. Denis, the first Bishop of Paris, had walked a hundred miles carrying his head in his hand, Madame du Deffand correctly observed, "In such a promenade it is the first step that is difficult."[5]

By analogy, if the beginning of the promenade of Mormon history, the First Vision and the Book of Mormon, can survive the crisis, then the rest of the promenade follows and nothing that happens in it can really detract from the miracle of the whole. If the first steps do not survive, there can be only antiquarian, not fateful or faith-full interest in the rest of the story.

When the historical crisis comes it can, of course, be addressed by fiat. Authority can invoke authority and silence the questioning, suppress curiosity, rule inquiry out of bounds, close off the sources, purge the questioners. Now and then rumors and reports of policies somewhere in this range of "heteronomy," to use Paul Tillich's term, reach the ears of Gentiles. If these occur, ecclesiastically, they are "none of our business." Intellectually, professionally, and personally, of course, one cares and feels sympathy for Mormon historians, who are believers and belongers through "secondary naïveté" or "after criticism" or "through interpretation." At the very least, one will also hear the whisper of those driven away or silenced: *eppur si muove*. Galileo kept integrity by murmuring such a truth after authority forced him to recant, to say that against all evidence the world did *not* move. "And yet it moves!"

Suppressed historians may busy themselves trying to comprehend the integrity of those who guard the tradition, eager as these are to protect the faith of Mormons who live in "primitive naïveté." Yet historians can be understandably frustrated if they feel that their gift, which would help people pass to another, secondary, mode of being and believing is a priori denied. Still, this is a matter of internal ecclesiastical concern, and it would come with bad grace for a guest to intervene or pursue the matter much beyond the point of observation.

It *does* belong to the historian's vocation, however, to say that alongside the unreflective faith of Christian believers who have not come to the crisis of historical consciousness there are reflective, historically conscious people who do believe. There may be something of worth in their history, a history of great complexity, which might serve Mormons through analogy and precedent. There can be more than one kind of integrity in faith and peoplehood.

FOCUSING ON THE MORMON CRISIS ISSUES

Having dismissed as secondary, late stages in the promenade, both what we might call "political embarrassments" and "borderline religious issues" (like the role of Masonry, the development and demise of polygamy) we can concentrate on what I will call the *generative* issues. They come down to what historians of religion call "theophany," the appearance of gods or godlike figures, and "revelation," the disclosure from one order of being and reality to another. The First Vision belongs to the category of theophany, the Book of Mormon to revelation.

The four accounts of the First Vision do not quite match, a fact no less and no more interesting than that details in the four Christian Gospels do not always match. What matters is the event, which is accessible only through these traces. It is hard to read Mormon history as I have for twenty years without coming to agree with Neal E. Lambert and Richard H. Cracroft, that this First Vision is "that pivotal event which is so central to the message of Mormonism that belief therein has become a touchstone of faith for the orthodox Mormon and Mormon convert." James B. Allen says that it is "second only to belief in the divinity of Jesus of Nazareth," and "next to the resurrection of Christ, nothing holds a more central place in modern Mormon thought than that sacred event of 1820."[6] Reflective Mormons have to cross Lessing's "ugly ditch" as they face up to such events.

Second, more urgently, the vision of 1823, the story of golden plates and seer stones and the text translated and published as the Book of Mormon is both theophany and revelation. While the book may go unread by many Mormons—it always surprises Gentiles to see how little awareness of much of its content there is among their Mormon neighbors—it is the event itself, the whole generative shape of the discovery, translation, and publication, which has made up a single base for Mormon history. When historians call into question both the process and the product, they come to or stand on holy ground. Not all Mormon historians devote their energies to these generative events, just as I as an historian of twentieth-century Christianity do not have to do research on the resurrection of Jesus: "It's not my period." Yet the basis for faith and concerns for events which follow are at stake when professional colleagues converge on these focal issues.

UNDERSTANDING THE MORMON ISSUES

After 150 years, when historians inside or outside the Mormon community focus on the generative events, it has become conventional to see them as concentrating on a direct, simple question. It is all supposed to come down to "Was Joseph Smith a prophet or a fraud?" To say "prophet" made one a Saint, for how could one then stay away from the history and people which issue from these events? To say "fraud" is precisely what made one leave Mormonism or never convert in the first place. That was that.

Then, two things happened. Many non-Mormon historians bracketed [put in brackets, suspended] that question. Seeing four million and more people shaped by Smith's theophanic and revelational vision, people who, in many cases, were as intelligent and "modern" as they, the historians asked a new range of questions. If they would get hung up on the prophet/fraud dialectic, however much it may have nagged or tantalized them, they could not get to another range of questions: what sort of people are these people, what sort of faith is this faith, what sort of prophet with what sort of theophany and revelation was Joseph Smith? His consciousness, his "myth" and his effect could be pursued if one refused to be tyrannized by the literal stark prophet/fraud polarity in the question.

Meanwhile, Saints historians asked more radical questions than before. They had to move through history and interpretation toward a "second naïveté" which made possible transformed belief and persistent identification with the people. They brought new instruments to their inquiry into Mormon origins; shortly I shall detail what strike me as the three main approaches used by outsiders and insiders alike.

For now, a very obvious and important point needs to be made. According to the norms and approaches of the historical profession, the "ground rules" accepted by historians, it would be impossible to prove that Smith was a prophet. As Renier reminds us, past events are, as events, wholly lost to us. We have only traces, testimonies, texts. As historians, we cannot get behind those testimonies to the New York hills where the visions occurred, and we cannot regress in time. There is no way in which empirical evidence can produce for our verification the "two personages" or the later angel of the visions. If by some now-inconceivable time machine device we could be there, we might be duly impressed that *something* was happening beyond the ordinary. But in 1820 and 1823, as in the present we would be suspicious of visions—and Smith called them that—because they can be contrived, can elude ordinary analysis without themselves being extraordinary. We can see some things more remarkable on television or on stage any day of a week, yet these do not inspire the response of faith.

Conversely, of course, historians may find it possible to prove to their own satisfaction that Smith was a fraud. This is hard to do with the First Vision, if we grant that somewhat different accountings of detail on four occasions are no more challenges to its integrity than are the four Gospel accounts to the Gospel event. It could be easier to do, and many have done so to their own and others' satisfaction, in respect to the Book of Mormon, both so far as its external circumstances and internal character are concerned. Yet this proving of fraudulence has not been compelling, not "proof," to millions of Saints, who do not really lie abed in suspense lest the next discovery or assault achieve what the first eight score years of attack could not achieve. For our purposes it is more important to note that the issue of fraud, hoax, or charlatanry simply need not, does not, preoccupy the historical profession most of the time.

It is not necessary here to detail fully two of the three approaches to questions beyond the prophet/fraud issue addressed to generative Mormon events. I need only cite them and point to major statements of the issue. The first family has been familiarly summarized in Klaus Hansen's *Mormonism and the American Experience*.[7] We might call the studies summarized and enlarged upon there "consciousness" studies, contributions to the question of the consciousness of a modern prophet. After reference to social and environmental contexts and explanations, Hansen moves to the consciousness sphere.

Quoting Jan Shipps, he develops first "the analogy of musical genius," and then, more speculatively, Julian Jaynes's hypotheses about consciousness as it relates to hemispheres of the brain. Other "possible explanatory frameworks for getting a handle on Smith's revelations" include non-Mormon T. L. Brink's summaries of four alternatives derived from "depth psychology." On their basis Brink can assume that Joseph Smith "was a man of sound mind and sincere religious convictions." Sigmund Freud, more plausibly C. G. Jung, and then Alfred Adler and Erik Erikson are called as witnesses to make plausible the prophethood and throw light on prophetic character.

Emphatically, in my understanding of the historical approach, none of these produce proof that Smith was a prophet or fraud. Instead they make possible a different level of urgent inquiry, make plausible the concepts of Smith's "soundness" and "sincerity." I should add that Larry Foster[8] has developed his own approaches to prophetic consciousness, approaches which have made it possible for him sometimes to speak up more emphatically for Smith than many Mormons can or do. These scholars show that one can use psychological instruments to illumine without falling into a reductionism which would insist that Smith was "nothing but" an exemplar of this or that stage of adolescent psychology, or whatever.

The second address to the crisis of Mormon historical consciousness comes from a cluster of scholars whose work is focused in and summarized by another non-Mormon, Jan Shipps. Aware as is Hansen from within that the issue of prophet/fraud is in many ways a question of faith which can be illumined by but not proven by historical inquiry, Shipps employs still another discipline for her work, *Religionsgeschichte*, which in America is usually translated as "History of Religion." (*History* here is not the same as ordinary *history of religions*, but implies a somewhat different set of methods, and has far less interest in narrative. It may be more taken with synchrony than diachrony, with structure than with happening.)

For Shipps's purposes, to begin with the First Vision casts the questions in an inappropriate light; the Book of Mormon here (as in Foster's work) is determinative. With the Book of Mormon the public career of the prophet began, and here it becomes accessible to the historian. Shipps is interested explicitly in shifting the focus from the prophet/fraud questions to the notion that Smith's story is "best understood in the context of his sequential assumption of positions/roles that allowed the Saints to recover a usable past." That was his *religious* function and achievement. She can go on to say that when one sees how this endeavor legitimated the prophetic task, "the question of whether Smith was prophet or fraud is not particularly important."

The fourth chapter of Shipps's book, "In and Out of Time," will suggest the promise of the History of Religion approaches for ordinary historians.[9] The sacred and nonsacred, wrote Mircea Eliade, are "different modes of being in the world." Historians using their ordinary canons have to be aware of this difference. They must be aware that the original Mormons saw their prophet and themselves stepping outside ordinary time and space, beyond the reach of conventional critical criteria. Temporally, they wanted to live "once again at the beginning, *in illo tempore*," the kind of time which lies beyond empirical evidence.

14. The Case of the Mormons

Guilford Dudley has written that "the mystic time of beginnings is sacred by definition." The experience on the hill in New York or, for Shipps more important, the Mormon entry into the Promised Land was "entry into sacred space" *and* sacred time. This did not mean that the Mormons ever were anything but practical people; they were not insubstantial or otherworldly. Yet their special kind of millennialism removed many of their claims beyond the realm of the mundane and practical and has served to provide extraordinary interpretations for the life of the people. Mundane Mormons even today "possess the means of reentering sacred time and space" in their temples and special times. These help endow their people-hood with value and guarantee that the mythic dimensions of their history, which remain beyond the range of historians' destruction, also become a part of their historical constructions. Shipps shows how creative it is to ask other than the prophet/fraud question of Smith and the Book.

A third approach, not yet fully developed but rich in promise, is the hermeneutical. This version of "interpretation theory" helps Mormon intellectuals make the passage from primitive to second-ary naïveté, or from belief before criticism to belief through criti-cism and interpretation. It also helps both Mormons and non-Mormons in the historical profession understand each other and do some justice to the generative events without being mired in the prophet/fraud polarity or posing. I will close with some references to it.

THE INTERPRETIVE ENTERPRISE AND ITS PROMISE

I propose a hermeneutical approach to the problem of Mormon texts. By texts I mean both those which impart Joseph Smith's vi-sions and the Book of Mormon itself. Contemporary hermeneutics, the focus of so much philosophical passion today, can be treated extremely technically, in ways which would seem alien to most his-torians. Yet the subject has on occasion been rather simply intro-duced, and I shall depend upon a summary by a noted literary critic, E. D. Hirsch, to outline it.[10]

Hermeneutics, he points out, is associated with *Hermes*, the di-vine messenger between gods and men. (The parallel name is *In-terpres*, from which we get "interpretation.") God's hidden message needs such a conveyor to ordinary people. In 1927 Martin Heidegger, in *Sein und Zeit*, borrowed a term from hermeneutics, *Vorverständnis*, or "preunderstanding," to launch the modern debate. He showed that unprejudiced, objective knowledge was not possible. All knowledge is bound in part by "pre-knowing" which is determined by our historical, social, and personal backgrounds. Such pre-knowing, for example, determines in large measure what attitudes we have toward and what we derive from Islamic, Marxist, Christian, or Mormon texts.

"Pre-understanding," to step back further, derives from Wilhelm Dilthey (1833–1911) who showed how understanding of a text is a circular process. As a non-Mormon I can discuss the Book of Mormon in such terms.

First, we encounter words and clauses which have no distinct meaning until we know how they function in the text as a whole. But since we can only know the whole meaning through the various parts of the text, and since we cannot know before what the parts mean or how they work together before we know the whole text, we find ourselves in a logical puzzle, a circularity. This is the famous "hermeneutical circle." It can be broken only by resolving the question of which came first, the chicken or the egg, the whole or the part. By general agreement, from which there has been virtually no dissent, the question of priority is decided in favor of the whole. The whole must be known in some fashion before we know the part. For how can I know that I am seeing a nose unless I first know that I am seeing a face? And from the doctrine of the priority of the whole came the doctrine of pre-understanding. Since we must know the whole before the part, we must assume some kind of pre-understanding in all interpretation.

Muslim children come to Muslim texts and Mormon children come to Mormon texts with pre-understandings which allow them to grasp the whole before they take apart the parts. These pre-understandings, no doubt often creatively, bias their understandings of the whole and the parts. Those who stand outside the circle have great difficulty sharing the understandings which come from the preunderstandings, though, of course, there can be and are conversions which bring illuminations of texts "from within," as it were.

14. *The Case of the Mormons*

Fortunately, for our purposes, philosophers Jean Nabert and Paul Ricoeur have developed the theme of a "hermeneutics . . . of testimony."[11] The philosophy of testimony evokes an enormous paradox. Nabert in *L'Essai sur le mal* asks, in the spirit of Lessing, "Does one have the right to invest with an absolute character a moment of history?" This must be addressed. Now, testimony begins with a "quasi-empirical meaning"; it "designates the action of testifying, that is, of relating what one has seen or heard." Then comes the sort of transfer on which all Mormon faith depends: "there is the one who testifies and the one who hears the testimony. The witness has seen, but the one who receives his testimony has not seen but hears," and it is in this hearing that faith or unfaith is decided. The statement and the story constitute "information on the basis of which one forms an opinion about a sequence of events, the connection of an action, the motives for the act, the character of the person, in short on the meaning of what has happened."

When, asks Ricoeur, do we give testimony and listen to it? In a form of discourse called "the trial," which, whether they have noticed it or not, defenders and attackers of Joseph Smith so regularly establish. "Hence the question: what is a true witness, a faithful witness?" Ricoeur connects witness with the Greek word *martus;* the witness is linked with the martyr. "A man becomes a martyr because he is first a witness. . . . It is necessary, then, that the just die." And "the witness is the man who is identified with the just cause which the crowd and the great hate and who, for this just cause, risks his life." Thus "testimony is the action . . . as it attests outside of himself, to the interior man, to his conviction, to his faith."

This is the point at which the religious meaning of testimony is most clear. Historical faith connects what one "testifies *for*" a meaning with the notion that he is testifying *that* something has happened which signifies this meaning. There is tension between confession of faith and narration of things seen, but it is this tension that means that faith is dependent upon testimony, not sight, not "proof."

Mormons are people who, though aware of many historical ambiguities in the record and fallibilities in the prophet Joseph Smith, also see in his character, vocation, career, and witnessing—finally, martyrdom—a credentialing which leads them to connect confession of faith with "something that has happened."

We have connected Jean Nabert and Paul Ricoeur with the hermeneutics of being the testifier, the witness. When one deals with the text of the Book of Mormon, the issue now becomes the hermeneutics of testimony. Ricoeur asks, "Do we have the right to invest a moment of history with an absolute character? One needs a hermeneutics, a philosophy of interpretation." Here Nabert remarks that "consciousness makes itself judge of the divine and consequently chooses its God or its gods." Testimony gives something to interpretation, but it also demands to be interpreted. There is the story of an event and a demand for decision, a choice that the testimony functions to awaken faith in the truth. "The judge in a court makes up his mind about things seen only by hearing said."

It is interesting to this Gentile to notice the Book of Mormon is not widely read in the church. People come to faith because living witnesses base their speaking and way of life on what they have read, "heard," there—and a new generation of children or converts comes to faith by "hearing." None of them see golden plates to authenticate this faith. There is "no manifestation of the absolute without the crisis of false testimony, with the decision which distinguished between sign and idol." The Mormon believer and the non-Mormon rejecter are on the same terms, so far as material traces of actual past events are concerned.

Nabert speaks of this norm for judging the divine "the expression of the greatest effort that consciousness can make in order to take away the conditions which prevent it from attaining complete satisfaction." Faith is *not* absolute knowledge of an event that is forever lost except through testimony. Here is the break between "reason and faith, . . . philosophy and religion." And "this is what signifies the 'trial,' the 'crisis' of testimony." We must "choose between philosophy of absolute knowledge and the hermeneutics of testimony." The enforcer of orthodoxy who limits the inquiry of the historian wants history to do what a "philosophy of absolute knowledge" would do. The historian, to whom past events are lost and for whom only traces in testimony remain, lives with "the hermeneutics of testimony" which is, in the end, at the basis of all faith.

I must add a word on *how* a text like the Book of Mormon ministers in the tension and authenticates itself as testimony. To summarize almost to the point of cliché a very complicated set of developments in "interpretation theory," let us say that one moves through and beyond both historical and literary criticism to the interpretive level. That is, one wants to understand "the world behind the text," the world of Joseph Smith and the events described in the Book of Mormon. Yet having learned all that can be learned is not what either brings about or destroys faith. Second, one can use literary tools to understand the world "of the text." What is its genre or form? Yet here, too, is not the birth or death of faith. Instead one deals with "the world in front of the text," for here testimony forces its challenge.

Not that Joseph Smith was a prophet or a fraud, but does the Book of Mormon connect confession and event in such a way that it discloses possible modes of being or thinking or behaving that the reader or, better, the listener (to a contemporary witness based on it) must entertain the risk of acceptance or rejection of the testimony? There is where faith or unfaith is born. David Tracy, employing an insight from Hans-Georg Gadamer, says that here is "the fusion of horizons";

> the reader overcomes the strangeness of another horizon not by empathizing with the psychic state or cultural situation of the author but rather by understanding the basic vision of the author implied by the text and the mode-of-being-in-the-world referred to by the text.[12]

One is henceforth freed of the burdens of "psychologizing" and is less burdened by concern over the exact reference to literal historical events.

Are there analogies in "ordinary Christians'" approaches to the issues of trace or testimony and event in respect to the resurrection of Jesus? How far does historical inquiry and doubt go and where must one make that leap "from trace to event" which is at the basis of narrative and, in some respects, of faith itself?

In a conservative Protestant survey, evangelical biblical scholar Daniel Fuller set forth a typology that began with "attempts to sustain knowledge of the Resurrection apart from historical reasoning," and then "partially from historical reasoning." Of greatest interest to Fuller is a third category, German theologian Wolfhart Pannenberg's "attempt to sustain knowledge of the resurrection wholly by historical reason."

Fuller's choice of Pannenberg was fortunate because Pannenberg is an extremely formidable and sophisticated theologian, not someone to whom the term *fundamentalist* could be applied in any pejorative sense. "True faith is first awakened through an impartial observation of events." Revelation is mediated only by history because "the events of history speak their own language, the language of events, [and] this language can only be heard in the world of ideas of the people in which these events occurred."

Pannenberg moves, then, from universal history to the testimony of the first witnesses and then and thus jumps to the events that presumably lie behind it. Fuller paraphrases this leap on the basis of a lecture by Pannenberg:

> While there is much in the resurrection reports that is mythical, yet it is impossible to explain them wholly as the work of the apostles' imagination. The apostles were too discouraged after the death of Jesus to have talked themselves into believing that Jesus was risen. The only satisfactory explanation for their sudden faith was that Jesus appeared to them. Furthermore, the early Christian community could not have survived if the tomb of Jesus had not been empty. An occupied tomb would not only have destroyed their faith, but it would have given the Jewish polemic against the church an invincible weapon. Hence it is impossible to charge off the Biblical reports of the resurrection wholly to the imagination, and, consequently, [we may arrive at] an historical verification of the resurrection.

Many critics have pointed out that Pannenberg as philosopher of history makes claims that no ordinary detective-historian would be content with. One body snatcher *could* have emptied the tomb. So Pannenberg does not have "material" evidence but only oral-and-then-written "testimony."

Fuller judges that Pannenberg has "provided some insights into how it is possible for historical reason to bridge Lessing's ugly ditch and therefore find a complete basis for faith in history." However there are at least two difficulties. Pannenberg's mode of reasoning to get to a basis for faith in history is extremely complex and abstruse. It is grounded in philosophies many believers would find alien. Therefore "only those can have an immediate knowledge of revelation who are trained historians." Or, only those can have faith who tend to be dependent upon sophisticated historians. For him, there should be no talk of supernaturalism, which is unacceptable for the critically oriented reason of the historian, because it arbitrarily cuts off historical investigation of immanental causes and analogies through the assertion of a transcendental intervention."

Fuller chooses to see the basis of faith better outlined by an earlier historian, the author of Luke-Acts. He contrasts how faith is born in the light of Luke's testimony or that of the early Christians about whom he writes:

> Pannenberg it will be remembered, wants to make faith the possibility for all men by having what is, virtually, a priesthood of historians. Theology's task, as he sees it, is to assert the credibility of the Christian proclamation, so that laymen can believe it because of the authority that the theologian, with special historical skills, can provide. It does not seem, however, that Luke, who finds the basis for revelational knowledge in history, makes historical reasoning the exclusive way to such knowledge. Acts 11:24 is a passage of particular interest in this connection because it tells how a number of people came to believe on the basis of the moral impact of the minister, rather than by accepting his authority or by employing historical reasoning to get back to the truth of the resurrection. "[Barnabas] was a good man, full of the Holy Spirit and of faith. And [as a result] a large company was added to the Lord."

So with Paul: the argument for the resurrection is made as a result of Paul's change in conduct.

> Thus it is understandable how Luke could have stressed that the faith of the apostles and of a Theophilus must come through a reasoning based on infallible proofs, and yet declare that many believed as Barnabas preached, for Barnabas was himself an infallible proof of his message. . . . Faith is possible for every man who is confronted with a Barnabas, for everyone who is rational is capable of seeing the infallible proof represented by such a man. Such a system of thought does keep Christianity as an historical religion, rather than one whose knowledge is immediately accessible to all. . . . But such a system does not make all men dependent upon a priesthood of theologians who can follow historical reasoning to know that Jesus rose from the dead.

The claim, then, is simple, bold, and emphatic: the historical craft never allows us to revisit *any events* except in and through and insofar as traces are satisfying. The empty tomb is not convincingly recoverable today to provide a basis for faith in the resurrection. The texts repeating the testimony of Paul, Barnabas, and other early witnesses and those dependent upon witness is all that Christians have—and that is enough. These texts disclose meanings and offer possible modes of thinking and being for those to whom faith in the resurrection and its fruits would otherwise not occur. So with Mormon texts, the testimony of Smith and witnesses.

CONCLUSION

How frustrating all this must be to someone who wants to prove Smith a prophet or a fraud, or to make the issue the only one to interest insider or outsider historians! We have argued that it is impossible for historians as historians to prove that Smith was a prophet and improbable that they will prove him a fraud. Instead, they seek to understand. That is a modest but still important task in the communities of both faith and inquiry. Similarly, historians cannot prove that the Book of Mormon was translated from golden plates and have not proven that it was simply a fiction of Joseph Smith. Instead, they seek to understand its revelatory appeal, the claims it makes, and why it discloses modes of being and of believing that millions of Saints would otherwise not entertain.

If what I have outlined makes any sense at all, it might be a contribution to a lowering of suspicions of historians by Mormon guardians. At the same time it does not try to pretend away the depth of the crisis of historical consciousness for history-based Mormondom. The motive for this all is not to commend Mormon history to the secular academy, as if the Mormon historians had to be driven by a push for relevance and respectability. The secular academy which despises Mormonism also has to despise Islam, Catholicism, Protestantism, all of which make theophanic and revelational claims similar to those of Mormonism. Yet Islamic, Catholic, and Protestant historians have found means of pursuing their work and displaying their integrity.

There are many kinds of integrity. Some of these are appropriate to insiders and others to outsiders, some to church authorities and some to historians, some to those with "primitive naïveté" and others to those who live in "second naïveté." Confusing these integrities is almost as destructive to them as is dismissing those sorts which are appropriate to other people in other callings. Discernment of them and empathy across the lines of the vocations of people who display them seem to be the most promising forms of address to the present crisis of historical consciousness.

DIRECTIONS

15   *Transpositions: A Place for Everyone*

Religious forces are positioned. Spiritually, West complements East. Spatially, Islam abuts Christendom. Maps locate Southern Baptists and Canadian Anglicans, while Utah is a Mormon domain. Displaced European Jews repositioned their Judaism in Israel or in urban America. Religious movements are also positioned with re- spect to their status and roles. Many are privileged while others are treated as outsiders. Some support the political establishment; oth- ers are in positions of dissent.

American religious forces and movements have been undergoing significant repositioning for decades. Of course there are continui- ties: about the same percentage of the population believes in God, belongs to and attends church, and cherishes chosen denomina- tions as it did at mid-century.[1] In the 1980s, however, public aware- ness of discontinuities due to shifts in place among the movements is widespread. It is possible to take advantage of this awareness by putting less energy into documenting the details of the changes and more into interpreting the moves. Seen in this context, the major religious event of the decade has been the transposition of forces.

CHANGING PLACES

To transpose, the *Oxford English Dictionary* reminds us, is "to alter the position of [a set or series of things]; to put each of (two or more

329

things) in the place of the other or others, to interchange." Here are six examples.

Secularists and Religionists

Secularists are in disarray, while religionists have regrouped. Of course, it would be wildly inaccurate to say that the secular dimensions of national society have diminished. The media, the academy, and most centers of power reveal an unreflective secularity to be in control. What has changed is the character of rationales. In colloquial terms, religions around the world have gotten their acts together. Whether in resentment or out of reasoned positive commitment, they have often become aggressive. Theologian Langdon Gilkey celebrated the two-century-old myth of progress with its promotion of democracy, science, and technology. He saw that it had functioned in American "social existence 'religiously,' that is, as the ultimate formative and authoritative symbolic structure of our commonality."

Now, he went on, "the disintegration of this *secular* myth—not that of the traditional Christian mythos—. . . constitutes the present religious crisis of American Society."[2] Public philosophy, even where plausibly expounded, gains little hearing. Religion, from Iran through India and Ireland to Israel and Washington, bids stridently for attention and power.[3] The religious rationales may all be wrong; indeed, being mutually contradictory, they cannot all be right. Yet they speak afresh to the passional sides of life, while the dispossessed keepers of the secular myth settle for relations chiefly with life's operative sides, by which I mean the practical running of things in spheres such as science, commerce, government, and daily affairs. Two two-century-long trajectories have begun to trade courses.

Protestantism: Mainline versus Evangelical-Moralist

The privileged Protestant mainline has become passive or dissenting, while Protestant evangelical moralism has become aggressive and culture affirming. During recent decades the heirs of colonial establishment—the Congregational, Presbyterian, and Episcopal denominations; of frontier achievement—the Northern Baptist, Methodist, and Disciples of Christ denominations; and of continental immigration—the Lutheran and Reformed denominations— ironically came to be called "mainline" at precisely the moment when their place was being challenged. They had long been custodians of the cultural lore, had had access to power all the way to the White House, and had occupied a privileged status in the national ethos, although not in law. They remained centers of experiment; for example, in these mainline churches feminist causes and agents keep getting their best religious hearing. But as early as 1972, with the publication of *Why Conservative Churches Are Growing*, National Council of Churches leader Dean M. Kelley was documenting mainline stasis or decline. Exactly ten years later, in the essay "Mainline Religion in Transition," Wade Clark Roof could take for granted such documentation and suggest how the mainline might find and meet new challenges in the future.[4]

Beneficiaries of the transposition, along with Mormons and several other latter-day American religions among the conservative churches of which Kelley wrote, were those Protestants who had often been regarded as culturally and societally marginal, despite their millions of adherents. Their earlier marginalization had been ironic, too, for they were heirs of another side of the very traditions to which the mainline Protestants also appealed. Though seen as old-time religion in the mid-twentieth century, these churches had often been experimenters and creators of novelty. Their ancestors were revivalists and innovators who challenged settled establishment and privilege as far back as the 1730s. Their parties were often called or devoted to the New Side, New Light, New School, or New Measures.[5]

Historians should not have been surprised at the recovery of this lineage, because after the 1730s the mainline was almost always in retreat, always being overtaken by new competing forces. Yet after the fundamentalist-modernist battles around 1925 or the time of briefly renewed mainliners' visibility just before 1965, few predicted that by 1985 the "evangelical-moralist" subculture—Daniel Bell's term[6]—would match active Catholicism and mainline Protestantism in size and outdo them in scope. Although self-portrayed and perceived as critical of some aspects of society—witness their attacks on legalized abortion and pervasive pornography—the evangelical-moralists have moved into positions of privilege. They have had the ear of or a voice in the White House during the presidencies of Ford, Carter, and Reagan. All of the Protestant celebrities now come from this camp. By 1984 it had come from apparently nowhere to hold the most visible and assertive political position in American religion.

Catholicism's Public Voice

Roman Catholic leadership interchanged position with mainline Protestantism with respect to the articulation of a social vision to its constituency and the public. Mainline Protestantism did not slink from the scene; however, it was being chastened by a realism acquired during social activist forays two decades earlier, preoccupied with regrouping, beset by backlashers all the way from its own pews to *Reader's Digest* and CBS television, and suffering reaction to bureaucratization. It had become virtually silent as a concentrated political force by the 1984 presidential campaign. Far from acquiescing to the terms of the present culture, it was seeking new symbols, vocabulary, and outlets, chiefly by a new responsiveness to local social justice concerns. Whereas in 1964 the mainline would have acted through pronouncements of world or national councils or denominational task forces and conventions, by 1984 it more readily dealt with issues of housing, aging, or sanctuary on local scenes even while its members became more aware of third world need.

Roman Catholic leadership meanwhile began to interchange positions with the mainline through a series of public advocacies culminating in May 1983 in "The Challenge of Peace"—a pastoral letter on nuclear weaponry—some intervention in the 1984 presidential campaign over the issue of abortion, and, immediately thereafter, a draft of a pastoral letter on the economy. Here was another major transposition in American religion. While the general social justice posture was not new, as the hierarchy drew on papal social documents from as far back as 1891 and on American bishops' programs dating from 1919, their leadership previously had always needed to be cautious and defensive about its role in national politics. Before the election of Catholic John F. Kennedy to the presidency in 1960 and the passage of the Declaration on Religious Liberty at the Second Vatican Council in 1965, the bishops had been wary of being accused of disrupting American civil life with the claims of Roman, and hence foreign, dogma and control.

Those cautions seemed gone in 1984 when New York's Archbishop John O'Connor and many other bishops and leaders all but implied that Catholics should not vote for candidates who did not work openly for legislation agreeing with the bishops' teachings against abortion. Yet most hierarchical representatives were still extremely careful to make distinctions regarding claims and audiences. Thus "The Challenge of Peace" began with the reminder that the letter on nuclear war was "an exercise of our teaching ministry . . . addressed principally to the Catholic community," yet, like the later letter on the economy, it was also to be "a contribution to the wider public debate in our country." The letter was "therefore both an invitation and a challenge to Catholics in the United States to join with others in shaping the conscious choices and deliberate policies required."[7] The once-suspect Catholic leadership had changed places in the public eye with mainline Protestants. It also challenged the ascendancy of evangelical-moralist New Right Protestantism as speaker to and, more ambiguously, for its own constituency in the context of the pluralist civil order.

Internal Unity of Blacks and Jews

Black religionists and Jews interchanged with respect to predictable public and partisan stands concerning their own interests. Ever since American blacks, usually under pastoral and local church leadership, shifted allegiance from the Republican to the Democratic party between 1932 and 1936, most of them represented both black and national interest through support of Democratic partisan and social causes. Therefore, their posture in the mid-eighties should have been seen as anything but new.

What was new was public perception and the organization of black religionists. Through the years of the civil rights struggle the black churches were seen chiefly as instruments of nurturing piety

among blacks and defending blacks' self-interest. This perception
began to change in the mid-sixties when Martin Luther King, Jr.,
began to enlarge the scope of his work to include efforts that would
lead the United States to disengage from the war in Vietnam, not a
specifically black issue. Over the next two decades blacks, again
with a base in the churches and the precincts that they dominated
or ministered to, became mayors of a large number of metropolises.
By 1984 on the national level—with the presidential primary candidacy and later campaign involvement of the Reverend Jesse Jackson, and the support of the Democratic ticket by nearly 90 percent
of blacks—it had become clear that these churches and their secular black counterparts held an inclusive vision and program for national and international life. They were massively united in support
of it, if not of a specific leader.

Jews, meanwhile, despite their century-old identification with
liberal movements and their half-century instinct for alliances with
mainline Protestants and Catholics in support of interfaith and social causes, were perceived to be deeply divided and ambiguous
over new causes and alliances. Much of the neoconservative movement, typified by the American Jewish Committee–sponsored
Commentary magazine, was under lay Jewish leadership. Many
more or less theological justifications for laissez-faire capitalism
were being encouraged by these neoconservatives, who were
clearly the most visible Jewish leaders in the media. Through a
decade and more they have moved or were moving into conservative Republican policy camps. More astonishing, Jews were finding
new alliance with the New Right evangelical-moralist leadership,
thanks to the vocal and unwavering support of Israel by these Protestant ultras. One says "astonishing" because in public perception
these Protestant conservatives had been anti-Semitic when it came
to relations with domestic Jews, and Jews had known only urban
mainline Protestants and Catholics.

In the 1980s, Israeli and American Jewish leaders were giving
and receiving honors in the sanctuaries of Protestant theological
intransigents and self-proclaimed political Far Right evangelists.
Many of these evangelical-moralists were Christian Zionists who,
to fulfill their understanding of biblical prophecy, saw the restoration of Israel as a modern political state to be a necessary prerequi-

site of the Second Coming of Christ.[8] *Commentary*'s Irving Kristol urged Jews to acquire a taste for association with Protestant fundamentalists. These advocated a strong anti-Soviet defense policy, were more reliable partisans of Israel than were mainline Protestants and Catholics, and were staunch defenders of capitalism.

Other Jews, however, in the course of 1984 began to be suspect of the fundamentalist support of Israel, as the fundamentalist view of the final act of history both rewrote the script of Jewish expectations and, sometimes through efforts at evangelizing Jews, called into question the integrity of Jewish faith. What is more, the evangelical-moralist calls and programs in support of a legally privileged theistic or Judeo-Christian culture and its traditional values were seen and heard to be an ever less covert and more overt call for a privileged Christian America, created on right-wing Protestant lines. Jews were in a new dilemma over political and religious alliances, and had become less partisanly predictable than blacks, less visibly organized around the specifically religious agencies of their people's lives.

A Conservative Civil Religion

Civil or public religion has been transposed in public perception, from moderate and liberal contexts to conservative and nationalist ones. Much of twentieth-century public religion had had the secular cast of John Dewey's *Common Faith*, a nontheistic but still ritualized public philosophy. In the era of Dwight Eisenhower's piety along the Potomac, it was to be an expansive and nondescript, generally benign faith for all. When Robert N. Bellah wrote his famed essay "Civil Religion in America," he was speaking out of a vision shaped during the liberal advocacies of Presidents Kennedy and Lyndon Johnson. Bellah revisited the theme after President Richard M. Nixon's more jingoistic second inaugural address. He then expressed second thoughts and, in *The Broken Covenant*, rued the direction the civil faith was taking.[9]

While moderates and liberals were as persistent as ever in claiming attachment to quasi-religious democratic values and symbols, the public media accurately chronicled the seizure of the symbols by un-selfcritical fortress-America nationalists who would move against the evil empires of their enemies. This transposition need not be permanent, for public and civil religions are episodic, subject to revivals and reforms. Yet the American conservatives' identification with their God and their own national purposes was consistent with what seemed to be a long-term and widespread international trend.

Entering the Mainstream

Extraordinary religion acquired an ordinary cast. Daniel Bell observed both traditional redemptive—read "mainline Protestant, Catholic, Reform and Conservative Jewish"—and evangelical-moralist faith complexes. He also saw a third complex, summarized by British sociologist Bryan Wilson as a "diffuse tendency to mythical and mystical thought, . . . a demand for colour in a world which has become drab," an effort to return to the sacred by routes seen as alternative or esoteric in the larger society. A generation earlier, as the old liberal synthesis was breaking up after the mid-sixties, this complex became more visible than ever before or since, both in respect to its promise and its threat. News magazines could write of occult explosions in astrology, cult formation, and support of Eastern religions. All of this looked extraordinary in Bell's gray-on-gray world.[10]

By the mid-1980s such extraordinary religion had established itself, although without essentially changing the map of American religion. Present in a number of thriving cults and persistent in holistic health movements, small-group therapies, and most of all in private spiritual pursuits, most of this religion had begun to fit quietly into the larger landscape. What the public called cults no longer made news as a harbinger of the spirit that might alter consciousness and national life, bringing in a new age. Instead they were seen as only slightly less conventional denominations among the denominations, study accents among other Great Book interests, or, most of all, as merely self-preservative groups constantly fighting for legal rights and privilege—and often thus winning support of both mainline and evangelical-moralist partisans. In other words, they made news on the familiar and ordinary church-state legal front, not on the horizon of extraordinary spiritual promise.

15. A Place for Everyone

Majority America had settled back into drab or chose to recolor only slightly its traditional and evangelical-moralist faiths.

One could point to any of a number of other transpositions, such as the dominance of the southern world over the northern.[11] Thus Christians were becoming aware that in their decade the Christian majority was in the southern world—sub-Saharan Africa, Latin America, Indonesia, and the like—for the first time in two millennia. Domestically, Sun Belt religious norms, long overlooked or seen as eccentric by media, historians, social analysts, and the northern public, were becoming determinative in the Rust Belt. Demography was on the side of the once-conservative churches of the newly prosperous and fast-growing American South. In various trickle-up ways, the music, ritual, evangelical experience, and programmatic life of southern Protestantism, beamed over television and made visible in the celebrity world, influenced the culture of the American North.

Yet to cite all such interchanges and transpositions would only further substantiate the main point: that long-term exchanges of position, privilege, role, and status were seen to be, if not a final new resolution, still a clearly established and probably long-term situation in America. After a period of such consolidation, interpretation of many sorts is in order.

OPPORTUNITY FOR APPRAISAL

Transposition allows for appraisal. When people are uprooted and change their position on the landscape, they tell us something special about their values and their landscape as they migrate, are exiled, conquer, or replace each other. When schism and disruption occur in history, scholars can gain special insight on what previous settlements and continuities have meant and what the new situation promises. When literary works are teased or subjected to the lever of deconstruction, when, in the fashionable language of the day, one can "disturb a poem along its own fault lines," there is a chance for new disclosures in a text.[12] In biblical parabolic terms, revelation can occur when there are reversals and transpositions: the last become first and the first last; the uninvited come to the banquet and the invited are outside; the smallest seed becomes the greatest tree; the righteous are scorned and the unrighteous are welcomed and honored. Then the hearer or reader stands the chance of being upset, dislocated enough to discern what is being disclosed.

Analogically, something similar goes on during the upheavals and interchanges in this time of fulfilled American transpositions. What might now be safely discerned? One must begin such an appraisal with a few observations about religion in the 1980s.

Religion's Strong Roles

In a secular and pluralist society, religion is playing and will play surprisingly strong private, spiritual, and public roles. In part this is simply an anthropological insight. It runs counter to a simpler secularization theory that predominated during the years when the myth of progress, with its faith in democracy, science, and technology, held sway. Around the world there is a larger quantity of passional expression and spiritual resource than the rational academy assessed or foresaw. Anthropologists and other social scientists have contributed to broader understandings and definitions of religion. Therefore, far more than religious institutions—which may indeed be in decline in many places—is involved in the category of religion.

Recent worldwide and American trends, meanwhile, have upset the prediction that the religion that survived would chiefly be, as Thomas Luckmann called it, privatized or invisible in the urban-industrial world.[13] Much of the new religious energy is poured into aggressive social movements that are often coextensive with huge subcultures, if not—in more coercive contexts—with both totalitarian states or a privileged Christian America. British sociologist Bryan Wilson may be right in his claim that a society is secular unless all its constituencies are responsive to a single set of spiritual symbols. Hence his critique of Daniel Bell's notion that in a society like America's the sacral can impinge through, say, the large traditional, evangelical-moralist, and mystical subcultures.[14]

True, it is easy to overdefine as religious many worldwide movements among peoples named by religions—Sikh, Muslim, Protestant fundamentalist, Irish Catholic, and others—for sometimes their religion is epiphenomenal, barnacled to secular economic and political vessels. Yet the force of religion is now more securely recognized. It is also possible to overestimate the power of the newly privileged or the weakness of recently upset religious movements in America—for example, by making too much of alignments in the political campaigns of 1980 and 1984. Yet politicians are less likely, through at least the rest of the 1980s, to underestimate the cohorts and caucuses of all sorts of religionists, including the New Right Protestants, black Protestants, Jews, at least two kinds of Catholics, regrouping mainline Protestants, and mystical advocates of their own rights. Church and state issues will be constant in the courts and polling places, and future decisions by judges and voters may not follow traditional lines.

This is not to say that the United States will join the new theocracies or, barring now-unforeseen social upheavals, turn coercively into Christian America and abolish the older terms of its pluralism. Instead, citizens are becoming aware of what we might call a multiplex consciousness to come to terms with what Robert N. Bellah and Benjamin R. Mariante have called a multiplex world and universe. Mariante described its focus well:

> Now when the world of religious institutions becomes the focus of the individual's consciousness in terms of his everyday experience, he is going to live, respond and act in that world. And about 96% of Americans respond positively in that institutional context, when this is the focus of consciousness. . . . Most individuals are willing to accept the religious institutional pattern in society as part of the real world, much as they accept the economic institution. Thus their responses will be to these institutions as separate, autonomous institutions, i.e., their responses will be in the pluralistic framework. What has occurred is pluralization not secularization; people are religious when religion is at the center of conscious life, as on a questionnaire, "Do you believe in God?" They are economic when the economy is at the center, as on a questionnaire, "What is the most important problem facing America today?"[15]

The disclosure of this unfolding multiplex consciousness is a result of this moment of transposition in secular-religious realms.

The Exploitation of Spiritual Resources

How does one account for the transposition of assertive Catholicism, in a time of many Catholic upheavals and setbacks, or of aggressive evangelical-moralist and New Right Protestantism and the recession of mainline Protestantism? And, further, what will be the role of that once-privileged and traditional mainline, which remains almost as large as before the transposition, and which is institutionalized and cherished in many tens of thousands of congregations and scores of denominations?

To respond to these questions I am going to make metaphoric and figurative use of two speculations or laws of cultural evolution. It is extremely important that this endeavor not be misunderstood. First, historians tend to be mistrustful of evolutionary models because of the models' determinism and long scale. They tend to be comfortable with evolution only or chiefly with respect to very general observations that everything develops and changes. Second, in the eyes of most historians, cultural evolution has normally been seen as progressive, though in the more recent vision of its most noted American advocates, Leslie White and his students, it could as well be linked to nonprogressive and even devolutionary understandings. It should be clear that the present article is not built on progressivist assumptions! Third, cultural evolution and ecology represent one challenged, perhaps ephemeral, episode or school in anthropology, questioned even by some scholars who earlier identified with it. Given those cautions, it should be clear that a metaphoric version is here being used for the task of teasing, creating leverage, disrupting texts, and understanding a spiritual landscape.

The first of the two laws comes in the context of an argument proposed by Marshall D. Sahlins and Elman R. Service in 1960.[16] This Law of Cultural Dominance says that "that cultural system which more effectively exploits the energy resources of a given environment will tend to spread in that environment at the expense of less effective systems." Sahlins and Service talked about the ecology of an actual physical landscape as environment. Metaphorically, one must insert the word *spiritual* before *energy resources* to gain leverage for insight. In these terms it now seems incontrovertible that mainline Protestantism misread three such spiritual energy resources in recent America. These were a passionate hunger for personal experience, a resort to authority in the face of a relativism and chaos, and the pull toward institutions and movements that provide personal identity and social location.

15. A Place for Everyone

Mainline Protestantism, protean Catholicism, and Reform Judaism, as three examples, do of course offer kinds of cherished religious experience, but these rarely have the competitive potency of the born-again or charismatic sort. They all do care about authority, but they see it in the context of reasoned inquiry, of critical approaches to texts and institutions, and of sophisticated interpretation theory. They are thus no match for the evangelists who assert a variety of contradictory messages but always under the banner of "the Bible says" and "thus saith the Lord." Similarly they are no match for Pope John Paul II asserting traditional papal authority or for Orthodox Jews. They do provide identities: an Anglican is as easy to spot as a Pentecostal, a Methodist as a Mormon or Muslim. Yet Pentecostals, Mormons, and Muslims are quite precise about personal and communal boundaries and walls; they are constrictive about the range of possibilities for expressing identity. Mainline Protestantism, Catholicism, and liberal Judaisms would work to create and nurture core personalities and coherent centers of social existence but with less sense of constriction and boundary. They thus are outdone by competitors who "more effectively [exploit] the [spiritual] energy resources of a given environment."

While this transposition exposes to view the ecological niches of this spiritual landscape, one hastens to note also that in many respects the evangelical-moralist and other putatively conservative religious subcultures have changed more than has the environment. Bell was right to think of the mainline as traditional, for its once-privileged people do reach back to symbols long identified with the culture for their *ressourcement,* their renewal. The old-time religion, in turn, after its selective critique of secular humanism, liberalism, and their effects, turns out to be the most world affirming of the competitors, even if the symbols of heaven, hell, and afterlife remain in its cognitive repertory.

A whole school of critics from within evangelicalism has effectively shown that evangelical-moralism, in its hypernationalism, materialism, success-mindedness, offering of more abundant life, identification with heroes and entertainers and athletes, and support of competitive capitalism, is probably the most worldly of the large options. Jon Johnston has written on a popular level, as have scholars on other levels, scoring evangelicalism for accommodation, hedonism, narcissism, materialism, faddism, "celebrityism," "youthism," and "technologism." Carol Flake speaks of the whole complex as "redemptorama" and demonstrates the this-worldliness of the movement.[17] Once upon a time, it was the liberal and mainline in Protestantism that overidentified with the success culture. In the neo-orthodox and critical-realist period in the middle third of the century, under the impetus of theologians like brothers Reinhold and H. Richard Niebuhr, this form of Protestant leadership began to adopt dissenting, critical, and prophetic stances, offering henceforth less uncritical support to citizens in their spiritual strivings.

To face this transposition, the second law, the Law of Evolutionary Potential, argues that "the more specialized and adapted a form in a given evolutionary stage, the smaller is its potential for passing to the next stage." Again used figuratively, this law refers not to the physical landscape but to an ecology that is at least partly spiritual, though adaptation to past given evolutionary stages in American life was even less figuratively the fate of the mainline, hence its smaller potential for adapting and passing to the new stage. The cultural evolutionists quote Thorstein Veblen and Leon Trotsky. Veblen spoke of "the merits of borrowing" and "the penalty of taking the lead" and Trotsky of "the privilege of historic backwardness." They all meant that underdeveloped complexes have certain potentials that advanced and adapted ones lack. Later comers are permitted or compelled to adopt "whatever is ready in advance of any specified date, skipping a whole series of intermediate stages."[18]

The mainline religionists, the early advocates of progressivism and modernism, later became wary of the dehumanization and depersonalization or technical reason and technological artifact. They carry the burden of identification with the earlier stages, and they are self-critical about that. The innovators and adapters of today, the advocates of old-time religion, in turn are thoroughly at home with the technology of electronic media and computers, less critical—with some very notable exceptions—of technical reason and capitalist rationalism. They plunge into politics with more self-assurance and less ambiguity than did the old mainliners in their prime. God and the party and cause of their choice are easily identified with each other. The mainline suffers the penalty of taking the lead and meets rejections that go with its inner uncertainties, while the borrowers and leapfroggers advance.

After the transposition, is there a mission for the once-privileged mainline? H. Stuart Hughes thought that among nations, late-starting, leapfrogging America would be to Western Europe as Rome was to Greece, for the ways it "raised certain aspects of that civilization to new levels of efficiency and specialization." Hughes then saw the United States becoming more like the later Byzantium than Rome itself.[19] Extending this analogy now, one can picture that mainline Protestantism, Catholicism, and Judaism will look on the newly efficient exploiters of their environment's spiritual energy resources in similar aristocratic ways. They will not disappear, convert, or lose all sense of mission.

Like latter-day Hellenists in an efficient and specialized spiritual Rome—by analogy—they will have renewals of their own tradition and will freshly ritualize their own symbols. They are likely to serve a more modest but still important role as advocates of sorts of tolerance in an increasingly tribal world. They will be bewildered by the acceptability of the evangelical-moralist culture and stunned by its worldliness under the very symbols of transworldliness. Mainliners will generate scholars and interpret texts, minister to a very large subculture, and represent aspects of the larger culture, confident that their philosophy is nobler than the near barbarianism of the newcomers. They are even likely to clarify their own views of experience, authority, and identity, and to minister to those who seek what they offer while also acquiring a new status as dissenters. The world of the late twentieth century is not arranged to promise that theirs can become a mass mission. Yet they will find articulators of selective missions in the awesomely rich and complex American spiritual environment. All the other movements will also be making adjustments after the transpositions of their age.

Epilogue

People in various disciplines can reflect on "Religion and Republic." One expects a certain number of philosophers, theologians, and publicists to do so. The case for the historian to do so is strong, though not always made in a time when some practitioners of the discipline cherish roles that keep them at some distance from the public scene. They serve the historical profession by their research, the purity of their endeavors, the standards they set, and their insistence that history has its own integrity. It can be pursued, as one humanist put it, in a spirit of "aggressive irrelevance."

Over against such purity I cite the title of an essay and book by Eugen Rosenstock-Huessy: "I am an impure thinker." It is possible, I believe, to hold to the highest standards of historical scholarship and to risk its results in the public sphere. In the Epilogue to his extended work on *Historiography: Ancient, Medieval, and Modern,* Ernst Breisach has given encouragement to this approach:

The reluctance of historians to acknowledge a public role for their discipline could well lead the public to conclude that history has little to do with human life beyond, perhaps, being a hobby or a source of entertainment. That would be an ironical situation for a discipline which by its nature has always been linked to the full reality of life and whose insights in turn have been of great value to the polity and to the individual alike, although these insights have lacked the simplicity of technological prescriptions."[1]

This is not the place, however, to turn the mirror back on the historian-writer. The closing word has to do with the reader, who may or may not be historically minded or professionally involved, but who must care considerably about "religion" and "republic" to persevere to this page. A book such as this is not a call for the whole public to turn into professional historians. Its author hopes, however, that it illustrates and gives impetus to the understanding that the past has much to do with shaping the future. With Hannah Arendt and William Faulkner, I believe that the past is not past. It is here to haunt us, to mark our days and ways, to serve as raw material for the concepts and terms with which we shape the future.

When does the public turn to the historian? G. J. Renier thought much about that, and said: when it must "stop to think." Individual humans have memories, but a society or a nation has no collective memory beyond the various ages of the people within it—until and unless it turns to the people who spend countless hours in libraries and writing desks, serving as custodians for materials that may not always look or be immediately relevant to circumstance. Then comes a moment of cultural uncertainty. It is easy at such a time for ideologues to make up stories, to create mythical pasts. The contribution of the historian then is to come forward with complications of such stories, with complexities that help question the myths.

In the 1980s, for example, the President of the United States and not a few political and intellectual supporters, conjured an image of an American past when "the little white church and the little red school house" dominated. Then, it was presumed, Americans truly shared consensus and promoted common values. They lived good and godly lives because they did not have to deal with the mess and muck of pluralism, with people who did not fit into a single pattern. We must voluntarily reproduce that order, it is said, and, for example in public schools, must "tilt" our teaching of values to give it privilege, and all will be well.

The historian revisits that scene and does, indeed, find homogeneities that elude us today. There were coherences that are now hard to find. Yet much of the projected picture is inaccurate and unsatisfying. The America of the "little white church and little red school house" was not, by any historical measure, more churchgoing, more religious, more literate, necessarily more moral, than is contemporary America.

More decisively for the present point, did the absence of pluralism solve much of anything? Take one test case. If ever in American history there was consensus over values, here is a time: when the Protestant empire produced "sameness" and homogeneity. When people across the nation agreed on the authority of the Bible, on God and Christ and heaven and hell and rewards and punishments and law and order. The peak of that consensus building came just before the 1860s, when this Protestant nation divided over the most profound social values and issues and engaged in the bloodiest imaginable civil war. Both sides, as Abraham Lincoln said, read the same Bible and prayed to the same God and claimed that God on their side and wanted to win. The Almighty, Lincoln reminded, had his own purposes.

The quest for coherence and consensus goes on and must go on. A complex society does not and need not cherish moral anarchy and incoherence in respect to values. This book, however, traces the record of a people that has grown ever more pluralist and has still found reasons to develop enough common spirit to have creative arguments—and has survived. The historian fulfils his or her mission by turning over accounts and stories to a public. Then, one hopes, the public takes that record into account as it sets out to effect what will become tomorrow's stories of "Religion and Republic."

Notes

CHAPTER 1: REDISCOVERY

1. The discussion of secularization was strongly influenced by European inquiry, where religious institutions were not prospering as in America. The literature on the subject is vast, of which Gerhard Szczesny's *The Future of Unbelief* (New York: Braziller, 1961) was typical. His kind of comment was born of cultural pessimism, while much of the American debate had a utopian aspect. In *Varieties of Unbelief* (New York: Holt, Rinehart and Winston, 1964) I attempted to assess the potency and validity of various secularizing tendencies and movements from a Christian theological viewpoint. Meanwhile, David Martin, in "Towards Eliminating the Concept of Secularization," in *Penguin Survey of the Social Sciences*, Julius Gould (ed.) (1965), pp. 169–82, was beginning to question the secularization motif.

2. See, for example, Daniel J. Boorstin, *The Genius of American Politics* (Chicago: University of Chicago Press, 1953), chap. 5, "The Mingling of Political and Religious Thought," pp. 133–60.

3. Seymour Martin Lipset, *The First New Nation: The United States in Historical and Comparative Perspective* (New York: Basic Books, 1963), chap. 4, "Religion and American Values," pp. 140–69.

4. John Murray Cuddihy, *The Ordeal of Civility: Freud, Marx, Levi-Strauss, and the Jewish Struggle with Modernity* (New York: Basic Books, 1974), pp. 3–14, especially p. 9.

5. Martin E. Marty, *The Fire We Can Light: The Role of Religion in a Suddenly Different World* (Garden City, New York: Doubleday, 1973), pp. 19–20.

6. Martin E. Marty, Stuart E. Rosenberg, and Andrew M. Greeley, *What Do We Believe? The Stance of Religion in America* (New York: Meredith, 1968), pp. 8–9.

7. The Gallup Opinion Index, *Religion in America 1977–78*, report no. 145 (Princeton, N.J.: American Institute of Public Opinion, n.d.), p. 43.

8. Robert Wohl, *The Generation of 1914* (Cambridge: Harvard University Press, 1979).

9. Ortega is quoted by Karl J. Weintraub, *Visions of Culture* (Chicago: University of Chicago Press, 1966), pp. 266–67.

10. David Hollinger, "T. S. Kuhn's Theory of Science and Its Implications for History," in *Paradigms and Revolutions: Appraisals and Applications of Thomas Kuhn's Philosophy of Science*, Gary Cutting (ed.) (Notre Dame: University of Notre Dame Press, 1980), p. 219.

11. Charles Y. Glock, "The Religious Revival in America," in Charles Y. Glock and Rodney Stark, *Religion and Society in Tension* (Chicago: Rand McNally, 1965), pp. 68, 84–85.

12. Michael Argyle and Benjamin Beit-Hallahmi, *The Social Psychology of Religion* (Boston: Routledge and Kegan Paul, 1975), pp. 25–29. This book also has the references to publication data of Luckmann, Marcus Lee Hansen, and Will Herberg, whom the coauthors discuss.

13. S. S. Acquaviva, *The Decline of the Sacred in Industrial Society* (New York: Harper and Row, 1979).

14. See ibid., pp. 7, 201–2.

15. Herman Kahn and Anthony J. Wiener, *The Year 2000: A Framework for Speculation on the Next Thirty-Three Years* (New York: Macmillan, 1967), p. 7. The authors do report that "almost all of the nineteenth- and twentieth-century philosophers of history seem to believe it likely that some new kind of 'religious' stage will follow a termination of Sensate culture" (p. 48).

16. Thus *New Yorker* writer Ved Mehta, after touring the world of avant-garde theologians concluded: "The New Theologian set himself the old task of equating faith and theology with reason and secularism, and doing so without any sacrifice on either side—a task, in its way, no less tantalizing than squaring the circle." *The New Theologian* (New York: Harper and Row, 1966), p. 209. Most of the scorn by Christian conservatives or "transcendence-minded" thinkers was heaped on William Hamilton and Thomas J. J. Altizer for their *Radical Theology and the Death of God* (New York: Bobbs-Merrill, 1966).

17. Larry Shiner, "The Meanings of Secularization," in James F. Childress and David B. Harned, *Secularization and the Protestant Prospect* (Philadelphia: Westminster, 1970), pp. 30–42.

18. For a contemporary summary of these debates about Gogarten and Bonhoeffer, and about Harvey Cox and Gibson Winter, see Martin E. Marty, "Does Secular Theology Have a Future?," in *The Great Ideas Today 1967*, Otto Bird (ed.) (Chicago: Encyclopedia Britannica, 1967), pp. 38–53.

19. Gibson Winter, *The New Creation as Metropolis* (New York: Macmillan, 1966).

20. Harvey Cox, *The Secular City* (New York: Macmillan, 1965), which quoted (p. 2) Dutch theologian C. A. Van Peursen: secularization was the deliverance of man "first from religious and then from metaphysical control over his reason and his language." Cox defined it as "the loosing of the world from religious and quasi-religious understandings of itself, dispelling of all closed worldviews, the breaking of all supernatural myths and sacred symbols."

21. David Martin, "Toward Eliminating the Concept of Secularization," in *Penguin Survey of the Social Sciences 1965*, Julius Gould (ed.) (Baltimore: Penguin Books, 1965), pp. 169–82.

22. Andrew M. Greeley, *Unsecular Man: The Persistence of Religion* (New York: Schocken, 1972), which is a polemic against propagators of the "secular paradigm"

in the interest of various theories of sacralization, and in the light of what Greeley presents as empirical evidence against the secularizers.

23. Peter Berger, *A Rumor of Angels: Modern Society and the Rediscovery of the Supernatural* (Garden City, N.Y.: Doubleday, 1969).

24. Harvey Cox, *The Feast of Fools* (Cambridge: Harvard University Press, 1969).

25. Brown was referring to a new trend in the black movement in America, with reference to the work of the Reverend Albert Cleage. See Clifton Brown, "Black Religion—1968," in Hart M. Nelsen, Raytha L. Yokley, and Anne K. Nelsen, *The Black Church in America* (New York: Basic Books, 1971), p. 18.

26. The literature on the new religiosity is extensive. For samples, see *Religious Movements in Contemporary America,* Irving I. Zaretsky and Mark P. Leone (eds.) (Princeton: Princeton University Press, 1974); *The New Religious Consciousness,* Charles Y. Glock and Robert N. Bellah (eds.) (Berkeley: University of California Press, 1976); Robert Wuthnow, *Experimentation in American Religion* (Berkeley: University of California Press, 1978); and *Understanding the New Religions,* Jacob Needleman and George Baker (eds.) (New York: Seabury, 1978).

27. Cuddihy, *Ordeal of Civility,* p. 10.

28. Robert N. Bellah, *Beyond Belief: Essays on Religion in a Post-Traditional World* (New York: Harper and Row, 1970), pp. 21, 39–45.

29. Sidney E. Mead, *The Nation with the Soul of a Church* (New York: Harper and Row, 1975), pp. 7–8, 118.

30. Thomas Luckmann, *The Invisible Religion* (New York: Macmillan, 1967), pp. 43, 49.

31. Clifford Geertz, "Religion as a Cultural System," in *The Religious Situation: 1968,* Donald Cutler (ed.) (Boston: Beacon Press, 1968), p. 643.

32. *The Culture of Unbelief,* Rocco Caporale and Antonio Grumelli (eds.) (Berkeley: University of California Press, 1971), a report on a symposium at Rome in 1969.

33. Both Hartt and Gustafson quotations are from James M. Gustafson, *The Contributions of Theology to Medical Ethics* (Milwaukee: Marquette University, 1975), pp. 97, 5. Phillip E. Hammond discusses the Court cases of the 1960s in the larger context of civil religion in *Varieties of Civil Religion* by Robert N. Bellah and Phillip E. Hammond (New York: Harper and Row, 1980), pp. 157–58.

34. Melford Spiro, in *Anthropological Approaches to the Study of Religion,* Michael Banton (ed.) (New York: Paragon, 1966), p. 89.

35. Daniel Bell, "The Meaning of the Sacred" in *The Winding Passage: Essays in Sociological Journals 1960–1980* (Cambridge, Mass.: Abt Books, 1981).

36. See the appended essay in the new edition of *The Triumph of the Therapeutic: Uses of Faith after Freud.*

37. Martin E. Marty, *The Search for a Usable Future* (New York: Harper and Row, 1969), chap. 4, "The Present's Twofold Sign," pp. 57–72, especially pp. 68, 72. See also Wilfred Sellars, "Philosophy and the Scientific Image of Man," in *Science, Perception and Reality* (Boston: Routledge and Kegan Paul, 1963), pp. 1–40.

38. Cuddihy, *Ordeal of Civility,* p. 10.

39. Dean M. Kelley, *Why Conservative Churches Are Growing: A Study in the Sociology of Religion* (New York: Harper and Row, 1972); see, especially, the grid on p. 84.

40. Quoted in James C. Hefley and Edward E. Plowman, *Washington: Christians in the Corridors of Power* (Wheaton, Ill.: Tyndale House, 1975), p. 195.

41. Harold R. Isaacs, *Idols of the Tribe: Group Identity and Poltical Change* (New York: Harper and Row, 1975), p. 1.

42. Robert Jay Lifton, *Boundaries: Psychological Man in Revolution* (New York: Vintage, 1969), pp. 43–44, 51–52.

43. William G. McLoughlin, "Is There a Third Force in Christendom?" in *Daedalus,* Winter 1967, p. 61. See also William G. McLoughlin, *Revivals, Awakenings, and Reform* (Chicago: University of Chicago Press, 1978), pp. 9–24, for the Wallace theories: pp. 211–16 for the projections.

44. Robert Heilbroner, *Business Civilization in Decline* (New York: Norton, 1976), pp. 112–24.

CHAPTER 2: TRADITIONS

1. Quoted in Art Spiegelman and Bob Schneider, *Whole Grains* (New York: Douglas Links, 1973), p. 52.

2. William L. O'Neill, *Coming Apart* (New York: Quadrangle, 1971).

3. *New York Review of Books,* June 26, 1975.

4. For an elaboration of experimentalism, see "Experiment in Environment," my paper in *Journal of Religion,* July 1976. That article, several of whose highlights are condensed here, accents foreigners' perceptions of the American experimental sense.

5. Alexis de Toqueville, *Democracy in America* (New York: Vintage, 1954), vol. 1, pp. 45f.

6. J. Milton Yinger, *Sociology Looks at Religion* (New York: Macmillan, 1963), pp. 70f.

7. Jacques Maritain, *Reflections on America* (New York: Scribners, 1958), pp. 37, 95f.

8. George Santayana, *Character and Opinion in the United States* (Garden City, N.Y., 1956), p. 29.

9. Quoted by Daniel Herr and Joel Wells, *Through Other Eyes* (Westminster, Md.: Newman, 1965), p. 204.

10. See Sidney E. Mead, *The Lively Experiment* (New York: Harper and Row, 1963), pp. 25f., 59; Philip Schaff, *America: A Sketch of Its Political, Social, and Religious Character* (Cambridge: Harvard, 1961), p. 213; for Hilaire Belloc, see Herr and Wells, *Through Other Eyes,* pp. 97f.

11. Ernest Bloch, *On Karl Marx* (New York: Herder and Herder, 1971), p. 131.

12. *Oeuvres completes,* ed. by J. P. Mayer, vol. 1 (2), pp. 262, 254, quoted in *New York Review of Books,* vol. 24, no. 1 (February 5, 1976), p. 6.

13. Chorus from *The Rock,* cited as epigraph by Daniel Bell in *The Cultural Contradictions of Capitalism* (New York: Basic, 1976), p. vii.

14. Jerald C. Brauer, *Protestantism in America* (Philadelphia: Westminster, 1965), p. 7.

15. Donald H. Meyer, *The Democratic Enlightenment* (New York: G. P. Putnam's, 1976), pp. 3, 79.

16. See, for example, George Wilson Pierson, *Tocqueville in America* (Garden City, N.Y.: Doubleday, 1959), p. 70.

17. Daniel J. Boorstin, *The Genius of American Politics.* (Chicago: University of Chicago Press, 1953), p. 141.

18. For these two choices see Thomas Luckmann, *The Invisible Religion* (New York: Macmillan, 1967); and Robert L. Heilbroner, *Business Civilization in Decline* (New York: W. W. Norton, 1976), pp. 119f.

CHAPTER 3: PUBLIC RELIGION

1. Quoted by George Wilson Pierson, *Tocqueville in America* (Garden City, N.Y.: Doubleday, 1959), p. 70 (abridged by Dudley C. Lunt from *Tocqueville and Beaumont in America* [1938]).

2. Alexis de Tocqueville, *Journey to America* (Garden City, N.Y.: Doubleday, 1971), p. 290.

3. Quoted by Pierson, p. 99.

4. Quoted ibid., p. 139; cf. Tocqueville, p. 15.

5. Quoted by Anson Phelps Stokes and Leo Pfeffer, *Church and State in the United States* (New York: Harper and Row, 1964), p. 61.

6. Quoted by Pierson, p. 139.

7. Quoted by Walter J. Ong, S. J., *American Catholic Crossroads* (New York: Macmillan, 1959), p. 20.

8. Quoted by Tocqueville, p. 132.

9. Quoted by Pierson, p. 322.

10. Quoted ibid., p. 70. Robert Heilbroner (*Business Civilization in Decline* [W. W. Norton, 1976], pp. 112ff.) develops the concept of "social morale."

11. Quoted by Pierson, p. 100.

12. Tocqueville, pp. 395ff.

13. Ibid., p. 270; cf. Pierson, p. 203.

14. John Dewey, *Human Nature and Conduct* (New York: Modern Library, 1930), p. 226.

15. Nathaniel Ward, *The Simple Cobler of Aggawam in America*, ed. P. M. Zall (Lincoln: University of Nebraska Press, 1969), p. 10. The first edition appeared in 1647.

16. For a sampling of the belief of peasants and bourgeois in France just before this period, see Bernard Groethuysen, *The Bourgeois: Catholicism vs. Capitalism in Eighteenth-Century France* (New York: Holt, Rinehart and Winston, 1968).

17. Perry Miller, "From the Covenant to the Revival," in *The Shaping of American Religion*, ed. James Ward Smith and A. Leland Jamison (Princeton: Princeton University Press, 1961), 1:365.

18. William James, *The Will to Believe* (New York: Dover Publications, 1956), p. 270. The image of a republic appeared frequently in the writings of William James. H. S. Levinson, then of Stanford University, traced it in *Science, Metaphysics, and the Chance of Salvation* (Missoula, Mont.: Scholar's Press [for the American Academy of Religion], 1978), p. 116. Even James's vision of a savable world is "conceived after a social analogy," that of a federal republic, which is "constituted as a 'pluralism of independent powers.'" James, according to Levinson, works out three analogies between the world and a federal republic: variety, novelty, and activity in universes of discourse and practice. Federal republics are constituted to generate social accommodation, the assimilation of novel proposals, and purposes held in common by constituents of this universe.

19. Cited by Sidney E. Mead, *The Nation with the Soul of a Church* (New York: Harper and Row, 1975), p. 39.

20. Gabriel Marcel, *Creative Fidelity* (New York: Farrar, Strauss, 1964), pp. 211, 214.

21. Quoted by Ralph Barton Perry, *The Thought and Character of William James* (Boston: Little, Brown, 1935), 2:266ff.

22. James, p. x.

23. Ibid., p. xii.

24. John Courtney Murray, S. J., *We Hold These Truths: Catholic Reflections on the American Proposition* (New York: Sheed and Ward, 1960), pp. 23, 74, 129, 74, 12, 15.

25. Bernard Crick, *In Defense of Politics* (Baltimore: Penguin Books, 1964), p. 176.

26. James, pp. 11, 3, 11.

27. Tocqueville (n. 2 above), pp. 70ff.

28. Chester E. Jorgenson and Frank Luther Mott, eds., *Benjamin Franklin: Representative Selections, with Introduction, Bibliography, and Notes* (New York: Hill and Wang, 1962), p. 203.

29. Ibid., pp. 69ff.

30. Thomas Jefferson, *The Writings of Thomas Jefferson*, collected and ed. by Paul Leicester Ford (New York: G. P. Putnam's Sons, 1899), 10:343.

31. See the discussion on this point in Joseph F. Costanzo, S. J., *This Nation under God* (New York: Herder and Herder, 1964), pp. 29ff.

32. Thomas Jefferson, *Notes on the State of Virginia* (New York: Harper and Row, 1964), p. 153.

33. Adrienne Koch and William Peden, *The Life and Selected Writings of Thomas Jefferson* (New York: Random House, 1944), p. 637.

34. Jefferson, *Notes on the State of Virginia*, p. 152.

35. Ibid., p. 156.

36. John C. Fitzpatrick, ed., *The Writings of George Washington* (Washington, D.C.: Superintendent of Documents, 1931–44), 35:229.

37. James D. Richardson, ed., *A Compilation of the Messages and Papers of the Presidents, 1789–1897* (Washington, D.C.: Government Printing Officer, 1897), 1:258.

38. For an important discussion of Lincoln's use of the declaration, see Glen E. Thurow, *Abraham Lincoln and American Political Religion* (Albany: State University of New York Press, 1976), chap. 4 and esp. pp. 72ff.

39. John Dewey, *A Common Faith* (New Haven: Yale University Press, 1934), pp. 87, 1, 61, 82.

40. J. Paul Williams, *What Americans Believe and How They Worship*, rev. ed. (New York: Harper and Row, 1962), pp. 486, 488, 491ff., 484.

41. Horace M. Kallen, "Democracy's True Religion," *Saturday Review of Literature* (July 28, 1951).

42. Will Herberg, *Protestant, Catholic, Jew* (Garden City, N.Y.: Doubleday, 1955), p. 102.

43. Donald R. Cutler, ed., *The Religious Situation, 1968* (Boston: Beacon Press, 1968), is one of a number of places in which Bellah published his essay "Civil Religion in America": see p. 331.

44. Ibid., p. 351.

45. Heilbroner (n. 10 above), pp. 112, 117, 119, 120.

46. Herbert A. Deane, *The Political and Social Ideas of St. Augustine* (New York: Columbia University Press, 1963), pp. 125, 122, 119ff., 127; see chap. 4 and esp. p. 120. I have found Deane's interpretation more convincing than that of Charles H. McIlwain.

47. See the discussion of this point in Glen Caudill Dealy, *The Public Man* (Amherst: University of Massachusetts Press, 1977), pp. 76ff. and esp. 77n.

48. Alexis de Tocqueville, *Democracy in America* (New York: Alfred A. Knopf, 1954), 1:314.

49. Sebastian de Grazia, *The Political Community: A Study of Anomie* (Chicago: University of Chicago Press, 1948), pp. 45ff.

50. Mead (n. 19 above), pp. ix, 19.

51. Voltaire is quoted by Stokes and Pfeffer (n. 5 above), p. 23.

52. Mead, pp. ix, 5, 33, 37, 115, 22, 124, 125, 127: interspersed also are sequences of quotations from Mead, *The Old Religion in the Brave New World* (Berkeley: University of California Press, 1977), pp. 2, 3, 42, 1.

53. William James, *The Principles of Psychology* (New York: Henry Holt and Co., 1904), 2:290.

54. Quoted by Crick (n. 25 above), p. 138.

55. Quoted by Charles Hampden-Turner, *Radical Man* (Cambridge, Mass.: Schenkman Publishing Co., 1970), p. 39. Sidney Mead, with manifest delight, called my attention to the "crack-up" context.

56. Gustave Weigel, S. J., "The Church and the Public Conscience," *Atlantic Monthly* 210 (August 1962): 116–17; quoted by Philip Kurland in *Church and State: The Supreme Court and the First Amendment* (Chicago: University of Chicago Press, 1975), p. 31.

57. John C. Bennett, *Christians and the State* (New York: Charles Scribner's Sons, 1958), p. 9.

58. Quoted by Kurland, p. 31.

59. Jorgenson and Mott (n. 28 above), p. 203.

60. Typical of Jewish works on this subject is Abraham I. Katsh, *The Biblical Heritage of American Democracy* (New York: Ktav Publishing House, 1977).

61. Hannah Arendt, *On Revolution* (New York: Viking Press, 1963), pp. 18–20.

62. For an example, see L. F. Greene, ed., *The Writings of John Leland* (1945: reprint ed., New York: Arno Press and New York Times Book Co., 1969).

63. See the discussion in Daniel J. Boorstin, *The Lost World of Thomas Jefferson* (Boston: Beacon Press, 1948), pp. 159ff.

64. Cited by Dorothy Dohen, *Nationalism and American Catholicism* (New York: Sheed and Ward, 1967), pp. 94, 96.

65. Isaac Hecker, *The Church and the Age* (New York: Catholic World, 1887), pp. 84, 71, 79, 96ff.; see Dohen, p. 102.

66. Quoted by Franklin H. Littell, *The Crucifixion of the Jews* (New York: Harper and Row, 1975); this does not appear in his prepared remarks, and I have not been able to confirm it.

67. On "common grace," see John T. McNeill, ed., *Calvin: Institutes of the Christian Religion* (Philadelphia: Westminster Press, 1960), 1:273. For an example of how a kind of "law of nature" enters the Puritan tradition, see the discussion of John Preston in Perry Miller, *Errand into the Wilderness* (Cambridge: Harvard University Press, 1956), pp. 74ff.

68. Paul Tillich, *Christianity and the Encounter of World Religions* (New York: Columbia University Press, 1963), p. 97; on the concept of "anonymous Christian" in Karl Rahner, see the full discussion, Robert J. Schreiter, "The Anonymous Christian and Christology," in *Occasional Bulletin of Missionary Research* 2, no. 1 (January 1978); 2ff.

69. I have reference here to the way Gallup polls and others show well over 90 percent of the people expressing themselves in theistic or deistic terms.

70. For a study of comparable issues in Israel, see Elihu Katz and Michael Gurevitch, *The Secularization of Leisure: Culture and Communication in Israel* (Cambridge: Harvard University Press, 1976).

71. W. Lloyd Warner, *The Family of God* (New Haven: Yale University Press, 1961), pp. 155–260 (based on writings from 1959).

72. Richard B. Dierenfeld, *Religion in American Public Schools* (Washington, D.C.: Public Affairs Press, 1962), pp. 45, 56, passim.

73. A discussion of the role of law in public religion and references to these court cases appear in Phillip E. Hammond, "Religious Pluralism and Durkheim's Integration Thesis," in *Changing Perspectives in the Scientific Study of Religion*, ed. Allan W. Eister (New York: John Wiley and Sons, 1974), pp. 129ff.

74. Richard E. Morgan, *The Supreme Court and Religion* (New York: Free Press, 1972), p. 198; see also Kurland (n. 56 above), p. 74.

75. Hammond, p. 131; Morgan, p. 170; and Kurland, p. 179, include references to the cited cases.

76. Daniel J. Boorstin (*The Genius of American Politics* [Chicago: University of Chicago Press, 1953], p. 170) first compared the situation.

77. Bellah, in Cutler (n. 43 above), p. 347.

78. Quoted by Franklin P. Cole, ed., *They Preached Liberty* (Indianapolis: Liberty Fund, 1976), p. 163.

79. Gustave Weigel, S. J., "The Present Embarrassment of the Church," in *Religion in America*, ed. John Cogley (Cleveland: Meridian Books, 1958), p. 234.

80. William Lee Miller, "American Religion and American Political Attitudes," in Smith and Jamison (n. 17 above), 2:93–95.

81. Perry (n. 21 above), 2:268.

82. Cited by Robert T. Handy, "The American Tradition of Religious Freedom: An Historical Analysis," *Journal of Public Law* 13, no. 2 (1964): 247–66, quotation from p. 251.

83. On Jehovah's Witnesses, see Morgan, pp. 58–74.

84. On the early years of the Black Muslims, see C. Eric Lincoln, *The Black Muslims in America* (Boston: Beacon Press, 1961).

85. A typical expression is Vine Deloria, Jr., *God is Red* (New York: Grosset and Dunlap, 1973).

86. George Santayana, *Character and Opinion in the United States* (Garden City, N.Y.: Doubleday, 1956), pp. 135ff.

87. See Cutler (n. 43 above), p. 357.

88. Quoted by Klaus Hansen, *Quest for Empire* (East Lansing: Michigan State University Press, 1967), p. 43.

89. John Courtney Murray develops the theme of "development" in his writings on this subject; see Walter M. Abbott, S. J., *The Documents of Vatican II* (New York: Herder and Herder/Association Press, 1966), pp. 672ff.

CHAPTER 4: CIVIL RELIGION

1. Luckmann's position is defined in *The Invisible Religion* (New York: Macmillan Co., 1967), chap. 4, pp. 50ff.

2. A sample basis for such inclusive definitions of religion appears in what strikes me as an admirable approach to symbolization in Clifford Geertz, "Religion as a Cultural System," in Donald R. Cutler (ed.), *The Religious Situation: 1968* (Boston: Beacon Press, 1968), pp. 639ff.

3. See Carlton J. H. Hayes, *Nationalism: A Religion* (New York: Macmillan, 1960), chap. 12, 164ff.

4. Ernest Gellner, *Thought and Change* (Chicago: University of Chicago Press, 1965), p. 123.

5. Sidney Mead, "The Post-Protestant Concept and America's Two Religions," in *Religion in Life*, vol. 33 (Spring 1964), pp. 191–204.

6. Will Herberg, *Protestant, Catholic, Jew: An Essay in American Religious Sociology* (New York: Doubleday, 1955).

7. Thus D. W. Brogan in his essay in Cutler, *Religious Situation*, pp. 356ff.

8. William L. Miller, *Piety Along the Potomac: Notes on Politics and Morals in the Fifties* (Boston: Houghton Mifflin, 1964) is the most detailed account of Eisenhower-era civil religion.

9. Edmund Wilson, *Eight Essays* (New York: Doubleday, 1964).

10. This approach to Jonathan Edwards is taken in Alan Heimert, *Religion and the American Mind* (Cambridge: Harvard University Press, 1966), pp. 96ff.

11. See William J. Wolf, *The Almost Chosen People: A Study of the Religion of Abraham Lincoln* (Garden City, N.Y.: Doubleday, 1959), chaps. 8 and 9.

12. *The Irony of American History* (New York: Charles Scribner's Sons, 1952).

13. Mark Hatfield is quoted in *The Christian Century*, February 21, 1973, p. 221.

14. "Civil Religion in America," in *Daedalus* (Winter 1967), pp. 15f.

15. Lowell D. Streiker and Gerald S. Strober, *Religion and the New Majority* (New York: Association Press, 1972), p. 179.

16. Charles B. Henderson, Jr., *The Nixon Theology* (New York: Harper and Row, 1972), p. 193.

17. For reference to J. Paul Williams and his colleagues, see Martin E. Marty *The New Shape of American Religion* (New York: Harper and Row, 1959), chap. 4, and "The Status of Societal Religion," in *Concordia Theological Monthly*, vol. 36, no. 10 (November 1965), pp. 687ff.

18. Sidney E. Mead, "The Nation with the Soul of a Church," in *Church History*, vol. 36, no. 3 (September 1967), pp. 275–83.

19. Robert N. Bellah, "Civil Religion in America," in *Daedalus* (Winter 1967), pp. 12, 18.

20. See also Robert N. Bellah, "Transcendence in Contemporary Piety," in Herbert W. Richardson and Donald R. Cutler (eds.), *Transcendence* (Boston: Beacon Press, 1969), p. 91.

21. Roger Garaudy, *From Anathema to Dialogue* (New York: Herder and Herder, 1966), p. 123.

CHAPTER 5: INTERPRETATION

1. First quotation from Reinhold Niebuhr and Alan Heimert, *A Nation So Conceived: Reflections on the History of America* (New York: Charles Scribner's Sons, 1963), p. 7 (hereinafter cited as *NSC*); second from Reinhold Niebuhr, *Discerning the Signs of the Times: Sermons for Today and Tomorrow* (New York: Charles Scribner's Sons, 1946), p. 10 (hereinafter cited as *DST*). Unless otherwise noted, all books cited are by Reinhold Niebuhr.

2. Edwards is quoted by Sidney H. Rooy (*The Theology of Missions in the Puritan Tradition* [Grand Rapids, Mich.: William B. Eerdmans Publishing, 1965], p. 294) in an extensive passage on *A History of the Work of Redemption*.

3. See, e.g., the somewhat dated James M. Stifler, *The Religion of Benjamin Franklin* (New York, 1925); Adrienne Koch, *Power, Morals, and the Founding Fa-*

thers (Ithaca, N.Y.: Cornell University Press, 1961); G. Adolf Koch, *Religion of the American Enlightenment* (New York: Thomas Y. Crowell Co., 1968 [first published in 1933]); Paul F. Boller, Jr., *George Washington and Religion* (Dallas: Southern Methodist University Press, 1963); Robert M. Healey, *Jefferson on Religion in Public Education* (New Haven: Yale University Press, 1962); Elton Trueblood, *Abraham Lincoln: Theologian of American Anguish* (New York: Harper and Row, 1972); William J. Wolf, *The Almost Chosen People: A Study of the Religion of Abraham Lincoln* (Garden City, N.Y.: Doubleday, 1959); Robert S. Alley, *So Help Me God: Religion and the Presidency, Wilson to Nixon* (Richmond, Va.: John Knox Press, 1972); John M. Mulder, "Wilson the Preacher: The 1905 Baccalaureate Sermon," *Journal of Presbyterian History* 51, no. 3 (Fall 1973): 267ff.

4. H. Richard Niebuhr, *The Social Sources of Denominationalism* (New York: Henry Holt and Co., 1929) is a particularly valuable study of class-based religious collective behavior.

5. The first quote is from *Does Civilization Need Religion?* (New York: Macmillan, 1927), dedication page (hereinafter cited as *DCNR*); the second from *Leaves from the Notebook of a Tamed Cynic* (New York: Living Age, 1957 [first published in 1929]), dedication page (hereinafter cited as *LNTC*).

6. "Intellectual Autobiography," in *Reinhold Niebuhr: His Religious, Social, and Political Thought*, ed. Charles W. Kegley and Robert W. Bretall (New York: Macmillan, 1962), p. 5.

7. "Ten Years That Shook My World," *Christian Century*, April 26, 1939, p. 545.

8. *The Nature and Destiny of Man: A Christian Interpretation* (New York: Charles Scribner's Sons, 1948 [vol. 1 first published in 1942, vol. 2 in 1943]) (hereinafter cited as *NDM*.) Significantly, this is the single major work by Niebuhr that is not cited in the present essay; the only other noncited Niebuhr book is the more ephemeral *The Contribution of Religion to Social Work* (New York: Columbia University Press, 1932).

9. See Kegley and Bretall, p. 3.

10. *Faith and Politics: A Commentary of Religious, Social and Political Thought in a Technological Age*, ed. Ronald H. Stone (New York: George Braziller, Inc., 1968), p. 41 (hereinafter cited as *FP*).

11. *The Children of Light and the Children of Darkness* (New York: Charles Scribner's Sons, 1945), p. 33 (hereinafter cited as *CLCD*).

12. *The Irony of American History* (New York: Charles Scribner's Sons, 1952), p. 49 (hereinafter cited as *IAH*).

13. Ibid., pp. 84–85, 91, 100.

14. *Man's Nature and His Communities: Essays on the Dynamics and Enigmas of Man's Personal and Social Existence* (New York: Charles Scribner's Sons, 1965), p. 14 (hereinafter cited as *MNHC*). The Thurber citation is from Holtan P. Odegard, *Sin and Science: Reinhold Niebuhr as Political Theologian* (Yellow Springs, Ohio: Antioch Press, 1956), p. 11.

15. *LNTC*, pp. 218–19.

16. *Moral Man and Immoral Society* (New York: Charles Scribner's Sons, 1960 [first published in 1932]), p. ix (hereinafter cited as *MMIS*).

17. Kegley and Bretall, p. 4.

18. *LNTC*, p. 59.

19. *The Self and the Dramas of History* (New York: Charles Scribner's Sons, 1955), pp. 92–93 (hereinafter cited as *SDH*).

20. *LNTC*, p. 45.

21. *DCNR*, pp. 12–16.

22. Harold R. Landon, ed., *Reinhold Niebuhr: A Prophetic Voice in Our Time* (New York: Seabury Press, 1962), pp. 61–62, 82.

23. Ibid., pp. 80–81.

24. Ibid., pp. 19–20; *Beyond Tragedy: Essays on the Christian Interpretation of History* (New York: Charles Scribner's Sons, 1965 [first published 1937]), p. 62 (hereinafter cited as *BT*).

25. *Essays in Applied Christianity*, ed. D. B. Robertson (New York: Living Age Books, 1958) (hereinafter cited as *EAC*), includes the following essays: in part 1, "The Weakness of Common Worship in American Protestantism"; in part 2, "Can the Church Give a 'Moral Lead'?" in part 5, "The Church and the Churches: The Ecumenical Movement."

26. *SDH*, pp. 47, 49.

27. *Christian Realism and Political Problems* (New York: Charles Scribner's Sons, 1953), pp. 109–10 (hereinafter cited as *CRPP*).

28. *IAH*, pp. 54–55.

29. *Reflections on the End of an Era* (New York: Charles Scribner's Sons, 1934), pp. 4–5, 30.

30. *SDH*, pp. 132, 143.

31. *EAC*, pp. 12–14.

32. *LNTC*, pp. 128, 74, 18.

33. *Love and Justice: Selections from the Shorter Writings of Reinhold Niebuhr*, ed. D. B. Robertson (Philadelphia: Westminster Press, 1957), p. 42 (hereinafter cited as *LJ*).

34. *EAC*, pp. 29–66, esp. pp. 29ff., 48, 52ff., 58.

35. *LNTC*, p. 50; *Faith and History: A Comparison of Christian and Modern Views of History* (New York: Charles Scribner's Sons, 1949), p. 156 (hereinafter cited as *FH*).

36. *LNTC*, pp. 162, 196, 82, 150–51.

37. *DCNR*, p. 36.

38. *REE*, p. 78.

39. H. Richard Niebuhr, chaps. 2, 3.

40. *Pious and Secular America* (New York: Charles Scribner's Sons, 1958), pp. 7–8 (hereinafter cited as *PSA*).

41. Ibid., p. 11; see *DCNR*, pp. 98ff.

42. *IAH*, p. 103; *DST*, p. 19.

43. *EAC*, pp. 102, 41.

44. *DCNR*, pp. 27–28.

45. *BT*, p. 107; *LJ*, pp. 44, 90.

46. *LJ*, pp. 44–45.

47. *PSA*, pp. 8, 11, 13, 31.

48. *MNHC*, p. 64; *LJ*, pp. 111, 113; *PSA*, p. 20; *LJ*, p. 91 (1930).

49. *IAH*, p. 10.

50. *PSA*, p. 6.

51. *MNHC*, pp. 122–23.

52. *FP*, pp. 119–20; *LNTC*, p. 117; *DCNR*, p. 67; *LJ*, p. 97.

53. *MNHC*, pp. 120, 11; *IAH*, p. 50.

54. *DCNR*, pp. 102–3.

55. *An Interpretation of Christian Ethics* (New York: Harper and Bros., 1935), pp. 15, 20, 22, 25, 186–87 (hereinafter cited as *ICE*).

56. *Christianity and Power Politics* (New York: Charles Scribner's Sons, 1940), p. 109 (hereinafter cited as *CPP*); *CRPP*, p. 109; *CPP*, p. 173.

57. *ICE*, p. 7; Kegley and Bretall, p. 13; *CRPP*, 163.

58. *ICE*, pp. 58–59; *CPP*, pp. 42–45.

59. *CPP*, pp. 75–78, 32.

60. Quoted by June Bingham, *Courage to Change: An Introduction to the Life and Thought of Reinhold Niebuhr* (New York: Charles Scribner's Sons, 1961), p. 310.

61. *NSC*, p. 7.

62. *CRPP*, p. 9.

63. Ibid., p. 111; *DST*, p. 30.

64. *BT*, pp. 53, 85; *LJ*, pp. 94–95.

65. *BT*, p. 86; *CLCD*, p. 124; *BT*, p. 86.

66. *IAH*, pp. 78, 7, 171.

67. Stephen Vincent Benet, *John Brown's Body* (New York: Farrar and Rinehart, 1928), p. 213; cited in *BT*, pp. 66–67.

68. *MMIS*, p. 119; *The Structure of Nations and Empires* (New York: Charles Scribner's Sons., 1959), pp. 214–15 (hereinafter cited as *SNE*); *LNTC*, p. 190.

69. *MNHC*, pp. 84–87; *LJ*, p. 127; *CLCD*, p. 140.

70. *MNHC*, pp. 28, 17; see also *PSA*, pp. 90ff., 88, 111; *DCNR*, p. 70.

71. *PSA*, p. 82; *MNHC*, p. 20.

72. *SDH*, p. 142.

CHAPTER 6: SPIRITUALITY

1. Paul Tillich, *Systematic Theology*, vol. 3: *Life and the Spirit, History and the Kingdom of God* (Chicago, 1963), pp. 21–30.

2. Quoted by Huston Smith, *Condemned to Meaning* (New York, 1965), p. 17.

3. Arnold B. Come, *Human Spirit and Holy Spirit* (Philadelphia, 1959), p. 72.

4. See Karl Rahner, "Wissenschaft als Konfession?" *Wort und Wahrheit*, vol. 9 (November 1954), pp. 811–13.

5. J. Milton Yinger, *Sociology Looks at Religion* (New York, 1963), pp. 36, 67ff.; see also, David Martin, "Towards Eliminating the Concept of Secularization," *Penguin Survey of the Social Sciences 1965*, ed. Julius Gould (Baltimore, 1965), p. 171.

6. John L. Thomas, S. J., *Religion and the American People* (Westminster, Md., 1962), pp. 67, 229; Gerhard Lenski, *The Religious Factor* (New York, 1961), p. 54.

7. Ralph Waldo Emerson, "The Method of Nature," in *The American Transcendentalists*, ed. Perry Miller (New York, 1957), p. 66.

8. Sidney E. Mead, *The Lively Experiment* (New York, 1963), p. 94.

9. *New Haven Gazette and Connecticut Magazine*, October 9, 1738.

10. Oscar Handlin, *The Americans* (Boston, 1963), pp. 65ff.

11. In John Wingate Thornton, *The Pulpit of the American Revolution* (Boston, 1860), p. 487.

12. Daniel J. Boorstin, *The Genius of American Politics* (Chicago, 1953), p. 44.

13. Alexis de Tocqueville, *Democracy in America*, vol. 1 (New York, 1954), p. 314.

14. Ralph Henry Gabriel, *The Course of American Democratic Thought* (New York, 1956), p. 14.

15. Max Lerner, *America as a Civilization* (New York, 1957), p. 715.

16. Perry Miller, *The American Character: A Conversation* (Santa Barbara,

Calif., 1962), p. 23. For Ayres, see Robert Theobald, *The Challenge of Abundance* (New York, 1961), p. 122.

17. James Ward Smith, *The Shaping of American Religion*, eds. James Ward Smith and A. Leland Jamison (Princeton, 1961), pp. 402, 404.

18. Walter Lippmann, *A Preface to Morals* (paperback edition; Boston, 1960), p. 327f.

19. James Bryce, *The American Commonwealth*, vol. 2 (New York, 1959), p. 487.

20. Quoted in Norman Foerster, *Image of America* (South Bend, Ind., 1962), p. 104.

21. Quoted by K. S. Inglis, *Churches and the Working Classes in Victorian England* (London, 1963), p. 8.

22. Ernest Gellner, *Thought and Change* (Chicago, 1964), pp. 194, 206.

23. H. Richard Niebuhr as paraphrased by Van A. Harvey in *The Historian and the Believer* (New York, 1966), p. 253.

24. *The Reporter*, January 13, 1955.

25. Boorstin, p. 135.

CHAPTER 7: SCRIPTURALITY

1. *Papers and Speeches of the Church Congress* (New York, 1897), 104.

2. Quoted in *Public Opinion* 14 (January 7, 1893), 333.

3. Walter A. Elwell ("Belief and the Bible: A Crisis of Authority," *Christianity Today* [March 21, 1980], 19–23), reports on the poll by Gallup.

4. Suzanne K. Langer, *Philosophy in a New Key* (New York: New American Library, 1952), 41, 39.

5. On Ortega's ideas, see Karl J. Weintraub *Visions of Culture* (Chicago: University of Chicago Press, 1966), 261, 263; and Harold C. Raley, *José Ortega y Gasset: Philosopher of European Unity* (University, Ala.: University of Alabama Press, 1967), 81.

6. George Boas, *The History of Ideas* (New York: Scribner's, 1969), 88.

7. Perry Miller, "The Garden of Eden and the Deacon's Meadow," *American Heritage* 7 (1955), 55.

8. George F. Parker, *Recollections of Grover Cleveland* (New York, 1911), 382.

9. Bernard Crick, *In Defense of Politics* (Baltimore: Penguin, 1964), 176.

10. Raymond T. Bond (ed.), *The Man Who Was Chesterton* (Garden City, NY: Doubleday Image, 1960), 131.

11. Daniel J. Boorstin, *The Genius of American Politics* (Chicago: University of Chicago Press, 1953), title page.

12. Elwell, "Belief and the Bible," 19–23.

13. Rosemary Gordon, "A Very Private World," in *The Function and Nature of Imagery*, ed. P. W. Sheehan (New York: Academy, 1972), 63.

14. Quoted by Andrew Greeley, *The Denominational Society* (Glenview, Ill.: Scott, Foresman, 1972), 51.

15. See Anson Phelps Stokes, *Church and State in the United States*, vol. 1 (New York: Harper Brothers, 1950), 293–99.

16. Paul F. Boller, Jr., *George Washington and Religion* (Dallas: Southern Methodist University Press, 1963), 40–41; Stokes, *Church and State*, 1: 486, 244.

17. Charles B. Sanford, *Thomas Jefferson and His Library* (Hamden, Conn.: Archon, 1977), 271. For Jefferson's interests in the Bible and religion, see Robert

M. Healey, *Jefferson on Religion in Public Education* (New Haven: Yale University Press, 1962).

18. On the Fisk Bible, see Elton Trueblood, *Abraham Lincoln: Theologian of Anguish* (New York: Harper and Row, 1973), 48–49, 55.

19. John Mulder, *Woodrow Wilson: The Years of Preparation* (Princeton: Princeton University Press, 1978), 49; Stokes, *Church and State*, 2: 549.

20. Bryan is quoted in the *Truth-seeker* 26 (June 29, 1929), 402. The exchange with Darrow is quoted in George Marsden, *Fundamentalism in American Culture: The Shaping of American Evangelicalism 1870–1925* (New York: Oxford University Press, 1980), 187. On the other attitudes of Bryan, see Lawrence W. Levine, *Defender of the Faith: William Jennings Bryan: The Last Decade, 1915–1925* (New York: Oxford University Press, 1965), 247, 281, 292.

21. *New York Times* (September 25, 1980), A27.

22. Richard B. Dierenfeld, *Religion in American Public Schools* (Washington: Public Affairs Press, 1962), chap. 4.

23. J. Paul Williams, *What Americans Believe and How They Worship* (New York: Harper and Row, 1962), 46.

24. Jerry Wayne Brown, *The Rise of Biblical Criticism in America, 1800–1870* (Middletown, Conn.: Wesleyan University Press, 1969), 158, 66, 164.

25. Henry David Thoreau, *A Week on the Concord and Merrimack* (Boston: Houghton Mifflin, 1906, 1961), 73–74.

26. John T. Morse, Jr., *Life and Letters of Oliver Wendell Holmes*, vol. 2 (Boston: Houghton Mifflin, 1896), 296–97.

27. Robert Jay Lifton, *Boundaries: Psychological Man in Revolution* (New York: Vintage, 1970), 43.

28. Eugene Goodheart, *Culture and the Radical Conscience* (Cambridge: Harvard University Press, 1973), 9–10.

29. Claire Cox, *The New-Time Religion* (Englewood Cliffs, N.J.: Prentice-Hall, 1961), chap. 15.

30. Folkloric treatment is in Donald E. Byrne, Jr., *No Foot of Land: Folklore of American Methodist Itinerants* (Metuchen, N.J.: Scarecrow, 1975), 85, 134.

31. Solomon Schechter, *Seminary Addresses and Other Papers* (Cincinnati: Ark. 1915), 48–49.

32. Ray Allen Billington, *The Protestant Crusade 1800–1860: A Study of the Origins of American Nativism* (Chicago: Quadrangle, 1964), 157–58.

33. William H. O'Connell, *Recollections of Seventy Years* (Boston: Houghton Mifflin, 1934), 120–22.

34. C. J. Jung, *The Integration of the Personality* (New York: Farrar and Rinehart, 1939).

35. Albert C. Moore, *Iconography of Religions: An Introduction* (Philadelphia: Fortress, 1977), 28; Moore quotes from John Philips, *The Reformation of Images* (Berkeley: University of California Press, 1973), 201.

36. Moore, *Iconography of Religions*, 34–35.

37. Hylan Lewis, "Blackways of Kent: Religion and Salvation," in *Hart M. Nelsen, Raytha L. Yokley and Anne K. Nelsen* (New York: Basic, 1971), 103.

38. See the section on "Bible Christians," in *Slave Religion: The "Invisible Institution" in the Antebellum South*, by Albert J. Raboteau (New York: Oxford University Press, 1978), 239–43.

39. Quoted by Will Herberg, *Protestant, Catholic, Jew* (New York: Doubleday, 1955), 236.

40. Victor Obenhaus, *Church and Faith in Mid-America* (Philadelphia: Westminster, 1963), 72–82.

41. Quoted in *The Ideas of the Woman Suffrage Movement, 1890–1920,* by Aileen Kraditor (New York: Columbia University Press, 1965), 78, 80.

42. Edward Robinson, *The Bible and Its Literature* (New York: Office of the American Biblical Repository, 1841), 17.

43. Winthrop S. Hudson, *The Great Tradition of the American Churches* (New York: Harper and Brothers, 1953), chap. 8.

44. Quoted by William R. Hutchison, *The Modernist Impulse in American Protestantism* (Cambridge: Harvard University Press, 1976), 94.

45. Reported on in *Chautauqua Assembly Herald* 17, no. 14 (August 4, 1892), 2, 3, 6, 7. For more on Harper's view, consult Robert W. Funk, "The Watershed of the American Biblical Tradition: The Chicago School, First Phase, 1892–1920," *JBL* 95 (1976) 4–22.

46. Sample titles of Bolce articles in *Cosmopolitan* 47 (June–November 1909) were "Polyglots in Temples of Babel," "Avatars of the Almighty," "Christianity in the Crucible," and "Rallying Round the Cross."

CHAPTER 8: EXPERIMENT

1. Hilaire Belloc, *The Contrast* (New York: Robert M. McBride, 1923), condensed and reprinted in *Through Other Eyes: Some Impressions of American Catholicism by Foreign Visitors from 1777 to the Present,* ed. Dan Herr and Joel Wells (Westminster, Md.: Newman Press, 1965), pp. 97–98; see also Sidney E. Mead, *The Lively Experiment* (New York: Harper and Row, 1963), frontispiece, pp. 25–26, 59; Philip Schaff, *America: A Sketch of Its Political, Social, and Religious Character,* ed. Perry Miller (1855; reprint ed., Cambridge: Harvard University Press, Belknap Press, 1961), p. 213. Benjamin Franklin is quoted in Donald H. Meyer, *The Democratic Enlightenment* (New York: G. P. Putnam's Sons, 1976), pp. 3, 79; the suggestion about a *Publick Religion* first appeared in 1749 in Franklin's *Proposals Relating to the Education of the Youth of Philadelphia*.

2. Jerald C. Brauer, *Protestantism in America,* rev. ed. (Philadelphia: Westminster Press, 1965), p. 7; see also Peter G. Mode, *The Frontier Spirit in American Christianity* (New York: Macmillan, 1923), pp. 12–14; William Warren Sweet, *The Society of Religion in America* (New York: Harper and Bros., 1950), pp. 2–3; Mead.

3. Milton Yinger, *Sociology Looks at Religion* (New York: Macmillan, 1963), pp. 70–71.

4. Hugh Dalziel Duncan, *Symbols in Society* (New York: Oxford University Press, 1968), pp. 5, 13, 241–42, and, esp., 25–26.

5. Quoted by Brauer, p. 19.

6. Edward W. Chester, *Europe Views America: A Critical Evaluation* (Washington, D.C.: Public Affairs Press, 1962), p. 114.

7. James Dixon, *Methodism in America* (London: for the author, 1849), p. iii. (This and a number of other observers' writings are excerpted and reproduced in Milton Powell, ed., *The Voluntary Church: American Religious Life, 1740–1865, Seen through the Eyes of European Visitors* [New York: Macmillan, 1967].) For the convenience of contemporary readers, pages in this source book will be referred to in the appropriate instances; in this case, for both quotations from Dixon see Pow-

ell, p. 176. For the reference to Tocqueville, see Joachim Wach, *Types of Religious Experience: Christian and Non-Christian* (Chicago: University of Chicago Press, 1951), p. 175.

8. Bryce is quoted in Carlton J. H. Hayes, *Nationalism: A Religion* (New York: Macmillan, 1960), pp. 20–21; for the definition of public theology, the quotation from Jonathan Edwards, and the reference to Abraham Lincoln, see Chapter 5 above, pp. 95–97 (see also William J. Wolf, *The Almost Chosen People: A Study of the Religion of Abraham Lincoln* [Garden City, N.Y.: Doubleday, 1959]).

9. José Ortega y Gasset is quoted in Julián Marías, *José Ortega y Gasset: Circumstance and Vocation* (Norman: University of Oklahoma Press, 1970), p. 362.

10. Alexis de Tocqueville, *Democracy in America,* in Powell, p. 90.

11. Kempert is quoted in Robert St. John, *Jews, Justice, and Judaism* (Garden City, N.Y.: Doubleday, 1969), p. 86; the Du Bois quotation is in J. Deotis Roberts, *A Black Political Theology* (Philadelphia: Westminster Press, 1974), p. 54: for Roman Catholic attitudes toward American nationalism, see Dorothy Dohen, *Nationalism and American Catholicism* (New York: Sheed and Ward, 1967).

12. Two versions of the story of white Protestantism "at business" in an environment it had helped shape are Robert T. Handy, *A Christian America: Protestant Hopes and Historical Realities* (New York: Oxford University Press, 1971); and Martin E. Marty, *Righteous Empire: The Protestant Experience in America* (New York: Dial Press, 1970).

13. William A. Clebsch, *American Religious Thought: A History* (Chicago: University of Chicago Press, 1973), pp. 1, 3f.

14. Alexis de Tocqueville, *Democracy in America* (New York: Random House, Vintage Books, 1954), 1:46, 45.

15. Herbert W. Richardson, *Toward an American Theology* (New York: Harper and Row, 1967), pp. 110–11.

16. Achille Murat, *Esquisse morale et politique des Etats-Unis de l'Amerique du Nord,* trans. and excerpted in Powell, p. 50.

17. Henry Sienkiewicz, *Portrait of America: The Letters of Henry Sienkiewicz* (New York: Columbia University Press, 1959), excerpted in Herr and Wells, p. 66.

18. Camille Ferri-Pisani, *Lettres sur les Etats-Unis d'Amerique* (1862), trans, and excerpted in Powell, pp. 89–90.

19. Tocqueville, *Democracy in America,* in Powell, p. 87.

20. Schaff, pp. 16, 210–11.

21. Jacques Maritain, *Reflections on America* (New York: Charles Scribner's Sons, 1958), pp. 37, 93–94.

22. James Bryce, *The American Commonwealth* (New York: G. P. Putnam's Sons, 1959), 2: 492.

23. D. W. Brogan, *The American Character* (New York: Random House, Vintage Books, 1956), pp. 78–81, 85.

24. Andrew Reed and James Matheson, *American Churches,* etc. (1835), excerpted in Powell, p. 106.

25. D. W. Brogan, "The Catholic Church in America," *Harper's Magazine* (May 1950), excerpted in Herr and Wells, pp. 166, 169.

26. George Santayana, *Character and Opinion in the United States* (New York: George Braziller, Inc., 1920), excerpted in Herr and Wells, p. 91; Evelyn Waugh, "The American Epoch in the Catholic Church," *Life* (September 19, 1949), excerpted in Herr and Wells, pp. 160–61, 162–63.

27. Harold J. Laski, *The American Democracy: A Commentary and Interpreta-*

tion (New York: Viking Press, 1948), excerpted in Herr and Wells, pp. 137–38, 140, 143–44.

28. Eric von Kuehnelt-Leddihn, "America Revisited," *Catholic World* (January 1954), excerpted in Herr and Wells, p. 204.

29. André Siegfried, *America at Mid-Century* (New York: Harcourt, Brace and World, 1955), excerpted in Herr and Wells, pp. 208–9; 211–12.

30. James Bryce, quoted in Winthrop Hudson, *The Great Tradition of the American Churches* (New York: Harper and Bros., 1953), pp. 27–28.

31. Harriet Martineau, *Society in America* (1837), excerpted in Powell, pp. 109ff.; see esp. p. 112.

32. For Ferri-Pisani, see Powell, p. 185.

33. William G. McLoughlin, "The Role of Religion in the Revolution," in *Essays on the American Revolution*, ed. Stephen G. Kurtz and James H. Hutson (Chapel Hill: University of North Carolina Press; New York: W. W. Norton, 1973), p. 248.

34. Philip Schaff, *America*, excerpted in Powell, p. 145.

35. Giovanni Antonio Grassi, *Notizie varie sullo stato presente della repubblica degli Stati Uniti dell' America* (1819); trans. and reprinted in *This Was America*, ed. Oscar Handlin (New York: Harper and Row, 1949), p. 148.

36. Lerner, p. 76.

37. See, for example, the quotation of Beaumont in George Wilson Pierson, *Tocqueville in America* (Garden City, N.Y.: Doubleday, 1959), p. 70.

38. Alexander Hamilton, *Gentleman's Progress*, excerpted in Powell, pp. 15ff.

39. For Murat, see Powell, pp. 53–54.

40. Francis Grund, *The Americans in Their Moral, Social and Political Relations* (1837), excerpted in Powell, p. 78.

41. For Martineau, see Powell, pp. 116, 118.

42. Tocqueville is condensed in Powell, pp. 90–91.

43. Quoted by Eugene Genovese, *Roll, Jordan, Roll: The World the Slaves Made* (New York: Pantheon Books, 1974), p. 270.

44. For Belloc, see Powell, p. 97.

45. Phillip E. Hammond, "Religious Pluralism and Durkheim's Integration Thesis," in *Changing Perspectives in the Scientific Study of Religion*, ed. Allen W. Eister (New York: John C. Wiley and Sons, 1974), pp. 133–35; see also Sidney E. Mead, *The Nation with the Soul of a Church* (New York: Harper and Row, 1975), p. 22.

46. D. W. Brogan, "Commentary," in Donald H. Cutler, *The Religious Situation: 1968* (Boston: Beacon Press, 1969), pp. 357, 359–60.

47. J. Hector St. John Crèvecoeur, *Letters from an American Farmer* (New York: Dolphin Books, n.d.), pp. 45–46.

48. Schaff, pp. 46, 51, 80–81.

49. See Robert N. Bellah, *The Broken Covenant: American Civil Religion in Time of Trial* (New York: Seabury Press, 1975).

CHAPTER 9: LAND AND CITY

1. José Ortega y Gasset, "Moralejas, III. La pedagogia del paisaje." *Obras* 1:35. Quoted by Julian Marias, *José Ortega y Gasset: Circumstance and Vocation* (Norman: University of Oklahoma Press, 1970), p. 362.

2. Nelson Klose, *A Concise Study Guide to the Frontier* (Lincoln: University of

Nebraska, 1961) is a helpful guide to Turner's themes and fortunately expands them to many other frontiers in other eras.

3. For example, see Edwin Scott Gaustad, *Historical Atlas of Religion in America* (New York: Harper and Row, 1962).

4. Samples of the literature are Roderick Nash, *Wilderness and the American Mind* (New Haven: Yale University Press, 1967); Peter N. Carroll, *Puritanism and the Wilderness* (New York: Columbia, 1969); Henry Nash Smith, *Virgin Land* (New York: Vintage, 1950).

5. H. Paul Douglass, *Church Unity Movements in the United States* (New York: Institute of Social and Religious Research, 1934), pp. 5f. On p. 443 Douglass admitted that regionalism was not an extreme problem in church unity movements, even if it was the main geographical characteristic of the churches.

6. See the map associated with Douglas W. Johnson et al., *Churches and Church Membership in the United States* (Washington, D.C.: Glenmary Research Center, 1974).

7. The Jewish figure is cited by Edwin Scott Gaustad, "America's Institutions of Faith," in Donald Cutler (ed.), *The Religious Situation* (Boston: Beacon, 1968), p. 844.

8. David E. Sopher, *Geography of Religions* (Englewood Cliffs, N.J.: Prentice-Hall, 1967), pp. 44f.

9. For a tracing of experimentality and altered mission in American religion and an argument that they are together a dominant motif in national history, see Martin E. Marty, "Experiment in Environment: Foreign Perceptions of Religious America," *Journal of Religion*, vol. 56, no. 3 (July 1976), pp. 291ff. That essay in revised form is Chapter 8 in this book.

10. E. H. Carr, *What Is History?* (New York: Random House, 1963), p. 16.

11. Robert F. Berkhofer, Jr., *A Behavioral Approach to Historical Analysis* (New York: Free Press, 1969), pp. 18f.

12. For a summary of the "consensus" and "conflict" debates, see Bernard Sternsher, *Consensus, Conflict, and American Historians* (Bloomington: Indiana University Press, 1975).

13. Harold R. Isaacs, *Idols of the Tribe: Group Identity and Political Change* (New York: Harper and Row, 1975), pp. 3f. Isaac speaks of over ten million such deaths between World War II and 1974.

14. James B. Allen and Glen M. Leonard, *The Story of the Latter-Day Saints* (Salt Lake City, Utah: Deseret Book Co., 1976), pp. 246f.

15. Edward T. Hall, *The Hidden Dimension* (Garden City, N.Y.: Doubleday, 1969), pp. 7–10.

16. Robert Ardrey, *The Territorial Imperative* (New York: Atheneum, 1966), p. 236.

17. Desmond Morris, *The Naked Ape* (New York: McGraw-Hill, 1968), pp. 176f.

18. See Konrad Lorenz, *On Aggression* (New York: Harcourt, Brace and World, 1966).

19. Dean Kelley, *Why Conservative Churches Are Growing* (New York: Harper and Row, 1972), p. 84, presents a chart of "strong" groups that would delight the eye of any ethologist or territorialist.

20. *The Spectator*, April 7, 1967, p. 398.

21. See Erich Fromm, *The Anatomy of Human Destructiveness* (New York: Holt, Rinehart and Winston, 1973), pp. 114ff., and Ashley Montagu, *The Nature of Human Aggression* (New York: Oxford University Press, 1976), for expressions

and collations of the refutations or counterarguments to territorialist instinctivism.

22. The negative reference to cultural evolutionary laws was by Berthold Laufer; the James quotaton is from an article he wrote in 1880. Both are quoted in Marshall D. Sahlins et al. (eds.), *Evolution and Culture* (Ann Arbor: University of Michigan, 1960), pp. v–vii.

23. I shall develop the concept of cultural evolution, especially with reference to David Kaplan's "The Law of Cultural Dominance," in chap. 15, drawing on Sahlins, *Evolution and Culture*.

24. Paul Tillich, "Migrations Breed New Cultures," *Protestant Digest*, vol 3, no. 2 (February 1940), p. 11.

25. Kaplan, p. 82.

26. For elaborations of these themes, see Chapters 4, 5 of Martin E. Marty, *Pilgrims in Their Own Land: 500 Years of Religion in America* (Boston: Little, Brown, 1984).

27. Hall, pp. 1, 4, 14f., 93. See also William Stephenson, *The Play Theory of Mass Communications* (Chicago: University of Chicago Press, 1966), p. 2.

28. Erving Goffman, *The Presentation of Self in Everyday Life* (Garden City, N.Y.: Doubleday, 1959), p. 106; Hall, pp. 131–64, "Proxemics in a Cross-Cultural Context."

29. Robert J. Lifton, *Boundaries: Psychological Man in Revolution* (New York: Vintage Press, 1976), pp. 37ff., 51.

30. Kurt H. Wolff (ed.), *The Sociology of George Simmel* (New York: Free Press, 1950), p. 333.

31. Lewis Coser, *The Functions of Social Conflict* (New York: Free Press, 1956), pp. 20, 21, 28, 31, 33, 38, 49, 55, 63, 70, 87, 104. These pages include the citations from Cooley, Weber, Lewin, Simmel, Frenkel-Brunswick, Malinowski, and Scheler.

32. Martin E. Marty, *The Infidel: Free Thought and American Religion* (Cleveland: World Press, 1961).

33. Ashley Montagu, *The Nature of Human Aggression* (New York: Oxford University Press, 1976), p. 252.

34. P. H. Klopfer, *Habitats and Territories* (New York: Basic Books, 1969), p. 105.

35. Originally published in 1895, this version appeared in Moscow in 1956; p. 121.

36. For Craig and Crook, see Montagu, p. 246.

37. H. Paul Douglass, *Church Comity: A Study of Cooperative Church Extension in American Cities* (Garden City, N.Y.: Doubleday, Doran, 1929), pp. 1, 16.

38. For the reference to Machiavelli see Floyd W. Matson, *The Idea of Man*, (New York: Delacorte, 1976), p. 65.

39. Isaacs, *Idols of the Tribe*, pp. 51f.

40. Vine Deloria, Jr., *God Is Red* (New York: Grosset and Dunlap, 1973), pp. 75–89.

41. Mircea Eliade, *The Sacred and the Profane: The Nature of Religion* (New York: Harper and Row, 1961), pp. 20, 31f.

42. Paul Tillich, *On the Boundary* (New York: Scribners, 1966), pp. 91f.

43. James Luther Adams, *Paul Tillich's Philosophy of Culture, Science, and Religion,* (New York: Harper and Row, 1965), pp. 101–3; Tillich's address was printed in *Die Form*, vol. 8, no. 1 (January 1933), pp. 11–12; Tillich was there identified as

an architect! See also Paul Tillich, *Political Expectations* (New York: Harper and Row, 1971), pp. 120, 150f.

CHAPTER 10: PEOPLES

1. Quoted in Lee Benson, Turner and Beard: *American Historical Writing Reconsidered* (Glencoe, Ill.: Free Press, 1960), p. 82.

2. Milton M. Gordon, *Assimilation in American Life* (New York: Oxford University Press, 1964), popularized the concept of *peoplehood*, which is the "sense" of an ethnic, racial, or religious group. The word turns up frequently in literature on ethnicity and new movements. Sometimes these movements, among them Women's Liberation, the New Left, "the counterculture," and the like, speak of themselves in the terms of "peoplehood," but this essay restricts itself to study of those groups which have at least a minimal claim on some sort of common ethnic origin and orientation. Significantly, the term worked its way into *Webster's New International Dictionary* during the 1960s; it did not appear in the second edition (1960) but is present in the third (1969): "Peoplehood: the quality or state of constituting a people: also: awareness of the underlying unity that makes the individual a part of the people."

3. The literature on black religion is rapidly expanding; Hart M. Nelsen, Raytha L. Yokley, and Anne K. Nelson, *The Black Church in America* (New York: Basic Books, 1971) is an excellent anthology on every major aspect of the subject. The suggestion that 1968 was a watershed year in black religious consciousness appears in this book, pp. 17ff. Cleage is quoted on p. 18 and Bishop Herbert B. Shaw, speaking of ties to Asia and Africa, on p. 21. James H. Cone, *A Black Theology of Liberation* (Philadelphia: J. B. Lippincott, 1970), is a representative charge that most of what had previously been seen to be a generalized and universal theology in America is actually an expression of "whiteness." See also James J. Gardiner, S. A. and J. Deotis Roberts, Sr., *Quest for a Black Theology* (Philadelphia: Pilgrim Press, 1971).

4. Vine Deloria, *We Talk, You Listen* (New York: Macmillan, 1970) was a widely noticed expression of new American Indian assertiveness; it included an explicit suggestion that our impersonal, homogenized America should relearn the tribal model from the original Americans.

5. Richard L. Rubenstein, "Homeland and Holocaust," in Donald R. Cutler, *The Religious Situation:* 1968 (Boston: Beacon, 1968), p. 45.

6. Arthur A. Cohen, *The Myth of the Judeo-Christian Tradition* (New York: Harper and Row, 1970), was written to help "break through the crust of harmony and concord which exists between Judaism and Christianity" and to help "destroy that in both communities which depends upon the other for authentication" (p. vii). Cohen believes that the myth of the common tradition was largely devised in America in the face of a secular religiosity; it induced two faiths to "join together to reinforce themselves in the face of a common disaster" (p. xix).

7. Armando B. Rendon, *Chicago Manifesto* (New York: Macmillan, 1971), uses figures (p. 38) from a survey taken in November, 1969; 9.2 million persons claiming Spanish descent would represent 4.7 percent of the population. Three-quarters of this number were native born; the rest were immigrants, with half coming from Mexico. See also p. 325.

8. Joseph P. Fitzpatrick, *Puerto Rican Americans: The Meaning of a Migration*

(Englewood Cliffs, N.J.: Prentice-Hall, 1971) is a brief but comprehensive survey of the situation of this minority.

9. Richard M. Scammon and Ben J. Wattenberg, *The Real Majority* (New York: Coward-McCann, 1970), p. 66. Andrew M. Greeley, *Why Can't They Be Like Us? America's White Ethnic Groups* (New York: E. P. Dutton, 1971) introduces this conglomeration of hitherto separate ethnic forces. He also points to the fact that in part because its members spoke English and were Catholic the large Irish immigrant group does not fit easily into "the white ethnic/white Anglo-Saxon Protestant" combination. Nor, it might be added, did Germans and Scandinavian Protestants, who did not speak English.

10. References to the church as "the new people of God" can be found throughout Walter M. Abbott, S. J., ed., *The Documents of Vatican II* (New York: Guild Press, American Press, Assoc. Press, 1966). In actual practice, ethnocentrism, competing ethnic subcommunities, and isolated or rival "national" parishes throughout American history have blurred the vision of their being a single "people of God."

11. Ben J. Wattenberg and Richard M. Scammon, *This U.S.A.: An Unexpected Family Portrait of 194,067,296 Americans Drawn from the Census* (New York: Doubleday, 1965), pp. 45f.

12. David Edwin Harrell, Jr., *White Sects and Black Men in the Recent South* (Nashville, Tenn.: Vanderbilt University Press, 1971), p. viii.

13. Lewis M. Killian, *The Impossible Revolution* (New York: Random House, 1968) p. 18. Richard L. Means, in *The Christian Century*, 78 (August 16, 1961), pp. 979–80, began to discuss the significance of *Anti-Protestant Prejudice*, a theme which subsequently received increasing attention, and which may serve to cause more WASPs to affirm the self-designation they had once shunned—if the experience of other more obvious victims of group prejudice is to be repeated in this instance. See also Peter Schrag, "The Decline of the Wasp," in *Harper's* Magazine, April 1970. While the WASPs "still hold power, they hold it with less assurance and with less legitimacy than at any time in history. . . . One can almost define their domains by locating the people and institutions that are chronically on the defense. . . . For the first time, any sort of settlement among competing interests is going to have to do more than pay lip service to minorities and to the pluralism of styles, beliefs, and cultures. . . . America is not on the verge of becoming two separate societies, one rich and white, the other poor and black. It is becoming, in all its dreams and anxieties, a nation of outsiders for whom no single style or ethnic remains possible. . . . We will now have to devise ways of recognizing and assessing the alternatives. The mainstream is running thin."

14. This definition and two subsequent definitions of *skeleton* are from the *Oxford English Dictionary*.

15. Charles H. Anderson, *White Protestant Americans: From National Origins to Religious Group* (Englewood Cliffs, N.J.: Prentice-Hall, 1971), p. viii. "Every American, as we shall use the term, is a member or potential member of an ethnic group—racial, religious, or national in origin."

16. See Max Weber, "Ethnic Groups," trans. Ferdinand Kolegar, in Talcott Parsons et al., *Theories of Society*, vol. 1 (Glencoe, Ill.: Free Press, 1961), pp. 305ff. "Any aspect or cultural trait, no matter how superficial, can serve as a starting point for the familiar tendency to monopolistic closure." "Almost any kind of similarity or contrast of physical type and of habits can induce the belief that a tribal affinity or

disaffinity exists between groups that attract or repel each other." "The belief in tribal kinship, regardless of whether it has any objective foundation, can have important consequences especially for the formation of a political community. Those human groups that entertain a subjective belief in their common descent—because of similarities of physical type or of customs or both, or because of memories of colonization and migration—in such a way that this belief is important for the continuation of non-kinship communal relationship we shall call 'ethnic' groups, regardless of whether an objective blood relationship exists or not." "Behind all ethnic diversities there is somehow naturally the notion of the 'chosen people,' which is nothing else but a counterpart of status differentiation translated into the plane of horizontal coexistence. The idea of a chosen people derives its popularity from the fact that it can be claimed to an equal degree by any and every member of the mutually despising groups."

17. Anderson, pp. 43ff, locates Swedes with WASPs. "They have been granted WASP status on the basis of their successful adaptation to Anglo-Saxon America. In a sense even today Scandinavians are second-class WASPs; nevertheless, Scandinavians know that it is better to be a second-class WASP than a non-WASP in American society."

18. Rudolph J. Vecoli, "Ethnicity: A Neglected Dimension of American History," in Herbert J. Bass, *The State of American History* (Chicago: Quadrangle, 1970), pp. 70ff, sets the stage for the present essay on religious historiography.

19. Quoted in Carlton J. H. Hayes, *Nationalism: A Religion* (New York: Macmillan, 1960), pp. 20f. Hayes provides one of the best analyses of the dimensions of national cultural religions in chap. 12, pp. 154ff.

20. Lyman Beecher, *Address of the Charitable Society for the Education of Indigent Pious Young Men for the Ministry of the Gospel* (Concord, Mass., 1820), p. 20.

21. Charles Hodge, "Anniversary Address," in *The Home Missionary*, vol. 2 (New York, 1829), p. 18.

22. Dorothy Dohen, *Nationalism and American Catholicism* (New York: Sheed and Ward, 1967) brings testimony of numerous nineteenth-century Roman Catholic leaders on this subject.

23. Philip Schaff, *America: A Sketch of Its Political, Social, and Religious Character* (Cambridge: Belknap Press of Harvard University Press, 1961), p. 51.

24. Quoted by Vecoli, p. 75.

25. John Dewey, *A Common Faith* (New Haven: Yale University Press, 1934). While the book uses the term *God*, it is nontheistic and advocates an imaginatively based synthesis or unification of values in which the many take part.

26. Robin M. Williams, Jr., *American Society: A Sociological Interpretation* (New York: Knopf, 1951), p. 312.

27. J. Paul Williams, *What Americans Believe and How They Worship* (New York: Harper and Row, 1962), pp. 477–592. The first edition appeared in 1952.

28. See especially Sidney E. Mead, "The Nation with the Soul of a Church," *Church History*, vol. 36, no. 3 (September 1967), pp. 262ff. Williams quotes Mead with favor, p. 479, in reference to the religion of the democratic society *versus* the religion of the denominations.

29. Sidney E. Mead, "The Post-Protestant Concept and America's Two Religions," in Robert L. Ferm, *Issues in American Protestantism: A Documentary History from the Puritans to the Present* (Garden City, N.Y.: Doubleday, 1969), pp. 387f. Following Paul Tillich's distinction, it might be said that Mead affirmed "the

catholic substance" in a common national religion because he trusted the presence of "the protestant principle" of prophetic protest. Those Mead criticized tended to stress "the protestant principle" even where they affirmed the common faith because they feared that its "catholic substance" could be idolized or imposed on people.

30. William Lee Miller, *Piety Along the Potomac: Notes on Politics and Morals in the Fifties* (Boston: Houghton Mifflin, 1964); Stephen C. Rose, *Sermons Not Preached in the White House* (New York: Baron, 1970).

31. Robert N. Bellah, "Civil Religion in America," reprinted in Cutler, pp. 331ff., especially p. 346. The paper was first presented at a conference in May 1966, before the liberal academic community had largely turned its back on the Johnson administration. After the escalation of the Vietnam War, the rise of the New Left and the intensification of Black Power movements, this community was somewhat less congenial to the expressions of a national religion once again.

32. Vecoli, pp. 74f. Crèvecoeur first published his *Letters from an American Farmer* in 1782.

33. Quoted by Stuart P. Sherman in *Essays and Poems of Emerson* (New York, 1921), p. xxxiv.

34. Marc Bloch, *The Historian's Craft* (New York: Vintage, 1964), p. 8. Such a "thrill of learning singular things" was not characteristic of Leibnitz, who tried to transcend variety and pluralism. Over against this, William James posed *A Pluralistic Universe* (New York: Longmans, Green, 1909), which may be seen as the philosophical grandfather of the American schools which tolerate or encourage particularisms.

35. John Courtney Murray, S. J., *We Hold These Truths: Catholic Reflections on the American Proposition* (New York: Sheed and Ward, 1960), p. 23.

36. In *America*, January 9, 1971, pp. 10f.

37. Secular and religious approaches to world integration are sketched by W. Warren Wagar, *The City of Man: Prophecies of a World Civilization in Twentieth-Century Thought* (Boston: Houghton Mifflin, 1963).

38. For a review of secular theologians' positions, see Martin E. Marty, "Secularization in the American Public Order," in Donald A. Giannella, *Religion and the Public Order*, no. 5 (Ithaca: Cornell University Press, 1969), pp. 33f, and "Secular Theology as a Search for the Future," in Albert Schlitzer, C. S. C., ed., *The Spirit and Power of Christian Secularity* (Notre Dame, Ind.: University of Notre Dame Press, 1969), pp. 1ff.

39. Bryan Wilson, *Religion in Secular Society: A Sociological Comment* (Baltimore, Md.: Penguin, 1966), pp. 40ff, and 121.

40. Seymour Martin Lipset, *The First New Nation: The United States in Historical and Comparative Perspective* (New York: Basic Books, 1963), pp. 151f.

41. Jefferson to J. Fishback, September 27, 1809, in Albert Ellery Bergh, *The Writings of Thomas Jefferson* (Washington, 1905), vol. 12, 314–16; the second reference is quoted by Anson Phelps Stokes, *Church and State in the United States* (New York: Harper and Brothers, 1950), vol. 1, 335.

42. Alfred North Whitehead, *Religion in the Making* (New York: Macmillan, 1926), p. 58.

43. William James, *The Varieties of Religious Experience: A Study in Human Nature* (New York: Longmans, Green, 1903), p. 31.

44. Thomas Luckmann, *The Invisible Religion: The Problem of Religion in Modern Society* (New York: Macmillan, 1967), pp. 97f., 105f. While Jefferson, White-

head, and James often advocated private limitations of religion, Luckmann merely observes it and regards it as a burden for moderns seeking an identity.

45. Quoted in Edgar S. Cahn, ed., *Our Brother's Keeper: The Indian in White America* (New York and Cleveland: World, 1969), pp. 184, 175.

46. Gerhard Lenski, *The Religious Factor: A Sociological Study of Religion's Impact on Politics, Economics, and Family Life* (Garden City, N.Y.: Doubleday, 1961), p. 11.

47. Will Herberg, *Protestant, Catholic, Jew: An Essay in American Religious Sociology* (Garden City, N.Y.: Doubleday, 1955), pp. 88–102. Lenski and Herberg did not regard the common religion of America with favor. Among those who did were Horace M. Kallen, in *Secularism Is the Will of God* (New York: Twayne, 1954) and Duncan J. Howlett, though they treated secularism or humanism as *The Fourth American Faith* (New York: Harper and Row, 1964), which still had to contend for place with Protestantism, Catholicism and Judaism. Samuel A. Mueller, "The New Triple Melting Pot: Herberg Revisited," in *Review of Religious Research*, vol. 13, no. 1 (Fall 1971), suggests that a new set of categories should be "white Christian, white non-Christian, and black." He bases this on a sociological study of lines between these and Herberg's three groups in the matters of "marriage, friendship, residence, occupations, and politics."

48. E. Digby Baltzell, *The Protestant Establishment* (New York: Random House, 1964), p. 53.

49. Arthur Mann, "Charles Fleischer's Religion of Democracy," in *Commentary*, June 1954, p. 557.

50. John Cogley, ed., *Religion in America: Original Essays on Religion in a Free Society* (New York: Meridian, 1958), p. 9.

51. John Meyendorff, *The Orthodox Church: Its Past and Its Role in the World Today* (New York: Pantheon, 1960), p. 107.

52. Mead's essay is reprinted in Sidney E. Mead. *The Lively Experiment: The Shaping of Christianity in America* (New York: Harper and Row), 103ff. Karl Hertz writes on denominationalism in "Some Suggestions for a Sociology of American Protestantism," in Herbert T. Neve and Benjamin A. Johnson, *The Maturing of American Lutheranism* (Minneapolis, Minn.: Augsburg, 1968), pp. 36, 42.

53. Wilson, pp. 47, 51.

54. Sidney E. Mead, *The Lively Experiment*, pp. 132f.

55. Charles Y. Glock and Rodney Stark, *Religion and Society in Tension* (Chicago: Rand McNally, 1965), pp. 86f.

56. Jeffrey K. Hadden, *The Gathering Storm in the Churches: The Widening Gap between Clergy and Laymen* (Garden City, N.Y., 1969), especially chap. 4, "Clergy and Laity View the Civil Rights Issue."

57. David Reimers, *White Protestantism and the Negro* (New York: Oxford University Press, 1965), p. 29.

58. Quoted in Benson Y. Landis, *Protestant Experience with United States Immigration, 1910–1960* (New York: Church World Service, 1961), pp. 12f.

59. Gordon, p. 38.

60. Vincent Harding, "Black Power and the American Christ," in Floyd B. Barbour, *The Black Power Revolt: A Collection of Essays* (New York: Collier, 1968), p. 97.

61. Denis W. Brogan, "Commentary," in Cutler, p. 357.

62. Robert Baird, *Religion in the United States of America* (Glasgow, 1843); see chap. 6, p. 35ff.

63. John Gilmary Shea, *The History of the Catholic Church in the United States* (New York, 1886–92), four volumes.

64. Daniel Dorchester, *Christianity in the United States* (New York: Hunt and Eaton, 1890), p. 765.

65. Leonard Woolsey Bacon, *A History of American Christianity* (New York: Scribners, 1898), p. 292.

66. Josiah Strong, *The New Era; or The Coming Kingdom* (New York, 1893), pp. 54–55; *Our Country: Its Possible Future and Its Present Crisis* (New York, 1885), pp. 178, 174–75.

67. Peter Mode, *The Frontier Spirit in American Christianity* (New York: Macmillan, 1923), pp. 6, 7, 14. Mode-Sweet-Mead represent a University of Chicago succession which is most familiar to me. See also William Warren Sweet. *The Story of Religion in America* (New York: Harper and Brothers, 1930); another student in this tradition, along with Robert T. Handy (see n. 68), is Winthrop S. Hudson, whose *Religion in America* (New York: Scribner's, 1965) pioneered at least in its sense of proportion, since it devoted much attention to black Protestantism, Judaism and other non-WASP religious groups.

68. New York: Oxford University Press, 1971. For another attempt to isolate WASP history and to treat WASPs as an ethnic group, see Martin E. Marty, *Righteous Empire: The Protestant Experience in America* (New York: Dial, 1970).

CHAPTER 11: LOCATIONS

1. See Ray Allen Billington, *Frederick Jackson Turner: Historian, Scholar, Teacher* (New York, 1973), pp. 124–31. Turner mailed the letter July 16, after he had read the paper.

2. John Tracy Ellis, "American Catholics and the Intellectual Life," in *Thought* 30 (Autumn 1955), 385–386.

3. Robert Leckie, *American and Catholic* (Garden City, N.Y., 1970), p. 323.

4. John Tracy Ellis, *American Catholicism*, 2d ed., rev. (Chicago, 1969), p. 167.

5. Donald B. King, "Catholics and a Ghetto Mentality," *Catholic World* 183 (September 1956), 424–27.

6. Thurston N. Davis, "Five Live Problems of Catholics," in *America,* vol. 95, no. 6 (May 12, 1956), pp. 158–59.

7. Don Brophy and Edythe Westenhaver, eds. *The Story of Catholics in America* (New York, 1978), p. 123.

8. Daniel Callahan, *The Mind of the Catholic Layman,* (New York, 1963), p. 32.

9. "Pius XII on the 'Ghetto,'" in *America,* vol. 98, no. 14 (January 11, 1958), p. 408.

10. Ellis, "American Catholics and the Intellectual Life," p. 354.

11. Quoted from a book by Colianni written in 1968, by James Hitchcock, *The Decline and Fall of Radical Catholicism* (Garden City, N.Y., 1972), p. 91.

12. Quoted from an issue of *Commonweal,* March 27, 1970, p. 60, by Hitchcock, p. 93.

13. David O'Brien, *The Renewal of American Catholicism* (New York, 1972), pp. 4–5.

14. John Cogley, *Catholic America* (New York, 1973), chap. 7, "The Ghetto Culture," especially pp. 168–69, 185.

15. Ellis, "American Catholics and the Intellectual Life," pp. 352, 362.

16. Bronislaw Malinowski, "An Anthropological Analysis of War," in *Magic, Science and Religion* (Glencoe, Ill., 1948), p. 285.

17. Georg Simmel, *Conflict*, trans. Kurt H. Wolff (Glencoe, Ill., 1955), pp. 43–44.

18. Ibid., pp. 87, 88.

19. John Henry Barrows, *The World's Parliament of Religions* (Chicago, 1893), p. 160, for Momerie: Müller is quoted in David F. Burg, *Chicago's White City of 1893* (Lexington, Ky., 1976), p. 285.

20. H. K. Carroll, "The Present Religious Condition of America," in Barrows, 2: 1162–65.

21. H. K. Carroll, *The Religious Forces of the United States* (New York, 1893), pp. 161–62.

22. Kaufmann Kohler, "Human Brotherhood as Taught by the Religions Based on the Bible," in Barrows, 1: 367.

23. Joseph Silverman, "Popular Errors about the Jews," in Barrows, 2: 1121.

24. Josephine Lazarus, "The Outlook of Judaism," in Barrows, 2: 705.

25. Joseph Hoffman Cohn, *I Have Fought a Good Fight* (New York, 1953), p. 42: for the Moody incident see Timothy Weber, *Living in the Shadow of the Second Coming* (New York, 1979), p. 145. On the Jewish-Irish ghetto conflicts, John Higham, *Send These to Me: Jews and Other Immigrants in Urban America* (New York, 1975), pp. 135–36.

26. For the Burroughs and *Harper's Weekly* quotations see Michael N. Dobkowski, *The Tarnished Dream: The Basis of American Anti-Semitism* (Westport, Conn., 1979), pp. 146, 149.

27. See Isaac Mayer Wise in *The American Israelite* 33, no. 31, p. 4 from January 28, 1887.

28. Carroll, p. xxix.

29. For the Pratt quotations, see Francis Paul Prucha, *American Indian Policy in Crisis: Christian Reformers and the Indian, 1865–1900* (Norman, Okla., 1976), p. 183, and Elaine Goodale Eastman, *Pratt: The Red Man's Moses* (Norman, Okla., 1935), p. 77.

30. Thomas Jefferson Morgan, *Studies in Pedagogy* (Boston, 1889), pp. 327–28, 348–50.

31. See Herman Hagedorn, *Roosevelt in the Bad Lands* (Boston: Houghton Mifflin, 1921), p. 355.

32. These four quotations are from *Northwestern Christian Advocate* 62 (April 23, 1913), 4–5; *Christian Index*, May 26, 1892; *Alabama Baptist*, April 26, 1900, p. 4; *New York Christian Advocate*, July 2, 1908, p. 1105.

33. John S. Chambers, "The Japanese Invasion," *Annals of the American Academy of Political and Social Sciences* 93 (January 1921), 26–27.

34. Carroll, pp. 79–82.

35. The Farcas-Podea incident is in Gerald J. Bobango, *The Romanian Orthodox Episcopate of America: The First Half Century, 1929–1979* (Jackson, Mich., 1979), pp. 20–21.

36. Quoted by Albert Camarillo, *Chicanos in a Changing Society* (Cambridge, Mass., 1979), p. 189.

37. Mario T. Garcia, *Desert Immigrants: The Mexicans of El Paso, 1880–1920* (New Haven, 1981), p. 186, is the source of the Escajeda quotation.

38. Milwaukee *Sentinel*, September 21, 1885, quoted in Anthony J. Kuzniewski,

Faith and Fatherland: The Polish Church War in Wisconsin, 1896–1918 (Notre Dame, Ind., 1980), p. 28.

39. Carroll, pp. 175–205.

40. See George H. Gerberding, *Problems and Possibilities* (Columbia, S.C., 1914), p. 171; Henry Cabot Lodge is quoted by C. S. Meyer, *Moving Frontiers: Readings in the History of the Lutheran Church—Missouri Synod* (St. Louis, 1964), p. 236.

41. Friedrich Bente, *Lehre und Wehre* 50 (January 1904), 1–20, quoted by E. Clifford Nelson, ed., *The Lutherans in North America* (Philadelphia, 1975), p. 378.

42. Richard Jensen, *The Winning of the Midwest: Social and Political Conflict, 1888–1896* (Chicago, 1971), pp. 83–84.

43. From an official address in 1912 by J. Wefel, quoted by Martin A. Haendschke, *The Sunday School Story: The History of the Sunday School in the Lutheran Church—Missouri Synod* (River Forest, Ill., 1963), p. 26.

44. On Finnish Lutheranism, see Arthur Edwin Puotinen, *Finnish Radicals and Religion in Midwestern Mining Towns, 1865–1914* (New York, 1979); pp. 271–88 deal with the Christmas Eve violence.

45. *Journal of the General Conference* (Southern Methodist Church, 1894), pp. 25–26.

46. J. S. Rogers, "A Symposium by Southern State Secretaries on the Union Movement," *Southwestern Journal of Theology* 3 (old series; January 1919), 23.

47. From a *Commonweal* editorial in 1953, quoted by Cogley, p. 192.

CHAPTER 12: OLD-TIME RELIGION

1. See the facsimile of the original title page in C. C. Goen, ed., *The Great Awakening: The Works of Jonathan Edwards,* vol. 4 (New Haven: Yale University Press, 1972), p. 128; the quotation from Edwards is on p. 19.

2. William G. McLoughlin, "Is There a Third Force in Christendom?" *Daedalus* 96:1:61.

3. William G. McLoughlin, *Revivals, Awakenings, and Reform* (Chicago: University of Chicago Press, 1978), pp. 213–14.

4. Jay P. Dolan, *Catholic Revivalism: The American Experience, 1830–1900* (Notre Dame: University of Notre Dame Press, 1978).

5. The literature on this subject is enormous; for a sample, see Joseph H. Fichter, *The Catholic Cult of the Paraclete* (New York: Sheed and Ward, 1975).

6. McLoughlin, *Revivals,* pp. 9–17.

7. For documentation of several sorts of "worldliness," see Richard Quebedeaux, *The Worldly Evangelicals* (New York: Harper and Row, 1978).

8. John Murray Cuddihy, *The Ordeal of Civility: Freud, Marx, Lévi-Strauss, and the Jewish Struggle with Modernity* (New York: Basic, 1974), pp. 9–10.

9. David Apter, *The Politics of Modernization* (Chicago: University of Chicago Press, 1965), pp. 3, 5, 6, 10.

10. See Edmund Morgan, *The Puritan Family: Religion and Domestic Relations in Seventeenth-Century New England* (New York: Harper and Row, 1966), p. 182; the phrase is Increase Mather's, from a sermon of 1678.

11. Alfred North Whitehead, *Adventures of Ideas* (New York: Mentor, 1955), pp. 30ff.

12. Perry Miller, *Errand into the Wilderness* (Cambridge: Belknap Press of Harvard University Press, 1956), pp. 167ff.

13. Cuddihy, *Ordeal of Civility,* p. 10.

14. See the essays by Bellah, Mead, and others in Russell E. Richey and Donald G. Jones, *American Civil Religion* (New York: Harper and Row, 1974).

15. Cuddihy discusses Bonhoeffer on this theme, *Ordeal of Civility,* pp. 235, 237–38.

16. For a psychological accounting, see Robert Jay Lifton, *Boundaries: Psychological Man in Revolution* (New York: Macmillan, 1967).

17. Thomas Luckman, *The Invisible Religion: The Problem of Religion in Modern Society* (New York: Macmillan, 1967).

CHAPTER 13: NEW-TIME RELIGION

1. There is no way, of course, to measure the number of fundamentalists for these reasons: (*a*) the distinction between fundamentalist and evangelical is too blurry; (*b*) very few church bodies are constituted around the name fundamentalism; (*c*) many fundamentalists are in church bodies that are not technically fundamentalist; (*d*) many people who might be classified as fundamentalists are not necessarily to be located on any church rolls at all. Gallup polls of the late 1970s made some efforts to assess evangelical sympathies, *evangelical* and *born again* being terms the Gallup people used to encompass fundamentalism as well. At that time, 60 percent of the public claimed to be Protestant, 48 percent of the Protestants claimed a "born again" experience, and 35 percent of the Protestants considered themselves "evangelical." It does not take much reckoning to find 10 million Americans out of this sector who could safely be described—or are self-described—as "fundamentalist." See the *Gallup Opinion Index* No. 145, American Institute of Public Opinion, Princeton, N.J., 1978.

2. Many sociologists of religion have pointed to the phenomenon of privatization; the most systematic account is Thomas Luckmann, *The Invisible Religion* (New York: Macmillan, 1967).

3. We now fortunately possess twin volumes that describe these polarities and parties; William R. Hutchison, *The Modernist Impulse in American Protestantism* (New York: Oxford University Press, 1982 [first published in 1976]) and George M. Marsden, *Fundamentalism and American Culture: The Shaping of Twentieth-Century Evangelicalism, 1870–1925* (New York: Oxford University Press, 1982 [first published in 1980]).

4. See Patricia Barrett, *Religious Liberty and the American Presidency* (New York: Herder and Herder, 1963).

5. In February 1981, an inclusive conference on this subject was held; proceedings are in Dean M. Kelley, ed., *Government Intervention in Religious Affairs* (New York: Pilgrim, 1982).

6. Definitions of politics on which I am here relying are elaborated upon in Bernard Crick, *In Defence of Politics* (Baltimore: Penguin, 1962), 15ff.

7. Martin E. Marty, *Righteous Empire: The Protestant Experience in America* (New York: Dial, 1970); see esp. chap. 17, "The Two-Party System," 177ff.

8. Timothy Smith, *Revivalism and Social Reform in Mid-Nineteenth Century America* (Nashville: Abingdon, 1957).

9. Donald W. Dayton, *Discovering an Evangelical Heritage* (New York: Harper and Row, 1976), is a popular account, see chap. 2, pp. 15–24, on Finney.

10. Details of the concept of the public are in Parker J. Palmer, *The Company*

of Strangers: Christians and the Renewal of American Public Life (San Francisco: Harper and Row, 1981).

11. See Timothy Weber, *Living in the Shadow of the Second Coming* (New York: Oxford University Press, 1981).

12. The first account of the second rise of fundamentalism was Louis Gasper, *The Fundamentalist Movement* (The Hague: Mouton, 1963); see also Joel A. Carpenter, "Fundamentalist Institutions and the Rise of Evangelical Protestantism, 1929–1942," *Church History* 49 (March 1980): 62–75.

13. Jerry Falwell, *Listen, America!* (New York: Bantam Books, 1981), outlines the program.

14. For a theoretical description of antimodernity in action, see John Murray Cuddihy, *The Ordeal of Civility* (New York: Basic, 1974), 9–10.

15. An excellent description is Harold R. Isaacs, *Idols of the Tribe: Group Identity and Political Change* (New York: Harper and Row, 1975).

16. A doomsday scenario with a socialist tinge is in Robert L. Heilbroner, *Business Civilization in Decline* (New York: Norton, 1976), 119–20.

17. A characteristic plea for "believers' rights" is to be found in Lynn R. Buzzard and Samuel Ericsson, *The Battle for Religious Liberty* (Elgin, Ill.: David C. Cook, 1982).

CHAPTER 14: HISTORY

1. For the dependencies upon Renier, see G. J. Renier, *History: Its Purpose and Method* (Boston: Beacon Press, 1950), chapter I:I (for the social or collective character of history); I:II (for its story character); II:I (for "events and traces"). See p. 14 on "stopping to think."

2. On "primitive" and "second" naïveté, see Paul Ricoeur, *The Symbolism of Evil* (New York: Harper and Row, 1967), pp. 351–53. His exact words on the second naïveté (p. 352): "For the second immediacy that we seek and the second naivete that we await are no longer accessible to us anywhere else than in a hermeneutics; we can believe only by interpreting. It is the "modern" mode of belief in symbols, an expression of the distress of modernity and a remedy for that distress. . . . This second naivete aims to be the postcritical equivalent of the precritical hierophany." Again (p. 351): "If we can no longer live the great symbolisms of the sacred in accordance with the original belief in them, we can, we modern men, aim at a second naivete in and through criticism. In short, it is by interpreting that we can *hear* again."

3. The Lessing passages are quoted in Daniel Fuller, *Easter Faith and History* (Grand Rapids, Mich.: William E. Eerdmans Publishing, 1965), pp. 33–35.

4. Morley, Meinecke, and Troeltsch are cited in Franklin L. Baumer, *Religion and the Rise of Skepticism* (New York: Harcourt, Brace, 1960), pp. 156–59.

5. Paul Elmen, *The Restoration of Meaning to Contemporary Life* (Garden City, N.Y.: Doubleday, 1958), p. 189.

6. See *Journal of Mormon History* 7 (1980): 31, 43. The articles are Neal E. Lambert and Richard H. Cracroft, "Literary Form and Historical Understanding: Joseph Smith's First Vision in Mormon Religious Thought," and James B. Allen, "Emergence of a Fundamental: The Expanding Role of Joseph Smith's First Vision in Mormon Religious Thought."

7. Klaus J. Hansen, *Mormonism and the American Experience* (Chicago: University of Chicago Press, 1981), pp. 15–27.

8. Lawrence Foster, *Religion and Sexuality: Three American Communal Experiments of the Nineteenth Century* (New York: Oxford University Press, 1981), pp. 128–30 and elsewhere in Foster's writings.

9. Jan Shipps, *Mormonism: The Story of a New Religious Tradition* (Champaign-Urbana: University of Illinois Press, 1984).

10. E. D. Hirsch, "Carnal Knowledge," in *New York Review of Books,* June 14, 1979, p. 18.

11. "The Hermeneutics of Testimony," in Paul Ricoeur, *Essays on Biblical Interpretation* (Philadelphia: Fortress Press 1980) pp. 119–54 passim.

12. David Tracy, *Blessed Rage for Order: The New Pluralism in Theology* (New York: Seabury Press, 1975), the section on "Interpretation Theory," pp. 72–79, especially p. 78.

CHAPTER 15: TRANSPOSITIONS

1. The best depiction of American religious positioning is Edwin Scott Gaustad, *Historical Atlas of Religions in America,* rev. ed. (New York: Harper and Row, 1976); see esp. an attached colored map. For updating, see Jackson W. Carroll, Douglas W. Johnson, and Martin E. Marty, *Religion in America: 1950 to the Present* (New York: Harper and Row, 1979).

2. Langdon Gilkey, *Society and the Sacred: Toward a Theology of Culture in Decline* (New York: Crossroad, 1981), pp. 23–24; see also the collection of twenty-five essays in Gabriel A. Almond, Marvin Chodorow, and Roy Harvey Pearce, *Progress and Its Discontents* (Berkeley: University of California Press, 1982).

3. Regarding aggressiveness, even of a lethal sort, on the part of religion in cultural complexes, see Harold R. Isaacs, *Idols of the Tribe: Group Identity and Political Change* (New York: Harper and Row, 1975).

4. Dean M. Kelley, *Why Conservative Churches Are Growing* (New York: Harper and Row, 1972); Wade Clark Roof, "America's Voluntary Establishment: Mainline Religion in Transition," *Daedalus* 3(1):165–84. The best accounting for change is a collection, Dean R. Hoge and David A. Roozen, eds., *Understanding Church Growth and Decline, 1950–1978* (Boston: Pilgrim Press, 1979).

5. A succinct, if controversial, history of these movements in respect to their revivalist roots is William G. McLoughlin, *Revivals, Awakenings, and Reform* (Chicago: University of Chicago Press, 1978), esp. pp. 5–24. See also McLoughlin's suggestion, depending upon an insight of Anthony F. C. Wallace's, that what we are seeing today may be only an early "nativist or traditionalist" stage in revitalization. Ibid., p. 14. I believe we are seeing a longer-term global trend.

6. Daniel Bell, "The Return of the Sacred: The Argument about the Future of Religion," in *Progress and Its Discontents,* Almond, Chodorow, and Pearce, pp. 501–23, esp. pp. 518–20.

7. Jim Castelli, *The Bishops and the Bomb: Waging Peace in a Nuclear Age: With the Text of the Bishops' 1983 Pastoral Letter* (Garden City, N.Y.: Doubleday, 1983), pp. 195–96.

8. For historical background on Christian Zionism, see Timothy P. Weber, *Living in the Shadow of the Second Coming: American Premillennialism, 1875–1982,* enlarged ed. (Grand Rapids, Mich.: Zondervan Academic Books, 1983), chap. 6, pp. 128–57, and chap. 9, pp. 204–26. An early assessment of the Jewish vote in 1984 and a reference to Kristol's call is TRB, "Still Chosen," *New Republic,* December 3, 1984, pp. 4, 42.

9. See John Dewey, *A Common Faith* (New Haven: Yale University Press, 1934); at the end of the Eisenhower era there was an assessment of the civil religion of that era and a reference to the literature in Martin E. Marty, *The New Shape of American Religion* (New York: Harper and Row, 1959). The literature on civil religion is assessed typically in Russell E. Richey and Donald G. Jones, *American Civil Religion* (New York: Harper and Row, 1974), which reprints Bellah's original essay of 1967 (pp. 21–44) and his revisionist probings of 1974 (pp. 255–72). The introduction and bibliographies are noteworthy.

10. For the paraphrases of Bell and argument with him, see Bryan R. Wilson, "The Return of the Sacred," *Journal of the Scientific Study of Religion* 18(3):268–80.

11. For statistics on Christianity, see David B. Barrett, ed., *World Christian Encyclopedia: A Comparative Survey of Churches and Religions in the Modern World, A.D. 1900–2000* (New York: Oxford University Press, 1982).

12. A popular summary of literary disturbances through transposition is in Robert Alter, "Deconstruction in America," *New Republic*, April 25, 1982, pp. 27–32. A reference to the ways uprooted and marginal people add insight to social process is in Hans Mol, *Identity and the Sacred: A Sketch for a New Social-Scientific Theory of Religion* (New York: Free Press, 1976), pp. 31–34.

13. I have commented on this broadening of the definition of religion in Chapter 1, p. 21, above. See Thomas Luckmann, *The Invisible Religion: The Problem of Religion in Modern Society* (New York: Macmillan, 1967), chap. 5, "Individual Religiosity," pp. 69–76.

14. Wilson, "Return of the Sacred," p. 271; see the longer argument in Bryan Wilson, *Religion in a Secular Society* (New York: Penguin, 1966), pt. 1, pp. 21–108.

15. Benjamin R. Mariante, *Pluralistic Society, Pluralistic Church* (Washington, D.C.: University Press of America, 1981), pp. 82–84.

16. Marshall D. Sahlins and Elman R. Service, eds., *Evolution and Culture* (Ann Arbor: University of Michigan Press, 1960), p. 75.

17. Jon Johnston, *Will Evangelicalism Survive Its Own Popularity?* (Grand Rapids, Mich.: Zondervan, 1980); Carol Flake, *Redemptorama: Culture, Politics, and the New Evangelicalism* (Garden City, N.Y.: Doubleday, 1984); James Davison Hunter, *American Evangelicalism: Conservative Religion and the Quandary of Modernity* (New Brunswick, N.J.: Rutgers University Press, 1983); Robert Booth Fowler, *A New Engagement: Evangelical Political Thought, 1966–76* (Grand Rapids, Mich.: Eerdmans, 1982).

18. Sahlins and Service, *Evolution and Culture*, pp. 97, 99–100.

19. Ibid., p. 102, cites Hughes.

EPILOGUE

1. Ernst Breisach, *Historiography: Ancient, Medieval, and Modern* (Chicago: University of Chicago Press, 1983) p. 409.

Index

Abel, Theodore, 242
Acheson, Dean, 86, 117
Acquaviva, S. S., *The Decline of the Sacred in Industrial Society*, 16–17
Adams, Henry, 253, 254
Adams, James Luther, 224
Adams, John, 1, 60, 61–62, 146
Adams, John Quincy, 60
Adler, Alfred, 315
Alabama Baptist, 260
Allen, James B., 313
America, 250
American Academy of Arts and Sciences, 7
American Council on Education, 68
Americanization, 168
American Jewish Committee, 334
American Legion, 79, 243
American Protective Association, 254, 255
Americans for Democratic Action, 243
Anderson, John B., 25
Anglican churches, 271
Annals, 8
Anthony, Susan B., 159–60
Anti-Semitism, 217, 218, 254
Apter, David, 278–79
Aquinas, Thomas, 65, 102
Ardrey, Robert, 207–8; *Territorial Imperative*, 208
Arendt, Hannah, 33–34, 68, 70, 346
Argyle, Michael, 15–16, 17
Aristotle, 65, 102
Asian ghettos, 261

Augustine, Saint, 1, 65, 102
Auschwitz, 135
Ayres, Clarence, 132

Bacon, Leonard Woolsey, 245
Baird, Robert, 245
Baltzell, E. Digby, 239
Baptists, 14, 74, 242, 266–67, 271, 288–89, 297
Beaumont, Gustave de, 43, 53–56, 65, 75, 187
Beecher, Lyman, 232
Begin, Menachem, 69
Behavior, categories of human: and cultural evolution, 209–12; evolutionary, 206–9; existential, 204–6; psychosocial, 212–21; religious, 221–25
Bell, Daniel, 22, 49, 70, 331, 336, 338, 341
Bellah, Robert N., 47, 63–64, 70, 79, 191, 192, 283; *The Broken Covenant*, 335; and civil religion, 72, 76, 80, 88, 89, 92–93, 234, 243–44, 335; on evolution, 19–20; on multiplex world and universe, 339
Belloc, Hilaire, 38, 167, 190, 192
Benet, Stephen Vincent, 119
Bennett, John C., 68, 103
Bente, Friedrich, 264
Benz, Ernst, 178
Berger, Peter, 70, 79; *Rumors of Angels*, 18
Berkhofer, Robert F., Jr., 203

381

Index

Bible, 41, 42, 49, 86, 136, 139; American historical figures and, 146–49; as icon in Republic, 139, 140–65; in the schools, 150

Birnbaum, Norman, 127

Black, Hugo L., 71

Black Muslins, 48, 73, 217

Black(s), 158–59, 175, 189, 202, 210; and denominationalism, 242; and fundamentalism, 229–300; ghettos, 260–61; internal unity of Jews and, 333–35; Niebuhr on, 121; peoplehood among, 227–28; religion, 271

Blackstone, William E., 298

Bloch, Ernst, 38, 88

Bloch, Marc, 235

Boas, George, 141–42

Bolce, Harold, 163

Bonhoeffer, Dietrich, 17, 126, 137, 178, 283

Book of Mormon, 74, 153, 311–24

Boorstin, Daniel J., 44–45, 143; *The Genius of American Politics*, 142

Brauer, Jerald C., 40, 170, 172; *Protestantism in America*, 169

Breisach, Ernst, *Historiography*, 345

Bremer, Frederika, 175, 189

Brewer, David J., 71

Briggs, Charles A., 140, 161

Brink, T. L., 315

Brogan, D. W., 74, 181–83, 191, 244

Brophy, Don, *The Story of Catholics in America* (with E. Westenhaver), 250–51

Brown, Clifton R., 18

Brownson, Orestes, 95, 183

Brown University, 273

Bruce, Lenny, 77

Bryan, William Jennings, 148–49

Bryce, James Lord, 133, 173–74, 181, 184–85, 231

Buber, Martin, 137, 221

Buckley, William F., 32

Buddhism, 78

Burckhardt, Jacob, 142, 171

Burke, Kenneth, 171

Burroughs, John, 259

Bushnell, Horace, 117, 180; *Christian Nurture*, 96

Callahan, Daniel, 251

Calvin, John, 65, 102

Calvinism, 127, 128

Camara, Dom Helder, 135

Camus, Albert, 136

Carr, E. H., 202–3

Carroll, H. K., 256–57, 259, 260, 261, 263; *The Religious Forces of the United States*, 257–58

Carter, Jimmy, 19, 69, 149, 332

Cassirer, Ernst, 171

Catholic Commission on Intellectual and Cultural Affairs, 248

Catholic Digest, 154, 159

Catholic Historical Review, The, 7

Catholicism, 75, 77, 79, 95, 131, 175, 217, 218; and the Bible, 145, 155–56, 164; changes in, 303–4; and common religion, 244; and crisis of historical consciousness, 306, 307–9; and denominationalism, 240–42; European observations of American, 179, 182–84, 190, 191; and evangelicalism, 273, 275, 278, 283; and fundamentalism, 290, 291, 295; and ghetto, 248–49, 250–57, 259, 261–63, 268; mainline, 341–43; and Mormonism, 303, 304, 324; Niebuhr on, 120, 121; public voice of, 332–33; traditionalist, 23, 24; transposition of assertive, 339–40; and Vatican II, 13, 24, 75, 137, 229, 251, 255, 273, 303, 306, 333

Catholic World, The, 250

"Challenge of Peace, The" (pastoral letter), 332, 333

Chambers, John S., 261

Chauncy, Charles, 276

Chester, Edward W., *Europe Views America*, 172

Chesterton, G. K., 190, 191, 233

Chicago Art Institute, 256

Chicanos, 228, 243

Christian Advocate, 260

Christian Century, The, 5, 98, 107, 116

Christian Index, 260

Christianity, 78, 132, 172, 225, 246, 307; and crisis of historical consciousness, 306, 307–9; European judgments regarding American, 178; mainline, 284, 300; Niebuhr on, 114–16; ties between American state and, 173

Christianity and Crisis, 116

Christian Reformed Church, 297

Christian Science, 265–66

Index

Index

Ellis, John Tracy, 248–50, 251, 253, 254, 255; *American Catholicism*, 249
Elwell, Walter A., 145
Emerson, Ralph Waldo, 62, 122, 128, 175, 234
England, John, 69
Enlightenment, 307; American, 42–43, 49–50, 130, 271
Episcopal Church Congress, 140
Episcopalians, 14, 19, 242, 270–71
Erikson, Erik, 315
Escajeda, J. A., 262–63
Ethnicity. *See* Race ethnicity
Ethnics, 228–29
Evangelical, evangel(ical)ism, 14, 24–25, 43–44, 269, 341–42; defined, 274–75; and fundamentalism, 273, 282, 287, 296–297; new face of southern, 270–86
Evangelical Alliance, 281
Evangelical Lutheran Synod, 264–65
Evolutionary category of human behavior, 206–9
Existential category of human behavior, 204; aesthetic, 205–6; mission, 204–5; practical, 204
Experiment, experimentalism, 36–40, 48, 166–69; perceptions of visitors to America from Europe of, 169–93

Falwell, Jerry, 292–93, 295, 298
Faulkner, William, 33, 41, 346
Federal Communications Commission, 291
Federal Council of Churches (FCC), 115, 116, 267, 281, 294
Ferri-Pisani, Camille, 179–80, 185
Fielding, Henry, 20
Fifield, James, 112
Finney, Charles Grandison, 112, 280, 294
First Amendment, 208
First Vision, 311, 312–13, 315, 316
Fitzgerald, F. Scott, 67
Flake, Carol, 342
Foley, Albert S., 250
Ford, Gerald, 19, 332
Fosdick, Harry Emerson, 163, 220
Foster, Larry, 315–16
Franklin, Benjamin, 1, 63, 66, 84, 96–97, 117, 182; *Autobiography*, 60–61; and the Bible, 146; and public religion, 42, 47, 60–61, 68, 75, 167, 219

French Revolution, 42
Frenkel-Brunswick, Else, 217
Freud, Sigmund, 315
Frontierization, 168
Frontier thesis, 198, 227, 232, 248, 252, 256
Fuller, Daniel, 321–23
Fundamentalism, 14, 24, 25, 74, 266, 269, 287; and changing Protestant "two-party" system, 294–95; defensiveness and aggressiveness of, 291–92; and evangel(ical)ism, 273, 282, 287, 296–97; future of, 300–302; groups similar to but differing from, 297; individual religiosity of, 287–88, 291; and legislated morality, 292–93; and Pentecostalism, 297; political dimension of, 289–91, 297–98, 299; as power among powers, 293–94; public/political distinction in, 295–96; reasons for contemporary visibility of, 299–300; as social phenomenon, 289, 290, 291, 293, 294, 297, 299; voluntary association in, 288–89

Gabriel, Ralph Henry, 131
Gadamer, Hans-Georg, 321
Galileo, 312
Gallup polls, 14, 87, 141, 144–45, 155, 156, 159
Garaudy, Roger, 93
Gaustad, Edwin Scott, 198
Geertz, Clifford, 21, 209
Gellner, Ernest, 78, 80, 83, 134–35, 268
Generation, concept of, 14–15
Gerberding, George H., 263–64
Ghetto(s): American Indian, 259–60; Asian, 261; black, 260–61; Catholic, 248–49, 250–57, 259, 261–63, 268; conflict within, 254–55; controversy over, 249–52; cosmopolitanism and, 255–57; culture and, 252–54; definitions of, 249; Jewish, 257–59; Protestant, 263–69
Gibbon, Edward, 138
Gibbons, James, 184, 256, 261
Gilkey, Langdon, 330
Glock, Charles Y., 15, 241
Gogarten, Friedrich, 17
Goldwater, Barry, 273
Goodheart, Eugene, 152–53
Gordon, Milton, 243
Gordon, Rosemary, 146

Index

John Paul II, Pope, 24, 341
Johnson, Lyndon B., 80, 88, 335
Johnston, Jon, 341
John XXIII, Pope, 124, 135, 137
Jones, Douglas, ed., *Civil Religion in America* (with R. Richey), 7
Joseph, Jacob, 258
Journal of Mormon History, 8
Journal of Religion, 7
Judaism, 23, 24, 44, 78, 95, 131–32, 307; and the Bible, 154–55, 164; and common religion, 244; and denominationalism, 240, 241; and evangelicalism, 283, 334, 335; and fundamentalism, 295, 335; and ghetto, 257–59; impact of death camps on, 135; and internal unity of blacks and Jews, 333–35; liberal, 341; mainline, 343; Niebuhr on, 120, 121; and peoplehood and tribalism, 228; and social issues, 137; Tillich on, 224–25
Jung, C. G., 156, 315

Kahn, Herman, 17
Kallen, Horace M., 63, 90
Kaplan, David, 211
Katz, Elihu, 70
Kaufmann, Walter, 163
Kelley, Dean M., *Why Conservative Churches Are Growing*, 331
Kempert, Ludwig, 174–75
Kennan, George, 86, 117
Kennedy, John F., 80, 88, 89, 291, 333, 335; death of, 135; efforts to thwart presidential candidacy of, 255; spiritual style of, 234
King, Donald B., 250
King, Martin Luther, Jr., 135, 227, 292–93, 334
Klopfer, Peter H., 219
Knight, Douglas A., ed., *Humanizing America's Iconic Book* (with G. M. Tucker, ed.), 7
Knights of Columbus, 219
Kohler, Kaufmann, 258
Kristol, Irving, 70, 335
Krutch, Joseph Wood, 163
Kuehnelt-Leddihn, Eric von, 38, 183–84

Lambert, Neal E., 313
Land and landscape, 200–201
Landon, Harold R., 103
Langer, Suzanne, 141
Laski, Harold, 183

Latter-Day Saints, 23, 74
Law of Cultural Dominance, 340
Law of Evolutionary Potential, 342
Lazarus, Josephine, 258
League of Nations, 115
Leckie, Robert, 249
Lee, Robert, 241
Leeuwen, Arend van, 129
Leibnitz, Gottfried Wilhelm, 235
Lenski, Gerhard, 127, 238–39
Lerner, Max, 186–87
Lessing, Gotthold E., 308, 313, 319, 322; *Nathan der Weise*, 307
Lewin, Kurt, 216
Lewis, Hylan, 158
Lifton, Robert Jay, 28, 152; *Boundaries: Psychological Man in Revolution*, 214–15
Lincoln, Abraham, 41, 63, 65, 68, 90, 96–97, 225, 347; on Americans as chosen people, 174; and the Bible, 147–48; and civil religion, 81, 83, 85, 86; and Jeffersonian self-evident truths, 62; Niebuhr on, 117, 119; and religious tolerance, 58; as representative of spirituality, 131; vision of, 182
Lippmann, Walter, 49, 117, 132, 136, 139, 163; *A Public Philosophy*, 90, 233
Lipset, Seymour Martin, 15, 26, 70, 237; *The First New Nation*, 12
Lodge, Henry Cabot, 264
Lolabrigida, Gina, 154
London Times Literary Supplement, 100
Lonergan, Bernard, 303
Lorenz, Konrad, 208
Luckmann, Thomas, 15, 20, 77, 79, 237–38, 338; *The Invisible Religion*, 46, 284
Lutheranism, 263–65, 297

McAuley Lectures, The, 250
McCarthy, Eugene, 32
McCarthy, Joseph, 32
McClellan, John L., 32
McGovern, George, 32
Machiavelli, Niccolò, 220–21
McIntire, Carl, 298
McKissick, Floyd, 32
McLoughlin, William, 28–29, 185, 273–74, 275–76
McLuhan, Marshall, 32
Macmillan, Harold, 94

Index

Index

Index

Quakers, 74, 158

Race ethnicity, 244–45; and religious history, 230–31
Rahner, Karl, 70
Ramsey, Ian, 87
Rauschenbusch, Walter, 99, 115–16, 117, 180; *Christianity and the Social Crisis*, 96; *Christianizing the Social Order*, 96
Reader's Digest, 332
Reagan, Ronald, 19, 80, 85, 89, 91, 234, 332; and the Bible, 149
Reed, Andrew, 182
Reformation, Protestant, 177, 280, 290, 307
Reimers, David, 242
"Religiocification," 18, 77, 227
Religion: diffusion of, 18–23; resurgent antimodern, 23–30; strong role of in 1980s, 338–39
Religious category of human behavior, 221–25
Renier, G. J., 304, 305, 314, 346
Republican banquet, 57, 58, 64, 70, 72–76
Reston, James, 117
Resurgent antimodern religion, 23–30
Revelation, 312, 313, 314
Review and Expositor, 7
Review of Religious Research, 7
Revitalization, 274, 275–76
Richard, Gabriel, 54
Richardson, Herbert, 178
Richey, Russell, ed., *Civil Religion in America* (with D. Jones, ed.), 7
Ricoeur, Paul, 306, 308, 319, 320
Rieff, Philip, 22
Robertson, D. B., 104
Robinson, Edward, 160
Robinson, John, 38, 165, 172
Rogers, Will, 93
Roof, Wade Clark, 331
Roosevelt, Theodore, 260, 264
Rosenstock-Huessy, Eugen, 345
Rousseau, Jean Jacques, 191
Ryan, John, 183

Sadat, Anwar el-, 69
Sahlins, Marshall D., 340
St. Exupéry, Antoine de, 213
Sandmel, Samuel, *Tomorrow's American*, 7
Santayana, George, 38, 74, 183, 267

Savannah, Georgia, *News*, 140, 141
Scammon, Richard M., *The Real Majority* (with B. J., Wattenberg), 229
Schaff, Philip, 38, 167, 180, 186, 192, 232, 245
Schechter, Solomon, 155
Scheler, Max, 217
Schlesinger, Arthur, Jr., 86, 117
Scofield Reference Bible, 298
Scopes trial, 24, 141, 148–49, 298
Scripturalism, 40–42, 48–49
Secular, secularization, defined, 17
Secularity, sameness through common, 236–37
Secular paradigm questioned, 15–18
Sellers, Wilfred, 23
Service, Elman R., 340
Seventh-Day Adventists, 23, 265–66
Shakespeare, William, 164
Shea, John Gilmary, 245
Shiner, Larry, 17
Shipps, Jan, 315, 317; *Religionsgeschichte*, 316
Siegfried, André, 184
Sienkiewicz, Henry, *Quo Vadis*, 179
Silverman, Joseph, 258
Simmel, Georg, 215–16, 217–18, 254–55, 257, 262
Skinner, B. F., *Walden Two*, 106
Smith, Adam, 279
Smith, James Ward, 132, 135
Smith, Joseph, 74, 311, 319, 321, 324; prophet/fraud controversy about, 313–17, 324
Smith, Page, 79
Smith, Timothy, *Revivalism and Social Reform*, 294
Social Darwinism, 131
Social Gospel, 114, 115–16
Society for the Promotion of Christian Knowledge (SPCK), 148
Society of Biblical Literature, 7
Sorokin, Pitirim, 171
Southern Baptist Convention, 289, 297
Spencer, Herbert, 99
Spencer, John Canfield, 54
Spirituality, 123–24; and disappearance of transcendent, 125–26; evidence of ongoing search for, 124–25; and exploitation of spiritual resources, 339–43; future agenda for, 136–38; impact of models, events, and features on, 135–36; and loss of cosmic sense, 131–33; and new setting in secular

Index

Index